Retailing

Retailing

R. Ted Will
Ronald W. Hasty
Colorado State University

CANFIELD PRESS / San Francisco

A Department of Harper & Row, Publishers, Inc.
New York, Hagerstown, London

Production editor: Thomas E. Dorsaneo
Cover and Interior Design: Brenton Beck
Interior art: Fifth Street Design Associates
Copy editor: Richard V. Aamodt

Retailing, Second Edition

Library of Congress Cataloging in Publication Data
Will, R. Ted
    Retailing
    Includes index.
    1. Retail trade—Management. 2. Middle managers.
I. Hasty, Ronald W., joint author. II. Title.
HF5429.W525 1977   658.8'7   √76-54897
ISBN 0-06-389403-3

77 78 79 10 9 8 7 6 5 4 3 2 1

Contents

Chapter 7   Information from electronic data processing   123

Chapter 8   Information from research   137

PART FIVE/STARTING A RETAIL STORE

PART SIX/OPERATING A RETAIL STORE

Chapter 12   Knowing how much to buy   203

Chapter 13   Knowing what to buy   221

Chapter 14   Retail pricing   247

Chapter 15   Retail advertising and sales promotion   265

PART SEVEN/THE ENVIRONMENT OF RETAILING: TODAY AND TOMORROW

Preface

In the first edition of *Retailing* we stated that the rationale guiding its development centered around particular needs of the retail businessman and the student of retailing.

In running their businesses, today's businessmen must understand the managerial techniques that will help them to:

1. plan for profits
2. plan and administer good control records
3. obtain productive performance from employees
4. obtain productive performance
5. follow through on useful merchandising techniques

In turn, businessmen need workers who understand the nature of business in general and who can provide immediate and productive input into the operation of a particular business. All too often businessmen say, "Give me somebody who can do something, and he'll be worth his weight in gold to me." What they are telling us is that there is no room for unproductive employees. Customers are too hard to acquire, and profits are too meager for firms to enjoy such luxuries. In no business is the requirement for productive employees more necessary than in retailing.

Unfortunately, however, the retailing courses offered by colleges throughout the country often appear to take a direction that is either highly descriptive, largely managerial, or basically theoretical. In addition, most courses are directed toward people in the top management level of large merchandising enterprises. Although there is clearly a need to provide students with the opportunity to study from the top management, policy-making perspective, there is also a need to recognize that not all college students aspire to be, nor do all businesses require, people with top management expertise.

This book, then, takes a middle management approach. In doing this, it strives to present a realistic, pragmatic approach to the studying of retailing. It is written on the assumption that both employees and employers want and need educational courses that will permit employees who have had relatively short periods of training to enter easily into middle management positions. The book emphasizes the conceptual, when the conceptual is directly relevant to decision making; it emphasizes the descriptive, when the descriptive contributes to effective retail employee performance; and it emphasizes the managerial. Our goal in the revision has been to strengthen this realistic, pragmatic approach.

Organization of the book

In this book, unnecessary frills have been eliminated in order to present the basics of retail store management. Every effort has been made to include information that will actually help management performance on the job.

The book begins with an introduction to retailing, the subject of Chapter One. It reveals the nature and scope of retailing and emphasizes the criteria for success in the retail business. Specifically it deals with the basics of retail planning and gives a foundation for later discussions of the decision-making environment in which all managers are expected to perform. In addition, this chapter highlights the career opportunities in which students of retailing may be interested.

Chapters Two and Three provide insights into the how's and why's of customer behavior. They stress the necessity for managers to identify with the needs of customers. A service, market-oriented firm can afford to do no less.

Because a midmanager's position in the retail store requires competency in managing employees as well as in other areas, Chapters

Four and Five deal with the essentials of supervision in retail stores. Chapter Four describes those management functions required of all retail managers and Chapter Five examines ways of developing prudent management characteristics.

Chapters Six, Seven, and Eight are designed to show the information base upon which retail store managers can rely to give them the kinds of information important to internal control of a retail store. The chapter on retail accounting develops the importance of keeping financial records, accounting for inventory, and maintaining surveillance over expenses. Chapter Seven shows how the computer can be of use to a retail manager of both small and large stores as a means of providing information. Chapter Eight examines ways that stores obtain information for decisions about themselves and their customers through the use of retail research.

Chapters Nine, Ten, and Eleven are concerned with the development of a new store. Chapter Nine is devoted to problems associated with store location while Chapter Ten addresses itself to determining the economic feasibility of setting up a given retail store. Chapter Eleven attacks the problem of store design and layout.

Chapters Twelve through Seventeen provide information and techniques concerning subjects that are the nuts and bolts of retail management, proceeding from the buying of merchandise, pricing, promoting and selling to the offering of store services. These chapters provide insights into how to actually operate a retail store.

The final two chapters explore the legal knowledge retail managers should have in offering their services and discusses trends and issues which informed and sensitive retail managers need to understand in order to be effective in operating their business.

There are seven appendices which appear at the end of selected chapters. These appendices are designed to provide valuable supplementary material for students who are going to be working in retailing. This material is treated as an appendice so that the students' reading of the text material will not be interrupted. Some of the work involves retail arithmetic while other is designed to develop techniques important to effective performance.

How to study from this book

You will notice that there is a set of behavioral objectives at the beginning of each chapter. The statements of objectives are intended to bring about increased achievement and a realization of the total nature of effective retail manager performance. In other words, the objectives tell you what you should learn from a chapter. Therefore, you should read the statements of objectives before beginning the chapter, and refer to them as you proceed through it. Review of behavioral objectives is absolutely necessary if you wish to gain as much from a chapter as possible.

To stimulate thinking and further study, each chapter concludes with questions, problems, situations, activities, and a bibliography. The bibliography is one way of giving other authors credit where credit is due; equally important, however, the bibliography provides you with a selected source of reading that you may use to build upon your knowledge of retailing. You should use the end of chapter questions to develop your own ability to solve retail problems. The situations and activities, in particular offer you an excellent opportunity "to make it all real."

Acknowledgments

We wish to acknowledge our gratitude to our former students for their feedback to us in the development of the revised manuscript. Our appreciation is extended to the many retail firms across the country who made suggestions and supplied materials for the book. For reviewing the manuscript and making suggestions to improve the organization, content, and readability of the book for their students, a special thanks to Professors A. Edward Spitz, Len Herzstein, Nathan Weinstock, Jeff Frates, Ed Robbins, Craig Wilson, Dale E. Helwick, Randy Busch, Richard J. Passage, Jacob Goodman, and Bruce S. Staff.

R. Ted Will
Ronald W. Hasty

one

INTRODUCTION

1

A General View of Retailing

contents

Retailing Today and Yesterday
Retailing in the Economy
Retail Institutions
Opportunities and Careers in Retailing
Choosing Retailing as a Career
Retail Management
Levels of Management
Problem Solving and Decision Making
Summary
Questions and Problems
Situations and Activities
Bibliography

behavioral objectives

Successful retailing requires an understanding and appreciation of the role and achievements of retailing in society. This knowledge provides a foundation from which the retail management process can be looked at in an enlightened perspective. The manager who fully understands the reasons for the existence of the business will develop retail plans that will meet customer needs and satisfactions.

Upon completing this chapter, you will be able to do the following:
☐ Define retailing.
☐ Compare the basic differences among a market socialism system, a central planning system, and a private enterprise system.
☐ Describe the advantages and disadvantages of a career in retailing.
☐ Know whether retailing is an appropriate career for you.
☐ Understand how to get a job in retailing.
☐ Describe the role of planning in retail management.
☐ Describe a target market.
☐ Use the retailing mix to appeal to a target market.
☐ Develop differential advantages.
☐ Describe the levels and jobs in retail management.
☐ Follow a sequential problem-solving process to arrive at a decision.

Retailing has been defined as the distribution of goods and services to the ultimate consumer. As such, retailing is the pivotal point around which all marketing of consumer goods revolves. Manufacturers and wholesalers rely on retailing to provide the structure in which their goods flow quickly, smoothly, and in large volume. Consumers depend on retailers to buy goods to meet their needs and to make it as convenient and enjoyable as possible to do the shopping that fills those needs. If you think about it for a moment, you will realize that a great deal is asked and expected of retailing.

Today some 1.9 million retail establishments perform the myriad tasks demanded of retailing, and in so doing face continually changing consumer purchasing patterns as well as strong competitive conditions within the industry.

Retailing Today and Yesterday

Most of us know retailing as that activity associated with selling goods in stores. These stores may be of several types: specialty stores (shoe, paint, clothing, jewelry, hardware, etc.), department stores, supermarkets, variety stores, and discount stores. Each type sells goods to household consumers over the counter. Some retail stores, such as shoe and TV repair shops, sell both goods and services over the counter. However, retailers may also sell goods to consumers through other means. Goods bought through mail order, door-to-door sales, in vending machines, and at roadside stands are also considered retail sales.

No matter how you look at retailing, it is dynamic. It *is* the world of merchandising, embodying a world of things and ideas, contributing to a world of excitement and beauty. Look at what you see all around you—beautiful, well-lighted, air-conditioned stores where you may leisurely shop. Look at the way stores are locating in areas near you and staying open at times most convenient to you. Look too at the way stores have adjusted their merchandise

offerings to provide for one-stop shopping.

But retailing hasn't always been this way. In the past retailing was often disdained or ignored as an honorable profession. In some societies it was just tolerated as a necessary evil. History records that during the Hellenic and Roman empires society scorned the trading occupations. In societies that emphasized the intellectual rather than the material, such occupations were held in contempt. Slaves and members of minority groups performed the retailing function for the economy.

Retailing was looked down upon in the United States and parts of Europe even as recently as the time of the industrial revolution. Some historians have suggested that the reason for this attitude lay not in the profit-making function of retailing but in the way profits were made. In this period some dishonest people engaged in whatever trickery would make a sale. Overstating, lying, passing off inferior goods, and overcharging were some of the dubious devices used to sell goods.

Although these condemnations apply only to some retailers of the time, in any field the few people who are dishonest seem to achieve prominence out of proportion to their numbers. In fact, it was the courage, foresight, and dedication of the great majority of retailers that helped shape today's new and improved environment for people to live in. Retailers have made important contributions—many times in difficult circumstances. A consideration of the number of small retailers who extended credit to farmers from early winter until harvest time and a knowledge of the amount of time large stores, such as Penney's and Macy's, have been in existence leads us to conclude that although retailing functioned differently in an earlier time, not all or even most retailers lacked integrity.

Historical interpretations aside, during the early part of the 1900's, retailing in the United States really began to come of age. The shift from an economy of scarcity to one of abundance made consumers more and more selective in their buying. Consequently, consumers tried to satisfy their needs through more than one retail outlet. For this and other reasons, market needs became a major concern of retailers. The result has been that today's retailers are, or better be, the epitome of service, because their survival depends on it.

In the American economy, it is generally held that it is the task of marketing to create as well as deliver a standard of living in the economy. Specifically, this means that marketers are sensitive to equating new and improved goods and services with the needs, desires and fancies of consumers. Retailing is the institution that is most closely in touch with consumers, and in many ways is best able to interpret these needs. To the extent that retailers are skillful in interpreting consumer needs, serving as the consumer's purchasing agent, and to the extent that they develop good assortments of merchandise (styles, materials, colors, prices, sizes) and present them in an effective manner so that consumers find it easy and attractive to buy, to that extent does retailing truly serve society.

Figure 1.1. An early American retailer—the Yankee peddler.

Retailing in the Economy

The type of economic system that exists in a country has a direct bearing on retailing's ability to be innovative and to change to meet the economic needs of society. In essence, there are three types of economic systems: market socialism, central planning, and private enterprise.

Types of economic systems

In a *market socialism system,* such as is found in some of the Scandinavian countries, most capital goods are owned by the state and are not bought and sold in actual markets. In general, however, consumers are free to spend their income as they wish, and workers are free to choose their jobs. Prices and wages are set primarily in response to the forces of supply and demand. Such an economic system does not make retailing much different from what it is in the United States.

In a *central planning system,* such as in the Soviet Union and the People's Republic of China, government and its agencies play a direct role in all business activities. A central planning body sets production requirements for both individual firms and industries, chooses among investment alternatives, and engages in financial planning. It influences the distribution of income to consumers and controls the rate that capital is accumulated. The key aspect of a central planning system is that the normal forces of supply and demand are not permitted to operate in the market.

Under this system, retailing involves simply selling the merchandise provided by state-owned and state-controlled firms at the price dictated. There is no way for retailers to respond effectively to the wants and needs of consumers.

In a *private enterprise system,* or, as it is also called, *capitalism,* businessmen make decisions concerning business activity. They provide products and services demanded by consumers and seek to make a profit by balancing income against costs. Consumer sovereignty is central to capitalism. In other words, suppliers of capital and land may use resources as they wish; workers may work where they please; and consumers are free to spend their income where, when, and how they desire. The foundations of capitalism are a free marketplace and the ownership of private property. The private enterprise system permits, and, in fact, requires retailing to respond to consumer's needs. If the demand for a product exists, manufacturers and retailers are free to try to meet the demand, with competition ensuring fair value for the price to the customer.

In the United States the private enterprise system has yielded a dynamic, growing economy powered by vast productive and natural resources and by talented, and knowledgeable private businessmen. This system of private enterprise has made possible America's supply of capital, trained people, industry, and overall productive capability—all of which have helped to establish the highest standard of living in the world. More importantly, the system is capable of expanding to provide for future needs of goods, services and jobs.

Importance of retailing to the United States

Retailing plays an important part in expanding the economy. Its importance in the American economy is revealed by the following facts. The 1976 Gross National Product (the total monetary value of the nation's business activity—the goods and services produced in the nation) exceeded $1.5 *trillion.* This business activity gave rise to about $1.3 trillion in personal income. $1 trillion of personal income left after deducting money for taxes and savings was spent for personal outlays, which included consumer goods and services, housing, interest, and donations. America's retailers had sales of over $500 billion, and they employed 12.5 million people, who earned $60 billion in salaries and commissions. This figure does not include the more than one million active proprietors of unincorporated businesses who devoted most of their time to their own business. The persons employed in retailing now constitute 15 percent of the employed civilian labor force. Figure 1.2 shows the growth, distribution, and size of the retailing industry based on the latest Census of Retail Trade.

Retail Institutions

To understand retailing as it exists today in the American Economy it is necessary to understand the institutions which comprise it. The total of these institutions is called the *retail trade,* and include establishments engaged in selling merchandise for personal or household consumption along with those which render services incidental to the sale of the goods. The institutions within the retail trade are generally characterized as: (1) having fixed places of business, (2) initiating activities which encourage the general public to buy, (3) both buying and selling merchandise, (4) possibly doing some manufacturing or processing (but these activities are incidental to their major function of selling), and (5) being in the retail trade by the trade itself.

The retail trade is made up of institutions which include store and nonstore retail activities.

Store retailing

Chain stores. Chain stores are retail organizations made up of two or more store units with common ownership. This type of organization has been particularly successful in the American economy, because it has many times resulted in lower prices for the consumer, offered broader lines and more customer services. These advantages have accrued through chain store type operations, because chains are characterized by standardized operations, centralized policy making, and better physical facilities resulting from better financing and stronger capital positions. Coupled with professional management and the advantages chains realize through large volume purchasing, it is easy to understand why they have

assumed a significant role in the retail scene. J. C. Penney, F. W. Woolworth, and Sears Roebuck and Co. are three well-known chains.

Discount stores. Discount stores use price as their major selling point by consistently pricing below the market averages. Reduced operational costs are a major characteristic of the way they operate. These cost advantages come about as a result of more narrow product lines than traditional type stores and they use self-service, whenever possible. Discount stores advertise extensively, minimize free customer service, utilize relatively inexpensive facilities, and provide ample parking. In addition, because discount stores are often chain store type organizations they realize the advantages of chains. Their primary differential advantage, however, exists in their "discount prices." Woolco and K—Mart are examples of two national discount stores.

Department stores. Strictly speaking, a department store could conceivably be any type of store which is divided into departments and which carries different kinds of merchandise. However, the true department stores are large retail operations facilities which are divided into departments for different kinds of merchandise. They generally include dry goods and housewares areas, with resulting advantages in merchandising, service, promotion, and operation control. By including dry goods and housewares in the description of a department store one eliminates departmentalized specialty stores such as those carrying only women's apparel.

Department stores have several distinctive operating advantages. Because of their size, they are able to buy in large quantities and hire managerial talent who specialize in various aspects of the store's operations; for example, buying, selling, promotion, traffic, store control, etc. This same size benefits customers by having all their merchandise needs provided under one roof along with special services and conveniences that they would not otherwise

Number of stores in 1972		Sales in millions of dollars (1967 / 1972)		Percent Change
Nonstore retailers	N/A	$7,623	$11,568	51.8%
Drug stores and proprietary stores	51,542	$10,930	$15,599	42.7%
Furniture, home furnishings, and equipment stores	116,857	$14,542	$22,533	55.0%
Apparel and accessory stores	129,201	$16,672	$24,741	48.4%
Building materials, hardware, farm equipment dealers	83,842	$17,200	$25,575	48.7%
Gasoline service stations	226,459	$22,709	$33,655	48.2%
Eating and drinking places	359,524	$23,843	$36,868	54.6%
Miscellaneous retail stores	500,480	$27,274	$39,097	43.3%
General merchandise group stores	56,245	$43,537	$66,676	53.1%
Automotive dealers	121,369	$55,631	$93,774	68.6%
Food stores	267,352	$70,251	$100,719	43.4%
United States Total	1,912,871	$310,214	$470,806	51.8%

Figure 1.2. Growth of retail trade in the United States between 1967 and 1972.

Source: U. S. Department of Commerce, Social and Economic Statistics Administration, Bureau of Census.

receive. On the other hand, these added services and advantages result in a higher cost of operation which tends to be reflected in higher prices. In recent years these higher prices have posed special problems for department stores as consumers appear willing to forego certain services in favor of price advantages.

Department stores in downtown areas also have suffered because of the difficulties customers have had to face in finding adequate parking facilities. [Add to this the fact that customers have been moving to the suburbs and shopping in shopping areas closer to their places of residence; it can be appreciated why department stores have been running hard just to keep what business they have enjoyed.] To combat the suburban shift in buying patterns, department stores have moved out into the shopping center and sought the customers who once shopped downtown stores and who now abound in the shopping centers. Although generally not as large in size as the downtown stores, "branch" stores have been established in the shopping centers to recover some of this lost business. These stores carry a representative assortment of the parent store's merchandise. Some department stores have also established "twig" stores. These are very small units typically containing about 30,000 square feet of selling area, and which carry about one classification of merchandise. For example, a department store might operate a twig store featuring only women's ready-to-wear. In areas where twig stores are located, department stores cannot justify the investment required of setting up a department or a branch store in a given market area. However, enough business may exist for some given line of merchandise that makes it feasible to operate a twig operation.

Limited line specialty stores. Specialty stores exist where merchandise requires individual selection and sale. Stores selling style and shopping-type merchandise such as appliances, automobiles, jewelry, shoes, and so on are characteristic of specialty-type stores. In the operation of these stores, personal contact with customers is fundamental to successful selling. In these situations the retailer is in a better position to learn of his customer's needs and to better tailor his merchandise offering and his services to accommodate them. The small specialty store retailer is free to choose his store location, handle different lines of merchandise, or even keep different store hours if he believes that these best meet the needs of his customers. The small store owner, however, is handicapped by the nature of his business. His small organization may not provide for experts to handle different aspects of the operation, and by the same token, this same smallness hinders his ability to buy merchandise at the lowest prices by taking advantage of quantity discounts.

Nonstore retailing

Nonstore retailing is concerned with purchases that occur at a different place from that of the seller.

Telephone sales. Increased use of credit cards has greatly expanded telephone sales. A store can verify a customer's credit status, immediately after the account number is read over the phone. Consequently, there can be less problems than when purchases are made with checks. Other advantages include: (1) bookkeeping costs are reduced by having transactions merely added to the credit account and, (2) there is a reduced risk of fraudulent usage when merchandise is sent directly to the address being recorded for the account.

Some reasons why consumers may prefer buying by phone include:

1. Convenience
2. Inclement weather conditions
3. Transportation problems
4. Dislike of shopping conditions or crowds
5. Illness, old age, or physical disability

Door-to-door sales. Door-to-door sales involve business exchanges in which the seller visits the buyer at home. Encyclopedias, vacuum cleaners, brushes, greeting cards, and cosmetics are examples of products in this category. Door-to-door selling is an alternative when established channels of distribution are unavailable to a manufacturer.

Three factors are important in this type of sales:

1. *Size of the market area.* Customers are usually located within a fairly small geographic radius. This type of marketing program requires large concentrations of potential customers in order to provide an adequate selling base. If customers are few in number and widely scattered, this system is economically unfeasible because salesmen must spend too much time traveling.

2. *Selling price of the product.* Selling price is an important factor in determining the feasibility of door-to-door programs. A product with a low price tag and small per-unit profit potential must be sold in large volume in order to be profitable. When salesmen contact customers personally on an individual basis, sales volumes in terms of units are not likely to be large. Thus, each item sold must have a relatively high profit potential and, therefore, a relatively high price.

3. *Scope of the product line.* Having a large number of products greatly increases the probability of a sale and also can enhance dollar volume, because customers may buy several different items. However, door-to-door salesmen normally carry samples of their products, and the salesman often must decide which items to carry because he cannot physically show all of them. In some cases this problem can be solved with photographs or drawings of the products rather than actual samples. However, demonstration is often necessary and there may be no suitable alternative to exhibiting the product in person.

Mail order sales. This retailing technique involves contact between the seller and the consumer by the postal system or a combination of the mail and a common carrier (e.g., truck-ing firm). Customers are made aware of goods available for sale through catalogs, mailing pieces, newspaper advertisements, magazines, and advertising on radio and television. Two major advantages of using a mail order system are (1) simplicity, (2) no large investment in marketing is needed. For a company just getting a foothold in the market that cannot make a large financial investment in marketing, selling by mail is an attractive distribution alternative.

The chief disadvantages are time delays in shipping, breakage, possible loss, and inconvenience and costs in returning merchandise. Because the customer cannot see or touch the product, he or she must rely on a description and picture to evaluate color, structure, size, and other features. To minimize this problem, sellers develop precise product descriptions and often use color pictures.

Vending. Vending is retailing in which products are sold through machines. There is no personal contact between the seller and buyer. Vending units can be built into buildings and plants to serve as automated shopping centers. Some carry up to 1,000 items, with almost no limit as to diversity of product. An example of a large vending machine is located in Stockholm, Sweden. The 100 foot-long machine has 1,515 compartments, 492 of which are refrigerated for various fresh foods.

Vending machines are manufactured that will accept credit cards, eliminating the problem of making change. The customer simply inserts a credit card, and the automatic vendor records purchases and arranges electronically for a bill.

Opportunities and Careers in Retailing

Retailing serves as an attractive career for many people. Its employment opportunities are quite diverse with jobs including positions for bookkeepers, stenographers, truckers, security personnel, sales people, stockers, display personnel, seamstresses, etc. And yet there are many who do not set their lifetime occupational goal to include a job in retailing. This is unfortunate.

Too many people when asked for their honest feelings about choosing retailing as a career, answer, "Oh, well, if I can't get another kind of job, I'll go into retailing." Or, "Who in their right mind wants to spend the rest of their working life running around a store with an apron around their middle and a pencil behind the ear?" If either of these attitudes has prevailed about a career in retailing, that person is missing one of the best opportunities of his or her life. Let's look at some reasons why one should seriously consider retailing as a career.

A good job

Consider for a moment what most of us look for in a good job: excitement, good pay, rapid advancement, job security, and probably many more things. Can retailing offer these? Can it offer them as well as or better than most other industries? Unequivocally, Yes!

You might say, "Now wait just a minute; that's an awful lot to swallow. No job is that glamorous or attractive." If you said this, you'd be half right, because retailing is not glamorous but it is attractive. For most of us a glamorous job is one that keeps us continually in the spotlight, being fascinated and fascinating everyone else. There are moments of glamour in retailing, but most of the time it is merely hard but challenging work. It is attractive, however, because it offers many of the requirements of "a good job."

The pay scale

What about pay? It is difficult to generalize about pay in retailing because pay levels vary considerably. Job responsibilities, the size and kind of firm, store location, and job seniority all affect pay levels. This difficulty notwithstanding, we have made the following appraisal of pay levels.

Large chain stores. On the whole, large chain stores have been especially generous to their store management group. To see how salaries compare with salaries in some other fields,

look at Figure 1.3. Many of these stores pay their managers salaries of $15,000, $20,000, $40,000, and, in the case of very large stores, $75,000 a year and up. Department store buyers, managers of the local J. C. Penney and Montgomery Ward stores, and, to some extent, managers of the local supermarket receive earnings in the $15,000 to $25,000 bracket and up. Most of these managers attain their positions after only eight to twelve years of employment with a company.

Small stores. On the whole, small stores do not pay as well as their chain counterparts. In general, pay levels are influenced by the kind of product or service sold and by the volume of business done. For example, the owner-manager of a store can usually realize about 12 to 18 percent profit on sales before taxes. He takes his salary out of this profit. If the owner-manager runs a family shoe store (say one of average size which does $120,000 worth of business annually), the owner's salary before taxes typically ranges between $14,400 and $21,600 (that is, 12 percent × $120,000 to 18 percent × $120,000). The assistant manager's

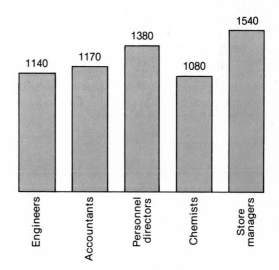

Figure 1.3. Comparison of average monthly income of variety store chain managers with that of other professionals.

Source: U. S. Bureau of Labor Statistics.

salary would probably range between $7,000 and $10,000. These salaries are not as attractive as that of the average chain store manager, but they fall within a respectable pay level. Furthermore, there are advantages to working in small stores. Many individuals enjoy its wider range of responsibility, flexibility, and closer personal contact.

Beginning salaries in retailing. One criticism levied against retailing is that beginning salaries are low. To a large extent, this criticism is justified. Some beginning jobs start as low as $5,500 per year. Retailers are reluctant to offer high beginning salaries because they have found that employee turnover is high during the first two years of employment. Recently, however, chain organizations have started to offer beginning salaries of $7,500 to $9,500. These salaries are comparable to beginning salaries offered in other industries.

Store support personnel. Up to this point our comments have centered largely on pay levels of store operations personnel. As we mentioned earlier, there are many kinds of jobs in a retail store. In some retail department store organizations, it is possible to find more than one thousand kinds of jobs. For people in these jobs it is impractical to talk about pay levels for such varied types of activities. But our observations, however, lead us to conclude that a person employed in retailing enjoys a pay level commensurate with, if not higher than, a similar position in other industries.

Advancement

Advancement opportunities in retailing are generally good, because there is a continuing need for employees. It is possible to understand this if one realizes that for every seven retail employees, there is one management employee, that stores are growing in size, and that there is new store development constantly taking place throughout the country.

Unlike some industries, in retailing it is possible to measure an employee's worth rather quickly. Some retail store managers feel that they can determine within a year or two

whether an employee has the capacity to advance in the organization. Therefore, employees who have the capacity to perform well are likely to find that advancement comes faster than it does in many other industries.

Some retail employees attempt to advance by moving from one retail organization to another, accepting greater responsibilities as they change jobs. Because of the geographical dispersion of retail organizations, the diversity of retail jobs, the continuing need for qualified retail management personnel, and the growth taking place within the industry, this is a practical way for many employees to move upward.

Women in retailing

What about jobs for women? In retailing, opportunities for women are usually quite good. Although there are only ten women who are presidents of large department stores, there are many women in high level management positions. Almost half the buyers in stores across the country are women. Considering the importance of fashion to today's customers, this should not be surprising. Aside from buyer positions, however, women occupy positions of responsibility in personnel, advertising, and, to some extent, in store operations supervision. In store supervision, such firms as the G. C. Murphy Company and the J. C. Penney Company have recently implemented programs that phase women into store operations management positions throughout their organizations. Women are also increasingly setting up and managing their own stores.

Retail training programs

Many large retail organizations have developed management training programs designed to increase employees' knowledge of business as well as to facilitate advancement within the organization. Most of these training programs follow a pattern. First, new employees spend a period of time, from several days to several weeks, receiving indoctrination. Indoctrination usually includes information on company policy and company benefits and instruction in the knowledge and skills necessary for effective performance on the first job.

The second step in training programs usually involves the assigning of the trainee to various departments. The trainee progresses through a series of assignments that may last one day or several months. After the trainee has become familiar with the different departments and their functions, he or she is permanently assigned to a particular department. Even though the new employee may ultimately want a job in personnel, advertising, or office administration, the first assignment is frequently on the sales floor. The experience the trainee gains on the sales floor with merchandise and customers helps to make an effective worker in other kinds of jobs.

Third, while the trainee is performing in the first assignment, he takes regular examinations that test and rate his knowledge. For example, Woolworth requires that management prospects participate in a two-year training program. In this program, Woolworth asks its trainees to study books and provides controlled work experiences. During their first year with the company, trainees learn stockroom procedures, basic merchandising, basic supervision, cost control, ordering and buying, promotion of new and seasonal merchandise, and office procedures. During the second year of the program, trainees study advanced supervision, office administration, customer service, display, advanced office administration, sales planning, advertising, sales promotion, and food operations. Throughout the two-year period, the trainees' advancements depend on their performance both on tests and on the job.

In most retail organizations an employee who has completed the formal training program is moved into a full-fledged mid-management position. From that point on, an employee's ability to advance in the organization depends on the ability to manage operations and to contribute to the profitability of the firm.

"The good life"

Many of us are looking for "the good life." We seek our share of social acceptance, ample food on the table, and time to be with our families. Retailing can become the basis for achieving some of these goals.

Social acceptance. Think for a moment of the town or city in which you grew up. Who were the leaders in the community? Who served as officers in local service clubs, deacons in the church, leaders of the local fund-raising drives, and boosters of high school sporting events? We're sure that the people you recall came from all walks of life, but notice how often the names of merchants and retailers came to mind. Retailers, because they are skilled in organization, in tune with customer needs, and interested in the welfare of the community, frequently become community leaders. Retailers are respected individuals within the community.

The pocketbook. You already know that retailing salaries are good. There are financial advantages in addition to salaries, however. Because there are 10 to 20 percent discounts on merchandise bought in the store, paid vacations of from two to six weeks (depending on length of service), generous retirement plans (some of which provide over $150,000 annuity at retirement age, free hospitalization, and life insurance coverage), net pay represents an even greater amount than base salaries show. Furthermore, all of these benefits compare favorably with those offered in other industries.

Leisure time. At one time retailing was an occupational field in which employees' time was never their own. They began work at 6:00 in the morning, left the store after closing at 6:00 P.M., and came back to work later in the evening to trim windows, work on the books, or plan next season's promotions. A six-day work week was common. Today, the retailing picture is different. Beginning employees may expect a forty-hour work week, with time and a half for overtime. To safeguard the forty-hour week, some retail firms will not even permit their employees to take work home with them at night. However, in any industry, the further up the ladder one travels, the more hours one spends working. In this respect, retailing is no exception. At certain times of the year, like Christmas, working hours may be very long. Despite seasonal upswings and the fact that some stores are open on both Saturday and Sunday, almost all stores operate with a five-day work week.

Job security. Retailing has been called a depression-proof industry. In some industries there are extensive layoffs during bad times, but retail stores are always open, and it is more necessary to maintain staffs of people. Furthermore, retailing exists everywhere—in big cities and in small towns, in the mountains and by the sea.

Some disadvantages

With all the advantages of retailing, it might be argued that everyone should be in it. Nothing, however, could be further from the truth. Even though there are more jobs than people available in retailing, there is no guarantee of success. A person must be suited to the field.

One disadvantage of retailing is that it is a hard taskmaster. It demands the best that people have, and if they can't or won't give their best, the results are apparent immediately. For this reason people who are suited to it advance into management positions very quickly. Those who are not suited to retailing discover this quickly and may take steps to find a career more in line with their abilities.

Before retailing is chosen as a career, some of the noticeable disadvantages should be taken into consideration. These disadvantages include the following:

1. Because retailing is a highly competitive field, the mental and physical pressures faced by managers are great.
2. Retailing is a seven-day-a-week, twelve-hour-a-day business. Thus, managers may be asked to work unusual and inconvenient hours.
3. Retailers must always try to satisfy customers, but some customers make this difficult.

4. Retailing requires physical exertion. Even management personnel may occasionally be called upon to sweep floors, open and stock merchandise, and prepare, in general, for business.
5. Retailing, particularly in chain stores, requires that people be willing to move from one locality to another. It is common for retail management personnel to be moved every two or three years. This is especially true while employees are gaining experience and assuming increasing responsibilities with the company.
6. Retailing never permits a person to relax. If a manager who has reached the age of fifty-five decides to work less, his doing so would weaken the business.

Choosing Retailing as a Career

Retailing involves people. Whether employees are involved in advertising, research, personnel work, data processing, or fashion merchandising, they must understand and plan to meet the needs of people, and they must work closely with people. People considering retailing as a career should genuinely like to be with and work with people and be interested in solving problems related to people. If they don't feel this way about people, they shouldn't be in retailing.

In addition to liking people one should be interested in products, checking to see what's new in fashions every season, searching for new products, walking through stores, and be interested in money and profits.

Finally, to be successful in retailing, one must be competitive. In other words, be alert, aggressive, and willing to accept constant change and innovation. Last year's sales and last year's way of doing business won't satisfy today's goals. With the vast growth of shopping centers and the introduction of new forms of retail businesses—all competing hard for the customer's dollar—the successful retailer must be active, imaginative, and persuasive to compete.

Harriet Wilinsky, in her book entitled *Careers and Opportunities in Retailing,* has suggested that you may determine whether a person is suited to retailing by answering the questions as they appear in Figure 1.4. The more often one answers these questions affirmatively, the more suitable retailing is as an occupational choice.

Starting out in retailing

A person's best entrée into retailing is a combination of formal education and work experience. Education may be obtained through four-year college programs, through two-year junior college vocational programs, or through high school programs. The distributive education programs at the high school level and the mid-management programs at the junior college level have been especially successful in providing formal education tailored to retailing.

It is one thing to study retailing and quite another to be able to perform successfully in it. Previous successful retail work experience provides a prospective employer with evidence of the following: (1) the person has more than a passing acquaintance with retail procedures, and (2) she (or he) probably enjoys working in retailing, or she would not be applying for another retail position. A combination of formal education and work experience will usually enable an applicant to command a higher salary and a position of greater responsibility than people who lack these qualifications.

A person interested in a retail position must usually secure one through his own initiative. Only a very few large retail firms visit high school counselors or college placement offices. Therefore, individuals interested in retailing obtain jobs by visiting or writing (submitting personal data sheets) to personnel officers of large organizations or to managers of small stores.

Retail Management

Retailing—successful retailing—is no game for the amateur. To be an amateur is to invite disaster. No longer is there as much room for family businesses as there was in the past.

Gone are the days when merchants succeeded in spite of their operating weaknesses. A stout heart and a little capital simply aren't sufficient for a retailer to maintain a business.

The people who are replacing amateurs are merchants who know what retailing is all about; they are professionals. They set objectives based upon predetermined customer needs and take advantage of new techniques of retail control, insights into the effectiveness of communication efforts, and sophisticated tools for analysis. They use an information system that helps them function in an increasingly competitive environment.

Tomorrow's successful retail operation, large or small, will be run by managers who are professionals in every sense of the word. They will be planners, they'll analyze, evaluate, and predict. They will not only work with many kinds of retail inputs, such as promoting, stocking, and pricing, but will also try to build their organizations into viable, innovative units receptive to change. Professional retailers will be products not so much of "the world of hard knocks" but of a world in which people believe in the value of formal educational programs.

Retail planning

Retailing centers around people. It serves customers, and it serves and uses the talents of employees. Both customers and employers expect retailing to fulfill many of their economic and psychological needs. By their very nature, retail stores are caught in the mainstream of a community's daily life. To make the kind of contribution to society demanded of them, retailers must plan, and plan well. They do this through enlightened approaches to management supervision and through attention to merchandising and operating. Later in this book, we will examine personnel management and store organization; now, however, we will devote our attention to the planning of merchandising and operations.

Merchandising is a term used to refer to the functions of merchandise buying, sales supervision, advertising, and customer service. Operations include the functions of office man-

Do you like things?
Do you find new products fascinating?
Do you like pretty clothes?
Are you interested every season in knowing what looks new in the stores?

Do you like people?
Do you like to figure out what makes them tick?
Do you like a lot of them around you?

Do you like change?
Change of scenery?
Change of activity?
Change in what you do every day?

Are you inquisitive?
Do you like to explore new ideas? New places?
Do you like to know the whole story?

Do you like action?
Do sedentary occupations bore you?
Do you like to be on the scene when exciting things take place?

Are you an extrovert?
Is it easy for you to strike up conversations with old friends?
And even with strangers?
Do you talk to strangers on planes, boats, wherever you're standing around in groups?

Are you energetic?
You don't necessarily have to be the best athlete on campus, but would you rather move than sit?

Is it easy for you to make decisions?
Do you enjoy making up your mind and going into action?
Do you like to help others make up theirs?

What's your leadership record?
Have you been Class President, or won an election for class officer?
Have you captained an athletic team, or led a group, or set a fashion trend in your crowd?
Do your colleagues seek your company—seem to lean on you for decisions?

How important is money to you?
If you were born with the silver spoon, will you settle for less than a gold one you insist upon earning yourself?
If you've been one of the hungry ones up to now, are material things important to you?

How hard are you prepared to work?
And are you willing to work hard, physically and mentally, to reach the top of the heap—or somewhere near the top?

Figure 1.4. Are *you* suited to a career in retailing?

Source: Harriet Wilinsky, *Careers and Opportunities in Retailing*, E. P. Dutton & Co., New York, 1970, p. 21.

agement, inventory control, maintenance, store security and personnel.

What does it mean to plan for merchandising and operations? To answer this question we must look at four different facets of planning: (1) the establishment of objectives, (2) the setting of goals, (3) the determination of the target market, and (4) the programming of strategies that make up a so-called retailing mix (see Figure 1.5).

Establish objectives. To establish objectives, one should describe the purpose of a business and its scope of operation. For example, a retail firm may be in business to fulfill customer needs for high quality ski apparel, equipment, and accessories. Defining the business in this way provides management with the guidelines necessary for effective formulation of operational policies. As management establishes its objectives, it must consider the future by anticipating the needs of the customers it seeks to serve; it must identify and assess the strengths and weaknesses of other retailers in the market; and it must make an evaluation of its own expertise and interests.

Set goals. An outgrowth of the establishment of objectives is the determination of company goals. Whereas objectives indicate the purpose and the scope of operation of a business, goals provide a basis for evaluating whether the company is meeting the objectives. Company goals, therefore, are the standards by which management measures its performance. A re-tail firm may, for example, set for itself the goal of becoming the largest supplier of skiing apparel, equipment, and accessories in a county. Goals may also be stated in terms of the profits, volume, and prestige that a firm hopes to attain at some time in the future.

Define the target market. As management determines objectives, it assesses the opportunities that exist in the market. Therefore, it will ultimately define the target market with which it can best identify; that is, it will select a particular group of customers to whom it wishes to appeal. Like any other marketer, a retailer has innumerable opportunities for directing his business toward a particular part of the market. Because there are many segments within a given market, a retailer must make a careful assessment of the segments before deciding to direct his business toward any one of them. In the ski business alone, a retail firm can strive to appeal to particular segments of the market based on age, sex, and shopping motivations and habits. A merchant must know to whom he wishes to appeal and develop strategies accordingly, or he runs the risk of "being nothing to everyone."

Program strategy. After objectives have been determined, goals have been set, and a target market has been selected, a retailer must select strategies applicable to his business. Before examining these strategies, however, it is important to remember that the hub of all policy decisions is the consumer. To say that stores

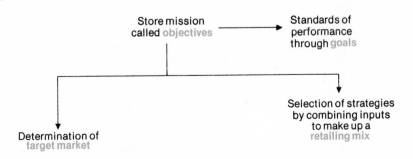

Figure 1.5. The essence of retail planning.

are in business to serve customers is to state the obvious. Nevertheless, too many retailers give only lip service to this seemingly obvious statement. If retailers sincerely attempt to serve customers by making them the focal point of all retail planning and programming, a proper tone will be established for all retailing activity.

Typically, the programming of strategies involves the construction of a retailing mix. As shown in Figure 1.6, a retailing mix is made up of a goods and services mix, a communication mix, and a physical distribution mix. (Notice the position of the consumer in this figure.)

Retailing mix. The *goods and services mix* in Figure 1.6 represents policy considerations relating to the variety and assortment of goods that will be sold and the customer services that will be offered in a retail store. In considering goods, a retailer must make decisions about the price lines, styles, and sizes to be carried by the store. In considering customer services, he must decide how to provide for credit, alterations and adjustments, deliveries, and sales service. Important to the goods and services mix is the recognition that all policy considera-

tions should be worked into an integrated whole, so customers can identify with the store in a consistent and unconfused manner. A store's image depends, in large measure, on consistent policies relating to the goods and services mix.

The *physical distribution mix* represents the policy considerations that relate to the distribution and handling of the merchandise for sale. Inputs into the physical distribution mix include policies involving store upkeep, warehousing, packing, and transporting. In addition, stores made up of more than one operating arm, such as branch stores, will include in their physical distribution mix policies relating to store location.

The *communication mix* represents policy considerations that relate goods and services to consumer demand. By communicating through personal selling, advertising, display, and store layout, the retail store provides information important for the sale of merchandise and services. In addition, the communication mix, like the goods and services mix, can provide the store with an identifiable, meaningful image.

Differential advantage. In developing a strategy that combines the various elements of the retailing mix, retail managers seek to obtain a differential advantage over their competitors. This advantage, which makes one store different or unique in the way it serves customers, may take the form of location, price, promotion, service, or buying advantage, or it may take the form of organizational efficiency. The following are some ways in which a differential advantage may be obtained:

1. The use of *location* as a differential advantage may lead to a site selection where access is convenient and driving time short or where parking is available for customers. A location may also be selected where complementary stores are available; in this kind of location, the customers of one store often become customers of neighboring stores.

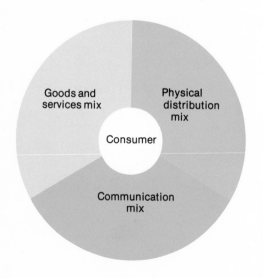

Figure 1.6. The retailing mix.

2. Seeking a *price advantage* may lead to the creation of discount operations that provide minimal service and facilities. Of course, a retailer may feature low prices without converting his store into a discount operation. In the long run, however, profits will suffer unless large volume is maintained and/or fewer services are provided.

3. Highly effective *sales personnel* and *advertising and promotion campaigns* have permitted some retailers to achieve a differential advantage. Many successful retail operations have been built on offering the best and most complete service to a group of consumers who shop where they are given delivery, credit, and extra attention and care.

4. *Buying strategy and ability* may create a differential advantage if retailers are able to interpret the desires of the customer accurately enough to consistently buy well-made, desirable merchandise.

5. Finally, *organizational efficiency* may permit retailers to use or combine successfully the other elements of differential advantage. Chains, for example, command tremendous buying power, have specialized expertise in management areas, and enjoy the advantages of centralized decision making. Retailers who can efficiently use the talents of their people and can develop an effective organization may be able to offer lower prices, more services, or engage in more promotion than their competitors do and still run their businesses as profitably.

Levels of Management

Because of the diversity of retail businesses and the diversity of jobs within a retail organization, any definition of the levels of management must be largely descriptive.

In large companies, there is a division of labor in management activities. This manifests itself in what are referred to as levels of management. Levels of management usually include top management, middle management, and operating management, as is shown in Table 1.1.

Top managers are responsible for developing objectives, establishing policies, controlling operations, and organizing and assembling resources for the firm at a high level or concerning its broadly based aspects. Middle managers are responsible for carrying out the policies formulated by top management; they work in a narrower sphere than do top managers, usually on a departmental level. Like any other management unit within a firm, mid-managers must assume reponsibility for retail planning. Without plans, effective administration is impossible. For most mid-managers the opportunities for personally developing overall company plans are minimal. Yet, they are expected to be aware of the kinds of plans being made because they will be asked to provide input for the development of company plans and to mirror them by formulating plans for their administrative unit. Operating managers develop procedures and regulations based on the policies made by higher levels of management.

Table 1.1. Levels of Management

Top management	Board of Directors, President, Heads of Major Functions (sales, promotion, finance, merchandise, etc.), Large Store Owners
Middle management	Buyers, Department Managers, Warehouse Managers, Divisional Managers, Section Managers, Small Store Owners
Operating management	Assistant Department Managers, Stockroom Managers, Office Managers, Floor Supervisors

At both the middle and operating levels of management, the basic knowledge required at the one level is, to a large extent, also required at the other. The differences between levels are primarily that the authority and responsibilities of operating managers are more narrow in scope than are those of mid-managers and operating managers are less likely to initiate changes.

Owner-managers of stores dealing in small volumes may also be considered middle managers, because the scale of operations in a small store does not require all of the different kinds of knowledge needed by executives faced with the problem of planning and coordinating highly stratified operations. The operating methods of an owner-manager of a small store are similar to those of a department manager in a large department store or a branch store manager of a large chain. Thus, owner-managers of small retail firms must perform many activities associated with the mid-management level as well as operating management.

Problem Solving and Decision Making

The essence of management is decision making. The best decision, of course, is one that results in the greatest sales and profits. It is the job of managers to evaluate alternatives and select a course of action that will result in the greatest return to the organization.

Any decision involves an element of risk or uncertainty, but by using a problem-solving process, managers can tip the balance between gains and losses in their favor. The problem-solving process one should use has six steps.

Identify the problem. Many times a problem may seem simpler than it is. Managers must be able to identify the specific cause of the problem. Take, for example, a store that is experiencing decreasing sales. Decreasing sales are not the real problem but are, instead, a symptom of some problem. It is a manager's job to determine the cause of decreasing sales. For example, are they caused by a poor advertising program, the stocking of inappropriate merchandise, or poor sales people?

Gather all relevant facts. If managers are to determine the extent and the implications of a problem, they must collect all the information needed to understand it. In this step of the problem-solving process, a hard look at the store, the environment, and the competition is vital to good decision making.

Determine possible courses of action. In light of the information gathered, managers must determine *all* possible solutions to the problem. Creative thinking is important in this phase, for innovations can make the difference between success and failure.

Determine the consequences of each course of action. After listing all alternative courses of action, managers must evaluate each from the standpoint of its benefits and its side effects. By viewing each alternative in terms of dollar return, increased efficiency, impact on employees, and so on, managers will be better able to select the best course of action.

Select and initiate the best course of action. In this step a course of action that will best serve the store's objectives is actually selected. After selection, the chosen course of action should be put into effect. This entails the delegating of authority and responsibility to subordinates who carry out the work requirements and the notifying of all interested parties that the course of action is in effect.

Evaluate the decision. How effective was the solution to the problem? What could have been done to improve the decision? If the problem still exists, what can be done to solve it, and why didn't the course of action selected solve it?

At the end of each chapter, you are asked to make a decision about a problem in a case study. Use the process we have described to make your decisions.

Summary

Retailing has had a varied existence. Although its primary purpose has been to serve society's needs for goods and services, it has not always enjoyed the best of relationships with society. Retailing is made up of many different types of institutions, both store and nonstore. The more important types of retail stores include chain, discount, department, and limited line specialty stores. Telephone, door-to-door, mail order, and vending machine selling are common types of nonstore retailing. These retail institutions offer many advantages (and some disadvantages) for those considering retailing as a career.

Managers of retail firms are concerned with developing a viable program that meets the needs of the customers they serve. Managers must understand that is their responsibility to develop this program in the most effective way possible, while taking into consideration the wishes and needs of customers. Attention to planning—beginning with the establishment of store objectives and concluding with the development of a retailing mix—will help the store to be of service to its customers. Crucial to planning is an understanding of the problem-solving and decision-making processes.

Questions and Problems

1. In your estimation, does our retailing system really work? Does it work to the advantage of everyone?
2. Would our system of retailing benefit if firms were larger or smaller than they are now? Why?
3. How might the retailing mix be different for a motorcycle shop and a teen specialty clothing shop? How might each shop achieve a differential advantage?
4. Explain the trends in retailing, as you see them. How could you obtain supportive data for your views?
5. What types of individuals are best suited to a career in retailing? For what reasons?

Situations and Activities

You are the owner-manager of a gift shop in a town of 40,000. Your stock consists of crystal, fine china, silver, bric-a-brac, candles, cards, artificial floral designs, kitchen crockery, woodware, metal sculpture, and an assortment of inexpensive gift items. The town has been growing rapidly, and two discount houses have recently purchased ground for stores which will open in a few months. You, and many other small retailers, feel threatened by these new competitors. You feel that you may lose as much as 15 to 20 percent of your business to the discount houses. What courses of action are open to you?

You are the white owner-manager of a service station in a predominantly black neighborhood. You have operated your station for only three months, but you are concerned that the sales volume you had anticipated will not materialize unless you act to alleviate some of the problems you are experiencing. These problems include the following: (1) There is substantial traffic flow going past your station, but no one is stopping. (2) Your prices continue to be 2 to 3 cents above those offered by your competitors in the immediate area, but you know that you're already getting rock-bottom prices from your supplier. What courses of action should you take to achieve the sales volume you had anticipated for your business?

Conduct a study of your community. Try to find the names of businesses which failed over the last five years, and to discover the reasons why they failed.

Try to find out why there seem to be so many service stations in your community. Ask consumers, service station owners, and gasoline company distributors why they believe there are enough or not enough such stations in existence. Then give your own conclusions.

Sketch out what you consider to be a "model" plan of your city by locating retail shopping facilities within the city. How does your model match with what exists? What things could you suggest to make "what exists" more nearly fit your model?

List reasons that can result in differential advantages for a retail store. Talk to a merchant and have him explain to you what he feels his differential advantages are.

Bibliography

Barksdale, Hiram C. and Darden, Bill. "Marketers' Attitudes toward the Marketing Concept," *Journal of Marketing,* October, 1971, pp. 29—36.

Buskirk, Richard H. *Principles of Marketing.* New York: Holt, Rinehart and Winston, 1970. pp. 280—283.

Franchising in the Economy, 1971—1973, U.S. Department of Commerce, 1972.

Kotler, Phillip. *Marketing Management: Analysis, Planning, and Control.* 2nd ed. Englewood Cliffs, N.J.: Prentice Hall, 1972. pp. 439—444.

Lazer, William, and Kelley, Eugene J. "The Retailing Mix: Planning and Management." *Journal of Retailing* Spring, 1961, pp. 34—41.

Leeman, Wayne A. *Capitalism, Market Socialism, and Central Planning.* Boston: Houghton Mifflin, 1963.

Nystrom, Paul H. *Economics of Retailing: Retailing Institutions and Trends.* 3d rev. ed. New York: The Ronald Press, 1930. Chapters 3—5.

Stern, Mark E. *Marketing Planning: A Systems Approach.* New York: McGraw-Hill, 1967.

Wilinsky, Harriet. *Careers and Opportunities in Retailing.* New York: E. P. Dutton, 1970.

two

UNDERSTANDING THE RETAIL CUSTOMER

2

The Customer's Ability to Buy

contents

behavioral objectives

A market represents customers who have both the ability and the willingness to buy. This chapter explores the factors that influence the ability to buy. The manager who is knowledgeable about such factors as population and income characteristics will be best able to adapt his store to meet customer needs. To understand the market, the manager must first become familiar with the totality of the retail environment, that is, with the national scene. However, the manager must also know and understand the community environment of which the store is a part.

Upon completing this chapter, you will be able to do the following:
☐ Define market.
☐ Explain the secret of serving customers.
☐ Describe the ways in which markets may be segmented.
☐ Explain how knowledge of population characteristics can help the manager make decisions.
☐ Explain how knowledge of income characteristics can help the manager make decisions.

Every employee in a retail store should have one central goal in mind. *It is his or her primary duty to make people want to patronize the store.* Unless each member of the management team works to bring customers into the store and strives to make them want to return with regularity, a successful retail operation cannot be sustained. This chapter, therefore, provides an understanding of the retail customer through an investigation of retail markets. The chapter first discusses the importance of the customer. It then shows how retailers may appeal to different groups, or segments, within a market. Following this is a description and discussion of the nature of retail markets.

The Sovereignty of the Customer

At various levels in the organization, retail personnel are responsible for observing and evaluating several operational factors:

Merchandise selection and display
Costs
Personnel
Sales
Business methods and systems
Competition

As important as these operational factors are, however, something else is more important to the retailer—the customer. The customer determines the ultimate success of a retail business. If customers are dissatisfied, they may easily find another store that serves them better.

It cannot be emphasized too strongly that consumers must be considered kings or queens by the retailer. As such, they present a challenge. Because consumers have a limited amount of money, they must decide how to spend it. Retailers compete with one another for each consumer dollar. Competition takes place not only among firms offering similar or substitute products but also among firms offering unrelated products. A woman walking down the main street of a city with fifty dollars

in her purse finds at least a thousand items she might buy. Merchants compete to tempt her to spend her fifty dollars in their store. Only she, however, can decide what she wants to buy, where she wants to buy it, and how much of the fifty dollars she will spend on each item. The customer, then, is sovereign—he or she has supreme power.

Attracting and Retaining Customers

There are two fundamental methods of attracting and retaining customers. These methods include (1) adapting operations to customer needs and (2) treating customers as individuals.

Adapting to the changing customer

Every day, there are increasing numbers of products and services from which customers may choose. Because shoppers' tastes, preferences, and habits change rapidly, retailers must keep abreast of trends in order to survive. Retailers must continually analyze customers' spending patterns and habits, to sell their products. They must adapt all parts of their operations to identifiable customer changes, and must consider the changes taking place in the local trading area as well as the changes taking place in the total consumer market.

Treating customers as individuals

Successful retailers must learn to relate to customers as individuals. The key to success is thinking in terms of individuals—not in terms of masses. Customers today have a greater sense of identity and individuality than ever before, and are, therefore, less concerned with conformity than they were in the past. Although customers still want approval, they are buying less frequently for reasons of status and more frequently to satisfy other needs.

Market segmentation

One way of treating customers as individuals is to take the total market available to the retailer and divide it into similar parts. The process of dividing a total market into parts, or segments, each of which has homogeneous or similar characteristics, is known as market segmentation. Examples of market segmentation include the following:

1. The shoe store owner that stocks a wide assortment of sizes for customers who desire and need uncommon sizes.
2. The discount house that serves customers who like the convenience of one-stop shopping, who are price conscious, and who do not expect a great many services.
3. The drive-in restaurant that gives customers quick service, convenience, and, in many cases, low prices.
4. The general merchandise store that provides shopping intimacy through the "shoppe" concept (for example, the ski shoppe) for customers who desire special personal attention.

Because few retail stores can cater to a total market, each retailer should try to identify one or a few segments that it can serve efficiently and profitably. The manager who segments the market must analyze and understand the segments with which he is dealing. Then he can tailor his merchandise offering, pricing strategy, and degree of service to the needs and desires of that segment.

Analyzing a Retail Market

How does the manager analyze the market? The approach is actually straightforward. It is based on the knowledge that a market is made up of people with both an ability and a willingness to buy. It is relatively easy for the retailer to examine and understand those aspects of population and purchasing power that affect people's ability to buy. To do this requires an analysis of the individuals making up the population, the location of the population, and the amounts of money being spent.

Understanding a market's willingness to buy is more complicated, requiring an examination of the complexities of consumer behav-

ior. The next chapter will deal with this aspect of retail markets. In Chapter 8 we will examine the role of research in providing information on retail markets.

Population characteristics

The following overview of population is designed to familiarize you with the important characteristics influencing retail markets. Specifically, this overview provides statistics and comments on population trends in the United States. The retailer is naturally most interested in the population characteristics of his community, but cannot fully understand that community without some knowledge of national characteristics. Every retailer is ultimately affected by changes that occur in the aggregate consumer market, and consequently, each must be aware of and ready to react to shifts and trends in the population characteristics of the nation.

Population characteristics are often referred to as demographic characteristics. Demography is the statistical study of the characteristics of human population, particularly with reference to size and density, growth, distribution, migration, births and deaths, and the effects these variables have on social and economic conditions.

The population of the United States. Throughout most of this century, the United States has been undergoing a population explosion. It was 1915 before the population reached 100 million. Thirty-five years later, in 1950, the population reached 151 million, an increase of over 50 percent; and by 1975 the population had reached 214 million, more than doubling the population of 1915—all in less than sixty years.

During the 1960's, however, population growth began to slow. Although absolute numbers increased, in each consecutive year it was less than in the year before, both in terms of absolute numbers and percentages. These declining rates appear to be leveling off and may even be reversing slightly. Nevertheless, the number of women today who are of child-bearing age is larger than it has ever been.

So even declining birth rates will not halt substantial population growth for some time.

But even a deceleration in population growth greatly affects retailers. In the past, many retailers relied on expanding population for sales growth. If the U.S. moves closer to the environmentalist's goal of zero population growth, sales growth in retailing will depend on growth in individual purchasing power and increasing a store's share of the existing market.

Regional population. Soon after the eastern seaboard was settled, the U.S. began to witness a steady westward population shift that still continues today. In all likelihood, the largest rates of growth will continue to occur in the Pacific Coast, South, and Mountain regions. Many retail operations have been successful because they moved with or in advance of population shifts to these areas.

Shifts in populations. As important as regional distribution changes have been, however, shifts among urban, suburban, and rural populations have had the most dramatic impact on retailing. Until the middle of this century, the cities experienced continuing population growth, partly as the result of rural migration. In the early 1950's, however, there began to be substantial migration from city to suburb, facilitated by automobile ownership and the growth of highway systems. Today the greatest growth is still in the suburbs, and the suburbs are moving farther out, away from the central core cities. Rural areas are also growing rapidly as the central cities stagnate or decline.

Like any rapid, unplanned, change, the population redistribution has created havoc throughout the business world, affecting retail and manufacturing facilities, many of which have followed the residential shift. Many major downtown retailers have been forced to move to suburban areas, or, at least, to open branch outlets. Some have been forced to close unprofitable downtown stores, while others, who did not anticipate the movement from the core city, have remained downtown although their market is now in the suburbs. As a whole,

however, retailers have been following population shifts by moving to locations accessible to customers' automobiles. This, in turn, has led to the formation of strip shopping areas and has accelerated the trend toward centralized suburban shopping centers.

Age distribution. Shifts in the age distribution of the population are also very important to retailers. Several events have had, and will continue to have, profound influence on age distribution. The depression of the 1930's caused the number of births to drop dramatically. As the GI's returned following World War II, the number of births increased as dramatically as they had dropped during the depression. During the 1960's, the birth rate again declined due to changing life styles, improved methods of birth control and the feminist movement. Figure 2.1 illustrates that as each group of people born during these periods moves up the age ladder the size of each level contracts or expands accordingly.

Important changes in age distribution will continue. For example, in 1975 approximately 44 percent of the population over fifteen years of age was in the fifteen to thirty year old group, in contrast to 39 percent in this group in 1965. Retailers must, therefore, plan to meet the needs of a rapidly growing portion of the population that is entering the market for the first time and has, of course, no preestablished store or brand loyalties.

Marriages. Another population characteristic that has an important influence on retail sales is the number of marriages. The formation of new families gives rise to a variety of needs for products and services. During the ten-year period from 1965 to 1975, the number of new families increased as much as it did during the fifteen-year period from 1950 to 1965. This increase occurred because the large number of children who were born in the post-World War II period reached marrying age. Marriages increased from 1.6 million annually in 1965 to 2 million in 1975.

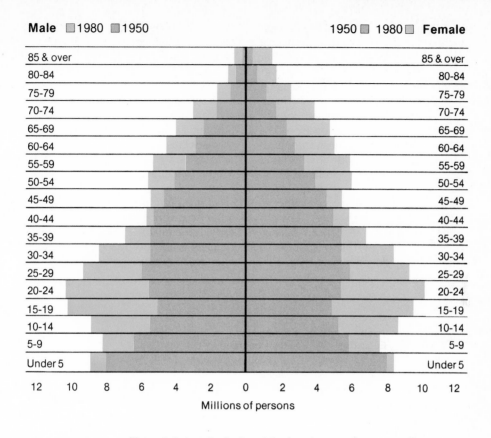

Figure 2.1. Age distribution of the American people.

Source: The Conference Board.

Birth rates. Retailers must also be aware of how current birth rates will affect the composition of tomorrow's population. Over the past two decades the birth rate has declined significantly. Although this seems paradoxical in view of the growing number of young people and the rising number of marriages, a significant part of the decline may be accounted for by couples who postponed having a second and third child. Births for each thousand women in the fifteen to twenty-four year old age bracket have decreased by over 30 percent.

Such postponements probably indicate trends toward smaller families. Young families today average only two children compared with three or four only a few years ago, and retailers will have to plan for substantial shifts in their merchandise offerings in the future. Young couples who have smaller families will have increasing amounts of disposable income to spend on homes, furnishings, recreation, and the like—income that previously would have been spent on raising and educating their children. Also, with fewer children, more money can be spent on each child and it is likely to be spent on more varied and higher quality merchandise.

Educational levels. Since World War II, Americans have been especially concerned with the amount and quality of their education.

More people than ever before want to obtain educations that involve in-depth study over a period of years. Figure 2.2 shows the number of students at various education levels over three decades. Notice the increasingly large numbers of students pursuing higher education. Students who forego immediate jobs in anticipation of higher earning capacity in the future will join the already large numbers of affluent Americans who provide the demand for products that satisfy a high standard of living.

College graduates represent only a minority of the total number of affluent Americans, however. The 13 million American college graduates of the middle 1970's constitute only 15 percent of the population over twenty years of age. Millions of other Americans will have extended their education through trade and technical programs, and many will achieve income levels exceeding those of college graduates. Not to be overlooked, too, are the estimated 65 million adults who participate in educational programs for job advancement, retraining, and cultural enrichment. These adults will also contribute substantially to the demand for products and services that contribute to a high standard of living.

Occupational shifts. A person's occupation influences not only his income but also his purchasing behavior. Of particular importance to retailers is the occupational shift that causes changes in purchasing behavior.

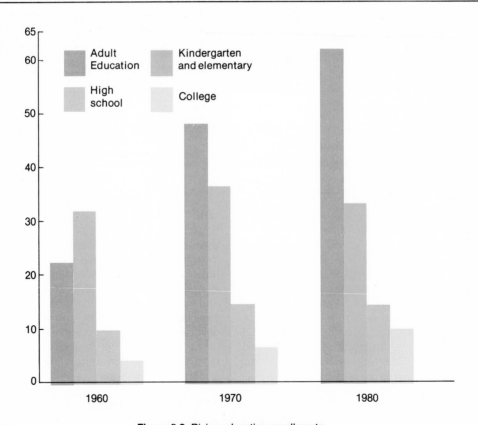

Figure 2.2. Rising education enrollments.

Source: U. S. Department of Commerce, Bureau of Census.

Today, occupational shifts are generally toward jobs that require a significant amount of higher education. Such shifts have been both the result and the cause of the rising educational level of people in the labor force. Occupational shifts also occur because of changes in the demand for goods and services and from changes in the level of technology. Automation and mechanization have enabled manufacturing industries to produce large volumes of products with fewer workers than in the past. Concurrently, the demand for services has increased rapidly, with an increased demand for white-collar workers in service industries, such as retailing and wholesaling, transportation, finance, education, health, and government.

As a result of occupational shifts, fewer people will spend their entire lives in one type of work or at the same job. The changing requirements of the working environment will require frequent retraining and additional education. Occupational shifts will also cause people to relocate frequently. As people improve their skills and move from job to job, numerous opportunities open up to retailers.

Another important change in the occupational world is the declining length of the work week. The average hours of work per week have declined from fifty-five in 1910 to thirty-seven in 1975. Large numbers of people with additional leisure time or time to pursue a second job and increase their income affect retailing.

There have also been significant changes in the number of women participating in the labor force. Increasing numbers of women, particularly in the over thirty-five group, are expected to hold jobs. Working wives bring additional income to families and increase the demand for services and laborsaving products.

Mobility. Americans are on the go and on the move. Occupational shifts are a major cause of increased mobility. Another cause is the weakening of cultural and social barriers. Figure 2.3 shows the mobility of the American population. In four years, over 37 percent of the

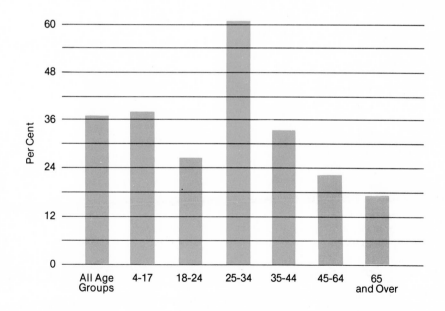

Figure 2.3. Proportion of each age group moving, March 1970 to March 1974.

Source: *A Guide to Consumer Markets, 1975/1976.* New York: The Conference Board, 1973, p. 39.

people have changed houses. Current statistics confirm that the U.S. population is still highly mobile. Mobility presents a challenge to the retailer, for every few years he may be faced with an entirely new group of customers, whose store loyalties, shopping habits, and even brand preferences are different from those of previous customers.

Income

A market's ability to buy is measured not only by the number of consumers (population) but also by the amount of money they have to spend (income). Income, then, is central to retailing. Income may be broken down into six basic divisions: personal income, disposable income, discretionary income, money income, real income, and psychic income.

1. *Personal income* is gross income before taxes.
2. *Disposable income* is income that remains after taxes are deducted; it is the amount of money available for expenditures for personal consumption and savings.
3. *Discretionary income* is income that is free of fixed commitments and is not needed for essential household needs.
4. *Money income* is income that an individual actually receives.
5. *Real income* is income that reflects actual purchasing power in relation to the purchasing power of income in some previous period. The importance of examining income changes in terms of real income versus money income is illustrated in Figure 2.4.
6. *Psychic income* is income that represents personal satisfactions, rather than money. If a person sacrifices a financial income to live in one place or to choose a job that he or she finds especially enjoyable, the person receives psychic income.

Levels and distribution of income. The income of Americans grew dramatically from 1950 to 1975. Per capita personal income is expected to continue increasing, with the result that by 1980, 67 percent of American families

will probably be in the over $10,000 income bracket (see Figure 2.5). In 1950 only 14.7 percent of families were in this bracket. The effects of a great number of families in high income levels combined with an increased number of consumer spending units will affect retailing profoundly. The demand for existing goods and services will increase, as will the demand for new ones.

The retailer should also be aware of differences in the distribution of income among regions. During the last two decades, personal income has been increasing most rapidly in the Far West, the Southwest, and the Southeast. However, in the Southeast per capita personal income is still 20 percent below the national average, while in the Far West it is 15 percent above the average. In addition to studying distribution within income levels, the retailer should be aware of the income levels of people in cities and in segments within cities. These considerations are important in making decisions concerning store locations, store image, merchandise offerings, and the like.

Credit and savings. The purchasing power of the individual consumer spending unit is made up of credit and savings, as well as current income. Americans use credit extensively for all types of retail purchases. In 1976 consumer installment credit passed $160 billion (up from about $14 billion in 1950). Noninstallment credit (charge accounts, single payment loans, and service credit) rose from less than $7 billion in 1950 to over $40 billion in 1976. These figures indicate one reason why the expanding population is able to translate needs and desires into demand for goods and services. The availability and use of consumer credit will continue to have a profound influence on the retailing industry.

In general, personal savings account for 6 to 7 percent of personal income. This creates a reservoir of funds available to the customer for major purchases.

Expenditure patterns

We have been considering population and income characteristics in an effort to understand consumer markets. Another useful ele-

1949	1975	
$10,000	$23,640	1975 income needed for equivalent 1949 purchasing power of $10,000
	10,544	Purchasing power lost through inflation.
1,112	4,208	Income and social security taxes.
8,888	8,888	Disposable income after taxes.

Figure 2.4. Real income in relation to money income.

Source: U. S. Department of Commerce.

ment has to do with *how* and *where* consumers spend their money. Analysis of consumer expenditure patterns allows the retailer to identify the dollar size of product and service markets, market growth rates, the proportion of the household dollar spent for various products and services, and the changes in expenditures associated with income changes.

Some changes that have taken place in consumer consumption expenditures are shown in Figure 2.6. The figure shows total dollar expenditures and the percent for each major expenditure category. Just as important as the aggregate expenditure data, which allows one to estimate total product-area sales potentials, is the trend and proportional expenditure data. Notice that some categories, such as toilet articles, are growing faster than disposable income, while others, such as shoes, have less growth.

A close study of consumer expenditure patterns leads to some useful generalizations about the relationship between income and expenditure patterns. In 1857 Ernst Engel, a

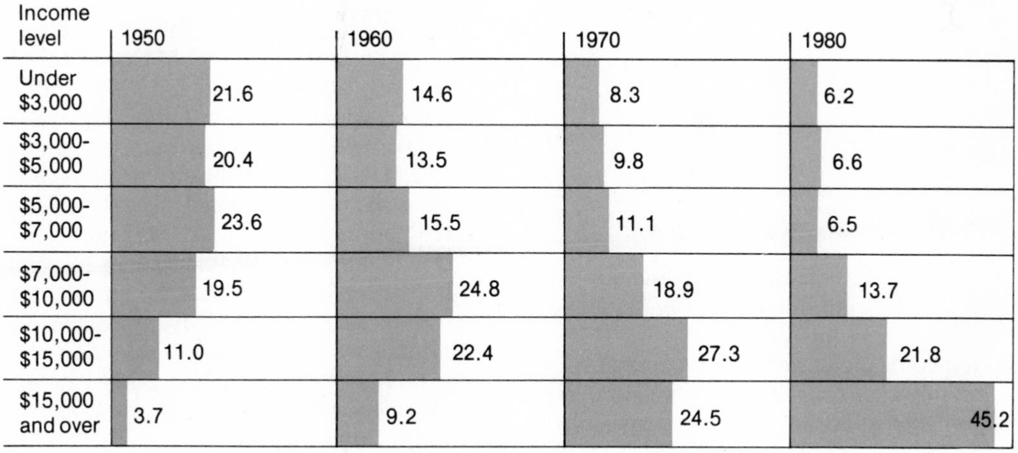

Income level	1950	1960	1970	1980
Under $3,000	21.6	14.6	8.3	6.2
$3,000-$5,000	20.4	13.5	9.8	6.6
$5,000-$7,000	23.6	15.5	11.1	6.5
$7,000-$10,000	19.5	24.8	18.9	13.7
$10,000-$15,000	11.0	22.4	27.3	21.8
$15,000 and over	3.7	9.2	24.5	45.2

Figure 2.5. Changing profile of family income distribution in 1971 dollars.

Source: U. S. Department of Commerce.

Type of Product	1960	1970 Amount	1970 Per Cent	Average Annual Growth Rate[1]	Income Elasticity[2]
Per capita disposable income	$1,938	$3,358			
Disposable personal income[3]	350.0	687.8	100.0	4.2	.97
Total consumption expenditures[3]	325.2	615.8	100.0	4.1	
Food for home consumption	62.0	100.5	16.3	2.6	.62
Purchased meals, beverages	16.2	28.4	4.6	2.1	.51
Women's, children's clothing	14.8	28.8	4.7	4.3	1.01
Men's, boys' clothing	8.0	15.5	2.5	3.8	.91
Shoes	4.5	8.1	1.3	2.5	.59
Toilet articles, preparations	3.0	6.1	1.0	6.3	
Personal care services	2.4	4.0	.7	3.2	
Housing	46.3	91.2	14.8	4.9	1.16
Furniture, bedding	4.6	8.0	1.3	3.3	.78
Household appliances	4.8	8.5	1.4	6.0	1.43
Household supplies	3.4	5.5	.9	4.0	.96
Drugs, supplies, equipment	4.4	8.6	1.4	6.3	1.49
Medical care services	14.7	38.7	6.3	4.9	1.16
Automobile purchase	17.7	31.5	5.1	5.6	1.33
Gasoline, oil	12.3	22.9	3.7	4.4	1.05
Radio, TV	3.4	8.3	1.4	9.3	2.21
Toys, sporting goods	4.5	10.6	1.7	7.2	1.71

[1]Average Annual Growth Rates, 1955 - 1970 based on constant dollars.
[2]Percentage change in personal consumption expenditures for each 1% rise in real disposable income.
[3]Billions of Dollars

Figure 2.6. Selected patterns of consumer spending: total dollars by category, growth rate, and income elasticity.

Source: *A Guide to Consumer Markets, 1975/1976.* New York: The Conference Board, 1973, pp. 162–170.

German statistician, after a study of Belgian workers' budgets, made four generalizations that have become benchmarks for the study of consumer expenditure patterns. The four generalizations known as *Engel's Laws* are as follows.

1. As income increases, a smaller percentage will be spent for food.
2. As income increases, the percentage spent for clothing will remain approximately the same.
3. As income increases, the percentage spent for housing and household operations will remain about the same.
4. As income increases, the percentage spent for miscellaneous items (recreation, religion, education, and so on) and savings will increase.

These laws, which are concerned with percentage changes (total expenditures for all categories increase with increasing incomes) have generally been confirmed by study of today's expenditure patterns except for some variations in laws 2 and 3. This is illustrated by the income elasticity figures in Figure 2.6.

The aggregate expenditure data and associations with changes in disposable income present only a part of the consumption pattern picture. There are significant variations associated with such factors as place of residence, family income, age of household, and so forth.

One of the most valuable sources of expenditure pattern information is the annual *Sales Management Survey of Buying Power.* This publication contains detailed breakdowns by the national, state, and local markets; income; and retail sales. The data in Figure 2.7, taken from the *Survey of Buying Power,* show the population breakdowns, income distributions, and retail sales by category for a particular metro area.

STATE OF KANSAS

KANSAS METRO AREAS COUNTIES CITIES	POPULATION—12/31/75								RETAIL SALES BY STORE GROUP 1975							EFFECTIVE BUYING INCOME 1975						
	Total Pop. (Thousands)	% Of U.S.	Median Age Of Pop.	% Of Population By Age Group				House-holds (Thousands)	Total Retail Sales ($000)	Food ($000)	Eating & Drinking Places ($000)	General Mdse. ($000)	Furnit-Furnish.-Appl. ($000)	Auto-motive ($000)	Drug ($000)	Total EBI ($000)	Median Hsld. EBI	% Of Hslds. By EBI Group (A) $8,000-$9,999 (B) $10,000-$14,999 (C) $15,000-$24,999 (D) $25,000 & Over				Buying Power Index
				18-24 Years	25-34 Years	35-49 Years	50 & Over											A	B	C	D	
LAWRENCE	63.0	.0293	24.0	30.9	14.0	14.2	17.2	20.4	163,471	32,640	10,184	21,197	16,141	31,362	3,421	304,088	12,299	8.1	20.9	27.1	11.3	.0283
Douglas	63.0	.0293	24.0	30.9	14.0	14.2	17.2	20.4	163,471	32,640	10,184	21,197	16,141	31,362	3,421	304,088	12,299	8.1	20.9	27.1	11.3	.0283
• Lawrence	50.2	.0234	23.6	35.5	14.2	13.2	15.2	16.2	153,967	30,883	9,613	21,104	15,841	29,231	3,161	244,620	12,126	7.8	20.7	26.4	11.5	.0238
SUBURBAN TOTAL	12.8	.0059	29.5	13.0	13.4	17.5	25.1	4.2	9,504	1,757	571	93	300	2,131	260	59,468	12,939	9.4	21.1	29.8	10.8	.0045
TOPEKA	183.8	.0857	28.8	13.5	13.5	16.5	25.1	63.9	554,985	94,090	43,707	80,143	24,049	100,311	14,690	940,936	13,124	8.2	22.6	30.7	10.7	.0888
Jefferson	13.6	.0063	30.1	12.7	10.8	15.5	29.2	4.6	17,206	4,950	1,712	446	554	2,158	647	61,308	11,729	8.8	21.7	27.6	8.1	.0051
Osage	14.3	.0067	32.8	13.0	10.2	15.2	32.6	5.2	25,261	6,659	2,523	139	1,128	6,348	609	63,662	10,547	8.3	21.7	24.9	5.8	.0055
Shawnee	155.9	.0727	28.4	13.6	14.2	16.7	24.0	54.1	512,518	82,481	39,472	79,558	22,277	91,805	13,434	815,966	13,464	8.1	22.6	31.6	11.5	.0782
• Topeka	131.7	.0614	29.4	13.4	13.8	16.0	26.3	47.8	479,500	80,143	36,224	72,265	21,531	90,545	13,434	709,729	13,185	8.2	22.0	30.6	11.4	.0695
SUBURBAN TOTAL	52.1	.0243	27.2	13.7	13.1	17.5	22.2	16.1	75,485	13,947	7,483	7,878	2,518	9,766	1,256	231,207	12,968	8.1	24.2	31.2	8.5	.0193
WICHITA	381.2	.1778	28.4	13.4	14.7	16.9	23.4	132.7	1,203,485	209,668	111,565	173,949	61,112	264,454	28,876	2,085,483	13,877	7.6	23.5	31.5	13.2	.1934
Butler	38.7	.0181	30.7	14.3	12.2	16.7	28.0	13.8	93,756	17,865	6,092	4,087	6,384	25,237	3,225	191,697	12,651	8.6	26.2	29.4	8.3	.0174
Sedgwick	342.5	.1597	28.2	13.3	14.9	17.0	22.9	118.9	1,109,729	191,803	105,473	169,862	54,728	239,217	25,651	1,893,786	14,037	7.5	23.1	31.7	13.8	.1760
• Wichita	263.2	.1227	29.0	13.9	14.5	16.5	24.8	95.8	1,006,421	175,872	96,365	163,213	47,134	217,695	24,365	1,504,434	13,823	7.6	22.5	30.8	13.9	.1452
SUBURBAN TOTAL	118.0	.0551	27.2	12.4	14.7	18.1	20.5	36.9	197,064	33,796	15,200	10,736	13,978	46,759	4,511	581,049	13,992	7.6	26.1	33.2	11.4	.0482

Figure 2.7. Example of expenditure data available from *Sales & Marketing Management of Survey of Buying Power.*

Sources such as the *Survey of Buying Power* and the *Survey of Current Business* contain much additional information on expenditure patterns and their association with education; occupation; residence in the central city, suburbia, or non-metropolitan areas; race; and sex. Careful study of expenditure patterns is an important part of the analysis necessary to understand and segment consumer markets.

Interpreting population and income information

The population, income, and expenditure information previously discussed tells retailers that the wants, needs, buying power, degree of education, and life styles of customers are different from what they were ten years ago, five years ago, or even last year. Continual changes make it necessary for retailers to adapt to the needs of their customers.

They must understand that customers expect and even demand that stores carry merchandise that meets their rising standard of living. Customers expect to shop in stores designed for comfortable and convenient shopping. They expect that stores will be able to accommodate large crowds and include appropriate display space for merchandise.

Retailers must understand that customers today want merchandise that emphasizes style and that appeals to the young. The young not only have more money to spend than ever before but also have more freedom to spend it. The young help determine what is bought, as well as where it is bought. Today's Americans are constantly on the move—from state to state, from country to city, and from the city to the suburbs. When Americans are not changing residences, they are traveling on business or for recreation across the country and around the world. A mobile population is a population that buys more products—sporting goods, housekeeping supplies, garden equipment, magazines, automobiles, and many, many more.

Finally, retailers must understand that population growth, mobility, high incomes, and increased amounts of education and leisure time will influence the life styles of consumers.

Summary

How does one assess a market's ability to buy? By now, you know the answer involves looking at the characteristics of the market's two components: population and income. Population (the number of people in the market) and income (the amount of money the people spend) are the retailer's criteria for assessing the profitability of a market. In the United States the ability to buy has been enhanced by a growing population and increased income. Population and income, in turn, have been influenced by increases in the number of marriages, the amount of mobility and leisure time, the number of young people, and the amount of education people receive. All these factors, operating both nationally and locally, must be taken into consideration by the retailer who wants to treat his customers correctly.

The retailer should also be able to divide the total market into segments so he can determine what group of customers he most wants to reach.

Questions and Problems

1. What factors may have contributed to the declining birth rate in the United States? Is this trend likely to continue? If so, what changes will retailers have to make?
2. The sales of which of the following products are likely to be influenced by urban, suburban, and rural population distribution?
   a. automobiles
   b. school supplies
   c. boats
   d. china dishes
   e. furniture
   f. foods
3. Has rising educational attainment influenced the popularity of discount stores? If so, why?
4. People of different ages purchase different products in differing quantities. Contrast the product and service needs of teenagers to the product and service needs of married couples whose children have left home.
5. Use population and income factors to define the target market segment represented by college students.

Situations and Activities

You are the owner-manager of a small specialty dress shop in a middle-class suburb of a major metropolitan city. You opened the store five years ago. The shop's merchandise is in the medium price range and consists of a few brand names but is made up mainly of a variety of good quality merchandise from relatively unknown manufacturers. After four years of success, you decided to open an identical store near the central business district of the city. You put the same merchandise in the new store because you thought that the shopping area in which it is located was as good as the shopping area in which the first store is located. At the end of the first year, the second store did not have even half the sales that the first store had during its first year of operation. Because you made sure that the two stores were similar in every way, you are perplexed by the poor showing of your new store. What factors did you most likely overlook?

You are the assistant manager in a medium-size junior department store located in the community in which you are now attending school. The store manager has asked you to explore the possibility of opening a subteen fashion boutique in the store. What factors will you include in your analysis? Where will you obtain the information you need?

Do the poor pay more? Conduct a survey of prices charged for food items within your community. Select stores frequented by the middle/upper-middle income families and stores frequented by the poor. Compare the results. What do books and magazines in your library have to say on this subject?

From what you know about population and income characteristics and trends within your community, predict which retail businesses will fail by 1980 if these trends should continue, and if the stores continue to serve customers much as they are doing today. What other factors may be forcing these failures?

Given the population and income trends presented in the chapter, how will each of these trends affect the following types of retail stores: variety stores, restaurants, and jewelry stores?

Bibliography

Cox, Reavis. *Consumers' Credit and Wealth: A Study in Consumer Credit.* Washington, D.C.: National Foundation for Consumer Credit, 1965.

Engel, James F.;Kollat, David T.; and Blackwell, Roger D. *Consumer Behavior.* New York: Holt, Rinehart, and Winston, 1973. pp. 120—142.

Foust, James D., and Southwood, Al D. "The Population Fizzle." *Business Horizons,* February, 1973, pp. 5—20.

Kessten, Charles. "Youth Market in Perspective." *Marketing Through Retailers.* American Management Association, 1967. p. 174.

Longman, Kenneth A., "Market Segmentation vs. Segmented Marketing." *TIMS Interfaces,* June, 1971, pp. 38—40.

McNeal, James A. *An Introduction to Consumer Behavior.* New York: John Wiley and Sons, 1973. pp. 23—28.

Saltzman, Maurice. "The Teenage Customer." *Marketing Through Retailers.* American Management Association, 1967. pp. 164—169.

"What Makes the New Consumer Buy." *Business Week, April 24, 1971, pp. 52*—58.

"Will the Real Youth Market Please Stand Up?" *Sales Management,* January 1, 1970, p. 36.

3

The Customer's Willingness to Buy

contents

behavioral objectives

Retail managers must understand the behavioral forces that influence customer purchasing. This chapter first explores individual behavior and behavioral concepts—attitudes, perceptions, motives. It then explores the environmental forces that may influence purchasing behavior. The presentation of a purchasing decision model follows this discussion. If you can relate your knowledge of internal and external forces to the way a particular consumer approaches a purchasing decision, you will have mastered the contents of the chapter and its implications for management.

Upon completing this chapter, you will be able to do the following:
☐ Explain what is meant by a dominance hierarchy of motives.
☐ Describe the classifications of motives.
☐ Define perception and attitude, and explain how they influence purchasing behavior.
☐ Describe the three major social variables that influence customer behavior, and explain how an understanding of these variables can aid retail managers.
☐ Explain how an understanding of the stages in the purchasing decision process can help retailers serve customers.
☐ Describe the characteristics of important market segments.
☐ Develop a general idea of the retail mix which will attract different market segments.

In the preceding chapter we discussed three influences on people's ability to buy: population, income, and expenditure patterns. The concept of population helps us to analyze the customers making up a market—who they are, how many of them exist, and where they live. The concept of expenditure patterns helps us analyze how customers spend their money.

It is also important to assess a retail market's willingness, as well as its ability, to buy. This is not an easy task. Different customers bring different experiences, habits, emotions, and thoughts to the market place.

Behavior-Influencing Forces

In this chapter we will discuss the forces that influence willingness to buy. First we will introduce a number of behavioral concepts on which retailers rely in an attempt to understand the customer. These behavior-influencing forces are: (1) motives and motivation, (2) learning, (3) attitudes, (4) perceptions, (5) social groups, (6) social class, and (7) culture. Demographic and income characteristics combine with these seven factors to determine consumer behavior. Figure 3.1 illustrates these forces. We will then turn to a brief look at an explanation of how buying decisions are made.

Motives

A motive is a need or desire that causes a person to behave in a particular way to fulfill needs, and is thus a directing force in purchasing behavior. For many years four motivation models dominated the basis for most thinking about buying behavior: (1) Alfred Marshall's economic motivation model, (2) Ivan Pavlov's learning model, (3) Sigmund Freud's psychoanalytic model, and (4) Thorstein Veblen's sociopsychological model.

Marshall's model of motivation suggests that man is a rational animal and that man's buying decisions are based on first carefully weighing the various costs of achieving any various satisfactions and then deliberately choosing the one that has the greatest value.

Pavlov, through his famous studies with dogs, concluded that motivation is largely based on learning, and that what we learn, and how we learn it, affects our motivation toward future goals. Freud saw most behavior as motivated by basic instinctive needs, particularly sex, and controlled by social, ethical, and moral considerations. Veblen saw man as a social animal, motivated by a desire to conform individual behavior to the norms of the culture and to the specific standards of the group to which he or she belonged or aspired.

Each of these motivational theories has made major contributions to an understanding of consumer behavior. However, each provides only a narrow view of motivation. They fail to account for the fact that motivation only initiates behavior and that many mental processes are involved in the purchasing process.

Maslow's classification of motives

One other useful concept of motivation is that provided by Maslow's[1] hierarchy of needs. Maslow postulated that at any given time a person may be faced with a number of motives, but probably can't act on all of them at the same time. Therefore, each person has a hierarchy of motives, with the motives arranged according to their importance. The most urgent motive, then, is acted upon first. Motives representing wants and desires lower in the hierarchy remain unsatisfied, at least temporarily. In the following classification, motives are arranged from the most to the least important.

Physical needs and security. Motives arising from physical needs, such as water, air, food, exercise, sleep, and freedom from pain and discomfort, are basic to the functioning of the body. Motives involving security result from the individual need to feel loved and safe. The word *security* sometimes suggests a striving for the financial security obtained through insurance, good wages, savings, and the like. However, financial security is not as important to

[1]Abraham H. Maslow, *Motivation and Personality*, New York: Harper and Row, 1954.

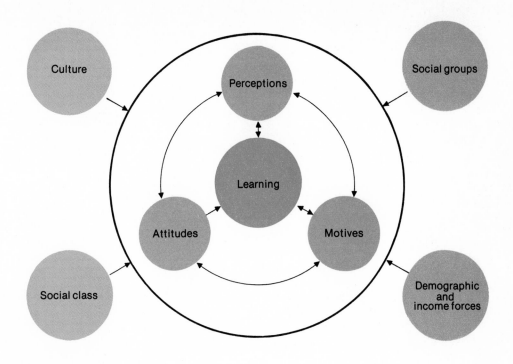

Figure 3.1. Behavior influencing forces.

humans as emotional security is. Emotional security makes us feel that we are needed by others and that we are confident in our own abilities and capacities for success and happiness.

Recognition and acceptance. The need for emotional security leads directly to motives involving recognition. We all need to be treated as unique individuals who are wanted and are important. Unfortunately, our society often makes the individual feel unimportant. Look at a credit card from your local department store. Is the account number larger and more prominent than the person's name? Does the importance of the individual seem to have diminished? Retailers must pay attention to such details.

Closely associated with the need for recognition is the need for acceptance: we all need to

be part of and to identify with groups. So strong is this motive that our primary means of punishment is to remove people from social contact, cutting them off from association with others. Ample evidence exists to suggest that much of our purchasing behavior is influenced by the motive to be a part of a group—to do that which is acceptable to our friends and associates.

Egoism. Egoistic motives involve the individual's need to be independent—to do things on his or her own and to obtain a sense of accomplishment. We all seek that inner feeling of enjoyment and accomplishment we experience when we have done a job well or when we achieve one of our goals. Egoism is closely linked to the need for recognition. Although egoistic motives may be satisfied even if no one else is aware of our accomplishment, most of

Your eight basic wants in life......you have them always!

Food and drink

Comfort

Freedom from fear and danger

To be superior

Figure 3.2. The basic wants.

us like others to know what we have done. Therefore, we may try to find a way of showing them. For this reason, egoistic motives are especially evident in purchasing behavior. We frequently look for products that help us let others know that we have accomplished our objectives and achieved our goals.

These motives classified by Maslow's hierarchy are presumed to be essentially the same for all people in a similar environment. However, they differ in intensity in different

people and are satisfied in different ways. In fact, the same purchase may be made by two people acting on entirely different motives. For example, in choosing an automobile, people are motivated by safety and comfort, prestige, and self-fulfillment. The product, then, serves as a mechanism for satisfying the particular motive.

Inventories of motives. Behavioral scientists who have been studying people have made

To attract the opposite sex

Welfare of loved ones

Social approval

To live longer

many inventories of what people want most. These inventories of people's wants and desires—motives—vary in the number of items. Hattwick[2] has itemized eight motives which seem to be common to all such inventories and that seem to be the basic wants—those desired most often and with the greatest intensity. See Figure 3.2. These eight are:

---

[2]Mel S. Hattwick, *The New Psychology of Selling*, McGraw-Hill, New York, 1960.

- food and drink
- comfort
- freedom from fear and danger
- to be superior
- to attract the opposite sex
- welfare of the loved ones
- social approval
- to live longer

People, of course, have many other wants. They want to be efficient, to have conveniences, to be healthy, and so forth, but these motives are more remote from the primary ones just listed. The secondary wants are learned or socially acquired. They are those we learn to value and satisfy in individualistic ways. They develop as we grow older and more experienced and become conscious of our role in society. An inventory list of the secondary motives would include the following:

- bargains
- information and knowledge
- cleanliness
- efficiency
- convenience
- dependability and quality
- style and beauty
- economy
- curiosity

Patronage motives. Whether the retailer considers motivation from the Maslow point of view or by studying an inventory of motives, the objective is to develop store characteristics that can be tied to a consumer motivation to shop at a specific store. The basic and secondary motives which influence product selection must be identified with factors which the store can use to influence consumer store choice. Motives which influence the choice of store are called *patronage motives*. There could be a long list of patronage motives, most of which can be summarized in the following list:

- good values
- price
- location
- convenience
- parking
- accessability
- friendly and helpful salespeople
- merchandise, assortments, varieties, and brands
- atmosphere
- store image
- services offered

Learning

Learning refers to changes in behavior that result from experience. These changes in behavior may be expressed in thoughts, words, or overt actions. Learning theory relies on the concepts of drive, cue, response, and reinforcement to help explain behavior. The drive or motive, as we have suggested, is the internal force that initiates action. The consumer has many possible responses or choices that will satisfy a given drive. Cues, or stimuli, exist in the environment and/or in the individual that serve to guide the nature of the response. If the response produces satisfaction, positive reinforcement occurs. If it is unsatisfactory, negative reinforcement occurs. Learning takes place because the response has satisfied some need or want, and an association is formed between a stimulus and the response. This association may be formed because of reinforcement (reward or punishment, mentally tied to the stimulus) or simply because the stimulus and response occurred together in time.

Learning theory suggests several roles for the retailer. Providing a product, at the right price, in the right place, and at the right time to satisfy drives is the retailer's role. Purchasing is the desired response. Sales personnel and advertising messages may provide the stimuli by suggesting solutions to the problem, heightening the relevance of the motive, or by reinforcing the response.

Attitude and opinion

The difference between an attitude and an opinion is subtle. Psychologists and sociologists often define an attitude as a predisposition or tendency to act in a particular way, and an opinion as the verbalization of an attitude. Thus, a person who says he prefers a Ford to a Chevrolet gives an opinion that expresses one aspect of his attitudes toward automobiles. Our cumulative experience in our total environment—in our family, our peer groups, our society, and our culture—causes us to develop preferences for and evaluate beliefs about the objects and ideas in our world.

The preconceived preferences and beliefs that all customers bring to the purchasing situation influence their decision making.

Holding attitudes perform several functions for consumers. As a person develops positive or negative attitudes towards products, services, or stores because of experience or other information, the decision process is expedited. Attitudes also serve to protect the self-image or ego of the consumer. Many attitudes may be held simply to enhance the ego. In other words, they are used to reduce tensions created by unpleasant stimuli. Further attitudes are formed to give expression to basic values. Finally, and perhaps most importantly, attitudes give meaning and organization to the world.

Perception

Every waking moment our five senses receive a great number of stimuli. We hear the radio announcer, see a billboard, taste a new product at a supermarket demonstration, feel the texture of a fabric, and smell a steak cooking. Thousands of times a day our brain is stimulated by inputs received by our senses. Perception is the complex process by which we select, organize, and interpret sensory stimulation so we receive a meaningful and coherent picture of the world. Let us examine the implications of perception.

In a single day a buyer may be exposed to over a thousand information messages. As one drives to work, there are hundreds of billboards and signs; the daily newspaper, television, and radio are filled with messages; and friends talk about stores and products. Obviously, an individual cannot receive all this information. Therefore, *selective perception* occurs, since the buyer unconsciously controls the reception of information, either paying attention to or ignoring the information.

Several things influence the buyer's willingness to receive information. The needs and desires of the moment make one sensitive to information that will help satisfy them. Attitudes also influence perception. In general, buyers tend to select information that reinforces attitudes they hold and reject information that conflicts with existing attitudes. Buyers are also likely to be receptive to information concerning areas about which they are uncertain or about which they lack knowledge. Products, packages, displays, store location, prices, advertising, signs, and so on are all information messages that may or may not be received by potential customers. If messages are to be received, they must first be made compatible with the needs, desires, and attitudes of customers. In addition, the messages should be designed to reduce uncertainty and to supply meaningful information.

When buyers receive information, they organize and interpret it during the perception process. In other words, once information is perceived, buyers distort it to make it consistent with their frame of reference and with previously received information. How the information is organized and interpreted is a function of thought processes that call on past experiences, on ideas of the product's desirability, and on an evaluation of the information received.

Culture

Customer behavior is strongly shaped by the interactions of individuals within groups and the values imposed by those groups. At the broadest level the behavior and values of the group are shaped by the culture in which that group exists. Culture is the "complex of values, ideas, attitudes, and other meaningful symbols created by man, and the artifacts of that behavior, as they are transmitted from one generation to the next."[3] Culture, then, encompasses everything acquired by a group of people in the form of knowledge, art, morals, law, customs, beliefs, and habits.

The United States has a larger number of subcultures with identifiable values than many other countries have. With the exception of the emphasis on youthfulness, the important but declining influence of the Protestant work

---

[3]Alfred L. Kroeber and Talcott Parsons, "The Concept of Culture and of Social Systems," *American Sociological Review,* 23 (1958): 583.

ethic, and the importance given to leisure time, retailers tend to look at more important influences identified with specific religious, ethnic, or geographical subcultures rather than to connect broad cultural values with purchasing behavior.

Because *culture* so strongly influences the patterns of motivation, the attitudes, and the perceptions of consumers, it has a direct bearing on purchasing behavior. What people accept and want largely reflects cultural values, particularly as they are filtered and transmitted to the individuals through social groups and social classes.

Social groups

A social group is made up of a number of individuals who, at a given time, stand in more or less definite status and role relationships to one another and who share a set of values or norms. Social-group influences comprise two types: families and reference groups.

Family. Because the family is a basic unit in American social structure, the family exerts a major influence on purchasing behavior. Three aspects of family life are especially important in affecting expenditures: (1) the family life cycle, (2) the family life style, and (3) family goals.

There are several identifiable stages in the family life cycle. These stages are characterized by the age of the head of the family and by the ages of the children. As a family goes through these stages, its needs and desires change. Usually, its income level also changes, particularly the level of discretionary income. Some of the purchasing behavior inferences that may be drawn for each of six representative stages are described as follows:

Stage 1. *Young singles.* The young singles have usually not yet realized their potential earning capacity, but have a relatively large discretionary income because they lack family responsibilities. They are heavy consumers of fashionable clothing, automobiles, and of products associated with recreation and leisure time.

Stage 2. *Young married couples, under forty, with no children.* With marriage, expenditure patterns begin to change. Young couples set up housekeeping in apartments or homes and purchase furniture and household appliances. At this stage, many wives work, and discretionary income may still be quite high.

Stage 3. *Young married couples, under forty, with youngest child under six, with or without older children.* With the birth of children, heads of households are still at the lower end of their potential income scale. Wives may no longer work; and needs of young children are added to the needs of their parents. With high needs and low income, such families tend to be highly conscious of price.

Stage 4. *Married couples, under forty, older children under eighteen at home, but no children under six years of age.* As children grow up, families' needs and income levels change. Family heads approach their peak earning capacity, and many wives return to work. Although the essential needs of the family have been met, many purchases represent replacement for products obtained during the family formation phase. Often, the replacements will be of higher quality than the originals.

Stage 5. *Older married couples, with no children living at home.* When children leave home, several major changes take place. The income of the heads may still be near its peak. However, the children's needs do not have to be filled, so discretionary income may increase dramatically. Couples travel and engage in other leisure activities. They may become involved in community activities to fill the gap in their lives left by the children's absence. There is no longer a need for a large home, and a move to a smaller house, an apartment, or a condominium may be made. This change creates the need for a new set of household furnishings.

Stage 6. *Older married couples, with family head retired.* When heads of households retire, the reduction in income may again cause major changes in consumption patterns. Needs and desires must decline to match the income level, and purchases are more likely to be made to fill basic necessities.

A family's characteristic manner of living is

called its *life style*. As a result of differences in, for example, values and resources, each family has unique qualities that distinguish it from other families. What a family purchases, the way it purchases, and the manner in which purchases are consumed reflect the family's life style.

Closely associated with a family's life style are its values and goals. Some families wait for sales and shop for bargains in order to save money for the unforeseen. Other families spend all of their paychecks as soon as they get them and may even be heavy credit users. The expenditures of two families with the same income may differ greatly: one may buy a boat or camper, whereas the other may save for retirement and the children's education or invest in life insurance.

The purchasing behavior of a family, then, is directly influenced by goals and values. Goals depend on the family's economic structure, its group of friends, the family members, and the needs of the family as a group. Some goals reflect the need for basic necessities. Other goals represent the particular desires of the family and its members. Decisions must be made, for example, as to whether the family most wants a new home, a cabin in the mountains, or a new car.

Purchasing behavior is affected not only by family life cycles, life styles, and goals, but also by the changes taking place in families today. Shorter work weeks, working wives, suburban living, and high incomes have weakened family unity, and have thus brought about important changes in family structure and family roles. In particular, the husband's role as family leader is lessening in importance. Decisions are frequently made jointly, by both husband and wife. The roles of all family members have been affected by the popularity and availability of the automobile, which has encouraged independence and mobility. Wives and children have become more independent than they were in the past; they often spend money without consulting anyone.

Reference groups. The family group, then, has great influence on purchasing behavior. So, too, does another kind of group—the ref-

erence group. A person's reference groups are made up of people to whom he relates or with whom he identifies. A person's reference groups may be groups he belongs to, or they may be groups he wants to join. Social psychologists believe that reference groups are a major source of values, norms, and perspectives.

Reference groups influence purchasing behavior in two major ways. First, they influence aspiration and achievement levels, and thus help cause consumer satisfaction or frustration. If, for example, a person's friends have a better home, he or she may be dissatisfied and try to obtain a similar home. Second, reference groups set standards of behavior; that is, they establish acceptable and approved patterns of using one's income and, therefore, produce conformity. The desire for conformity is one explanation for the existence of fads.

Social classes

Societies may be stratified into groups called *classes*. Sociologists have suggested a six-level social class system based on occupation, source of income, type of housing, and location of residence. Figure 3.3 shows the six levels described, along with representative membership and percentages of people. A person's self-perception as a member of a particular social class influences motives and attitudes. Members of the same social class share similar values and standards of behavior.

The Purchasing Decision Process

The search for a better understanding of consumer behavior has led to the development of a number of models representing theoretical explanations of the purchasing decision process.[4,5]

One simplified purchasing decision process

---

[4] John A. Howard and Jagdish N. Sheth, *The Theory of Buyer Behavior,* New York: John Wiley and Sons, 1969.

[5] James F. Engel; David T. Kollat; and Roger D. Blackwell, *Consumer Behavior,* rev. ed., New York: Holt, Rinehart and Winston, 1973.

Social Class	Membership and Occupation	Basic Values	Purchasing Behavior
Upper-upper (.5 to 1.0 percent of the population)	Locally prominent families; third or fourth generation wealth; merchants, financiers, or professionals	Live graciously; maintain the family reputation; reflect excellence of background; have reputations in the community	Heavy consumers of services; are interested in quality and associate it with the old and traditional; do not behave ostentatiously; fashion-setters
Lower-upper (1.5 to 2.0 percent of the population)	Newly arrived in upper class but are not accepted by it; executive elite, founders of large businesses, doctors, and lawyers	Pursue an upper-upper style of gracious living; maintain upper-middle class drive for success	High expenditures for travel and prestige extras: foreign cars, boats, stereo sets
Upper-middle (10 to 12 percent of the population)	College-educated moderately successful professionals; top salesmen, advertising professionals; owners of medium-sized businesses, and members of middle management; people in their twenties or very early thirties who are expected to arrive at this occupational-status level are also included	Child and home centered; status-conscious; want success in their careers; reflect success tastefully in social participation and home decor; cultivate civic or cultural interests	Spend large share of resources on housing, rather than on expensive pieces of furniture; buy clothing from quality stores; have club memberships and intangible investments, such as stock and insurance
Lower-middle (30 to 35 percent of the population)	The top level in the world of "the average man"; non-managerial office workers, owners of small businesses, and blue-collar workers	Desire respectability; live in well-maintained, neatly furnished homes; dress in clothes from nice stores; save for college education for children	May have a better house than some upper-middle but in a less elegant neighborhood; have more furniture than upper-middle but none of brand-name designers; have full wardrobe with less expensive clothes and more in savings account than upper-middle
Upper-lower (40 to 45 percent of the population)	Ordinary working class, semiskilled workers; income often as high as next two classes above	Enjoy life; keep in step with the times; desire to be at least modern, if not middle class; are able to keep themselves out of slum levels	Own big, late-model cars, many expensive appliances, big TV sets in living rooms; spend proportionally less on furniture and clothing; make large expenditures on sports (baseball, hunting, boating, etc.)

Social Class	Membership and Occupation	Basic Values	Purchasing Behavior
Lower-lower (15 percent of the population)	Unemployed and unassimilated ethnic groups, unskilled workers	Fatalistic, apathetic; take the point of "getting your kicks whenever you can," which characterizes their approach toward life and toward spending money	Have less than 7 or 8 percent of the total purchasing power; must buy primarily to provide for necessities

Figure 3.3. Characteristics of the American social class structure.

Source: W. Lloyd Warner, Marcia Mecker, and Kenneth Eels, *Social Class in America,* Chicago: Science Research Associates, 1949; Richard P. Coleman, "The Significance of Social Stratification in Selling," *Proceedings of the 43rd National Conference of the American Marketing Association,* ed. Martin L. Bell (1960), pp. 171–184; Pierre Martineau, "Social Class and Spending Behavior," *Journal of Marketing* 23 (1958): 121–130; Joseph A. Kahl, *The American Class Structure,* New York: Holt, Reinhart and Winston, 1957.

is illustrated in Figure 3.4. The segment on the left, labeled *Forces that Influence the Purchasing Process* (Figure 3.1) was introduced to help the reader visualize aspects of the purchasing process that influence consumer behavior.

The segment on the right, labeled *Stages in the Purchasing Process,* shows the stages of a purchasing decision and what happens after the decision is made. The four basic stages are (1) motive, (2) prepurchase activity, (3) purchasing decision, and (4) postpurchase activity.

Need arousal

The motive for a purchasing decision may range from basic physiological needs for food to psychological needs for group approval. Regardless of the nature and strength of the motive, the individual's attitudes and perceptions will interact with external, or environmental, forces to cause him to begin to fill his need. If the need can be filled by purchasing, the buyer engages in prepurchase activity.

Prepurchase activity

After the problem is identified, the buyer moves into prepurchase activity. If the buyer relies on habit, he or she may be able to avoid prepurchase activity by moving directly to a purchase decision. In other words, if the same motive has arisen before, the buyer has previous experience and may know that satisfaction can be achieved by a specific action.

Uncertainty. In general, prepurchase activity may be divided into two phases. In Phase 1, shown in Figure 3.4, the buyer is uncertain about the best course of action. The source, kind, and degree of this uncertainty is evaluated and weighed against the strength of the motive. The source of uncertainty may arise from choices of products and/or brands, places of purchase, or methods of purchase. The kind of uncertainty may be classified either as sociopsychological or rational. Sociopsychological uncertainty involves considerations such as reference-group identification, self-esteem, and social class. Uncertainty concerning value, price, quality, and performance involves rational considerations. Finally, the degree of uncertainty is determined by the likelihood of making a wrong purchasing decision. The buyer knows that making a wrong decision is worse than making no purchase at all. To resolve these uncertainties, the buyer searches for information before making the purchasing decision.

The search for information. In the phase involving a search for information, the buyer

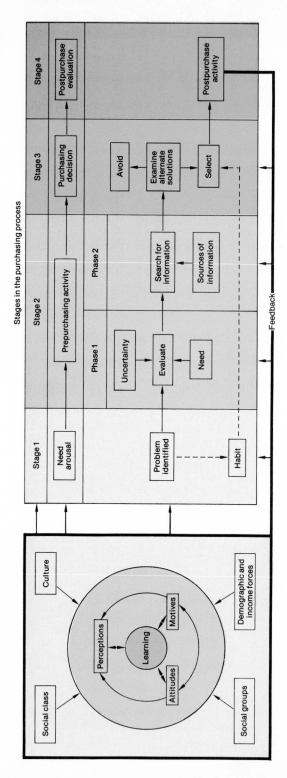

Figure 3.4. The purchasing decision process.

tries to find out about particular aspects of the product, and during this period, is influenced by many factors. A list of the most common ones appears in Figure 3.5. As the buyer collects information and considers other factors, the amount of uncertainty surrounding the purchase decision begins to decrease.

The purchasing decision

At some point the buyer must develop and examine alternative solutions to the problem. The buyer must compare and decide on factors such as product, brand, price, store, service contract, guarantee, credit, and delivery. At this point the buyer can either select from the alternatives, seek additional information, or once again avoid a decision of any kind.

Postpurchase activity

After the purchase is made, the consumer begins to use the product, and doing so, develops attitudes about it. The buyer may, at this point, begin a critical reevaluation of the decision. During this period, she or he may also look for ways to obtain postdecision reinforcement; that is, may seek additional information that confirms the wisdom of the decision. For example, a person who has recently purchased a new Ford may read and pay close attention to Ford advertisements but avoid looking at Chevrolet advertisements. A buyer who does this is trying to obtain postdecision reinforcement.

Feedback

Throughout the decision-making process, the buyer records and stores information that may change motives, attitudes, and percep-

tions. The decision also influences the decision-making process the next time a motive arises. Feedback is that phenomenon by which an outcome becomes input that may generate another outcome.

A Look at Some Market Segments

In these two chapters we have shown how retailers must adapt to specific market segments if they are to meet the needs and wants of their customers. The following discussion selects certain consumer segments that emerge from an analysis of population, income, and expenditure pattern characteristics. Our examination will include subteens, teenagers, singles and mingles, college students, working women, middle-majority families, poor people, minorities, and affluent families.

Subteens

Early subteens exert direct influence on parental purchases. Their influence is directed, to a slight degree, toward the type of products advertised on television. Furthermore, children of this age are beginning to respond to social influences at school and among their peers. This influence is also passed on from the child to the parent.

Retail experiences for children begin at a very early age. Even if five-year-olds have only a few pennies for chewing gum, they are consumers as soon as they buy the first stick. Children aged five to nine receive small amounts of money from their parents. Until five, children may rely entirely upon their parents to satisfy their needs, but soon after this, they be-

1. Brand loyalty	8. Peer group behavior
2. Major brand	9. Endorsements
3. Store image	10. Private tests
4. Shopping	11. Expensive models
5. Free samples	12. Money-back guarantees
6. Government testing	13. Advertising
7. Recommendations from friends and family	14. Salesmen

Figure 3.5. Factors influencing the buyer in search-for-information phase.

come aware of stores and their functions.

Although five-year-olds may visit stores primarily for gum and candy, the influence of seven-year-olds spreads to toys. Their experience with different kinds of stores and merchandise has broadened. By the time children reach the age of nine or ten, their influence has expanded to include clothes, even if it affects only the selection of a pair of sneakers.

Nine- and ten-year-olds have allowances, and therefore they have spending power. Meager as their allowances may be, their position has changed from one involving only influence on family spending to one in which they have become consumers. At this age they begin to shop independently—a trend that accelerates as they grow older.

As children's allowances increase, so does their spending. Along with their new power come their first definite consumer demands. They are now spending their own money—a fact reflected in their careful selection of stores. Although parental influence still plays an important role, subteens begin to strike out on their own. The subteens begin to understand the value of money and the functions of a store. By the time they reach the teens, young people are well on their way to being customers in their own right.

Teenagers

Teenagers are important to retailers, not only for purposes of present consumption, but also for the business they will provide in the future. They also influence overall family spending and selection. There are some twenty million American teenagers. They spend $10 billion a year and influence 15 percent of total consumer expenditures. Their individual spending power increases with their age and with national economic growth. Since 1944 the average purchasing power of teenagers has increased fourfold. Thus, the direct buying power of teenagers is approaching their level of influence, and they now influence their parents' purchases in more expensive areas than in the past.

Teenagers are influenced by their families, but even more so by other teens. They are quick to try something new and equally quick to drop it; are spontaneous and unpredictable; and switch brands and change interests rapidly, confusing retailers. To complicate the matter, teenagers undergo attitude and fashion changes in each year of growth.

Although teenagers have some degree of loyalty to specific stores and brands, they reject standardized products and seek variety in numbers, brands, sizes, and prices. They are very conscious of styles and often influence the total market. Retailers must appeal to their sophistication and discrimination. Furthermore, teenagers are fine judges of sincerity, and can easily sense respect and disrespect, interest and distaste, trust and distrust. Therefore dealings with teenagers must be fair and honest. A firm should be sure that any product sold to a teenager will perform exactly as stated or the entire market may be affected now and later, when the teenagers become young adults. Teenagers will purchase at a store or in a department that they feel is specifically designed for them. They feel the need to be individualistic and independent in their selection of merchandise, yet peer group attitudes still force a tendency toward conformity.

Singles and mingles

The group of singles, as a marketing phenomenon, has been developing for a number of years. Now it is coming to the forefront of retailers' awareness, especially for the swelling *young adult* age group. Mingles form a parallel phenomenon, but are not as well known. *A mingle is a person living with non-relatives in a single household.*

The young singles segment of the population is growing over five times as fast as the nation as a whole. In the past decade the single and divorced age group between twenty and thirty-four has risen 52 percent; today they make up over a quarter of the forty-eight million single adults in the United States. One factor in this rise is that young people, particularly young women, are marrying later. Adding to the growth of this segment is a skyrocketing divorce rate. Couples under thirty-four are divorcing at just about double the rate of a decade ago, and are staying single longer thereafter. Households headed by singles under thirty-four increased by 55 percent—to 2.7 million—between 1970 and 1973, while all such units were up 16 percent to fourteen million. The traditional family grew by only 6 percent in the same period. Also, the number of unmarried couples living together increased by 800 percent in the last decade as against a 10 percent growth in households of married couples.

Compared to the population as a whole, the singles segment tends to be:

- More affluent
- Highly mobile
- Very self-concerned
- Oriented to immediate enjoyment as opposed to long-term concerns
- Fashion and appearance-conscious
- Active both in life style and leisure pursuits

The impact singles of both sexes are having on the market is to be found in the establishment of dwelling complexes for singles and mingles; of social organizations such as Parents Without Partners; of special tours, cruises, and social functions; and of eating places seeking their patronage.

New product and service opportunities are opened up in a wide range of categories. The smaller household of the future—involving both families and singles—means more apartments and condominiums and fewer homes, more furniture suitable for apartments. Practicality, rather than status and prestige, will be stressed. A continued trend to smaller automobiles will emphasize sporty styling and many options such as stereo. Food retailers will see more one- and two-person packages, cans, plastic bags, and so on. Convenience and disposability will be the prime benefits of such items, rather than economy. Appliances that are portable and practical rather than stationary and expensive will be in demand.

Isolating the singles and mingles market from the total market is a challenge to the retailer. The national advertisers have experi-enced a boom in print media providing an editorial climate suiting the life styles of such young adults—ranging from *Viva, Playboy, Playgirl,* and *Oui,* to such activity-oriented publications as *Boating, Flying, Skin Diver,* and *Hot Rod.* Both sexes tend to be working and therefore unavailable for daytime television and radio advertising. Broadcasters are developing specialized television programs such as *Midnight Special* and *In Concert* that are run after prime time to catch the young with "their" music. And there has been a proliferation of FM radio stations programming a variety of youth-oriented music. The retailer has less advertising flexibility. He is generally restricted to radio and local newspapers in reaching his audience. His adaptation must be in store design and product selection.

College students

There are 8.2 million students enrolled in over 2,600 higher-education institutions in this country. These college students are often the first to accept new ideas. Furthermore, they have money to spend; the average college student has 37 percent more discretionary income than has the average American. In clothing purchases alone the expenditures of college girls far exceed those of all other groups. College students are strongly oriented toward consumption. They spend a significant portion of their money on travel and other leisure activities: on dining out, clothing, television and radio sets, and on automobiles. They frequently like individualized products and services, and they look for fairness and honesty from stores. They tend to choose a variety of brands in a variety of sizes and price categories. And although they seek advice and acceptance from friends, they are individualistic and independent in their selection of products and stores.

College students are a real challenge to the retailer. They often lead unconventional life styles and hold values that may conflict with the social norm. They are often critical of the business system and of advertising; many of them do in fact have relatively low media-consumption patterns.

The working woman

Perhaps no sociological trend in the last twenty years has had more influence on consumer markets than has the increasing entry of women into the labor force. Today some thirty-three million, or close to 48 percent of the adult women, work outside the home. This compares to 33 percent in 1950.

About 25 percent of the working women are between eighteen and twenty-four years old and over 25 percent of them have attended college. Especially important to the retailer is the fact that one half of the women from households whose income is over $10,000 are working. In many of these households the supplementary pay check of the working woman represents discretionary income.

The working women are an especially important part of the market for products such as cosmetics, apparel, convenience and prepared foods, and labor-saving appliances.

The middle-majority families

Today about 60 percent of the families comprise a group that might be called the *middle majority*. They have a median income of about $10,000, with a range from $9,000 to $15,000. This group is able to acquire an acceptable standard of living. They are no longer solely concerned only with providing the basic necessities and can afford luxuries such as durable goods, travel, recreation, and entertainment. Most of the demand for such luxuries is generated by the middle majority.

Because many of the middle majority families live in a highly uniform suburban environment and have a large discretionary income, they show increased individuality in consumer buying habits. More and more they are buying goods and services that reflect their own image of themselves rather than goods and services that impress the group.

Members of the majority want shopping to be fast, easy, and convenient. To save time, they may make routine decisions, buying familiar brands to avoid making new decisions. The majority often spends little time in prepurchase planning, as illustrated by the trend to-

ward impulse shopping. Retailers are adjusting to this phenomenon by providing self-service facilities, as well as informative advertising, and by offering well-known, sought-after brands.

Members of the majority are better informed about products than ever before. They are never deceived for long. Some majority consumers may be temporarily persuaded to buy a useless or wasteful product, but they seem to quickly realize their mistake. Although majority consumers may not be ideally rational, they are sensible. Because these customers are well informed and demand information about goods, they expect advertising to be truthful and informative. And they want goods that perform as promised.

The poor and minorities

There are an estimated thirty-four million people in families that have incomes of less than $5,000 a year and seventeen million people in families that have incomes of less than $3,000 a year. The median income of these families is $3,500 a year, of which 15 percent derives from welfare payments, 13 percent from pensions, and 72 percent from earnings. Members of such families often live in urban areas and either belong to ethnic minorities or are old, blind, or disabled.

The poor represent a small market because they have low disposable incomes. They have little money and are often unwise consumers. One unwise aspect of their buying is compensatory consumption. The poor live in a land of abundance. Our society values status and is based on the possibility of social mobility. In reality, however, many poor people realize that they have little chance to better their position. Therefore, they compensate for their lack of upward mobility by purchasing items that represent security or that have great social value.

In making retail purchases, the poor also suffer from a low level of education. They have little experience in shopping and lack the sophistication required of today's shopper. Furthermore, the poor lack mobility. The stores at which they shop are usually in their neighborhood. Poor people either do not know where else to go, or lack the means of getting there. Moreover, poor people frequently have such limited funds that they must shop in their local area in order to obtain credit from merchants who know them and who will take high risks. Poor people's lack of shopping sophistication and low mobility make them especially susceptible to unethical selling practices. The poor are therefore often exploited in the marketplace.

The affluent families

Some 37 percent of the families, twenty million, have an income of over $15,000 each year. The habits of these affluent consumers can vary greatly, depending on their level of status and income. The affluent are, for the most part, however, responsive to new ideas, conscious of quality and style, willing and able to pay, individualistic, and sophisticated. The retail store they patronize must be neat and clean, and the personnel must be courteous, but not too friendly. The affluent exhibit high shopping mobility (most families in this class own two or more automobiles). They tend to change brands at a whim, especially if displeased with the product. Their time, if they socialize often, is limited, and they want to shop as fast as possible. If a product is out of stock, these hurried consumers are exasperated and may well accept a substitute product.

When affluent men or women shop, they look for quality and are willing to pay for it. They like interesting items, but they avoid sensationalism. They do not mind spending money, but they are conscious of price. Stores best serve their interests by offering only first-rate merchandise and by providing sophisticated communication.

Summary

A number of behavioral concepts are important to the retailer's understanding purchasing behavior. Motivation is the directing force in purchasing behavior. Marshall saw man motivated to achieve the maximum value through conscious economic calculations. Pavlov suggested that motivation was the result of learned responses. Veblen suggested that man was motivated to conform to the norms of behavior set by his culture and reference groups. Freud saw most behavior motivated by basic instinctive needs. Maslow postulated that each person has a hierarchy of motives, arranged in order of importance.

Learning refers to behavioral changes resulting from experience. Learning theory relies on the concepts of drive, cue, response, and reinforcement to help explain behavior. Attitudes refer to the preference and beliefs that individuals bring to a decision situation. Perception refers to the process by which we select, organize, and interpret sensory stimulation to provide a meaningful and coherent picture of the world. Cultural values influence purchasing behavior as they are transmitted to individuals through social groups. The family is the most important social group. The family life cycle, life style, and goals strongly influence purchasing behavior. Other reference groups influence aspiration and achievement levels. A person's perception of himself as a member of a particular social class influences his motives and attitudes.

The purchasing decision process can be described in a number of different ways. One model describes four stages: need arousal, prepurchase activity, the purchasing decision, and postpurchase activity.

If a need can be filled by purchasing, the buyer engages in prepurchase activity which involves an evaluation of uncertainty and a search for information. At some point the buyer must examine alternative solutions to fulfilling the need and make a decision. After a decision is made, the buyer may engage in a search for post-decision reinforcement.

Questions and Problems

1. How do the social groups that we identify with influence the way we perceive an advertising message?

2. The sales of which of the following products

are likely to be influenced by stages in the family life cycle? by social groups?
a. automobile
b. boats
c. school supplies
d. china dishes
e. furniture
f. food
3. What different motives might influence your choice of a restaurant?
4. Explain why two families of the same size with the same income might spend substantially different amounts of money on recrea-

tion and on the type of recreation chosen. Would stages in the family life cycle be important? In what way? Would social class be important? In what way?
5. What information sources might be used to reduce each of the following uncertainties?
a. least expensive product
b. fear of product failure
c. peer group approval
d. product quality
e. store reputation
6. Why do you think some people develop strong brand loyalties and others do not?

Situations and Activities

You are the owner of a medium-size downtown sporting goods store. You are considering opening a new suburban branch store, and you know that it is critical that the customer motives important to potential target markets be correctly identified. What customer motives should be considered? Why? How do the customer motives relate to customer buying habits? to the buying process?

You are the store manager of a gift shop located in a large suburban shopping center. The center manager has proposed that it be a matter of policy that all stores in the shopping center stay open until 9:00 P.M. Monday through Saturday. How will you respond? What factors might have prompted the center manager to make this suggestion?

Specify how you would go about measuring the market in your town for alcoholic beverages by the bottle.

Using the stages in family life cycle classifications describe how purchasing behavior and product/service needs might be different for: housing, recreation, automobiles, clothing.

Describe a purchasing process that might be followed by a college student purchasing an automobile for the first time. The purchase is made with savings from summer employment.

Make a list of all of the groups that you perceive as being "reference groups." Take the view that reference groups influence aspiration and achievement levels as well as kinds of purchasing behavior. Indicate ways that each group you listed influences you.

List three different cultures or subcultures and identify culture-based characteristics for each. Explain how the characteristics affect motives, attitudes, and purchasing decisions.

Bibliography

Bennet, Peter D., and Kassarjian, Harold H. *Consumer Behavior.* Englewood Cliffs, N.J.: Prentice-Hall, 1972, pp. 76—95.

Engel, James F., and Blackwell, Roger D. *Consumer Behavior.* New York: Holt, Rinehart, and Winston, 1973, pp. 27—30.

Howard, John A., and Sheth, Jagdish N. *The Theory of Buyer Behavior.* New York: John Wiley & Sons, 1969.

Katz, Daniel. "The Functional Approach to the Study of Attitudes," *Public Opinion Quarterly,* 24 (1960): pp. 163—191.

Kotler, Philip. *Marketing Management.* Englewood Cliffs, N.J.: Prentice-Hall, 1972. pp. 101—107.

Lazer, William. "Life Style Concepts and Marketing." In *Toward Scientific Marketing.* Edited by Stephen A. Greyser. Chicago: Proceedings of the Winter Conference of the American Marketing Association, 1963. pp. 130—139.

Martineau, Pierre. "Social Classes and Spending Behavior." *Journal of Marketing,* Vol. 23, No. 2 October, 1958, pp. 121—130.

Stafford, James E. "Effects of Group Influences on Consumer Brand Preferences." *Journal of Marketing Research,* Vol. III February, 1966, p. 69.

Walters, C. Glenn, and Paul, Gordon W. *Consumer Behavior.* Homewood, Illinois: Richard D. Irwin, 1970. Chapters 20—28.

Warner, W. Lloyd., Meeker, Marcia, and Eels, Kenneth. *Social Class in America.* Chicago: Science Research Associates, 1949.

three

RETAIL ORGANIZATION AND SUPERVISION

4

The Management Functions

contents

behavioral objectives

This chapter is designed to help you develop a basic knowledge of the management functions that supervisors must perform. You should not only understand each of the management functions but you should also be able to perform them in a work situation.

Upon completing this chapter, you will be able to do the following:
☐ Explain the basic requirement for being a supervisor and explain why it is a requirement.
☐ Explain the importance of objectives in retail planning.
☐ Explain the eight essentials of a good plan.
☐ Describe the structure of an organization.
☐ Describe the supervisor's responsibilities in staffing, directing, and controlling.

This chapter and the one following are concerned with retail supervision. The chapters offer no pat solutions and do not attempt to substitute formal instruction for practical experience. They do, however, present the basic concepts and specific techniques of management.

This chapter is designed to explore the management functions all supervisors must perform: planning, organizing, staffing, directing, and controlling. The next chapter is designed to give insights into the most important aspect of the job of a supervisor: leadership.

The Retail Supervisor

Retail supervisors are persons who are responsible for (1) the conduct of others in the achievement of a particular task, (2) the maintenance of performance standards, and (3) the protection and care of merchandise. Their job is to integrate and coordinate these responsibilities so that the store's overall objectives are met. They provide a link in an organization to ensure a smooth flow of work activity. They do this by implementing decisions made by people above them and by making decisions themselves.

The jobs of all retail supervisors involve working with people. Laborers are usually responsible for materials and equipment. Sales employees work with people but are not responsible for the actions and the performance of these people. Supervisors, on the other hand, are responsible for achieving goals by motivating and directing employees. The human factor is, then, emphasized.

Supervision is present in all fields and in all groups. There are leaders in groups as dissimilar as the Green Bay Packers, small town gangs, and retail establishments. All supervisory decisions have a common basis. Only the environment in which they are made differs.

The Supervisor's Primary Concern

As we have said before, retailing has become more and more directed toward the ful-

fillment of people's needs. Nowhere is this more apparent than in relations between supervisors and employees. The viewpoint that the primary role of the supervisor is to control the behavior of his subordinates is being replaced; today the primary concern of the supervisor is to develop the self-directing capacities of his subordinates. In other words, the supervisor's role is essentially that of a teacher. Management training is designed to enable supervisors to serve as resource persons for their subordinates and as facilitators of their continuing self-development.

Methods for applying this concept are explored in depth in the next chapter. However, no supervisor can successfully develop the subordinate's abilities who cannot handle the basic management functions.

Planning

Planning is an important supervisory function. Without planning, there is no predetermined course of action, and without some predetermined course of action, supervisors do not know what to do, where to do it, or why it should be done. They waste their own energies and the resources of the store. Planning involves selecting objectives and developing specific programs, policies, and procedures for achieving them. "If supervisors don't know where they're going, different roads can take them anywhere."

Store objectives and planning

All planning should begin with a consideration of the objectives of the store. Stores have many different objectives. These include survival, growth (market share increase), return on investment, service to the public, and the maintenance of the store image. Some objectives are more important than others. Profit, of course, is the primary objective of retail organizations.

Profit maximization—the attainment of the greatest possible profit—is, however, not necessarily the primary objective. Stores cannot afford to deliberately neglect their social responsibilities and service offerings in an attempt to increase profits. Most retail stores attempt to balance their service and social objectives—and even the personal objectives of their employees—with their profit objective to attain something less than maximum profits. Today a practical approach to the setting of objectives entails profit suboptimization rather than profit maximization (see Figure 4.1).

Whatever a store's objectives are, however, they are vitally important to management, because they provide direction for the store. To do this, they must be clearly formulated so all levels in the organization can work together toward the same goals. Take, for example, a store in which one of the objectives is "to give the best customer service in the county." Employees, attempting to achieve this objective, in their own perception, may be reprimanded by superiors for giving liberal credit on exchanged or returned items. In other words, because the objective is not formulated clearly enough at all levels, it may be interpreted differently by supervisors and employees.

Objectives must be stated in a manner that provides direction for employees at all levels. Simply stating an objective of profit maximization, for example, gives little direction to a sales person. Broad statements are difficult to apply to daily operating procedures. Therefore, if different supervisory levels are to make consistent and integrated plans, the objectives of the organization must be translated to apply to each position involved.

Reasons for planning

If supervisors do not plan, they might as well make their decisions by flipping a coin or rolling dice. Leaving the destiny of a company to the whims of "chance" doesn't make sense. Therefore, planning is necessary.

Planning offsets uncertainty and change. All decisions are subject to change and uncertainty. Because of constant changes in fashion, changes in the competition, and customer desires, planning is of the utmost importance. Planning helps a store forecast and adapt to

such changes. Planning forces supervisors to consider the future and to revise and reevaluate operating plans in the face of it.

Planning focuses attention on objectives. Because all planning is oriented toward the attainment of company objectives, planning focuses attention on these goals. Well-constructed plans unify the activities of all departments and of all units in departments, and direct their activities toward store objectives.

Planning increases economic efficiency. Planning minimizes costs. Take, for example, retailers who are faced with deciding what spring fashions to order. They can consult trade magazines and fashion experts to determine what consumers want and then make an estimate as to what and how much they can expect to sell, or they can avoid planning an order until the season begins. By planning in advance, retailers can buy the quality, styles, and designs they want in the appropriate quantities, and they will have the merchandise well in advance of the selling season. If, however, retailers decide to wait until spring to order, they will probably have difficulty obtaining what they want, will have to have their orders

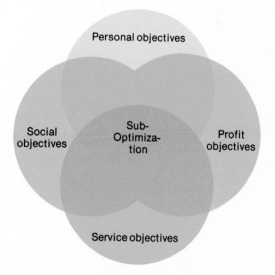

Figure 4.1. Profit suboptimization.

sent "rush" to them (at extra cost), and will probably lose sales to their competitors as they wait for the merchandise.

Planning facilitates control. Supervisors have no way to evaluate and check on their operation unless they have plans against which to measure performance. Without plans and accountability devices to serve as criteria of performance, supervisors would not be able to tell who was doing his or her job or even what jobs should be done. They would not know which products were meeting expectations and which were not.

The elements of good plans

Good plans have several elements:

1. Plans should be capable of accomplishing the objectives.
2. Plans should be realistic in respect to the capabilities of the organization. For example, it would be foolish for a store to plan on increasing sales through the use of television advertising, if its advertising budget were only large enough for newspaper ads.
3. Plans should be defined in (comprehensive but simple) terms so employees will understand what is required of them. Employees must be able to determine what specific role they will play in a plan.
4. Plans must be economical. They should save time, space, material, and personnel. Unless planning increases profits, the money spent on it is wasted.
5. Plans should have continuity. They must be coordinated with the store's objectives.
6. Plans should be built around (a) forecasts of future events and (b) estimations of the probable outcome of the plan.
7. Plans should contain creative approaches to the solving of problems. Too many times supervisors are blinded by traditional thinking.

Organizing

Retail planning is of little value unless members of the organization coordinate their efforts effectively to implement plans. In this section we examine formal and informal organizations and the elements of organization.

Formal and informal organizations

Organizations establish relationships among people, materials, and other resources to get a job done. There are two organizations in all firms. One is the formal organization—the planned structure created by management. Informal organization, the other, refers to aspects of the system that are not formally planned, but rise naturally out of the activities and interactions of personnel.

The formal organization. Retail stores usually develop organizational charts. These charts show the formal lines of responsibility and authority existing within the firm; that is, they show who reports to whom. In small retail stores, organizational charts are similar to the one shown in Figure 4.2 with functions as illustrated in Table 4.1. In large stores, organizational charts look like the one shown in Figure 4.3.

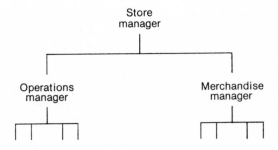

Figure 4.2. Organizational chart showing the functional breakdown of a small store.

The two figures reveal that the same general functions must be performed in both small and large stores. The four main functions are operations, promotion, merchandising, and control. However, the smaller an organization is, the more likely it is that some of these functions will be combined and administered by one manager. The reverse is also true: The larger

Table 4.1. Small Store Organization

Responsibilities:

Management	Head Salesperson	Other Salespersons	Stock and Delivery Personnel
Plan business	Operates stock control	Sell products	Correct, on-time deliveries
Develop teamwork	system	Arrange stock	
Supervise	Supervises and trains	Observe/report slow	Report all delivery complaints
buying	subordinates	moving items and stock	
displays	Sells products	shortages	Watch for new customers on delivery routes
advertising	Assists in buying	Check invoices received	
selling	Analyzes credits	Supervise outgoing delivery and shipping	Keep delivery equipment clean and in good mechanical condition
credits	Plans advertising		
deliveries	Plans window and interior displays	Price-mark new merchandise	
office			Collect delinquent accounts under instructions
Analyze records	Effects price changes	Stock shelves	
Control expenses		Maintain price markings and price tickets	
Financial collections			Maintain stock and help sell during rush periods
Increase market share		Maintain stock reserve	

Source adapted from: Type of organizational chart suitable for smaller independent stores (National Cash Register Company).

an organization becomes, the more likely it is that some of the functions will be broken apart and administered by more than one manager. It depends on how much work there is for a manager to handle. And the work is great. Considering all the various activities which take place in a retail store, management by necessity must establish an organization which divides up the work load and gives direction to each activity. Figure 4.4 shows the organization chart of one large department store's breakdown of its functions.

In a very large retail organization, the organization may separate the personnel function from the operations function and the buying function from the selling function. Separate provisions for branch store operations also

may be made. As retail organizations grow, personnel requirements increase, one person may not be able to administer both the buying and selling functions, and provisions must be made to handle satellite organizations, or branches.

The informal organization. There are informal, as well as formal, organizations. The idea of an informal organization refers to the natural flow of authority and communication that develops as people work together. These flows may or may not be the same as reflected on the organization chart. The informal organization can't be seen in any of the organizational charts, but it exists in every firm. It can be a powerful force that either works for or against a

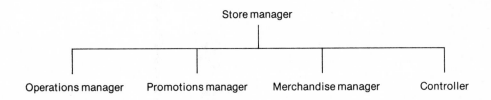

Figure 4.3. Organizational chart showing the functional breakdown of a large store.

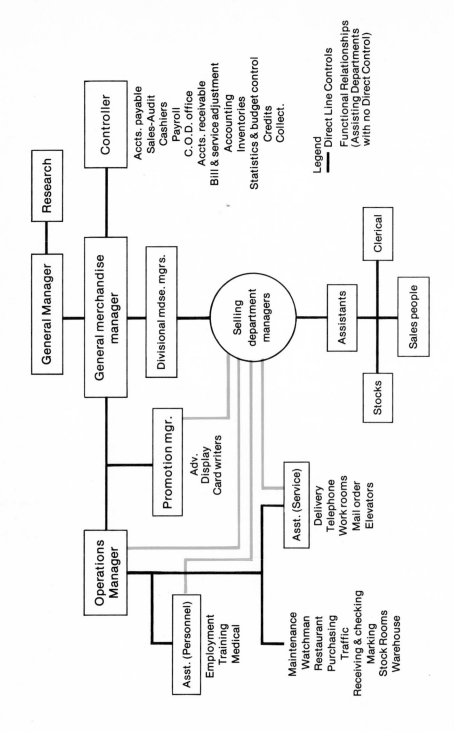

Figure 4.4. Typical functional breakdown of a large department store.

firm. If supervisors understand and utilize the informal organization, they can greatly increase work performance. If informal groups work against them, they face serious problems. One way of working with the informal organization is to recognize its existence and cultivate its support.

The elements of organizations

Supervisors must know the elements that make up an organization. This means studying organizations in terms of division of labor, authority, responsibility, delegation of authority, unity of command, span of control, and line and staff functions.

Division of labor. Division of labor is job specialization that increases efficiency. As an organization grows, the tasks to be performed become more and more complicated. It is more efficient to have employees work at only part of a task than to have each employee perform a whole task. Take, for example, the proprietor of a small town grocery store. When he first went into business, he was the only employee; he ordered, stocked and sold the goods. When the town grew, his sales volume increased, and ordering, stocking, and selling became more and more complicated. Because of the increased complexity, he decided that he could work more efficiently if he hired a stock boy and a sales clerk. In hiring these employees, the store owner divided the labor and introduced job specialization.

Authority. Authority is the right to give orders and to be obeyed. There are three types of authority: formal, technical, and personal. Formal authority is the authority conferred on the supervisor by the organizational-hierarchy. This refers to the right to rule based upon position. Technical authority is the authority that comes from the knowledge and skills of the supervisor. Personal authority (charismatic authority) is based on leadership ability, and depends more on personal characteristics than position. However, supervisors have none of these kinds of authority unless employees rec-

ognize that they have the right to give orders. Supervisors can be delegated a large amount of authority and can possess outstanding leadership qualities, but unless their employees acknowledge and accept their authority, they actually have none.

Responsibility. Responsibility is the obligation to perform duties to the best of one's ability. When supervisors assign their employees a task, the employees are obligated to perform this task, and they can be held accountable if they fail to do so.

Delegation of authority. Supervisors delegate authority, because they cannot perform all tasks themselves. Through the delegation process, supervisors encourage employees to act as they themselves would if they had the time and energy to perform the job. Supervisors, in delegating authority, free themselves of small tasks and, thus, can concentrate on making plans and decisions. Delegating authority also helps employees gain experience in supervising. It improves morale, because employees' attitudes improve when they believe they are making vital contributions to a firm's success.

In delegating authority, supervisors should remember two things. First, although a supervisor makes an employee responsible for a task, the ultimate responsibility is still the supervisor's. The employee is responsible to the supervisor, but the supervisor is held accountable by his or her superiors for the accomplishment of the task. Second, authority must be commensurate with responsibility. In other words, an employee should not be asked to do a job who doesn't have the authority necessary to get the job done.

The amount of delegation depends on the physical distance separating the supervisor and the employer, the complexity of the tasks to be performed, the amount of time available for performing them, the confidence the supervisor has in the employees, and the number of employees the supervisor has under his or her control.

Unity of command. Unity of command means that employees should have one, and only one, boss. Every employee should know to whom she or he is responsible and to whom to report.

Span of control. Span of control refers to the number of employees a supervisor can effectively manage. Some sources say that no supervisor can control more than seven employees and that he or she must have control over at least three to keep busy. This, of course, depends on the characteristics of the supervisor, and the characteristics of the employees, and the business situation. If employees depend greatly on the skills and knowledge of the supervisor there must be a great deal of interaction between the supervisor and the employees. Therefore, a narrow span of control is required. If supervisors work according to stringent time schedules, again, the span of control should be narrow. If the employees' work is complex, close control is required, but if the work is repetitive, the span of control can be wide. If employees are highly skilled and are proficient at their jobs, again, a wider span of control can be employed.

Line and staff functions. Line functions contribute directly to the accomplishment of the organization's goals, whereas staff functions are supporting activities because they, in some way, serve line functions. An example of a typical staff function is an "assistant to" position. Employees occupying these jobs help line supervisors to accomplish their duties. Staff members serve as advisors in specialized areas. Whereas line supervisors have formal responsibilities to those above and below them, staff employees have responsibilities only to their immediate supervisors (see Figure 4.5).

Staffing

The staffing function involves the recruitment and selection of employees. The human resources of a retail firm constitute its most important asset. Success and failure is determined mainly by the caliber of the work force and the efforts it exerts. Therefore, the policies and methods that a retail firm adopts to meet its manpower needs are of vital significance.

It is very costly to hire new employees. This cost is, in reality, an investment amortized over the length of time the person is employed by the company. Personnel turnover is very expensive. If a wrong selection is made and a replacement must be hired, the increased costs of training can significantly affect the store's financial picture. For example, it may cost from $200 to $1000 to add a salesperson to the payroll, but for middle and upper management, the costs may reach as high as $10,000.

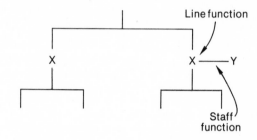

Figure 4.5. Line and staff functions.

Although we discuss staffing as the third of the supervisory functions, we are not implying that staffing is performed after planning and organizing. In a new store, staffing may take place after these other functions, but in an ongoing operation staffing is a continuing function.

Determining staff needs

Before carrying out staffing functions, a firm must identify its needs. Job descriptions can help accomplish this. A job description is a written record of the duties, responsibilities, and requirements of a particular job. The job description has several important uses. It is the guide for testing and selecting prospective employees. It describes to employees exactly what is expected of them. And it provides standards of performance by which employees can be judged.

To obtain the information for the job description, firms conduct a job analysis, which is a report giving pertinent information on a specific job. A job analysis usually provides answers to questions like these:

1. What specific work should be accomplished?
2. How much work is expected?
3. What quality of work is expected?
4. What are the best ways to accomplish the expected work?
5. What do the working conditions involve? For example, is physical effort necessary? Are physical hazards involved?
6. What responsibilities are associated with the position?
7. What authority is associated with the position?
8. What characteristics should an employee have to fill the position?
   a. Experience and training
   b. Attitude
   c. Mental abilities
   d. Leadership qualities.

Some large retail firms use the information obtained from job analyses not only to develop job descriptions but also to make job evaluations. A job evaluation determines the value of a job in relation to other jobs. It establishes minimum and maximum salaries for each job, based on its relative value. The civil service system used by the federal government is based on job evaluation. Jobs are graded and classified according to the skills and knowledge needed to perform them, and salary ranges are established according to classifications such as these: Grade I, clerk; Grade II, clerk typist; Grade III, stenographer.

Recruiting and selecting employees

Several widely used sources are available to employers who are seeking applicants for jobs. One such source is local trade and high schools. Alert supervisors talk to school principals and guidance counselors in secondary schools and inform them of job opportunities and employment practices in their firms.

Today there is also large-scale recruiting at junior colleges, colleges, and universities. Such institutions are excellent sources of potential management trainees and personnel for specialized positions.

Employment agencies are another source of personnel. Every state in this country has an employment service that maintains offices in cities and large towns. Employers may use their services by placing job orders by telephone or in person. There are also large numbers of privately operated employment agencies. Many of these agencies do a careful job of interviewing, testing, counseling, and screening applicants to meet employer specifications.

The handicapped represent a labor source sometimes overlooked by employers. State employment services and state offices of vocational rehabilitation do a good job of screening the handicapped for placement. The Veterans Administration offers similar services for disabled veterans.

Newspaper and trade magazine advertising is another widely used method of recruiting. The most common type of advertising involves the placement of classified ads in newspapers. In placing such ads, supervisors should remember that advertising for personnel is no different from other kinds of advertising. Jobs must be sold in the same way that products and merchandise are sold. When placing an ad, it is also important to spend enough money to give complete information about the job opening. Failure to do this causes supervisors to waste their time screening applicants who are unqualified or who are not interested in the job.

Most retailers rely, to some extent, on people who walk in the store and fill out applications. This source of personnel is uncertain because the candidates display a wide range of abilities. If, however, a company has demonstrated that it treats employees well, pays adequate wages, and has fair personnel practices, qualified applicants will be attracted to the company.

After applicants have been recruited, selections must be made. The selection of employees involves an evaluation of an applicant's capabilities in relation to the requirements stated in the job description. Retail firms may draw on several sources to help them make such evaluations.

A well-designed application provides information on an applicant's personal and family history, his or her education and work experience, the type of work the applicant desires, and the reason the applicant wants to work for a particular firm. The application form may also ask the applicant to list the names of people who will give him or her references. References include evaluations of previous work, educational experiences, and character.

Interviews provide additional information about applicants and give prospective employees an opportunity to learn what is involved in the job to be filled. The interviewer can explore the areas covered on the application blank by asking why the applicant left a previous position or why some of the lines on the application form were left blank. Interviewers can evaluate personal appearance, self-confidence, and speaking ability. Many firms follow up on initial pre-screening interviews by giving the applicant tests that evaluate skills, aptitudes, and sometimes personality traits.

Giving directions

The purpose of giving directions is to orient employee behavior toward accomplishment of organizational goals. In short, directions tell the employee what the supervisor wants done. Not all directions are the same, however; some are general and some are specific.

Whether a direction is specific or general depends on the preference of the supervisor, his or her ability to foresee the consequences of the order, and the response made by the employee. If supervisors want their employees to participate in the decision-making process, they give general, rather than specific, orders. General orders permit employees to use their imagination and initiative to determine how to accomplish a task. General directions are also given when the employee who is to perform a task is not in personal contact with the supervisor or when the supervisor cannot possibly

foresee all the contingencies that may arise. In almost all circumstances, general directions are preferable to specific ones because employee participation enhances implementation of actions. If employees show initiative, possess the skills and experience required, and are willing to accept the responsibility for their actions, they should be permitted to act as independently as is possible.

There are also different ways of giving directions. Written directions are usually more precise and accurate than are oral ones. Furthermore, written directions are permanent communications. However, they are usually more time-consuming than oral directions; they require more effort; and they can create inflexibility if employees try to follow them too closely.

Written directions are used in the following cases:

1. When the task will take a long time to perform
2. When precise or complicated figures and specifications are involved
3. When activities must be performed in sequence
4. When a permanent record of the direction is required
5. When the direction must be known by everyone in the entire organization.

Oral directions are used in the following cases:

1. When the action to be performed is simple or repetitive
2. When the purpose of the direction is simply to clarify some aspect of a written direction
3. When there is an emergency, and it is impossible to prepare written directions
4. When the supervisor and the employee are continually in close contact.

Studies have shown that a combination of oral and written directives enhance communication flows.

Whether directions are general or specific, written or oral, supervisors must know how to give them properly. Almost everything a supervisor does or says can be interpreted in different ways by different employees. Therefore, supervisors must make certain that their words and actions clarify their intentions. A framework for giving effective directions is provided in the following four-point guide:

1. Make directions clear, complete, and concise. Supervisors should state clearly the who's, what's, when's, where's, and how's of a job assignment. They should check their directions to be sure that they state the specific requirements of the job and that there is little chance for misunderstanding.
2. Tailor directions to the knowledge and experience of the employee who is to handle the job. Make certain that the employee has the ability and authority to carry the job through to completion.
3. Give businesslike directions. Many times directions are taken personally. Supervisors should realize this and make their directions factual. When dealing with employees, supervisors should put their emotions in the top left-hand drawer of their desk.
4. Make directions easy to accept. When giving directions, supervisors should attempt to explain the reasons for them. If employees know why they have to do a particular job, they will usually perform well. Furthermore, if supervisors keep their employees informed, they will earn their respect and confidence.

Controlling

Supervisors must follow up to make sure the work that has been planned, organized, and delegated is being carried out in the proper manner. To do this they must establish standards of performance. Then they can measure actual performance and compare it with planned performance to determine whether activities are progressing according to schedule. If the system is not under control, the supervisor can isolate the troublespot by evaluating the deviation between actual and planned performance.

Exception Principle

One way to help keep things under control is by operating on the exception principle. This means that routine matters should be handled at the lowest management level possible. For example, an executive spending time reordering toilet paper for the restrooms represents a misallocation of upper level resources. The executive is paid to make higher level decisions and should spend time in those areas. To the extent that executives can keep from concentrating on details at the expense of more fundamental, difficult, and abstract issues better control of the organization can be maintained.

Management by Objectives

Management by objectives (MBO) is an approach to control which emphasizes better leadership, motivation, and communication as a way of achieving store goals and objectives. It is a system of management best described as a process whereby superior and subordinate managers of an organization jointly identify its common goals. The MBO approach is designed to define each worker's major area of responsibility in terms of results expected of him or her and uses these measures as guides for operating the unit and assessing the contribution of each of its members. Its usefulness as a control device is founded in the way that it assesses results. MBO concentrates on what should be and actually is achieved rather than on the ways in which things should be achieved. In other words, it concentrates on the outputs that subordinates and superiors have agreed will be desirable and will be set out as objectives for achievement.

The approach to management by objectives is relatively simple. It basically involves three steps: (1) superiors and subordinates get together and discuss jobs which need to be performed and under which they have some control and relate this to the objectives of the department and the overall organizational goals, (2) the subordinates and superiors mutually agree upon a set of goals (usually quantifiable if possible) and the results that subordinates are to achieve, (3) subordinates and superiors at some future date need to analyze whether their performance has been achieved.

In the next chapter, we will discuss elements of leadership which contribute to better motivation of employees. The MBO approach can be used to get more enlightened performance from an employee while at the same time it provides an element of control for the organization. As an instrument for improving leadership, the participatory aspects of the approach between subordinate and superior leave subordinates with a good feeling about their jobs and the involvement that they had in the goal setting and review process.

complish these objectives. They fulfill the organizing function by developing an organization in which labor is properly divided and responsibility is delegated. They fulfill the staffing function by recruiting and selecting employees. They give directions to let employees know what must be done. And they perform a controlling function by checking on all aspects of operational performance.

Questions and Problems

1. *What is the distinction between formal and informal organization?*
2. *Discuss the relative value of different sources for recruiting applicants for buyers, for sales people in specific departments (for example, the camera or the toy department), and for an assistant store manager trainee.*
3. *What conflicts might exist between members of the formal organization and informal organizations?*
4. *Are there advantages in giving directions in the form of suggestions instead of orders? If so, what? Are there potential problems? Does it depend on the type of authority?*
5. *Evaluate this statement: Good supervisors have similar personality traits. What personality traits do you think make for a good supervisor?*

Summary

Supervisors are managers—their job consists of working with employees in such a way that necessary tasks are accomplished. As managers, supervisors must perform certain functions. They fulfill the planning function by setting objectives and developing plans to ac-

Situations and Activities

You are a department manager. You recently returned from a district sales meeting. The district sales manager discussed the problem of relating in some meaningful way to consumerism. One of the suggestions was to improve the sales force's ability to relate to and work with customers. You question this suggestion because you believe it is an oversimplified approach to the problem. You wonder whether the typical organizational structure and staffing programs are consistent with today's consumer orientation. How would you look at this problem from a total management approach?

You are the salesman in a men's wear department that pays on the basis of salary plus commission. You have been in the department for three weeks, and you have noticed that another salesman in the department makes higher commissions than you do. You suspect that the reason he does is that he is the first sales person to approach each customer who comes into the department. If the customer wants a suit, he is happy to wait on him. If the customer wants a pair of socks, he directs him toward the back of the department, and other salesmen wait on him. In thinking about this, you know that it sometimes takes as long to sell a pair of socks as it does to sell a suit. Your boss will do nothing about this situation. If you were a supervisor, what courses of action would be open to you? What would you do?

Interview four retailers in an effort to identify the basic management needs of retailers. How are these needs being met? Are there better ways to meet these needs?

One problem that continually plagues retail supervisors is disciplining employees. List three discipline problems. Indicate at least two alternatives for handling each problem. Evaluate the pros and cons of each alternative.

List three different positions you might be interested in at three different organizational levels.
a. Write a job analysis and job description for each position.
b. Describe the commonalities in each of the positions. What requirements change as you move up the organization ladder?

Bibliography

Bruel, Grady D., and Bonjen, Charles M. "Self-Actualization Among Retail Sales Personnel." *Journal of Retailing,* Vol. 45 No. 2, 1969, pp. 73—84.

"Can You Qualify as a Supervisor?" *Goodall News,* Vol. XXVII, June-July, 1969, pp. 1—2.

Hays, Colonel Samuel H., and Thomas, Lieutenant Colonel William N. *Taking Command.* Harrisburg, Pennsylvania: Stackpole Books, 1967, pp. 67—68.

Hood, Robert C. *Ansul's Aggressive Marketing Concept.* Ansul Chemical Company's Corporate Marketing Function, October, 1964, pp. 6—7.

Kast, Fremont E., and Rosenweig, James E. *Organization and Management.* New York: McGraw-Hill, 1974. p. 437.

Killian, Ray A. *Managers Must Lead!* New York: Comet Press, 1966, pp. 261—263.

Koontz, Harold, and O'Donnell, Cyril. *Principles of Management.* New York: McGraw-Hill, 1964. pp. 79—81.

Kotler, Phillip. *Marketing Management.* Englewood Cliffs, New Jersey: Prentice-Hall, 1967. pp. 152—155.

Longenecker, Justin G. *Principles of Management and Organizational Behavior.* Columbus, Ohio: Charles E. Merrill Books, 1964. pp. 146—147.

Miller, M. S. "What Are the Principles of Leadership?" *Journal of Systems Management,* June, 1969, p. 11.

National Association of Retail Grocers. *Procedure Manual for Recruiting, Interviewing, Selecting, and Guiding New Staff Members.* Chicago, Ill.

Rubin, Leonard, "Today's Retailer Must Be a Man for all Seasons." *Stores,* October, 1969, p. 27.

Spriegel, William R.; Schulz, Edward; and Spriegel, William B. *Elements of Supervision.* New York: John Wiley & Sons, 1958. p. 1.

5

The Essentials of Leadership

contents

behavioral objectives

No organization is successful if it lacks effective leadership. The leadership capabilities of supervisors are demonstrated not only in how well they manage operations but also in how well they train, motivate, and communicate with their employees. This chapter is designed to encourage you to think about ways to become a more effective leader.

Upon completing this chapter, you will be able to do the following:
☐ Describe the qualifications for supervisory success.
☐ Explain the three types of supervisory skills.
☐ Recognize the key elements in a framework designed to help trainees learn.
☐ Discuss the best ways to motivate employees.
☐ Explain some of the communication barriers that supervisors face.

The art of leading people has been a fascinating topic throughout history. Although an endless number of theories have been proposed to explain why some people are good leaders and why others fail miserably, all theories possess a common theme: Successful leadership depends on one's ability to influence others for a specific purpose. It is the ability to induce psychological or behavioral change.

Supervisors should be leaders. They should understand the needs and wants of their employees, and be able to use this knowledge to motivate them. Supervisors should be interested in helping employees achieve their maximum potential while, at the same time, accomplishing organizational goals.

This chapter examines the leadership aspects of a supervisor's job. It begins by exploring the qualities of leadership and ends by examining some of the activities supervisors must perform as leaders.

Learning to Be a Leader

For many years, people believed that the traits of leadership were inherited. Today this theory of leadership has been abandoned. Almost everyone agrees that leadership can be learned.

People are often puzzled when one person is promoted to an executive position over others who seem brighter, but who remain in less important jobs. One answer is that people who desire success know their goals and go after them. These people are highly motivated and have developed plans to channel their motivations. Part of this planning involves learning how to be a supervisor. Fortunately, there are unlimited ways for people to learn. Some of the more obvious include the following:

1. Learn from your own supervisor.
2. Learn from top management.
3. Take advantage of all training offered by the company.
4. Avail yourself of formal course offerings.
5. Schedule a reading program for yourself.

6. Learn from your own mistakes and avoid repeating mistakes of others.

To determine your qualifications for leadership, you may want to take the following test.

The qualifications for supervisory success might be viewed as positive answers to the following questions.[1]

Do you like to deal with people? Of prime importance to supervisory success is the ability to get along with people. Leaders must be able to cooperate with all organizational leaders and receive needed cooperation from all organizational levels. Their job does not necessarily entail winning popularity, but involves gaining group cooperation so that an integrated effort can be made to accomplish the goals of the company.

Have you completely mastered your job? Before people can expect to be promoted to a higher level, they must have performed to the best level of their ability and at a high level of competence at their present position.

Do you look for better methods? Supervisors must be alert to possibilities of improving company image, improving employer-employee relations, decreasing costs, increasing quality, saving time, etc. Supervisors must use creative thinking and be able to visualize, understand, and develop new methods to replace outdated ones.

Do you reach out for responsibility? Supervisors must be able to assume the responsibilities of their job in terms of their own performance and the performances of their subordinates. Supervisors must follow a job through even though it requires extra time and effort. They must be able to delegate duties to others and share their knowledge and experience with their co-workers. Training subordinates is an important supervisory function.

---

[1] "Can You Qualify as a Supervisor?" *Goodall News*, Vol. XXVII (June-July, 1969), pp. 1—2.

Are you willing to keep learning? The learning process never stops. Whether one manages a large store or a corner newsstand, all jobs require up-to-date knowledge. Supervisors must constantly gain current information about their store, its products, its competition, customer needs, and the marketplace.

How do you react to criticism? Successful supervisors must be able to accept failure without anger or resentment and not let their pride sway the facts.

Do you express yourself clearly? If supervisors cannot get ideas across and communicate them effectively, their ability as supervisors will be severely hampered. Supervisors must develop speaking skills and writing skills to enable themselves to be understood.

Do you think positively? Although every problem faced has both good and bad aspects, the supervisors cannot let themselves develop pessimistic attitudes. If workers see their "leader" with a negative attitude, they, too, will develop one.

Do you thrive on competition? By the nature of their job, supervisors must thrive on competition. They are constantly in competition with others for their job, their workers, and their products.

Leadership Skills

To be an effective supervisor, a person must make a never-ending attempt at developing and improving knowledge of leadership. The success of the supervisor's leadership will be measured by the ability to lead others in accomplishing organizational goals. Supervisors must be motivated to learn everything they can about their jobs, the needs and activities of their subordinates, and the overall activities of the firm. Learning to be a supervisor, therefore, should involve development of the skills necessary for leadership. These skills are basically of three types: human skills, technical skills, and conceptual skills.

Human skills

Human skills involve the ability to work with people. Supervisors must understand human relations. They must be able to motivate people, satisfy their needs, and promote cooperation between and among them so that the goals of the organization can be accomplished. They have to be able to "sell" an idea to their employees and coordinate their activities into an integrated network.

To understand some of the important ways in which supervisors must work with people, see Figure 5.1.

Technical skills

Whereas human skills concern the supervisor's ability to lead people, technical skills involve the supervisor's abilities to perform specific duties and tasks required by his or her position. Knowledge of specific job processes and administrative duties is essential if the supervisor is to perform the job. Take, for example, the manager of a grocery store. This supervisor must know the specific managerial requirements of the position, as well as the duties performed by the employees. As a store manager, he must know what to order, when to order to avoid being out of stock, how to price the merchandise, and how to display it. In addition, the manager must know how the produce department should be set up and how many facings should be given to spiced tea and floor wax. If the supervisor doesn't know what to do, who does?

Conceptual skills

In addition to human and technical skills, every supervisor must have conceptual skills. These skills may be viewed as the ability to see the big picture. Supervisors must be able to see how their particular department or division relates to the overall organization. If supervisors see their department as the entire store rather than a portion of it, serious problems can arise. Supervisors who "see trees instead of the forest" lack the perspective to make a total contribution to the firm.

The actions of supervisors are at least as important as their intentions. The adage that actions speak louder than words never held truer. In discharging their duties, good supervisors:

—demonstrate organized thinking.
—use good judgment.
—know what and when to delegate.
—set goals and build work schedules.
—are fair.
—are consistent.
—act on facts.
—accept changes.
—give recognition.
—treat everyone as individuals.
—let their people know how they are doing.
—do not pass the buck.
—answer questions honestly and fully.

For the most part, poor performance can be attributed to employee discontent, which can stem from a variety of causes:

—failure to receive credit for ideas and suggestions.
—not knowing where he stands with regard to his performance.
—not being kept informed on changes, procedures, etc.
—failure to have grievances recognized or acted upon.
—favoritism.
—being criticized in the presence of others.
—a supervisor who is too aloof and does not accept the opinion of others.
—not being held accountable.
—being part of a poorly disciplined work force.

There is really no magic in improving poor work performance. Just talk with people. Talk about some very simple questions that most people want to discuss. Follow this with guidance, encouragement and recognition, and the job will get done.

Figure 5.1. People working with people.
Source: Rich's, Atlanta, Georgia, *Head of Sales Manual*.

Training

One activity that requires the supervisor to apply all of the human, technical, and conceptual skills possible is the training activity. As stated previously, training is an important part of the supervisor's job.

Training also must go on continuously. When a new employee is hired, when a job operation is changed, when equipment is introduced or new procedures are to be used, the supervisor must train the people involved. It is the supervisors' skills and abilities that determine the success of the company. The extremely important function of training, then, increases the basic skills and abilities of all employees, and therefore, increases efficiency in all store operations.

How employees learn

Increasing the basic skills and abilities of employees through training is difficult. There are no definite rules to follow in determining how employees learn because employees are all individuals and are, therefore, very different. There are also no specific rules to follow in training employees. There are, however, some guidelines that will apply to most employees in retail training situations:

Guideline 1. People learn when they are ready and willing to learn. Supervisors will find it difficult to teach employees unless they are ready and willing to learn. Because learning is difficult and requires attention and concentration, supervisors should always try to provide an environment that is conducive to learning. Especially in on-the-job training, learning suffers from the distractions of a noisy store.

Guideline 2. Employees learn when they see a need to know. The desire to learn must be present in employees before they will learn. They must see a need to know that which is being taught. Supervisors must create a situation in which employees will see a direct personal value in learning and recognize that the new knowledge and skills being taught will help them satisfy a direct personal need in the day-to-day job.

Guideline 3. Employees learn through involvement. Learning requires both involvement and thinking. Depending on what they are attempting to teach, supervisors should try to use as many training techniques as possible. In this way, they will be able to adjust to the individual differences of the trainees. It is important to recognize that the more of the five senses that can be involved, the greater will be the comprehension and retention of what is presented. Every effort should be made to use charts, graphs, blackboards, outlines, pictures, diagrams, and other training aids that can reinforce what is said and what is done, and therefore, promote learning.

Guideline 4. Employees learn by participating. There can never be any lasting effects to the training process unless the employee actively participates. In on-the-job training employees must follow the presentation mentally as well as physically. In classroom training employees must be forced to use their powers of reasoning to integrate their new knowledge and skills with those they already possess. Only then can the new knowledge and skills become a part of their thought processes and, thus, direct and influence their future behavior. There is increased interest and motivation in exercises in which the actions taken closely duplicate actual job conditions.

Guideline 5. Employees learn through associations and impressions. Supervisors should try to find out about the interests and the past experiences of employees and relate what is being taught to what they already know. When working with an experienced employee, an "as you know" approach can be used; this indicates that the employee already knows the material and needs only to be made conscious of it once again.

Every aspect of what supervisors do and say makes an impression on employees. First impressions must be good impressions. Cover the important subjects first, because employees remember first impressions. Impressions should be made strongly. When possible, use a striking example or put drama into the subject that is being discussed. For example, if the importance of safety is the subject of a training session, refer to situations in which failure to follow safety measures resulted in serious injury.

The effectiveness of the supervisor's ability as a trainer is measured by the learning that takes place in employees. If employees have not learned, the supervisor has not taught.

Techniques for promoting learning

Learning, as we said earlier, is a difficult process. It requires patience and careful preparation on the part of the supervisor. When supervisors train, they should follow a basic framework designed to promote good learning:

Guideline 1. Have clearly defined objectives. Supervisors must have clearly defined objectives in mind. Throughout the training period, supervisors should know in what way the things they are saying or doing help employees meet the training objectives. Each day employees should show personal progress, whether the progress is in the learning of a new skill, new knowledge, or the overcoming of an earlier weakness.

Guideline 2. Know what you are going to teach. Supervisors should study their material carefully, reviewing it as often as necessary to make sure that they understand it completely. Training materials must be used skillfully. It is also important that sufficient time for training has been budgeted for the subject matter to be taught.

Guideline 3. Know why employees should learn. Throughout the training period, supervisors must know the importance of what is being taught and why employees should want to learn it. If employees understand why they are learning something, they will be motivated to learn it. Supervisors should outline for employees the material that they will teach. This will help employees establish their own goals as well as strengthen their desire to learn.

Guideline 4. Divide training into small parts. Supervisors should decide what they want to teach; then they should break the subject down into small segments and teach the parts, moving through the sequence of segments only as rapidly as employees can grasp and comprehend the new material. Supervisors must use their judgment in fitting the breakdown to each individual. For those who learn slowly, the material must be divided into small parts. For those who understand quickly, larger segments can be used.

Guideline 5. Arrange the material in logical sequence. The material supervisors want to teach should be arranged in a logical teaching-learning sequence. Supervisors should proceed from what is known and understood by employees to unknown material and new skills. Training should proceed from the simple to the complex.

Guideline 6. Let learners practice and participate. Employees should fully understand that which has been taught. Supervisors can learn quite a bit about the effectiveness of their training by observing employees as they apply their new knowledge and skills.

Guideline 7. Test, correct, and retrain. Employees must be tested throughout the learning process to make certain they are prog-

ressing and learning on schedule. If they have not mastered the material, they should be corrected and retrained. Employees have no way of knowing whether their performance is good or bad unless they are told. Employees who know that they are doing the job correctly and that their efforts are appreciated will be receptive to future training. In making corrections, some of the following suggestions may be of help:

(a) Mistakes should be corrected tactfully.
(b) Criticize the way the job is being performed, but avoid criticizing the individual. Correcting performance rather than the individual will maintain goodwill and cooperation.
(c) Give praise before criticism.
(d) Correct errors indirectly by making comparisons with what employees have done correctly.
(e) Avoid criticizing a trainee in front of other employees or customers. Always counsel in private.
(f) Supervisors should refrain from emphasizing their own abilities.
(g) When employees demonstrate good performance, indicate to them that it is the result of a well thought-out procedure.
(h) Avoid pettiness. Supervisors should not pick at an employee's performance by pointing out every minor mistake. Select the two or three most important weaknesses, and work on these.
(i) Keep a sense of humor by placing errors in their proper perspective.
(j) Avoid laughing at employees, but help them laugh with you.
(k) Stress courtesy, and be courteous.
(l) Avoid personal topics during training sessions.

Guideline 8. Follow up and smooth out the job. When employees start applying what they have learned, weaknesses will appear. These may be the result of overemphasizing some aspect of what they have studied to the detriment of an overall performance. Supervisors must recognize such weaknesses and help employees work more smoothly by giving additional instructions when they are needed.

Guideline 9. Rebuild the segments into a total unit. Because training was conducted by teaching the parts, supervisors should summarize and put the parts back into the whole. This will help employees understand the totality of what they have been studying and will help them to simplify it in their own minds.

Motivating Employees

If supervisors are to lead, they must be able to motivate employees to perform tasks that are asked of them. Many times employees have to perform tasks that are boring and have little interest or challenge. In spite of the monotony of the work, however, the work must be performed. It is the supervisor's job to motivate employees to perform all of their duties. Motivating involves guiding employees' efforts toward the accomplishment of the firm's objectives. Management's success depends upon the ability: (1) to understand its employees on a personal basis, and (2) to know and understand the nature and source of job satisfaction.

Alternative approaches to motivation

Retailers use many ways to try to get employees moving in ways beneficial to the organization. Some shout, others coax; some have contests, others give time off from work; and some praise while others threaten. Any of these and other possible methods can be categorized into three alternative methods to motivation.

The human need approach. The human need approach to motivation is based on the premise that the most effective motivators are those that act as satisfiers of employee needs and goals. Figure 5.2 illustrates this point of view through the stairway to effective motivation.

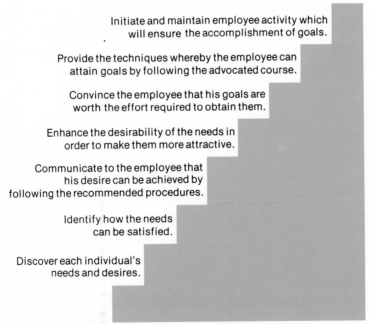

Figure 5.2. The stairway to effective motivation.

Source: Text from Ray A. Killina, *Managers Must Lead!* New York: Comet Press, 1966, p. 93.

It is important that the supervisor recognize two assumptions underlying this view. First, each individual may have different needs, and second, different motivational devices may satisfy the same need for different individuals.

The authority approach. The authority approach is based on the assumption that the supervisor's authority and position are the only factors necessary to motivate subordinates. Authority is the right to take action and the right to expect others to perform. In other words, subordinates will do the assigned tasks because they are told to do them and because they fear the consequences of doing otherwise. This is really a negative incentive view of motivation. It is doubtful that negative incentives such as loss of promotion, demotion, reprimands, or even loss of a job are motivation devices in the true sense of the concept. They may cause an employee to do an adequate job but seldom will they inspire him or her to perform to the best of ability.

The financial approach. The financial approach to motivation is based on the assumption that employees work to maximize their economic position. To some extent, this economic man concept has been discredited today. Money is only one of many factors important to the employee. Today, when people are relatively affluent and much of the work environment has become depersonalized, other factors, such as social and higher level ego needs, may be much more important than additional money.

Motivation in practice

Supervisors have many motivational tools available to them: pay increases, promotions, prizes, paid vacations, insurance plans, praise, recognition, and added responsibility for deserving individuals. The key to successful motivation is to use one or a combination of these tools. Unfortunately, the supervisor may at times be forced to resort to the use of negative incentives.

Supervisors also can use competition to motivate. Most people have a strong desire to win, and this can be channeled into a motivational device. It's amazing how monotonous jobs gain appeal and excitement when people are in competition with their peers.

Communication

Communication is the key to understanding others. It is only through communication that individuals are able to interact and relate to each other. If supervisors are to be effective leaders, they must be able to communicate, thereby influencing the performance of their employees.

Forms of communication

Although communication is usually viewed as written or spoken, there are other ways in which people communicate. Lack of communication can be a form of communication. In many situations, nothing communicates better than dead silence. In oral communication a person's voice inflections can indicate feelings. One of the best communicators is facial expression. Physical appearance and "body language" also serve as communication tools. One of the best known forms of communication is a person's actions. The parable that "Actions speak louder than words" is true.

Barriers to communication

There are, unfortunately, barriers to communication, and supervisors must overcome them if they are to be effective leaders. There is, for example, the poorly expressed message in which the supervisor uses words or illustrations that have no meaning to the employee. There are the semantic and cultural differences that take place when words have different meanings to different individuals. There are the role expectation differences between superior and subordinate. Subordinates, for example, may fear their supervisor and, thus, tell her what she wants to hear. Or subordinates may have little skill in expressing themselves whereas supervisors, because of the nature of their jobs, have considerable experience in communication.

These barriers to communication are serious enough that it is important to overcome them. To do this supervisors must, first, make a conscious attempt to break the barriers created by their organizational role. By transmitting ideas frankly and by encouraging their employees to make suggestions and offer opinions, supervisors can greatly reduce organizational tensions. Encouraging employee participation and feedback can enhance communication flow and reduce status and role tensions.

Second, supervisors can greatly increase understanding if they transmit their messages in the employee's frame of reference. By viewing the world as their employees do, supervisors can make their messages more effective.

Third, supervisors should listen more. Everyone talks, but no one listens. If supervisors are to communicate effectively, they must listen so that they understand what is being said. The best listener often turns out to be the best communicator.

Summary

Most leadership qualities can be learned. By developing human, technical, and conceptual skills and by applying problem-solving techniques, most people can learn to be leaders. Supervisors must master these skills and should also learn how to train employees, how to motivate them, and how to communicate with them.

Questions and Problems

1. *How might supervisors gain and improve their human, technical, and conceptual skills? Are different methods required for each of the three types of skills?*
2. *How is the process of decision making related to the supervisory function of planning? How is it related to the training situation?*
3. *Are the guidelines for learning consistent with your formal education experience?*
4. *Should different motivational devices be used for the new employee and the veteran employee? Why or why not?*
5. *Why do you think most people are poor communicators?*

Situations and Activities

You are assistant to the divisional merchandise manager of a large general merchandise store doing $1.5 million of business. You are asked to take the responsibility for conducting the yearly white-goods sale. Every January this store makes an all-out effort to sell (or promote) sheets, pillow cases, and bedspreads. In the past some unusual and interesting ideas have been successfully used to motivate all employees to work for bigger and better sales. How would you proceed to obtain the total involvement of all employees?

You are the newly appointed personnel manager. One of the first problems that you face is a request by a department head to dismiss an employee. The employee has been with the firm for eighteen years and until a year and a half ago was very productive. Recently, however, the employee has frequently been late to work, and his absenteeism is increasing. The department manager's report suggests that the employee may have family problems and/or an alcoholic problem. How will you proceed? What will you do?

One of the key parts of the supervisor's job is changing employee attitudes. For each of the following broad categories identify an attitude that might need to be changed and describe things you could do to change the attitude.
   a. Toward customers
   b. Toward employer
   c. Toward fellow employees
   d. Toward oneself.

Develop a formal method for self-evaluating one's effectiveness as a supervisor. Identify those things which a manager is called upon to do before suggesting ways in which to measure the performance.

Bibliography

Blum, Milton L., and Maylor, James C. *Industrial Psychology: Its Theoretical and Social Formulations.* New York: Harper & Row, 1968. p. 352.

"Can You Qualify as a Supervisor?" *Goodall News,* Vol. XXVII, June—July, 1969, pp. 1—2.

"Equal Pay for Women Retailers." *Business Week,* January 29, 1972, pp. 76—78.

Hays, Colonel Samuel H., and Thomas, Lieutenant Colonel William N. *Taking Command.* Harrisburg, Pennsylvania: Stackpole Books, 1967.

Herzberg, Frederick; Mausner, Bernard; and Synerman, Barbara. *The Motivation to Work.* New York: John Wiley & Sons, 1959. p. 82.

Hogan, Charles. "A Systems Approach to Manpower Planning in Department Stores." *Journal of Retailing,* Vol. 44, No. 3, 1968, pp. 18—22.

Hood, Robert C. *The Art of Managing.* Ansul Chemical Company. Mairneth, Wisconsin.

Killian, Ray A. *Managers Must Lead!* New York: Comet Press, 1966. pp. 67—68.

Longenecker, Justin G. *Principles of Management and Organizational Behavior.* Columbus, Ohio: Charles E. Merrill Books, 1964. p. 241.

Maslow, Abraham. "A Theory of Human Motivation." *Psychological Review,* Vol. 50, 1943, pp. 370—393.

Miller, Max S. "What Are the Principles of Leadership?" *Journal of Systems Management,* June, 1969, pp. 11—13.

Rubin, Leonard. "Today's Retailer Must be a Man for All Seasons." *Stores,* October, 1969, p. 27.

"Who'll Run the Stores of the 70's." *Chain Store Age* (Variety Stores Executive Edition), November 1970, p. 40.

four

INFORMATION
FOR RETAILING

6

Retail Accounting

contents

behavioral objectives

No retail manager can escape the often tedious but very important task of maintaining good records. The task consists of setting up a system that will give good information and maintaining the system to ensure that it yields accurate information. The retailer, then, must know what kinds of records to keep and for what purposes; must understand how inventory is accounted for in a store; and must know how to analyze this information in developing plans for a store.

Upon completing this chapter, you will be able to do the following:
☐ Establish balance sheet and profit and loss statements.
☐ Explain why percentages help the retail manager analyze profit and loss statements.
☐ Name the accounting records that retail managers should keep to run their stores.
☐ Explain why having too much or too little invested in inventory is bad for a business.
☐ Find operating data information that is important to various types of retail stores.
☐ Describe how a store's ending inventory position affects gross margin.
☐ Develop procedures for taking inventory.
☐ Explain the differences among the cost, the book, and the retail methods of inventory.
☐ Develop a cost code.
☐ Explain how overages and shortages might occur in a retail business.
☐ Name the types of expenses a retail store may incur.
☐ Build a sample cash budget.

No retailer "flies blind" for very long. An airplane pilot quickly learns that the plane can come to an abrupt halt if there aren't instruments to tell when it is flying too low, toward a stall, or with too little fuel. Instruments are the source of information, for visual references are inadequate if the pilot is flying in bad weather or through clouds. The experienced pilot knows that relying wholly on senses may cause a premature abortion of the flight.

To this extent, flying an airplane is similar to running a retail business. Although it is possible to run such a business by relying solely on one's senses or intuition, the odds of doing so successfully are not favorable. Reliable, objective sources of information are needed. Like the pilot who needs instruments to steer a plane, the merchant needs instruments to guide her or him. These instruments must inform where the business has been and where it is now.

In business we call such instruments records. In a very real sense, they become the basis for guiding and controlling the operations of a retail organization. They tell how much is owed employees, the government, and suppliers. They tell whether the business is making a profit. They tell when, how much, and what types of merchandise are needed in the store. And they help the merchant make plans for the future. They are the tools of the trade, providing information vital to the making of everyday decisions. To fulfill their functions, records must be as timely, accurate, complete, convenient to use, and neat as one can possibly make them.

To keep inadequate records is to court disaster. Retailing is becoming too complex, competition too keen, and products too numerous for a merchant to lose sight of the details of the business. Overwhelming evidence shows that managers who operate with less than complete information are the ones whose businesses are most likely to fail. In fact, a study has shown that in the records of one U.S. District Court, 90 percent of the firms adjudged bankrupt failed to keep adequate records. Therefore, a manager should be able to compile, understand, and use records effectively. Working with records may not be the most exciting or glamorous part of running a business, but it is vital!

This chapter begins by providing information on the development of profit and loss statements and balance sheets—information that is useful for the analysis of retail store operations. It introduces the minimum set of records that should be kept by any retail business along with information on how to use them. Special attention is devoted to problems connected with accounting for inventory. The first appendix deals with a problem that plagues the keeper of accurate records—shortages—and suggests control procedures for reducing them. In addition, a second appendix sets forth some "how to" techniques for analyzing information contained in profit and loss statements and balance sheets. It is recommended reading for students who need detailed information on financial data.

Financial Statements

An evaluation of the financial condition of a retail store should tell three things: whether the store can pay its bills on time, whether it is making a profit, and whether it has a healthy balance between debt funds and ownership funds. To assess these factors, managers use two summaries, called statements. They are the profit and loss statement and the balance sheet statement.

The profit and loss statement

The profit and loss (P & L) statement shows how successful the buying and selling of goods has been and how well expenses have been controlled over a period of time. In summarizing sales and expenses, it reflects the profit situation. If gross margin—the difference between net sales and cost of goods sold—exceeds expenses, a profit is made; if expenses exceed gross margin, a loss is generated. A sample retail profit and loss statement is shown in Table 6.1.

Table 6.1. Profit and Loss Statement

Gross sales	$11,000	
Sales returns and allowances	− 1,000	
Net sales	10,000	100%
Cost of goods sold		
Opening inventory	5,000	
Purchases	10,000	
Total merchandise handled	15,000	
Ending inventory	− 8,000	
Total cost of goods sold	7,000	70
Gross margin	3,000	30%
Expenses		
Payroll	1,500	15
Rent	500	5
Advertising	200	2
Other expenses and taxes	300	3
Total expenses	2,500	25
Net profit	$ 500	5%

Gross sales = consists of the record, in the form of sales slips and/or cash register readings, of all merchandise sold.

Sales returns and allowances = consists of the record kept of all merchandise returned by customers.

Net sales = difference between gross sales and sales returns and allowances.

The P & L statement shown tells how much profit was made, how much was spent on total expenses, and how much gross margin was earned. Notice also that accounts are represented in terms of both dollars and percentages. Percentages are calculated by using net sales as the base figure, or the 100 percent figure. All other figures within the statement are expressed as a percentage of the net sales figure. For example,

$$\frac{\text{Rent}}{\text{Net sales}} = \frac{\$500}{\$10,000} = 5\%$$

$$\frac{\text{Profits}}{\text{Net sales}} = \frac{\$500}{\$10,000} = 5\%$$

The percentage figures establish relationships that show the effect of management's decisions on various operating accounts. The relationship of accounts such as cost of goods sold, expenses, and profits to the net sales figure permits managers to compare their store's performance with its performance in previous years or with the performance of similar stores. (Percentage figures make comparisons much easier than do dollar amounts.) Managers may use this information to make adjustments that affect operations.

The balance sheet statement

A balance sheet statement tells management how efficiently the business is operating by showing whether the firm is overcommitted or undercommitted in asset holdings or is too far in debt. As such, it gives the value of all assets, debts, and the net worth of the business at a particular time (see Table 6.2). In other words, it shows (1) everything a business owns, called *total assets,* (2) everything a business owes, called *total liabilities,* or debts, and (3) *net worth.*

Table 6.2. Balance Sheet

Current assets		Current liabilities	
Cash	$ 1,000	Accounts payable	$ 5,000
Accounts receivable	5,000	Accrued taxes	1,000
Inventory	25,000	Salaries payable	5,000
Fixed assets		**Fixed liabilities**	
Furniture and equipment		Notes payable	20,000
(less depreciation)	10,000		
Property (less depreciation)	20,000	Net worth	30,000
Total assets	$61,000	Total liabilities	$61,000

Assets. Assets are broken down into current and fixed assets. Current assets are those that will be converted into cash during the normal operation of the business within an accounting period, usually a fiscal or calendar year. Cash, accounts receivable, and merchandise inventories represent such assets.

Other types of assets include land, equipment, and fixtures—assets which are not sold but are retained and used in operating the business. They are considered fixed assets because they will not be converted into cash in the normal yearly operations of the business. Other assets such as deferred charges (for example, prepaid insurance) and good will are found in many retail balance sheets, but for our purposes they are of little significance.

Debt liabilities. Liabilities show the amount of money a company owes to its creditors and net worth shows the amount it owes to its owners. Debt liabilities may be broken down into debts that will mature within a year and debts that will mature within a longer period of time. As is true of asset accounts, liabilities that mature within a year are called current liabilities; they include items such as accounts payable, accrued taxes, and salaries payable. Long-term debt liabilities are called fixed liabilities and include obligations such as payments on the mortgage of the building.

Net worth. The net worth of a business is simply the difference between total assets and total debt liabilities. In a large retail firm net worth may include preferred stock, common stock, earnings retained in the business, and reserves set aside from earnings for special purposes. The net worth of a small retail firm is usually the owner's capital. In any event, whether net worth includes many accounts or only one, it is still the difference between the value of assets and of debts.

A Minimum Set of Records

It is difficult to say what constitutes an adequate set of records. The adequacy of records depends on several variables:

1. The type of retail business being conducted
2. The financial and human resources available to the firm
3. The type and extent of the manager's informational needs
4. The manager's ability to make good use of the information in the records
5. The information necessary for the Department of Internal Revenue office to assess the business's tax liability.

There are, however, three areas in which it is absolutely essential to keep records: sales, merchandise inventory, and expenses. A minimum set of records includes information that falls in these categories (see Table 6.3).

Sales Records

Managers should have at their disposal, on a regular basis, three different types of sales information—store cash and charge sales, department sales, and sales by individual sales people. Managers who record less information cannot find out what is contributing to the business.

With sales information available, managers, such as department heads and store managers, can compare last year's sales with this year's. They have one of the essential pieces of information necessary for the preparation of profit and loss statements. They can forecast needs for personnel, inventory, and facilities.

Cash and charge sales

There are two basic ways of recording sales. The first is based on the capability of modern cash registers to record both cash sales and charge sales. Store managers who have such cash registers need only read the cash registers or their tapes at the end of each day, or more often if desired, to determine both cash and credit sales. Stores that have cash registers equipped to record only cash sales may have sales people record charge sales by making out charge sales tickets or processing credit cards. Then, charge sales are tallied and added to the cash register readings to obtain total sales for the day.

The second way to record sales is to use sales tickets to keep track of both cash and charge sales. This method is usually practical only when total unit sales per day are relatively small, as in appliance stores.

Table 6.3. Records Kept by the Average Retail Store

Allowances given customers	Rent	Money put into business
Allowances received from suppliers	Light, heat, water	Money received on account
	Telephone	Notes discounted
Average sale	Losses from bad debts	Notes given bank
Store	Depreciation	Notes given by merchant when buying goods
Departments	Delivery	
Sales people	Repairs	Notes paid by merchant when due
Cash sales	Equipment rentals	
Charge sales	Donations	Notes paid to merchant when due
Checks drawn	Services purchased	
C.O.D.'s	Interest	Notes—part payment to merchant, with interest and renewal
Customer count	Pensions	
Delivery equipment bought	Insurance	
Delivery equipment sold	Sundry expenses	Notes renewed by merchant and interest paid
Departmental information	Freight and express	
Sales	Freight and express reimbursements	Other income
Expenses		Outstanding charge accounts of customers
Profits	Furniture and fixtures bought	
Deposits	Furniture and fixtures sold	Refunds (paid out)
Discounts earned	Inventory	Returns by customers for credit
Discounts given customers	Invoices paid	Returns to wholesalers
Discounts given employees	Invoices received	Sales people's sales
Employees' employment and earnings	Layaways	Shortages and overages
	Merchandise bought	Taxes paid
Expenses	Money borrowed	Sales
Advertising	Money drawn from business	Income
Salaries and wages	Money paid out	Excise
		Property
		Taxes withheld

Department sales

Receiving a breakdown of sales by department or product is a necessity. It is impossible for a manager to keep abreast of the performance of each department or even of all merchandise within one department without some systematic method for doing so. A manager who lacks knowledge of a department's performance frequently misses sales opportunities and does a poor job of buying merchandise.

Some stores have cash registers that key sales to individual departments or products. Another method of recording department sales is to set aside one register in each department. A reading of the cash register at the end of the day gives total sales for the department. The ringing up of sales in other departments on the same register should require a departmental sales tally sheet which identifies sales by department (see Figure 6.1).

Sales may be further divided into categories within each department. Table 6.4 shows examples of such divisions.

Employee sales

Notwithstanding the impact of self-service on today's retailing, personal customer contact still plays a dominant role in retailing. It is often personal contact that alienates or retains customers. In the absence of self-service, it is the sales person who brings in the dollars. Therefore, managers should determine whether they are obtaining maximum performance from their sales people. Because payroll expenses in a retail store are usually greater than all other operating expenses combined, managers are foolish if they ignore employee performance.

One of the many ways to assess each sales person's performance is to determine his or her average sales over a particular period of time. The typical procedures for recording sales person's sales include (1) identifying the maker of each sale by establishing a system involving, for example, the coding of each transaction with employee name or number or (2) assigning separate cash register drawers to

Sales by Department

Date 4/18/77
Register No. 23

	Dept. #16 / Amt.	Dept. #19 / Amt.	Dept. #23 / Amt.	Dept. # / A	ept. / Amt.	Dept. # / Amt.	Dept. # / Amt.	Dept. # / Amt.
	1.29	2.20	5.79					
	.69	.80	4.31					
	.58	.60	8.10					
	5.98	.42						
Totals	8.94	4.22	18.20					

Figure 6.1. Daily tally sheet of sales by department.

each sales person. The latter method gives the manager an opportunity both to assess the person's sales and to determine how he or she handles money.

Merchandise Inventory Records

In most retail businesses the largest investment is in merchandise inventory, that is, in merchandise that is available for sale. In fact, small retail firms often have 60 to 70 percent of their total assets invested in inventory. Obviously, it is important that managers be regularly informed of the merchandise inventory situation.

Knowing one's merchandise inventory situation includes (1) knowing what purchases have been received and (2) keeping an accounting of in-stock or on-hand inventory. It is relatively simple to set up accounts that record purchases received. The obvious procedure is to establish a "Purchases" account and enter in it the amounts of merchandise received.

It is more difficult to keep track of the in-stock situation. Yet, knowledge of this situation is fundamental to management's appraisal of a retail store. The in-stock situation provides information on the store's investment in inventory and on its gross margin position (gross margin is equal to the net sales minus the cost of goods sold).

The investment in inventory

There are disadvantages to having an inventory that is either too large or too small. Having too much merchandise may lead to excessive markdowns if all the goods can't be sold or if they become soiled or obsolete before people can buy them. Overstocking is also expensive because of increased handling, storage, and insurance costs. On the other hand, having an inventory that is too small leads to lost sales because items are not in stock when customers ask for them.

One way to measure whether there is too little or too much invested in inventory is to compute the number of times stock turns over

Table 6.4. Departmental Divisions

Hardware	Men's Clothing ˙
Hardware	Suits and sport coats
Housewares	Topcoats and overcoats
Sporting goods	Jackets and sweaters
Lawn and garden	Slacks
Paint and paint sundries	Shoes
	Hats and caps
Plumbing and electric	Sportswear
	Dress shirts and neckwear
Hand and power tools	Hosiery and underwear
Gifts	Belts, jewelry, gloves, and miscellaneous

in a given period; this computation is called the rate of stock turnover. The rate of stock turnover may be found in either of two ways, both of which involve the calculation of average inventory. (Average inventory is calculated by adding the inventory at the beginning of the period and the inventory at the end of the period and dividing by two.)

1. Divide net sales by the average inventory at retail prices.
2. Divide cost of goods sold by the average inventory at cost.

Suppose, for example, that the net sales for a year were $100,000. On January 1 (the first of the year) the inventory was $40,000, and on December 31 (the end of the year), the inventory was $60,000. The rate of stock turnover is determined in the following manner:

$$\text{Average inventory} = \frac{\text{beginning inventory} + \text{ending inventory}}{2}$$

$$\text{Average inventory} = \frac{\$40,000 + \$60,000}{2} = \$50,000$$

$$\text{Rate of stock turnover} = \frac{\text{net sales}}{\text{average inventory at retail}}$$

$$\text{Rate of stock turnover} = \frac{\$100,000}{\$50,000} = 2$$

Whether a stock turnover of 2 is good or bad depends on the type of retail business being run. Some retail businesses such as supermarkets operate at turnover rates as high as 12. Others such as clothing stores operate at turnover rates as low as 2.

The reason for differences in stock turnover rates should be obvious. Supermarket sales may be so rapid (how long, for example, does it take to sell three hundred cans of green beans?) that markets must replenish stock as often as twice a week. (Imagine how much space and investment would be necessary if stores were to stock for several months' sales.) Fortunately for supermarket managers, supplies are shipped quickly from nearby distribution points, and merchants do not have to keep too much stock on hand. The fast turnover, therefore, is caused by small in-stock inventories and large numbers of sales.

The situation in clothing stores is, however, different from that in supermarkets. First, customers demand extensive choice; they want to examine different styles, colors, and sizes before they buy even one item. Second, the system for distributing clothing forces most merchants to order the bulk of their merchandise only two or three times a year. Therefore, it is necessary to carry a backup stock. Backup stocks slow down the rate of stock turnover.

Table 6.5 lists some sample stock turnover rates for selected retail stores and for departments within stores. To a large extent, overall turnover rates are of limited use to managers in making operational decisions. The turnover rates of departmental stock or, in some cases, of different kinds of merchandise are much more useful than figures for the store as a whole.

In determining stock turnover, it is important to understand that the rates for particular stores and departments are compared to the so-called average stock turnover rate for that kind of store or department. Obviously considerations must be made for businesses that operate in ways significantly different from the average.

Throughout this book, we will emphasize the importance of comparing one's own business with similar types of businesses. Such comparisons are necessary if one is to assess the position of his business. Stock turnover rates, profit to sales, current ratio, stock sales ratio, and average transactions are only a few of the comparisons that may be made.

There are many sources that provide the data necessary to make comparisons. Trade associations, trade periodicals, government

---

Table 6.5. Average Stock-Turnover Rates for Various Businesses

Kind of Business	Turnover Rates per Year
Bars and taverns	13.7
Camera and photographic supplies	3.2
Confectioneries	13.8
Department stores	4.4
Drugstores	3.9
Florists	11.5
Furniture stores	2.6
Grocery stores	11.8
Hardware	2.3
Jewelry	1.1
Lumber and building materials	4.6
Men's wear	2.7
Package liquor	6.0
Office supplies and equipment (stationery stores)	3.1
Shoe stores (family)	1.8
Specialty stores (women's apparel)	4.8
Toys	3.0

agencies, and manufacturers are all sources of data on different areas and businesses in retailing. The *Expenses in Retail Businesses* offered by the National Cash Register Company, the *How to Operate and Establish a Retail Business* series offered by the Small Business Administration, and the *Merchandising and Operating Results (MOR) of Department and Specialty Stores* offered by the National Retail Merchants Association are excellent sources. (*See* Tables 6.6 and 6.7 for examples of data found in these publications.)

The effect of the inventory situation on gross margin

To know the amount of profit a firm is making, it is necessary to know the amount of gross margin, or gross profit. The number of sales made and the cost of goods sold are the two components of gross margin. (Because we have already shown how sales are recorded and computed, we will show how the cost of goods sold is calculated.)

Cost of goods sold is the difference between the cost of the total merchandise handled during a period (beginning inventory plus purchases—all the goods that have been in the store at one time or another during the period) and the cost of the ending inventory (what is left in inventory at the end of the period). If a retailer knows how much merchandise he had during a period and how much was left at the end of the period, he can calculate the difference between the two to determine how much was sold. Note, however, that he must calculate the merchandise at cost prices, not retail prices, because gross margin is figured by subtracting the cost of goods sold from retail sales.

The following illustration clarifies how gross margin is calculated:

Beginning inventory	$ 400—cost
Purchases	+ 600—cost
Total merchandise handled	$1000—cost
Ending inventory	− 300—cost
Cost of goods sold	$ 700—cost
Sales	$1000—retail
Cost of goods sold	− 700
Gross margin	$ 300

Although the idea seems simple enough, the problem is one of collecting the data with which to make the calculations. To obtain the figure for total merchandise handled, one must keep records of the beginning inventory plus all purchases received at cost price. Ending inventory is found by taking a physical count, at

---

Table 6.6. Operating Information for a Motel

	Number of Units					
	20	21-40	41-60	61-100	101-125	126 ↑
Income:						
Room rentals	92.80%	83.84%	84.18%	74.43%	70.68%	63.36%
Food service	2.36%	10.80%	5.60%	13.17%	17.41%	22.68%
Sundry sales	.40%	.50%	.74%	3.37%	.55%	.37%
Rents, concessions, etc.	2.12%	3.56%	6.85%	7.78%	9.99%	11.12%
Other income	2.32%	1.30%	2.63%	1.25%	1.37%	2.47%
Total Income	100.00%	100.00%	100.00%	100.00%	100.00%	100.00%
Operating Expenses:						
Salaries and wages	10.87%	17.48%	19.20%	27.90%	27.88%	26.62%
Executive salaries	1.80%	3.81%	5.31%	3.91%	3.85%	3.55%
Laundry	2.16%	2.02%	1.18%	1.53%	1.24%	1.18%
Linen, chinaware, glassware	2.07%	1.73%	1.08%	1.10%	1.24%	.71%

Table 6.6. Continued

	Number of Units					
	20	**21-40**	**41-60**	**61-100**	**101-125**	**126↑**
Advertising, printing, stationery	2.36%	2.38%	4.37%	3.06%	3.86%	4.02%
Payroll, taxes, insurance	1.28%	1.97%	1.66%	2.72%	2.66%	4.20%
Heat, light and power	9.13%	7.43%	6.34%	6.73%	5.84%	4.82%
Repairs and maintenance	5.02%	4.49%	3.46%	4.22%	2.71%	3.67%
Cleaning and other supplies	3.89%	3.33%	3.34%	2.66%	2.71%	1.63%
Telephone and telegraph	2.52%	2.51%	2.74%	2.42%	2.08%	1.59%
Other operating expenses	4.45%	4.36%	7.36%	6.51%	8.93%	12.65%
Total operating expenses	45.55%	51.51%	56.04%	62.76%	63.00%	64.64%
Gross operating profit	54.45%	48.49%	43.96%	37.24%	37.00%	35.36%
Capital Expenses:						
Real estate and property taxes	4.78%	3.77%	3.20%	3.85%	4.56%	4.54%
Insurance	2.30%	2.78%	2.23%	1.68%	2.23%	.74%
Interest	10.39%	10.77%	8.93%	9.36%	13.78%	4.89%
Rent	1.83%	3.91%	3.78%	4.46%	3.53%	4.88%
Depreciation & amortization	14.52%	14.34%	13.88%	11.26%	12.47%	7.18%
Total capital expenses	33.82%	35.57%	32.02%	30.61%	36.57%	22.23%
Net Profit	20.63%	12.92%	11.94%	6.63%	.43%	13.13%
Average Investment Per Motel:						
Buildings	$ 95,199	$226,401	$350,251	$566,725	$1,014,741	$1,871,490
Furniture & fixtures	22,539	58,758	84,166	150,239	333,492	547,387
Sub-total	$117,738	$285,159	$434,417	$716,964	$1,348,233	$2,418,877
Land	25,331	54,051	89,819	128,284	113,925	223,309
Total Investment	$143,069	$339,210	$524,236	$845,248	$1,462,158	$2,642,186
General Statistics:						
Percentage of occupancy	67.44%	67.98%	70.64%	70.46%	74.15%	70.60%
Avg. daily rate per rented room	$13.00	$15.80	$14.35	$15.45	$16.35	$23.66
Avg. daily rate per guest	$ 7.10	$ 8.41	$ 7.93	$ 8.30	$ 9.73	$13.37
Avg. no. guests per room	1.83	1.88	1.81	1.86	1.68	1.77

Table 6.7. Performance by Volume of a MOR Merchandise Group: Aggregate Company Data

Men's Clothing

VOLUME CODE	MOR Mdsg. Group Volume $000 (Omitted)	Merchandising and Inventory Data—Aggregate Company									Sales Data—Aggregate Company						Expense		
		Cumulative Mark-on %	Mark-downs	Stock Shortage	Net Workroom Cost	Cash Discounts % of Net Cost Purchases	Gross Margin % of Net Sales	$ Return per $ Average Cost Investment	$ per Square Feet of Selling Space	Stock Turns (Times)	Net Sales % of Last Year	Number of Sales Transactions % of Last Year	Sales Returns % of Gross Sales	Sales % of Total MOR Merchandise Division	Selling Area % of Total MOR Merchandise Division	$ Sales per Square Feet of Selling Space	Newspaper Space Costs % of Sales	Selling Salaries % of Sales	Number of Reporting Companies
			% of Net Retail Sales																
1	up to 120 Median	44.9	13.3	1.6		0.9	36.4	1.19	35	1.7	103.5		6.4	42.0	35.5	97			25
	Goal	45.5	9.9	0.3		1.8	38.4	1.59	48	2.6	115.4		3.8	50.5	48.6	123			
2	120 to 310 Median	45.1	10.4	1.2	3.2	0.7	37.0	1.43	35	2.1	104.6		7.8	37.5	46.8	95	2.8	7.2	29
	Goal	45.7	8.3	0.6	1.5	1.6	38.8	1.95	42	2.8	116.9		6.9	47.3	63.1	116	2.1	6.6	
3	310 to 600 Median	45.0	10.3	2.1	4.0	0.9	35.8	1.35	43	1.9	104.7		5.9	41.8	43.5	131	2.1	7.6	25
	Goal	46.8	8.3	1.0	3.0	1.7	38.3	1.77	63	2.4	122.0		4.8	55.6	56.1	153	1.7	6.6	
4	600 to 1250 Median	45.6	8.7	1.6	2.9	1.0	38.9	1.87	52	2.8	110.0		8.0	46.9	46.8	141	2.3		27
	Goal	46.8	7.7	0.4	1.8	1.3	42.1	2.35	68	3.0	113.7		6.1	49.0	49.2	160	1.6		
5	1250 up Median	44.5	9.0	4.1	4.2	4.0	36.5	1.69	46	2.6	105.7	101.1	7.9	45.2		125	2.0	7.3	25
	Goal	46.0	7.6	2.1	3.3	6.3	37.5	2.15	56	3.2	109.3	104.2	7.0	53.8		158	1.5	6.6	
6	Median Goal																		
	All Companies Median	45.0	9.9	1.7	3.5	1.1	36.7	1.55	43	2.3	106.1	103.9	7.3	41.8	44.1	114	2.2	7.3	131

Source: Merchandising and Operating Results, Controllers' Congress, National Retail Merchants Association.

cost prices, of the inventory in stock. Obviously, gross margin can be determined only if a physical inventory is taken. Most firms take a complete count of their goods once a year.

Accounting for inventory

There are three ways in which managers keep track of inventory. These methods are called the cost method, the book method, and the retail method. Before these methods may be used, however, one must know the basic mechanics of taking inventory and know how to assign dollar values to the inventory in stock. Knowledge of both of these things is necessary if one is to understand the cost, book, and retail methods of inventory.

Taking inventory. Ending inventories are determined by taking a count of the merchandise in stock. During the counting there must be certainty that merchandise movements (occurring as a result of sales or replenishment of stocks) do not affect inventory totals. Management must, then, either (1) close down the store during the period in which inventory is taken, (2) take the inventory at night or on weekends, or (3) keep the store open and establish a system to control merchandise movements. Let's look at the procedures used by retailers who take inventory during business hours.

The first step is to see that the understocks (merchandise stored under the counter) and counter tops are filled. This ensures that no one will move merchandise from the stockroom to the floor to replenish stocks. The movement of merchandise is dangerous because of the possibility of double counting (counting the same merchandise both in the stockroom and after it has been moved to the floor).

The second step is to count the merchandise in the stockroom. This is usually done by assigning individual employees to selected departments to count the merchandise in the bins and record information such as price, item number, and quantity. For this an inventory slip like the one shown in Figure 6.2 is used. To control errors, it is best to assign this job to

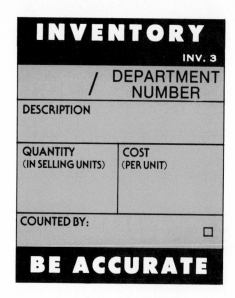

Figure 6.2. Inventory slip.

employees who are familiar with the merchandise in the department. After inventory slips have been made up and inserted alongside the merchandise already counted, the manager or an assistant pulls the slips, checks their accuracy, and sees that the information is entered onto inventory sheets like the one shown in Figure 6.3. Some managers do not use inventory slips but have their employees record the counts directly on the inventory sheets.

The third step is to count merchandise in the understocks and on the counter tops, in that order. (After all merchandise has been counted, understocks and counter tops will need to be replenished since they have not been filled during the counting period.)

The fourth step is to tally the totals on the inventory sheets, probably by department, and add the departmental totals to obtain a grand total that represents the ending inventory for the store.

Assigning a value to inventory. Fundamental to the taking of inventory is the assignment of some value to each item. Up to this point, you may have assumed that inventory values are recorded on inventory sheets at the cost price actually paid for the goods. This valuation of

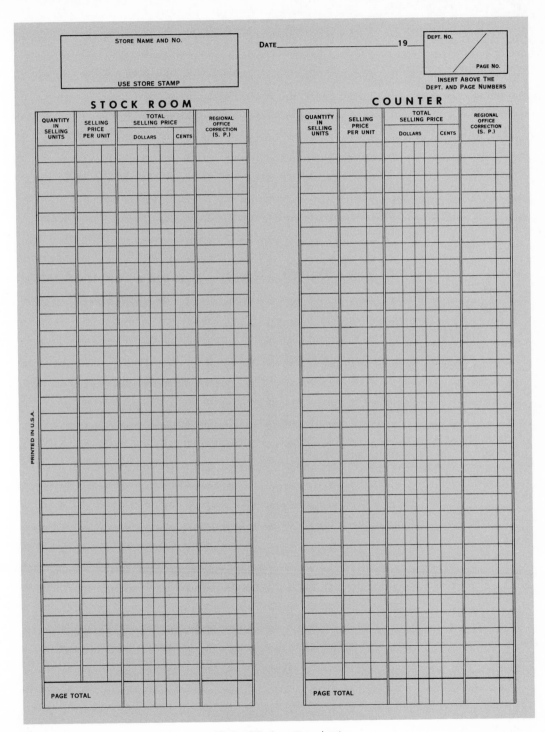

Figure 6.3. Inventory sheet.

inventory would be based on the assumption that present in-stock goods have the same worth as they had when they were bought. This, of course, is not always the case. Inventories can depreciate in value.

For example, a motor bike bought for $200 and priced at $300 might have to be sold for $250 if it were still on the floor when new models appeared. If this were the case, the merchant would not want to valuate the motor bike at its original cost but at some lower value—probably at one that would give the same markup planned for the $300 price. The inventory value of the bike could be determined in the following manner:

$$cost + markup = retail\ price$$

old pricing $\$200 + \$100 = \$300$ 33-1/3% markup

new pricing $\$167 + \$83 = \$250$ 33-1/3% markup

where: retail	$250
times desired markup percentage	= 33-1/3%
new dollar markup	$83

In other words, the bike would be valued at $167.

Goods may become soiled or damaged; wholesale price may move downward after goods are bought; or customers may lose interest in particular items. Any one of these reasons makes the goods less valuable to the retailer. To value goods at the original cost despite these considerations is to overvalue the inventory. The overvaluing of inventories inflates profits.

You might ask, "Why is it bad to show inflated profits?" The answer is that it is not bad as long as profits are earned. However, in accounting for inventory, it is possible to show unearned profits. That is why inventories are usually valued at *cost or market value, whichever is lower.* Thus, any inventory loss is recognized and accepted in the period in which it occurs and does not inflate profits.

For example, let's assume that two store managers operate in exactly the same way except that they carry their inventories differently. Store Manager A always carries his in-

ventory at the cost that he originally paid for the goods. However, Store Manager B carries his inventory at the original cost or at a cost (market value) that he would pay for the goods today if he were to buy them. Store Manager A's ending inventory, then, is, in general, higher than Store Manager B's. The following illustration shows how gross margin is affected by the different ways of valuing inventories.

	Store A	Store B
Beginning inventory	$ 50	$ 50
Purchases	50	50
Total merchandise handled	100	100
Ending inventory	− 60	− 50
Cost of goods sold	$ 40	$ 50
Sales	$100	$100
Cost of goods sold	− 40	− 50
Gross margin	$ 60	$ 50
Taxes at 50 percent	$ 30	$ 25

The only difference between Store A and Store B is that Store B's ending inventory was justifiably depreciated, because the goods were no longer worth their original cost value. Assuming there are no expenses and the tax rate is 50 percent, Store A pays $30 in taxes, whereas Store B pays $25 in taxes.

To summarize, a valuation of inventory at cost or market, whichever is lower, reduces the value of the ending inventory. This, in turn, increases the cost of goods sold, which reduces the gross margin. Because the amount of gross margin earned has a direct bearing on the amount of taxes paid, a reduction in gross margin reduces taxes and saves cash for the firm.

Some retail businesses don't have to be concerned about reducing the value of their inventories, because the inventories do not depreciate in value. Merchandise that does not easily become shopworn or is not subject to changes in fashion is not likely to depreciate. But, for merchandise that does depreciate, a lowering of cost or market is a reasonable objective.

Methods of accounting for inventory. Now that we have investigated the mechanics of taking inventory and briefly explored the way inventory values are assigned, we can describe the methods used in accounting for ending inventories. These methods are called the cost method, the book method, and the retail method.

The underlying assumption of the *cost method* of inventory is that all goods are recorded at cost and that ending inventory values are determined by actually counting the goods in stock and recording values at cost prices (see Figure 6.4). This gives the manager of a firm knowledge of (1) how much money is invested in inventory and (2) what the firm's gross margin position is. Recall that if ending inventories are not figured at cost, it is impossible to calculate the cost of goods sold—a necessary step in calculating gross margin.

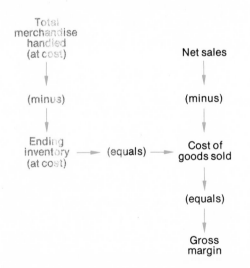

Figure 6.4. The use of the cost method of inventory in calculating gross margin.

When inventories are counted according to the cost method, the cost price of the article is usually recorded on an inventory slip. The person counting the merchandise will usually find the cost information on the price ticket. For example, a price ticket might be printed up as shown in Figure 6.5. The cost price is printed in code so its value is hidden from customers and

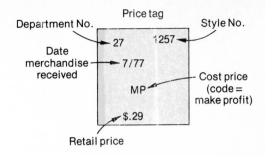

Figure 6.5. Price ticket.

even from employees who do not need to possess such information. Most cost codes are expressed with letters from a word or phrase that is easily remembered. The following are illustrative of cost codes:

Make Profit (example: AKT = $2.30)
1234 567890

Young Blade (example: OUGE = $23.50)
12345 67890

Black Horse (example: CS = 49¢)
12345 67890

Chemistry X (example: MYXX = $49.00)
123456789 0

Cost codes may also be expressed as 100151; that is, the 1's at the beginning and end of the number have no meaning, whereas 0015 represents the cost price—in this case, 15 cents. If cost information is not printed on the price ticket, the cost of the item usually may be obtained from stock books located in the office.

In using the cost method of inventory, it is important to realize that calculations of inventory investment and gross margin are impossible unless a physical count of goods in stock is made. If a business is small and the inventory stock is small, management may be able to keep abreast of its inventory investment and its profit situation through observation and the taking of inventory once a year. If observation isn't reliable enough, businesses with a small inventory may count it more often than once a year. Liquor, appliance, jewelry, and garden supply stores may count all their goods as many as six times a year without causing the manager undue hardship.

Large stores, however, face different problems. Obviously, stores stocking thousands of items cannot actually count the total inventory very often. Merchants, however, may want to make regular assessments of inventory investment and gross margin so they can take corrective action, if necessary. Waiting until the end of the year to take an inventory may endanger the store. How, then, might variety stores, supermarkets, drug stores, and department stores receive inventory and gross margin information even though it is impractical for them to take physical inventory more than once a year?

The *book method* of inventory provides a way of recording inventories so that a person may, at any time, look at the record books to obtain information on the amount of merchandise handled and sold. No physical counting of the merchandise is required. The book inventory method is a running, or more properly, a perpetual inventory.

In recording information for a book inventory, values may be recorded at either cost or retail prices. Firms usually employ the book method at retail prices. The illustration below shows that beginning inventory and purchases have been recorded at retail prices and added to yield a total figure for the merchandise handled at retail prices. Since the amount of inventory handled during the period is known, it is necessary to know only the amount sold to determine the amount remaining in inventory at the end of the period. The store's sales record shows how much was sold.

	At retail
Beginning inventory	$ 700
Purchases	+ 500
Total merchandise handled	$1200
Sales	−1000
Ending inventory	$ 200

Once again, a knowledge of the ending inventory position helps the firm to evaluate how well it's handling its inventory. The retail book inventory method provides a means of obtaining this information without taking a physical inventory.

Using the book method at retail prices to obtain information on gross margin is a different matter, however. In fact, it can't be done unless cost information on inventory is available. One way to get such information is through the cost method of inventory, but this procedure requires the counting of inventory.

Information on inventory investment and gross margin may be obtained without counting through the use of the book method at cost prices. The procedure for recording information is essentially the same as that for the book method at retail prices. The exception is the recording of cost prices. The illustration below shows the same format that was used in the book method at retail prices:

	At cost
Beginning inventory	$200
Purchases	+ 300
Total merchandise handled	$500
Cost of goods sold	− 400 ←
Ending inventory	$100

The problem with this method arises at the point designated by the arrow. To obtain the figure for the cost of goods sold, every time a sale is made, the cost of the goods must be entered, usually on the sales ticket. Such a procedure is cumbersome when many sales are made each day. Therefore, stores that sell high ticket items such as automobiles, appliances, and furs usually benefit the most from the book method at cost prices.

The third way of maintaining inventory records is through the use of the *retail method* of inventory. The advantage of this method is that it provides information on both inventory investment and gross margin but does not require a physical inventory. Combining elements of the cost method of inventory with those of the book method of inventory at retail prices permits us "to have our cake and eat it too"—as often as we want it.

Crucial to the procedures underlying the retail method of inventory is the recording of (1) component parts of total merchandise handled at cost and (2) retail prices. The illustration at the bottom of this page shows a standard format for deriving gross margin through the retail inventory method.

The following steps were used to arrive at the $240 gross margin figure shown in the illustration:

Step 1. Record all merchandise handled at both cost and retail prices.

Step 2. Compute the average markup percentage, called cumulative markup, for total merchandise handled.

	Cost	+ Markup	= Retail
Total merchandise handled	$480	+ $320	= $800

$$\text{Cumulative markup} = \frac{\text{Markup}}{\text{Retail}} = \frac{\$320}{\$800} = 40\%$$

Step 3. Subtract the net sales from the retail value of total merchandise handled to derive ending inventory at retail.

Step 4. Convert the ending inventory at retail to cost by using the percentage figure derived from the cost and retail figures of total merchandise handled.

Ending inventory at retail	$200
times cumulative markup (%)	40%
= cumulative markup ($)	$ 80

Ending inventory at retail	$200
minus cumulative markup ($)	$ 80
= ending inventory at cost	$120

Step 5. Subtract ending inventory at cost from the cost value of total merchandise handled to derive the cost of goods sold.

Step 6. Subtract cost of goods sold from net sales to derive gross margin.

Notice that the total merchandise handled was recorded at retail prices (as in the book method at retail prices) and again at cost prices (as in the cost method of inventory). Immediately, it is possible to determine that with a cost of $480 and a retail of $800 yielding a markup of $320 ($800 − $480), the average markup on all the goods handled during the period would be 40 percent.

Step 3 calls for a deduction of the net sales figure from the total merchandise handled at retail to derive ending inventory at retail. This is exactly what is done under the book method at retail prices. As in the book method at retail prices, however, it is impossible to calculate further until a cost value is given to the ending inventory. Only then can the cost of goods sold be derived. If, on the average, the total merchandise handled reflects a markup of 40 percent, any inventory left in stock should also have an average markup of 40 percent. Applying this average markup to the ending inventory at retail permits us to derive the ending inventory at cost and, ultimately, the gross margin figure. All this may be done without a physical inventory.

	At cost	At retail	Cumulative markup percentage
Beginning inventory	$ 180	$ 200	
Purchases	300	600	
Total merchandise handled	$ 480	$ 800	40%
Net sales		−600	
Ending inventory	−120	$ 200	
Cost of goods sold	$ 360		
Sales	$ 600		
Cost of goods sold	−360		
Gross margin	$ 240		

A more sophisticated format used in the retail method of inventory involves adding factors such as freight in and net additional markups to total merchandise handled. Next net markdowns, employee discounts, and a provision for shortages are included, along with net sales as total deductions from the retail figure of total merchandise handled. This results in a format like the following:

	At cost	At retail
Beginning inventory	$ 100	$ 200
Purchase	200	400
Freight in	50	
Net additional markups		100
Total merchandise handled	$ 350	$ 700
Net sales		−200
Employee discounts		− 50
Estimated shortages		− 80
Net markdowns		− 50
Total retail deductions		$ 380
Ending inventory at retail	$ 160	$ 320
Cumulative markup percentage		50%

The procedure is similar to the one described above, in that beginning inventory and purchases are entered at both cost and retail figures. Then freight in (entered at cost) and net additional markups (entered at retail) are added to beginning inventory and purchases to arrive at total merchandise handled for both cost and retail columns. Later in Chapter 14 you will learn that net additional markups include markups (price changes upward after goods have been originally priced) less markup cancellations (additional markups which have been cancelled). At this point the cumulative markup is calculated.

To obtain the value of the inventory at the end of the period, total retail deductions are subtracted from total merchandise handled at retail. Total retail deductions are the summation of (1) the net sales figure, (2) net markdowns, which include markdowns (prices changed downward after goods have been originally priced) less markdown cancellations (markdowns which have been cancelled), (3) employee discounts, and (4) estimated short-

ages. If a physical inventory is taken, shortages (or overages) do not have to be estimated, but are known as a result of a discrepancy between physical and book figures.

The cost of the ending inventory ($160) is found by multiplying the cumulative markup percentage times the ending inventory figure at retail and subtracting the product from the ending inventory at retail.

The advantages of using the retail method of inventory are significant, especially for larger stores. First, since a physical inventory is taken at retail prices, fewer errors occur, and it can be done in less time than by taking inventory at unmarked or coded cost prices (as under the cost method of inventory). Second, it serves as a merchandise management device. Because markups, markdowns, etc. are regularly compiled, these figures can be compared with industry norms or past company performances and therefore give management a basis for control. Third, at some time, the merchandise in the entire store must be physically counted, if for no other reason than the requirements of the Internal Revenue Service. It is highly unlikely that a count will show agreement between the book inventory and the physical inventory. If the book inventory exceeds the physical inventory, there is a shortage. If the reverse occurs, there is an overage. Differences between the two figures result from clerical errors and/or loss of merchandise. Note, however, that only when book inventory figures are available can shortages or overages be detected. Therefore, an advantage of the book method of inventory is that it yields information on shortages and overages. And fourth, it automatically gives conservative values for the inventory by forcing computation of the cumulative markup percentage to include net additional markups and exclude net markdowns. In other words, as in the earlier example with the motor bike, the cumulative markup percentage is held constant because markdowns will not affect it. If markdowns were taken into account in arriving at the cumulative markup percentage, the result would be a value approximating the original cost of the goods—not the market value.

Expense Records

The third item that merchants must record is expenses. Expenses for a business (exclusive of depreciation expenses) are cash outlays made in operating the store. Expenses are different from cost of goods, which represent cash outlays made for goods the firm expects to sell. Cash outlays that are not part of expenses nor goods for sale include payments made to reduce debt and to buy nonmerchandise inventory, such as fixtures and equipment.

No one runs a business without incurring expenses. In fact, in department and specialty stores, expenses run as high as 33 percent of sales. For each dollar of merchandise sold, then, 33 cents are spent on expenses. Interestingly enough, in the same department and specialty stores, 64 cents out of each dollar of sales are spent to pay for the merchandise sold. The 33 cents for expenses and 64 cents for cost of goods sold leave a net profit of only 3 cents after taxes. It is obvious that good records are a must; it isn't possible to be a sloppy merchant and still make money.

Table 6.8 shows the minimum set of expense records that retail stores should keep.

Table 6.8. A Minimum Set of Expense Records

Salaries and wages	Taxes and utilities
Advertising	Supplies
Delivery	Insurance
Maintenance	Telephone
Depreciation	Donations
Rent	Miscellaneous
Bad debt losses	(postage,
Travel	professional
Interest paid	fees, etc.)

Because the list in the figure represents a minimum number of expense records, a much more expansive list could obviously be developed. A dry cleaner might want information on production expenses such as overhead on buildings and machinery, and an automobile dealer might want information on expenses involving make ready costs, delivery, and warranty adjustments.

Because expenses directly affect profits, management should frequently check and analyze them. A comparison of the expenses of one's own store with those of other stores or a comparison of last year's expenses with this year's provides a basis for analysis. Because it is important to compare one's own business with similar kinds of businesses, one should use generally accepted expense classifications. Trade associations and suppliers are good sources of expense classifications, as is the *Retail Accounting Manual* of the Controllers' Congress of the National Retail Merchants Association.

Financial Planning Through Budgets

It is probably obvious that all firms should plan for the future. Good managers do this by analyzing the information found in profit and loss and balance sheet statements and by making projections based on budgets. Financial budgets then, are of great importance to managers.

Budgets are plans of operation that increase the efficiency of management. Only by using a budget can management conserve resources, establish the proper relationship between income and expenses, and identify trends in time to adjust to them before money is lost. If a retail store is to be profitable, managers must spend time on numerous details and must have definite goals in mind.

The budget of a retail business should include everything having to do with finances: income, expenses, cash, inventory, capital equipment. It's natural, therefore, that some budgets are based on profit and loss statements and balance sheets. Table 6.9 shows a comparison between hardware stores considered to be "profit-makers" and average hardware stores. Although the differences between the stores may seem small, these differences, when combined, add up to a big difference. Small differences are not detected unless management looks for them, and budgets provide a systematic way of finding them.

Table 6.9. Hardware Stores

Income Statement Data	All Hardware Stores	Low Profit Stores	High Profit Stores
Number of Stores	760	253	243
Net Sales Volume	$254,029	$252,721	$208,283
Current year's sales vs. previous year	+ 9.21%	+ 6.42%	+ 9.27%
Gross sales	102.07%	102.03%	102.24%
Less: total deductions	2.07	2.03	2.24
Net sales	100.00	100.00	100.00
Cost of goods sold	66.84	67.35	65.02
Margin	33.16	32.65	34.98
Payroll and Other Employee Expense			
Salaries—owners, officers, managers	6.87	8.24	5.27
Salaries—sales personnel	8.02	8.97	7.55
Salaries—office help	1.02	1.13	.88
Salaries—other employees	1.22	1.04	1.06
Federal and state payroll taxes	.86	.98	.77
Group insurance	.30	.39	.22
Benefit plans	.29	.26	.19
Total Payroll and Other Employee Expense	18.58	21.01	15.94
Occupancy Expense			
Heat, light, power, water	.76	.82	.74
Repairs to building	.25	.26	.22
Rent or ownership in real estate*	2.81	3.13	2.41
Total Occupancy Expense	3.82	4.21	3.37
Other Costs of Doing Business			
Office supplies and postage	.46	.51	.44
Advertising	1.64	1.79	1.50
Donations	.07	.06	.09
Telephone and telegraph	.30	.35	.26
Bad debts	.29	.26	.28
Delivery (other than wages)	.44	.53	.41
Insurance (other than real estate and group)	.68	.78	.63
Taxes (other than real estate and payroll)	.64	.70	.55
Interest on borrowed money (other than mortgages)	.54	.77	.35
Depreciation (other than real estate)	.63	.69	.52
Store and shop supplies	.34	.36	.33
Legal and accounting	.29	.36	.24
Dues and subscriptions	.09	.10	.08
Travel, buying, entertainment	.19	.20	.18
Unclassified	.47	.56	.36
Total Other Costs of Doing Business	7.07	8.02	6.22
Total Operating Expense	29.47	33.24	25.53
Net Operating Profit	3.69	.59	9.45
Cash discounts and other income	1.18	1.02	1.30
Net Profit (before Federal Income Tax)	4.87	.43	10.75

Source: Adapted from National Retail Hardware Association, "Management Report '72."

Pro forma statements

Two common budgets used in retailing are the projected, or pro forma, profit and loss statement and the pro forma balance sheet statement. These statements include information that will appear on future statements. Pro forma statements are based on two elements: (1) historical data (figures for last year) and (2) forecasts (figures planned for this year). These elements are included in all budgets.

Cash budgets

Another budget commonly used in retailing is a cash budget. It is one of the best ways to avoid becoming overextended. A cash budget forecasts on a week-to-week or month-to-month basis all cash receipts and payments. It is similar to a personal budget, which shows the income one expects to receive during a period and compares it with the expenditures one expects to make during that period. The purpose of a personal budget is to pinpoint *in advance* any cash surpluses or shortages so plans for taking care of them may be made.

Retailers need the same kind of knowledge. They must know whether they are going to have enough cash on hand to meet their payments. If they aren't, they may either cut back on their planned expenditures or seek additional capital, usually through a short-term loan. (By the way, it is much easier to get additional debt money to meet future needs than it is to bargain when the financial position is already precarious.) If merchants find that they will enjoy a cash surplus, they can bank the money or take advantage of other investment opportunities. A merchant who prepares a cash budget is ten steps ahead of one who doesn't.

The preparation of a cash budget requires planning. It requires knowledge of the present situation and of the future. It requires the estimation of sales, receivables turnover, and expense and other cash outlays. The following steps are used in the preparation of a cash budget:

1. Estimate cash sales and cash collections on previous charge sales, and total them to achieve total receipts.
2. Estimate cash disbursements and total them.
3. Find net receipts or disbursements by subtracting disbursements from receipts.
4. Add the beginning cash balance to net receipts or disbursements to find the ending cash balance.
5. Assuming it is necessary to maintain a minimum balance in the cash account, adjust the funds needed to take into account this minimum balance.

Only cash in-flows and out-flows are recorded in the cash budget. For example, if a cash budget is prepared by months (a typical approach), only the cash expected to go in and out of the business in a particular month is entered in that month's cash budget. An example of a cash budget for a retail store is shown in Table 6.10.

Summary

A retail business depends on good records. Records give information on sales, merchandise, and expenses. In merchandise inventories, two things are of special importance. Retailers must know how much stock they have in inventory and must have some idea of their gross margin position. Gross margin may be calculated only after information on merchandise inventories is collected. To supply their informational needs, retailers rely on physical counts of inventories and running, or book, accounts of inventories.

Management may use the information found in records to make summaries (profits and loss and balance sheet statements) that assess the financial position of the business. Management uses budgets to plan its operations and therefore, can adapt innovatively to change instead of simply reacting to it.

Two appendices follow this chapter. The first, "Shortage Control," presents an account of the problem of shoplifting and employee pilferage. Because it is a costly problem for

Table 6.10. Cash Budget for Three Months (January 1–March 31, 1977)

	January	February	March
Receipts			
Cash sales	2000	1500	2000
Charge sale collections	500	400	300
Total	2500	1900	2300
Disbursements			
Purchases	1000	1500	2000
Payables (wages, expenses, rent, etc.)	1200	1200	1200
Taxes	—	—	100
Total	2200	2700	3300
Net receipts (disbursements)	300	(800)	(1000)
Beginning cash balance	200	500	500
Ending cash balance	500	(300)	(500)
Minimum cash balance needed	200	200	200
Cumulative funds needed	0	500	1200

retailers, you would be well advised to read this appendix. The second appendix, "Financial Analysis of a Retail Store," provides additional knowledge about some financial aspects of managing a retail enterprise. In particular, it shows how management can assess its ability to (1) pay bills, (2) make a profit, and (3) live with its net worth position.

Questions and Problems

1. Is a department store buyer likely to purposely overvalue or undervalue the inventory at the end of the year? Why or why not?

2. Would you advise the owner of a shoe store doing $80,000 of sales to use the retail method of inventory? If so, why? If not, what should be used?

3. Treating additional markups before and markdowns after the total merchandise handled has been calculated yields a conservative evaluation of inventory. Explain.

4. Financial statements and a cash budget are interrelated. What are some of the interrelationships, as you see them?

Situations and Activities

You have recently established a small pet store. One of your initial problems is to determine the minimum set of records that you should keep for your business. You are aware that the Internal Revenue Office has an interest in the records of retail businesses. What is the absolute minimum set of records that will satisfy the needs of the IRS? What additional records might you want to maintain to satisfy your need for management information?

You are the floorwalker in a general merchandise store. Early one morning, you see a teenager shoplifting a tie off of one of your displays. Before you can do anything, he has left the store through the front exit. What alternatives are open to you? If you decide to run after the shoplifter and you subsequently catch him, what should you do? What courses of action might you take to minimize shoplifting in your department?

You are the manager of a local drugstore which is part of a large chain of drugstores. Recently, you have been receiving pressure from your district manager to raise your gross margin. The district manager has told you that your gross margin is 30 percent, whereas other stores in his district have gross margins of almost 32 percent. The district manager argues that your store should also earn 32 percent because it pays the same price for merchandise that other stores in the district pay and it sells at identical prices. Will you have to agree with him, or can you give other reasons for the differences in gross margin? Explain.

Arrange the following as it might appear in a profit and loss statement and a balance sheet. Eliminate those items which should not appear. Compute the percentage breakdowns in the profit and loss statement.

net sales	$9,000
wages	2,000
gross margin	7,000
beginning inventory	1,000
ending inventory	2,000
gross sales	10,000
accounts receivable	$1,000
cash	1,000
depreciation	1,000
debt	3,000
interest	1,000
purchases	$1,000
rent	1,000
miscellaneous expenses	1,000
fixtures and equipment	3,000

Given: net sales $1,000; closing book inventory $300. *Find:* total merchandise handled.

Given: total merchandise handled at cost $70,000; at retail $140,000; closing inventory at retail $30,000. *Find:* closing inventory at cost.

Given: gross sales $410,000; sales returns and allowances $10,000; purchases at cost $100,000, at retail $300,000; total merchandise handled at cost $200,000, at retail $500,000; physical inventory $90,000. *Find:* net sales, beginning inventory at cost and retail, and shortages.

The assistant manager of the Outlet Shoe Store is directed to set up the inventory-taking procedure for a business doing $120,000 yearly. The store is a family shoe store with both counter and backroom stock. One of the things at issue is whether to use a cost or book inventory method or both. Analyze both methods and then set up steps in the inventory-taking procedure that you would use.

You have been asked to prepare a cash budget for the Whoopee Cowboy Shop for the period January 1 to March 31. Given the following information, will there be enough cash available during the period to pay bills?

Sales are 80%, 20% on open account
Credit sales are collected in the first month following the sale
Gross margin on sales is 40%
Cash on hand January 1 is $1,000
Sales are forecasted at $7,000—$4,000—$10,000 for January, February, March, respectively
Purchase invoices will be paid in the amounts of $4,000, $5,000, and $2,000 for January, February, and March, respectively.
Cash expenses will run 10% of sales for the month

Prepare a balance sheet on your personal financial condition.

Bibliography

Astor, Saul D. "One Customer in 15 is a Shoplifter." *Stores,* April 1971, p. 8.

Bell, H. F., and Mascarello, L. *Retail Merchandise Accounting.* 3d ed. New York: The Ronald Press, 1961.

Corbman, Bernard P. and Kreiger, Murray. *Mathematics of Retail Merchandising.* New York: The Ronald Press, 1972.

Denver Police Department. *The Shoplifter Manual.* Denver, Colorado.

"The How and Why of Successful Retailing." *Hardware Retailer,* October, 1966.

McNair, Malcolm P., and Hersum, Anita C. *The Retail Method of Accounting and Life.* New York: McGraw-Hill, 1952.

The National Cash Register Company. *Expenses in Retail Businesses.* Dayton, Ohio, 1968.

The National Cash Register Company. *Profiting by Adequate Business Records: A Chapter of Better Retailing.* Dayton, Ohio, 1961.

The National Retail Merchants Association. *Merchandising Arithmetic for Retail Training.* New York, 1960.

The National Retail Merchants Association. *Departmental Merchandising and Operating Results.* Published annually. New York.

The National Retail Merchants Association. *Expense Center Accounting Manual,* rev. ed. New York, 1962.

"Security: Can It Keep up with Crime?" *Stores,* January, 1961.

Definitions of accounting terms used in this chapter:

Profit and loss statement (also called income statement) summarizes the effect of the transactions of a business in terms of profit or loss over a period of time.

> *Gross Sales* represents products, services or merchandise sold to customers over a period of time.
>
> *Sales returns and allowances*—"returns" represent goods physically returned by customers, "allowances" are deductions from original sales price permitted to customers for damaged goods, imperfect goods or similar causes.
>
> *Net sales*—difference between gross sales and sales returns and allowances.
>
> *Cost of goods sold*—the cost of the goods which a company has sold to its customers during a period.
>
> *Gross margin*—the difference between net sales (the quantity of goods sold at net selling price) and cost of goods sold (the same quantity of goods at cost).
>
> *Expenses*—all expenditures for services or supplies required in the operation of a business.
>
> *Depreciation*—the gradual reduction in use value of a fixed asset.
>
> *Net Profit or Loss*—difference between net sales and cost of goods sold plus expenses or the difference between gross margin and expenses.

Balance Sheet—(also called statement of condition) A statement showing the nature and value of the assets, liabilities, and net worth of a business at a specific time.

> *Current Assets*—assets that will be converted into cash during the normal operation of the business within an accounting period, usually a fiscal or calendar year.
>
> *Accounts receivable*—an account used to record the indebtedness of customers for merchandise or services supplied to them on credit.
>
> *Inventory*—value of the merchandise held for sale.
>
> *Fixed assets*—assets of a more or less permanent nature which are not sold but are attained and used in operating the business.
>
> *Current liabilities*—debts of the business which have to be paid within a limited time—usually one year.
>
> *Accounts payable*—amounts owed by the business to creditors for purchases of goods and services.
>
> *Accrued* (taxes) (salaries)—accrued amounts owed to various agencies and/or individuals.
>
> *Fixed liabilities*—Liabilities which do not have to be paid within a year.
>
> *Net worth*—the investment of the owner in the business. It is the difference between total assets and total debt liabilities.

Physical inventory—the actual count of merchandise inventory in stock.

Perpetual inventory—a system by which all merchandise movements in and out stock are recorded on a day to day basis, sometimes called running inventory.

Stock turnover—the number of times the average stock level will be sold in a given period of time—usually a year. It is found by dividing net sales by the average inventory at retail or by dividing cost of goods sold by the average inventory at cost.

Cost or market whichever is lower—A method of inventory valuation where inventory will be valued at its market price if the replacement cost of an article is lower than its invoice cost or at its cost price if the invoice cost is the same or higher than the market price.

Cost method of inventory—a method of accounting for inventory where all goods are recorded at cost at the time a physical count is made.

Book method of inventory—a perpetual inventory (running inventory) of merchandise at either their retail or cost prices.

Retail method of inventory—a method for determining merchandise values by recording purchases at both cost and retail prices. Under the retail method, inventories are taken at retail prices and their cost value is determined at each fiscal period by the application of the cumulative markon percentage.

Cost code—the cost of an item printed on a sales ticket in the form of a hidden code such as "make profit"

Markup—the amount added to cost to determine the original retail price for a specific article.

Cumulative markup—the average markup for a department, store, and/or merchandise classification.

Additional markup—price changes upward after goods have been originally priced.

Markup cancellations—additional markups which have been cancelled.

Net additional markups—the difference between additional markups and markup cancellations.

Markdowns—price changes downward after goods have been originally priced.

Markdown cancellations—Markdowns which have been cancelled.

Net markdowns—the difference between markdowns and markdown cancellations.

Freight in—incoming transportation charges on goods for sale.

Shortage—when book inventory exceeds physical inventory.

Overage—when physical inventory exceeds book inventory.

Pro forma statements—profit loss statements and balance sheet statements which are based on projections of an upcoming period.

Cash budget—a forecast listing all cash receipts and payments for a given period.

Appendix A
Shortage Control

One of the benefits resulting from accounting for inventory by the book and retail methods is the ability to identify shortages. This is important because shortages are one of the most serious problems facing retailers today. Some retailers even hold a monthly store-employee meeting to discuss ways to prevent shortages.

Shortages

In retailing, shortages are losses for which there is no determinable source. Shortages result when the accounting books indicate that (1) a quantity of merchandise should be in stock but a count reveals a lesser quantity or (2) the amount of cash that should be in the register is less than the reading of the register shows. Whatever the cause of shortages, the profits are reduced. If shortages amount to 2 percent of sales (a common estimate) in a store having a sales volume of $150,000, a profit reduction of $3,000 will result (2 percent × $150,000 = $3,000). Shortages of 2 percent further reduce the already slim profits earned by retail stores.

The Causes of Shortages

Shortages occur for many reasons. Customer shoplifting combined with theft by dishonest employees account for the largest share of the losses, with employee pilferage accounting for over half. Shortages also result from improper accounting, breakage, damaged merchandise, errors made in recording stock, errors made in giving customers change or merchandise, and failure to record markdowns.

It's difficult to determine what makes a person steal. Many people might argue that need is the motive for stealing or that thieves belong to the so-called criminal element in society. Yet most of the shoplifters apprehended are from middle-class families. Merchants, then, are hurt more often by their friends and neighbors than by impoverished people.

Much of what goes out the front door unpaid for is taken by people considered to be basically honest. The teenager who steals a pencil in preparation for tomorrow morning's exam or perhaps because there is nothing else to do, the shopper who eats an unpaid-for apple while shopping, and the salesgirl who snagged her hose on a store counter yesterday and decides to replace them with a pair of unpaid-for hose today are ordinary, generally law-abiding people. Unfortunately, they often feel justified in what they are doing; after all, "It's a big store with lots of money." Add to these people those who steal for need and/or gain, and you can understand why shortages are a serious problem for merchants.

The Responsibility of the Merchant

In some respects merchants have only themselves to blame for shoplifting. They have either refused to establish the necessary safeguards against stealing, and/or they have refused to take action against people who have been apprehended. Evidence accumulated by authorities shows that shoplifters who are apprehended have stolen ten times on the average, before they are caught. Almost all of them are amateurs who steal on impulse rather than by premeditation. The price of an item stolen is, on the average, $3.00 to $5.00.

In one community with a population of 40,000, 575 cases of juvenile shoplifting were reported to the police in the first six months of one particular year. All of the people tried were found guilty, but less than 1 percent of the cases were actually heard in court. Is it possible that merchants encourage the attitude that shoplifting is not really wrong?

Although merchants complain about theft, there are several reasons why they may be slow to act against it. First, they may not realize there is a problem. Second, if they catch someone, they may not want to be responsible for causing a "black mark" on someone's record. Third, insurance companies may discourage merchants from pursuing thieves because of possible lawsuits. Fourth, merchants who prosecute offenders may have to spend many hours away from their stores in litigation proceedings. Fifth, they may not know the provisions of the law that establish their rights and responsibilities regarding shoplifting.

The Colorado statutes regarding shoplifting are representative of those appearing in other states (see Figure 6.6). Notice Section 9, 40-5-31. Does your state provide similar protection for its merchants?

Minimizing shortages

There is no one answer to the problem of minimizing shortages in a store. The remedy or remedies will, of course, depend on the cause of the loss. Needless to say, safeguards and constant vigilance aid in reducing shortages. In general, the departments which suffer the most from shoplifting losses as reported in *Watch Out For That Thief,* National Retail Merchants Association, 1969 are

Jewelry Cosmetics Records Small Leather Goods	The first three are favorites of teenage shoplifters, who usually want them for personal use.
Sportswear Dresses Sweaters Blouses Teenage Outerwear Men's Furnishings	Again the favorite targets of young thieves, but well up on the "wanted" list among shoplifters of all ages.
Lingerie Gloves Hosiery Handbags	Useful—and often expensive—accessories for all kinds of thieves.
Sportings Goods Cameras and Camera Equipment Small Electrical Items Tools and Other Hardware Items	More often taken by the male shoplifter and the professional, but attractive to many thieves.

The remaining part of this section deals with pointers that management might find useful in shortage control. Some or all of these pointers might be used, depending on the nature of the business and the seriousness of the shortage problem.

Most people are honest. Controls are necessary only for those few who are not. Controls are not a threat to honest people, who usually accept them gracefully.

Spotting a shoplifter

Watch for persons who act in these ways:

1. Leave an area or a store with undue haste.
2. Frequent the washroom.

Section 1, 40-5-2, Colorado Revised Statutes 1963, is amended to read:

40-5-2. Theft. (1) (a) Any person commits theft when he knowingly:

(b) (i) Obtains or exerts unauthorized control over anything of value of another; or

(ii) Obtains by deception control over anything of value of another; or

(iii) Obtains by threat control over anything of value of another; or

(iv) Obtains control over any stolen thing of value knowing the thing of value to have been stolen by another; and

(c) (i) intends to deprive another permanently of the use or benefit of the thing of value; or

(ii) Knowingly uses, conceals, or abandons the thing of value in such manner as to deprive another permanently of such use or benefit; or

(iii) Uses, conceals, or abandons the thing of value intending that such use, concealment, or abandonment will deprive another permanently of such use or benefit.

Section 1, 40-5-2, Colorado Revised Statutes 1963, is amended to read:

(2) (a) Any person who commits theft where the value of the thing involved does not exceed one hundred dollars, and any person who commits theft twice or more within a period of six months and from the same person where the aggregate value of the things involved does not exceed one hundred dollars, is guilty of a misdemeanor and, upon conviction, shall be punished by a fine of not more than three hundred dollars, or by imprisonment in the county jail not to exceed six months, or by both such fine and imprisonment.

(2) (b) Any person who commits theft where the value of the thing involved exceeds one hundred dollars, and any person who commits theft twice or more within a period of six months from the same person and has not been placed in jeopardy for the prior offense, where the aggregate value of the things involved exceeds one hundred dollars, is

guilty of a felony and, upon conviction, shall be punished by imprisonment in the state penitentiary for not less than one year nor more than ten years.

Section 8, 40-5-30, Colorado Revised Statutes 1963, is amended to read:

40-5-30. Concealment of goods as prima facie evidence of the crime of theft. If any person shall willfully conceal unpurchased goods, wares, or merchandise owned or held by and offered or displayed for sale by any store or other mercantile establishment, whether such concealment be on his own person or otherwise and whether on or off the premises of said store or mercantile establishment, such concealment shall constitute prima facie evidence that such person intended to convert same to his own use without paying the purchase price therefor within the meaning of Section 40-5-28 COMMIT THE CRIME OF THEFT.

Section 9, 40-5-31, Colorado Revised Statutes 1963, is amended to read:

40-5-31. Questioning of person suspected of theft without civil liability. If any person shall commit the offense of shoplifting, as defined in Section 40-5-28, or if any person shall willfully conceal upon his person or otherwise any unpurchased goods, wares, or merchandise held or owned by any store or mercantile establishment, the merchant or any employee thereof or any peace or police officer, acting in good faith and upon probable cause based upon reasonable grounds therefor, may question such person, in a reasonable manner for the purpose of ascertaining whether or not such person is guilty of shoplifting as defined in Section 40-5-28 THEFT. Such questioning of a person by a merchant, merchant's employee, or peace or police officer shall not render such merchant, merchant's employee, or peace or police officer civilly liable for slander, false arrest, false imprisonment, malicious prosecution or unlawful detention.

Figure 6.6. Representative statutes concerning shoplifting.
Source: Colorado Revised Statutes, 1963.

3. Enter the store carrying bundles, bags, boxes, topcoats over arms, briefcases, newspapers, umbrellas, or have an arm in a sling. All these provide opportunities for concealment of merchandise.
4. Come in wearing heavy outer garments out of season, baggy clothes, or full or pleated skirts.
5. Have unusual walks, tug at a sleeve, adjust socks, rub the back of the neck, or act in other unusual ways that might help them to hide articles.
6. Reach into display counters or walk behind sales counters.
7. Don't seem to know what they want and exchange articles frequently.
8. Don't appear to be interested in articles about which they have inquired.
9. Wait for a friend or companion to shop.
10. Are nervous, flush-faced, dry-lipped, or perspire in a room with normal temperatures.
11. Keep one hand constantly in an outer pocket.

The preceding actions may be evidence of shoplifting. The following are some methods used by shoplifters:

1. Carrying packages, newspapers, coats, gloves, and other things to aid in the palming of small articles.
2. Using umbrellas, knitting bags, diaper bags, large purses, briefcases, paper sacks, booster boxes, and similar devices to conceal merchandise.
3. Using a slit in a pocket of an outer garment. The hand is placed through the slit as though the hand is in a pocket and the stolen merchandise in it is concealed by the outer garment.
4. Wearing a skirt, trousers, or other garments with elastic waistbands; wearing "shoplifter bloomers."
5. Trying on a garment, placing an outer garment over the stolen one, and wearing it out of the store in the conventional manner.
6. Using hooks on the insides of coats, pants, dresses, or slips, and using them in

much the same way as a magician would use them.
7. Entering a store without jewelry or accessories and wearing or carrying items of this kind out of the store in the conventional manner.
8. Wearing a long outergarment and concealing articles between legs.
9. Walking to an unattended section or an area near a convenient exit, then grabbing merchandise and hastily departing from the store.
10. Working as a shoplifting team, that is, one or more occupy the attention of the clerks while the others, who appear to be just waiting, are actually shoplifting.

Employees may take the following protective actions:

1. Greet all customers when they enter a department.
2. Display shoplifting warning posters.
3. Keep high value and appeal merchandise in conspicuous spots and/or in safe places.
4. Watch customers' hands.
5. Keep the selling floor well lighted.
6. Use store detectives, trained personnel, one-way or convex mirrors, peek-a-boo vents, and electronic detection devices for surveillance
7. Keep the store neat, preferably with displays below eye level.
8. Maintain strict surveillance of customers trying on articles of clothing.
9. Pay attention to customers wearing bulky clothes or carrying container devices, such as large coats, sweat shirts, umbrellas and knapsacks.
10. Never leave the store, department, or customers unattended.
11. If possible, give each customer a receipt for every purchase. This will help prevent shoplifters from obtaining cash refunds for stolen merchandise.
12. Keep areas clear of discarded sales checks. Shoplifters may use them as evidence of purchases.

13. Develop a warning system so that all employees can be alerted when suspected shoplifters are present. In a small store, a code word might be used.
14. Arrange merchandise so customers must pick it up. Then, a thief cannot push it off the counter into some kind of container.
15. When merchandise is made up of pairs, display only one of a pair.
16. Place the telephone so sales persons can view their sales area while using it.
17. Return to stock any merchandise that was taken out for a customer's inspection and was not sold.
18. Keep service fast and efficient, especially when waiting on juveniles.
19. Follow suspects; they might either get rid of the merchandise or give themselves away in some other fashion.
20. Put small items in conspicuous places where other customers might notice someone stealing.
21. Machine or rubber stamp all prices and price changes onto price tickets, and keep checkout personnel informed about prices.

Many retail employers are experimenting with electronic detection devices. When an attempt is made to remove merchandise from a store without authorization, an audible signal is generated electronically. This alarm notifies the store that the customer is leaving the store with tagged merchandise. To preclude this from happening, store personnel are trained to remove special markings from the merchandise at the time of purchase. This system accomplishes two things: it detects shoplifters in the act and it discourages would-be shoplifters who realize the merchandise is marked and leave without trying to take something.

There are words of caution that you should remember when dealing with shoplifters. First, your responsibility to the store does not extend to the physical capture of a shoplifter. Leave that to authorities, who are trained. Shoplifters who become physically belligerent (and some do) are best left alone; you should observe as much as you can about them so you may give

information to the police. Some store shoplifting policies prohibit employees from challenging shoplifters but leave this to security people. Second, if you do accuse a customer of taking merchandise, take the merchandise back right away. One management trainee who caught a thief led him back to the manager's office and found that the shoplifter didn't have the merchandise on him when he arrived at the office. Of course, the thief claimed that he had not stolen any merchandise. On the following morning, an employee who was straightening up a department found the stolen merchandise on a counter board with other merchandise. Obviously, the store could have faced a liability suit. In this case the manager wasn't cowed by the shoplifter, and he sent him out of the store.

Spotting employee thefts
Watch for these signs:

1. Empty containers found in unauthorized areas or hidden in warehouses are signs of employee stealing.
2. Overly enthusiastic employees, who *may* be trying to find out all the different angles.
3. Employees who break petty rules.
4. Employees who do not associate with other employees.
5. The cash handling procedures of individual employees.
6. The popular employee, because free gifts *may* be one reason for this popularity.
7. Phoney bookkeeping errors, which may indicate that something is wrong.

Employees may use such methods as the following:

1. Pocketing money.
2. Ringing up sales for more than the actual amount to cover up shortages.
3. Not ringing up the sale or giving, for example, three dimes as change for a quarter.
4. Hiding merchandise in trash containers.

Employers may take the following protective actions:

1. Follow up on rules for employees.

2. Set up a system of counter checks and balances to reduce dishonesty.
3. Demand excellence in performance and conduct.
4. Release immediately and *prosecute* any employee caught stealing.
5. Do not suspect old employees any less than new ones. They may rely on this and be more tempted than new employees.
6. Store security forces, merchants' protective associations, and off-duty policemen may often be used for control.
7. Respect your employees so they, in turn, will respect you.
8. Set reasonable rules for employees.
9. Establish clear lines of authority.
10. Hire only honest employees. Investigate applicants carefully, checking references and employment history.
11. Make certain that a good example is set for employees. Ethical conduct and fair dealing on the part of the management will encourage employee honesty. Strive for zero shortages.
12. Remove the temptation to steal. Preventive measures such as uniforms without pockets, individually assigned cash drawers, an employee check out system at night, lie detector tests, and information on the physical and moral consequences of giving in to temptation are some techniques used to thwart temptation.
13. Keep the back door locked. Spot-check trash containers. Keep a careful accounting of all stockroom keys. Double-check incoming and outgoing shipments.

Maintaining records control

Management should be constantly alert to shortages caused by employees' lack of attention to details, violation of store policy, and/or carelessness. Management should be especially careful to:

1. Maintain thorough record-keeping procedures. Establish a system for recording markdowns, additional markups, breakage, and damaged goods.
2. Tighten up records. Start by prenumbering sales slips, checks, and purchase orders.
3. Have markers affix price tickets to merchandise.
4. Check any price discrepancy between purchase order and invoice with the buyer prior to release for payment.
5. Clear each cash register at the end of the day.
6. Check measuring machines and scales frequently for accuracy.
7. Not allow merchandise to be transferred out of a department without transfer, loan, or sales slip forms.
8. Insure that returned merchandise be checked in to reflect current prices if required, handled as a markdown, or a charge to expense.

Appendix B
Financial Analysis of a Retail Store

Businesses differ in many ways. From a financial standpoint, however, there are some things common to all businesses. Typically, these things are expressed in terms of ratios, that is, a numerical relationship between one figure and another. The profit and loss statement and/or the balance sheet statement provide the figures for computation.

To determine how well a business is doing, management needs information. This information may be broken down into three major categories. Management wants to know if it can pay its bills, if it's making a profit, and if it can live with its net worth position.

Solvency

Solvency is a firm's ability to meet its cash obligations as they become due. Insolvency, which can lead to bankruptcy, exists when a firm cannot pay its bills on time. Obviously, firms that become overextended are most likely to become insolvent.

The cash budget discussed in Chapter 6 measures solvency. So do three commonly used ratios. Although the ratios must be considered in conjunction with other variables, they do give some indication of the financial soundness of a firm and can help management to determine future policies. To compile these ratios, both the profit and loss statement and the balance sheet must be used. (See Tables 6.11 and 6.12).

$$\text{Current ratio} = \frac{\text{current assets}}{\text{current liabilities}} = \frac{3,000}{1,000} \quad 3{:}1$$

Table 6.11. Profit and Loss Statement

For the Period Ending December 31, 1977

Sales	$5,000
Cost of goods sold	3,000
Gross margin	$2,000
Expenses	1,000
Profit	$1,000

Table 6.12. Balance Sheet

As of December 31, 1977

Current assets		Current liabilities	
Cash	$1,000	Accounts payable	$ 400
Accounts receivable	1,000	Accrued expenses	500
Inventory	1,000	Taxes payable	100
Total current assets	$3,000	Total current liabilities	$1,000
Fixed assets		**Fixed liabilities**	
Fixtures and equipment	$2,000	Notes payable	$1,000
		Net worth	3,000
Total assets	$5,000	**Total liabilities**	$5,000

A current ratio of 3:1 indicates that for every dollar of current liabilities the firm has $3.00 of current assets with which to make payment. Because cash is usually generated through the turnover of merchandise inventory and the collection of accounts receivable, it is desirable to have more current assets than current liabilities. For a retail firm, a current ratio of 2:1 is considered satisfactory. The 3:1 ratio above indicates a firm's ability to meet its current obligations.

Another measure of a firm's solvency is the speed with which its accounts receivable are collected and converted into cash. Because accounts receivable, a current asset, represents a large investment by the retail firm, any delay in the collection of these accounts withholds cash that could be used to pay bills. A measure of the speed with which accounts receivable are collected is found by dividing them by the amount of sales, preferably charge sales if available, and multiplying the quotient by the number of days in the period, usually 365 days for the year:

$$\text{Average collection period} = \frac{\text{accounts receivable}}{\text{sales}} \times 365$$

$$\frac{\$1,000}{\$5,000} \times 365 = \begin{array}{l}\text{73 days on the average that} \\ \text{accounts receivable are out-} \\ \text{standing}\end{array}$$

If the store above sells on terms of 30 days and if the average receivable is paid within 73 days, then the conclusion may be that its credit policies are too liberal or it has poor collection procedures. In any event, the longer it takes to collect on receivables, the less money it has immediately available to meet current obligations.

A final measure of a firm's solvency is its ability to turn over merchandise inventory. As in the case of accounts receivable, merchandise inventories often represent a sizeable investment. Therefore, it is important for management to turn these assets into cash as soon as possible. Inventory turnover rate, or stock turnover rate, is derived by dividing net sales by average inventory at retail. The average inventory is found by adding available ending inventory figures and dividing by their number:

$$\begin{array}{l}\text{Rate of} \\ \text{stock} \\ \text{turnover}\end{array} = \frac{\text{net sales}}{\begin{array}{c}\text{average inventory} \\ \text{at retail}\end{array}} = \frac{\$5,000}{\$1,000}, \text{ or } 5$$

Whether the above inventory turnover figure of 5 is satisfactory depends on the nature of a business. For a hardware store this turnover would be good; for a supermarket, however, it would be unsatisfactory—the turnover of a supermarket should be closer to 12. A slow turnover indicates that the firm is slow to receive cash for its inventory, and therefore, may find it difficult to meet payments on obligations.

Profitability

Because the main purpose of any business is to make profits, management must attempt to determine how well it is accomplishing this purpose. The most common way to do this is to compare net sales with net profits. By dividing net profits by net sales, management can determine how well it has been running the business.

$$\text{Profitability} = \frac{\text{net profits}}{\text{net sales}} = 20\%$$

The case of a 20 percent profit on sales shows that for every dollar's worth of business, the firm realizes a 20 cent profit. Again, the evaluation of percentages depends on the kind of retail business, but a 20 percent profit on sales is good in any business. Usually, retail firms make a 2 to 3 percent profit.

One other way to measure the profitability of a retail firm is to compare its net profits with its net worth. By so doing, management can determine whether its investment in the business is yielding an adequate return. The comparison is made by dividing net profits by net worth:

$$\begin{array}{l}\text{Net profits} \\ \text{to net} \\ \text{worth}\end{array} = \frac{\text{net profits}}{\text{net worth}} = \frac{\$1,000}{\$3,000} = 33\text{-}1/3\%$$

Table 6.13. Ratios of Retailing

Line of Business (and number of concerns reporting)	Current assets to current debt	Net profits on net sales	Net profits on tangible net worth	Net profits on net working capital	Net sales to tangible net worth	Net sales to net working capital	Collection period	Net sales to inventory	Fixed assets to tangible net worth	Current debt to tangible net worth	Total debt to tangible net worth	Inventory to net working capital	Current debt to inventory	Funded debts to net working capital
	Times	Per cent	Per cent	Per cent	Times	Times	Days	Times	Per cent	Per cent	Per cent	Per cent	Per cent	Per cent
5531 Auto & home supply stores	1.90	1.88	7.63	12.17	4.32	5.48	**	5.7	27.4	81.4	99.0	115.6	104.7	44.5
5641 Children's & infants wear stores	2.18	1.92	8.16	10.07	4.56	5.15	**	4.9	22.7	58.0	90.6	106.4	76.2	26.9
5611 Clothing & furnishings men's & boys'	2.83	1.79	6.11	7.69	3.32	3.69	**	4.2	11.1	50.5	103.7	96.4	65.9	34.0
5311 Department stores (269)	2.78	1.72	5.22	7.01	3.44	4.20	**	5.4	32.2	45.2	88.4	81.5	72.5	38.0
Discount stores	2.06	1.47	9.44	11.06	5.93	7.23	**	4.9	32.3	81.3	136.5	146.4	65.2	37.0
Discount stores, Leased departments	2.06	1.51	6.91	7.17	5.80	5.90	**	5.0	23.8	81.8	139.5	140.2	66.7	31.5
5651 Family clothing stores	3.02	1.69	6.04	6.96	3.12	3.58	**	4.4	13.5	40.0	94.8	81.2	67.3	41.1
5712 Furniture stores	2.68	2.16	6.54	6.73	3.03	2.99	91	4.5	11.9	60.0	125.5	67.3	82.5	19.9
5541 Gasoline service stations	2.08	5.86	21.71	52.21	3.59	8.11	**	10.0	37.8	43.4	66.7	85.5	115.1	42.7
5411 Grocery stores	1.58	1.00	11.57	25.60	12.43	24.75	**	15.4	82.0	73.4	120.6	167.9	95.4	74.1
5251 Hardware stores	3.11	1.93	7.45	10.07	3.03	3.64	**	4.1	13.6	39.8	57.7	87.5	54.6	18.1
5722 Household appliance stores	1.92	1.27	8.66	9.09	5.25	6.20	28	5.0	20.0	96.3	202.0	121.3	94.5	32.5
5944 Jewelry stores	3.22	3.50	7.93	8.15	2.23	2.37	**	3.2	6.5	38.0	78.5	82.8	56.5	28.7
5211 Lumber & other bldg. mtls dealers	2.80	2.93	9.78	12.87	3.99	5.11	40	5.9	28.1	42.6	94.4	82.6	77.0	42.6
5399 Miscellaneous general mdse. stores	3.15	1.98	8.59	10.25	3.09	3.82	**	3.9	19.3	38.7	98.2	92.5	51.5	36.4
5511 Motor vehicle dealers	1.58	1.12	7.68	11.33	8.33	11.50	**	5.8	23.0	125.7	180.9	189.8	87.1	36.1
5231 Paint, glass & wallpaper stores	4.18	2.10	9.23	14.29	3.05	4.11	**	6.1	18.7	20.0	59.1	75.3	49.3	41.4
5732 Radio & television stores	2.62	2.86	10.84	11.54	5.24	6.43	**	4.6	18.8	62.3	200.7	114.1	60.0	34.2
5261 Retail nurseries, lawn & garden supp. stores	2.09	4.27	18.50	30.91	4.59	7.06	**	7.6	30.6	52.6	83.0	85.8	113.8	34.7
5661 Shoe stores	3.22	1.60	4.71	5.77	3.39	4.51	**	3.8	14.6	41.8	93.7	108.9	46.0	34.5
5331 Variety stores	3.19	2.25	9.09	10.28	3.82	4.47	**	3.9	24.7	38.5	86.3	121.3	40.4	37.0
5621 Women's ready-to-wear stores	2.52	1.77	6.93	7.48	4.31	5.02	**	6.4	18.9	52.4	132.8	80.9	88.3	36.5

Source: "The Ratios of Business" *Dun's Review*, October 1975, p. 83. Reprinted by courtesy of *Dun's Review*. Copyright 1975, Dun and Brandstreet Publications, Inc.

The 33-1/3 percent indicates that every dollar invested by management earns approximately 33 cents in return. Considering that the national average is around 8 percent, a 33 percent return on investment is very good.

Net Worth Position

A store's net worth position influences both the ease with which management can finance its operations and the cost of financing. The usual way of assessing a firm's net worth position is to compute the firm's total debt to its net worth. This is done by dividing total debt by net worth:

$$\frac{\text{Total debt}}{\text{to net worth}} = \frac{\text{total debt}}{\text{net worth}} = \frac{\$2,000}{\$3,000} = 66\text{-}2/3\%$$

The percentage shows the financial relationship between creditors and owners. A general rule of thumb for a retail firm is that owners should have as much invested in the business as creditors; in other words, there should be a 1 to 1 relationship. Firms that have a small amount of ownership funds compared to debt funds are less likely to weather periods of stress. In other words, when sales drop and inventories pile up, the firm has to count on its permanent source of ownership funds to see it through. In the example shown, 66-2/3 to 1 indicates that the firm's total debt is 66-2/3 percent of its net worth, and is, therefore, satisfactory.

Other Ratios

There are additional ratios that managers may use in evaluating their business. Some of the more common ones are shown in Table 6.13 for twenty-four kinds of retail businesses.

7

Information from Electronic Data Processing

contents

Electronic Data Processing
Information Gathering
The Computer System in Retail Operations
EDP Applications in Retailing
Summary
Questions and Problems
Situations and Activities
Bibliography

behavioral objectives

Because electronic data processing has become a major force in retail operations today, managers should have a basic understanding of computer operations. The manager must be alert to the possibilities of applying electronic data processing (EDP) to retail operations.

Upon completing this chapter, you will be able to do the following:
☐ Explain why computers were first used in retailing in accounting departments.
☐ Discuss the factors that caused retailers to hesitate to adopt EDP.
☐ Describe the basics of a computer system.
☐ Discuss what factors determine the kinds of data gathered for EDP.
☐ Explain alternative methods of collecting data when sales are made.
☐ Identify the areas of retailing that are most in need of improved EDP applications.

In the previous chapter we examined retail accounting and its importance in providing information for making decisions. In this chapter we will show how the electronic data processing facilitates the collection of data for merchandising, accounting, and control. In the next chapter we will examine the research process and its role in providing information for many retailing decisions.

Electronic Data Processing

The heart of electronic data processing is the computer—a machine that touches our lives in some way every day. Computers are used in designing automobiles, guiding space shots to the moon, calculating department store bills, transmitting long-distance telephone calls, and so on. The impact of the computer has been so great that the computer has become recognized as one of man's greatest inventions.

Even though the computer has changed our way of life, many people think of it as a mysterious, magical black box. Yet, a computer is simply a device capable of accepting and processing data and supplying the results of the processing at a very rapid rate. Computers are made up of complex electrical circuits, but the concept according to which they function is a simple one. Computers accept data which are converted to electrical impulses which are then either added, subtracted, stored, or moved from one location to another. Because multiplication can be performed by a series of additions, and division by a series of subtractions, computers can also perform these operations. The ability to store data gives computers a memory capability.

The importance of computers lies in their electronic circuitry which permits them to calculate and process data at great speeds and with exceptional accuracy. Internal speeds vary from milliseconds (one thousandth of a second), to nanoseconds (one billionth of a second). Such speed and accuracy in handling information is vitally necessary for the smooth functioning of today's dynamic businesses and for scientific and technological advancements.

Only a few years ago many businesses were almost drowning in the sea of paperwork generated by their organizations. Businesses were expanding, new markets were opening up, consumers were demanding new products and services, and government was demanding more and better records. Growth and efficiency were jeopardized because businessmen could not keep pace with the paper work necessary to support the business nor could they obtain the kind of information needed for decision making. Electronic data processing, or the computer, provided the answer to businessmen's problems. During the 1960's and early 1970's the computer became a basic tool which was used by many businessmen. In 1975 computer equipment worth over $30 billion was in service in the United States. The tens of thousands of computers represented by this investment spews forth daily an uncountable number of facts, figures, compilations, and computations.

Information Gathering

As you study each of the operational functions in retailing, you will be impressed by the necessity for fast, accurate, complete data. Yet, retailers fell behind other industries in adapting and using computer technology to achieve such information.

Computers were first used in retailing in accounting departments. This is logical, for accounting is responsible for many detailed clerical and repetitive functions of retail store operations. Accounting activities are usually carefully defined and highly structured.

In areas other than accounting, retailers were slow to adopt electronic data processing (EDP). One reason for this was that EDP technicians found input, output, and control procedures too poorly defined to permit an EDP system to work. Information was often loosely controlled, and few systems existed for obtaining and analyzing data. Unit merchandizing records were incomplete, inaccurate, and not timely, because stock counts were taken sporadically, and poorly trained sales people created inaccuracies in sales reports.

Retailers were slow to adopt EDP for another reason. Almost every retailer participates in a large number of transactions of which the details are obscure. Because obscurity had always been a part of the business, most retailers were accustomed to it. They realized that their competitors had precisely the same problem. Furthermore, many retailers feel that retailing is essentially an art, to which accurate and timely information can contribute little.

In the 1970's, however, conditions have changed rapidly. Large retailers are using EDP to develop reports that provide answers to many important questions. Such reports can tell them who their most effective salesperson is, who their most profitable supplier is, or which seasonal items sell best in January and which in February. Retailers are using this kind of information to meet the needs of their customers, and customers are rewarding them with increased business. Small retailers are fighting back by using data processing centers, which provide services at prices consistent with the benefits received. For example, the National Cash Register service centers can provide retailers with computer-generated financial statements, sales and salesperson analyses, inventory control reports, and accounts receivable analyses. A retailer may sign up for one report or for any combination of reports, from a system especially designed for the specific type of retail business.

The Computer System in Retail Operations

A computer system is made up of the three basic components shown in Figure 7.1.

1. *Input devices* receive data, perform the transmission, and transform data and instructions into machine-recognizable form.
2. The *central processor* has three components:

Memory devices store the data to be operated on and give instructions on what is to be done with the information.

Control devices regulate and coordinate all elements of the system.

Arithmetic and logic devices perform arithmetic operations and logical comparisons.

3. *Output devices* print, transmit, or display the results of computer processing.

Figure 7.1 also shows data selection and preparation being fed into the computer system, and reports being fed out of it. These two elements are not part of computers, but they represent fundamental areas that retail managers must consider when they work with a computer system.

There are particular ways in which a retailer must work with an EDP system. First, the retailer must decide what reports are to be received. Then he will know what input information to use. Second, he must decide how data will be collected and fed to the computer. A computer program contains instructions that tell the central processor what operations to perform on the input data in order to obtain the output information. Finally, the retailer must also decide whether the information resulting from processing is to be printed out in report form or returned to the central processor for comparison with another entry.

The input and output devices and the central processor are hardware. The retail manager is usually not concerned with the details of their operation. The concern is with selecting data for input, deciding how the data will be fed to the computer, and selecting the applications and reports that are wanted. The balance of the chapter is concerned with these areas.

Selecting data for input

Every purchase or sale generates data that can be used for some kind of analysis. To make the data meaningful, retailers must carefully

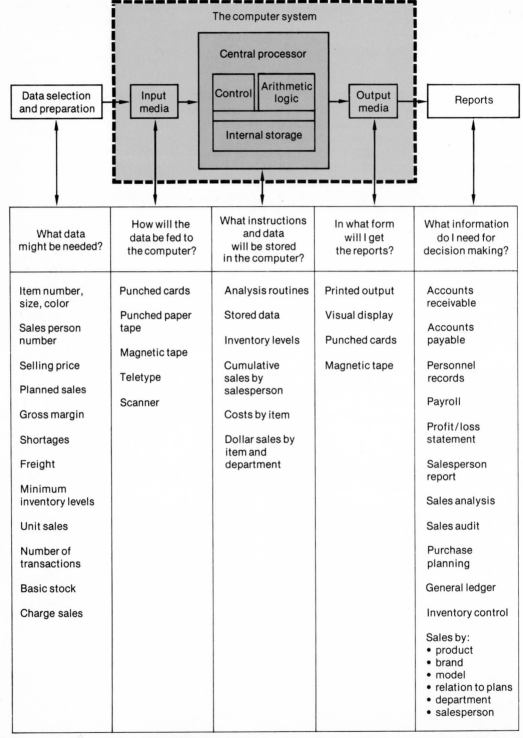

Figure 7.1. The electronic data processing system.

evaluate the kinds of information and reports they need. They must answer questions such as the following:

What key reports do I need?
Why do I need these reports?
What decisions will I make on the basis of the information?
How often do I need these reports?
Can I manage if I receive a report only when an operation deviates from expectations or standards?
How detailed must the information be?
Do I need to know only how many toothbrushes I sold last month, or do I really need to know that on Tuesday the average sale of Brand X in Size Y was so many dollars?

When the necessary output is carefully defined, selection of data for input is fairly straightforward.

The input media problem

Before the retailer can obtain the necessary information, the computer must be supplied with facts in a language it understands.

These facts should be gathered by machine. (Obviously, hand recording all of a store's transactions for only one day would be prohibitive because of the employee costs involved.)

Sales information. Sales information is usually taken from cash registers. Unfortunately, mechanical cash registers are slow and inefficient. For this reason, manufacturers spent years developing a cash register that could rapidly and efficiently gather information for computers. Today a complete marriage of the computer and the cash register exists; retailers have a system for checking customer credit, computing the sale, furnishing customer receipts, providing inventory control, automatically reordering items in short supply, producing regular up-to-date financial statements, and supplying sales analyses and sales audits. This is possible because of the electronic cash register and the data it is capable of providing for computer analysis.

The electronic cash register is a major step in making sales transactions more accurate and faster. Operations are simplified and information requirements are more easily satisfied. The electronic cash register performs many functions automatically, such as sales tax calculation, computing customer change, extending quantity purchases, and subtracting credits. These automatic functions improve accuracy, increase productivity, eliminate tedious repetition, and build customer confidence. And, by tying into a central computer they are the basic instrument for instant credit and check verification and eventually automatic funds transfer in a "cashless society."

There are several means for entering information into the cash register. At the most basic level, salespeople manually depress keys to record the required information at the time the sale is made. Item amounts are entered on a conventional 10-key pad and other data is entered on department and transaction keys conveniently surrounding the pad. (See Figure 7.2.) All of the data is stored on magnetic tape for input into a computer for merchandising, accounting, and control reports.

In another system, price tags are printed on a tag printer in the store or at a central location. Each tag contains readable information and

Figure 7.2. The electronic cash register.

Source: NCR Corporation, Dayton, Ohio.

color bar encoded information that is readable by a wand reader. (See Figure 7.3.) A sweep of the wand across the encoded tag and all data necessary for control and reporting is captured. The retail terminal to which the wand is attached automatically computes the sales total, the sales tax, and the change due to the customer. Data from the tag and terminal is recorded on magnetic tape and is available for inventory and accounting reports.

Other systems provide a batch answer for inventory control. Merchandise information is imprinted on tags and price labels in both a machine readable linear bar code and human readable form. When a sale is made the salesperson simply removes the tag and places it in a box. At the end of the day stubs are sent to a central location. A reader automatically records data onto computer-compatible magnetic tape. The data is then ready for computer processing and timely merchandise reports

can be ready each day reflecting the previous day's transactions.

Data may also be entered into an electronic cash register by a laser beam scanning device that can read a code from a rectangle of thick and thin linear bars.

The use of scanner systems is furthest advanced in the food industry, primarily because of the industry's adoption of the Universal Product Code and Symbol. The Universal Product Code (UPC) is a numbering system that assigns a unique number to every product in current distribution. The code system for the grocery industry has 10 digits. The first five identify the manufacturer and the second five identify the specific item. See Figure 7.4.

In the supermarket, at each check out lane there is an electronic cash register hooked up to a computer. Built into each counter is the laser beam scanner which can read the code. The cashier slides each item's UPC symbol

RETAIL TERMINAL

MODERN STORE

7 4 2
DEPT

9 3 4 2 8 6
SKU

S M A L L
SIZE

$5.69

COLOR BAR
CODE TICKET

WAND READER

Figure 7.3. The encoded tag and wand reader.

Source: NCR Corporation, Dayton, Ohio.

Figure 7.4. The universal product code.

over the scanner which sends the code to the store's computer. See Figure 7.5. Each code is unique and has only one corresponding price in the computer. Almost immediately the item's price and description is flashed on a viewing screen at the checkout counter. If the code marking is damaged or smudged the scanner will not read it. The cashier must then read the code number into the keyboard of the cash register. The cash register prints a receipt for the customer which can show the item by department and description in addition to the price. Automatically the system can separate food stampable from non-stampable items, calculate sales tax, and for meat and produce show pounds and ounces bought and the cost per pound. And, of course, the computer has stored vital shelf movement data to be used for inventory control and management.

The scanner systems being implemented in the food industry are likely the prerunner of complete systems that will be adopted by other retailing segments. The only major barrier, other than capital investment cost, is the development of product codes for each segment.

Other information. Information that does not

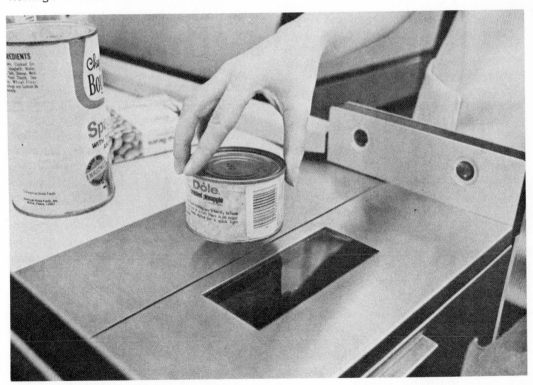

Figure 7.5. An optical scanner reading the universal product code.
Source: NCR Corporation, Dayton, Ohio.

involve sales includes preparation of budgets, warehousing requirements, order processing, delivery scheduling, minimum sales level, work measurement, investment analysis, vendor evaluation, and personnel scheduling. Such information is usually entered off the selling floor. Equipment in the back office may be used to punch cards or paper tape, record data on magnetic tape, or to transmit data directly to the computer.

EDP Applications in Retailing

We now want to examine some of the applications that retailers may make of computer based information systems.

Applications in merchandising

Many retailers are reaping the benefits of using electronic data processing. Most of the benefits have been in the areas of savings in costs and in accuracy in records and reports. These benefits are associated with financial and accounting functions such as expense distribution, accounts receivable, and accounts payable. However, accounting has never been a problem in retailing; the soft spot has always been inventory control. In fact, there are countless potential EDP applications in the merchandising area.

In recent years, retailers have been faced with a growing selection of merchandise and a fashion explosion. Fashion and style lines have proliferated in both depth and breadth. Even staple items are made in numerous sizes, colors, and shapes. This increase in the number of different items that must be stocked has made control extremely difficult. Ideally, a completely computerized merchandising system would provide information on the complete inventory, the distribution of fast and slow moving items, the items that are moving and those that are not, the vendors who supply the merchandise that is selling, customer buying patterns in terms of styles, colors, prices, and fashions, and rates of sale. The system would also make it possible to maintain reliable open-to-buy and assortment plans and to achieve improved stock-to-sales ratios. Some major retailers are making tremendous strides in developing a system that can do what has been suggested.

Initially, some buyers resist computers because they are afraid the machines will replace them. However, this doesn't happen. Computer systems give buyers time to analyze their markets and to seek out new and better products and suppliers. Computers help buyers identify troublespots and define what is wrong. When computer systems show a dramatic mistake in overbuying, steps can be taken to correct the problem.

Applications in accounts receivable

Today computerized accounts receivable programs go beyond the typical accounting function. Good customer credit systems not only establish regular dunning and collection procedures but also improve credit application policies so bad debt losses are decreased and charge sales to paying customers are increased. New total credit systems review a customer's account and his or her open-to-buy balance and simultaneously transmit this information to the selling floor.

Possible future applications

Many additional nonselling activities can be handled by computers. Programs can be developed to build seasonal merchandise plans, write purchase orders and reorders, forecast future needs, hypothesize whether a depleted item should be reordered, and note trends on what is selling.

Furthermore, programs can be developed to find correlations among the type of product sold, its brand name, and the sales volume. Other programs can be established to design and test reorganizational structures, analyze current market conditions, select customers for direct mail advertising campaigns, specify store layout and warehouse design, and simulate operations for customer contact.

Does this sound as if we are dreaming? All that is necessary to achieve these applications is good data collection systems and creative and innovative retail managers.

Examples of applications

To provide a clear picture of some existing applications, we present a few examples of the capabilities of a National Cash Register system that can be used by both small and large stores.

Although it is not alone in the EDP field, NCR has been a leader in helping retailers solve their information needs.

Examples of reports that NCR can generate for almost any retailer are illustrated in Figures 7.6 to 7.10. Figures 7.6 and 7.7 provide cost and retail value of inventories. Figures 7.8 and 7.9 illustrate income and balance sheet statements. Figure 7.10 shows a salesperson productivity report.

NCR PROFITABLE STORE   RETAIL INVENTORY MANAGEMENT REPORT ALL STORES   (CN123456)   9/30/7-   PAGE 1

CL. NO.	DESCRIPTION	ST NO	UNITS SOLD	NET SALES	GROSS MARGIN AT	ADDITIONS AT COST	ADDITIONS AT RETAIL	MARK-DOWNS	END/COST END/RETL	ON HAND ST/SL	% OF MKDN	% INV TURN	% OF SALES	% MARG	INT MU CUM MU
1436	MERCHANDISE A	1	10	791	419	0	0	5	2223	59	.6	28.4	20.6	52.9	.0
			90	6300	3232	1249	1580	230	4732	6.0	3.7	1.9	19.7	51.3	53.0
1436	MERCHANDISE A	2	9	713	401	316	680	0	2081	52	.0	29.3	22.8	56.2	53.5
			80	5714	2918	901	1304	201	4137	5.8	3.5	2.1	19.4	51.1	52.9
CLASS 1436 ALL STORES			19	1504	820	316	680	5	4304	3	.3	28.8	21.6	54.5	53.5
			170	12014	6150	2150	2884	431	8869	5.9	3.6	2.0	19.6	51.2	52.9
DEPT. 11 ST 1 TOTAL			48	3831	1817	429	850	30	9053	208	.7	72.5	43.2	47.4	49.5
			447	31906	13792	9879	17577	734	16654	4.3	2.3	1.7	71.5	43.2	47.8
DEPT. 11 ST 2 TOTAL			39	3121	1503	545	1080	0	7190	176	.0	62.6	50.9	48.1	49.5
			376	29408	12042	7085	12659	481	14109	4.5	1.6	1.9	72.2	41.0	47.4
DEPT. 11 ALL STORES			87	6952	3320	974	2780	30	16243	384	.4	67.6	46.4	45.6	49.5
			823	61314	25834	16964	30236	1215	30763	4.4	2.0	1.8	71.8	42.1	47.5

NCR PROFITABLE STORE   RETAIL INVENTORY MANAGEMENT REPORT ALL STORES   (CN123456)   9/30/7-   PAGE 20

CL. NO.	DESCRIPTION	ST NO	UNITS SOLD	NET SALES	GROSS MARGIN AT	ADDITIONS AT COST	ADDITIONS AT RETAIL	MARK-DOWNS	END/COST END/RETL	ON HAND ST/SL	% OF MKDN	% INV TURN	% OF SALES	% MARG	INT MU CUM MU
DIV.	ST 1 TOTAL	1	108	8858	4055	889	1680	160	12325	287	1.8	17.8	27.3	45.8	47.1
			665	44623	19389	16317	29674	2040	22970	2.5	4.6	1.6	17.0	43.5	46.3
DIV.	ST 2 TOTAL	1	82	6131	2904	655	1260	0	11313	304	.0	15.5	16.8	47.4	48.0
			535	40733	17634	11574	16973	1254	22553	3.7	3.1	1.8	13.7	43.3	47.1
DIV.	ALL STORES	1	190	14989	6959	1544	2940	160	23648	641	1.0	16.6	21.7	46.4	47.5
			1200	85356	37023	27891	46647	3294	45523	3.0	3.9	1.8	15.3	43.4	46.7
GRAND TOTAL STORE 1			1884	32384	14799	1193	2000	178	70378	7594	.5	47.0	46.9	47.5	47.2
			19633	262855	108043	140273	250255	19717	129100	3.9	7.5	2.0	47.0	40.1	46.5
GRAND TOTAL STORE 2			2124	36529	16688	1345	2256	0	79362	8563	.0	53.0	52.8	45.7	48.1
			22140	296410	121836	158180	282202	22235	145580	4.1	7.5	1.9	51.0	42.0	47.2
GRAND TOTAL ALL STORES			4009	68924	31487	2539	4257	178	149741	16157	.3	100.0	100.0	45.7	47.5
			41773	559266	229880	298454	532458	41953	274681	4.0	7.5	1.9	100.0	41.1	46.8

Figure 7.6. The retail inventory management report shows gross profit by percentage and dollars and margins being maintained in each classification. Inventory at cost and retail, total markdowns, and a classifications' percentage of total sales compared with inventory investment, is provided.

Source: NCR Corporation, Dayton, Ohio.

NCR PROFITABLE STORE   COST/DIRECT COST   (CN123456)   9/30/7-   PAGE   1
                                        INVENTORY MANAGEMENT REPORT

CLASS STORE NO. / NO.	SALES AT RETAIL	%SLS /TOT	GROSS PROFIT	G.P. %	ST/SLS BOM	ADDTONS AT COST	DIR.COST OF SALES	CAL.COST OF SALES	CLOS INV AT COST	ON HAND UNITS	TURN	YEAR TO DATE SALES	%SL/TOT	G.P.%
2101 1	3040	4.41	1298	42.71	4.92	.00	.00	1741	6830	28	2.2	25406	4.54	42.71
2101 2	2295	3.33	1111	48.42	3.48	.00	.00	1184	2937	12	1.3	8451	1.51	48.52
CLASS TOTAL	5335	24.0	2410	45.0	1.83	.00	.00	2925	9767	40	1.8	33857	30.0	45.61
2202 1	2245	3.26	992	44.19	4.35	.00	.00	1253	4201	44	1.9	5256	.94	44.19
2202 2	2230	3.24	896	40.18	1.52	.00	.00	1334	699	7	1.3	6941	1.24	50.18
CLASS TOTAL	4476	20.0	1888	42.0	1.09	.00	.00	2587	4901	51	1.1	12197	10.0	47.18
2303 1	560	.81	293	52.43	2.19	.00	.00	226	315	7	.5	1861	.33	48.76
2303 2	592	.86	322	54.37	5.75	.00	.00	270	1285	29	2.1	1780	.32	53.55
CLASS TOTAL	1153	5.0	909	79.0	1.39	.00	.00	497	1601	36	1.3	3642	3.0	51.15
DEPT 1 ST 1	11692	57.0	5169	44.2	1.94	1750	226	2995	22696	237	1.9	65049	52.6	47.4
DEPT 1 ST 2	10237	53.9	4660	45.5	1.93	1540	270	2518	19844	144	1.9	34345	52.6	48.1
DIV 10 ST 1	20480	76.2	9675	47.2	1.99	2380	440	5990	40950	474	1.9	123593	97.0	45.1
DIV 10 ST 2	18990	79.2	8250	43.4	1.94	1950	390	5016	36865	273	1.9	65255	95.2	44.7
STORE 1	26850	52.8	15520	57.8	2.0	3900	590	1074	53700	513	2.0	127300	50.0	57.0
STORE 2	23975	47.1	13845	57.7	2.0	3900	540	9590	47950	390	2.0	127300	50.0	56.5
ALL STORES	50825	100.0	29365	57.8	2.0	7800	1130	10664	101650	903	2.0	254600	100.0	56.5

Figure 7.7. The cost inventory merchandise report shows each merchandise classifications' percentage of total sales and its gross profit. Information on stock turns and inventory changes contribute to a detailed profile of the entire merchandise inventory.

Source: NCR Corporation, Dayton, Ohio.

CLIENT NO. XXXXXX   THE VILLAGE STORE   DATE XX/YY/ZZ

INCOME STATEMENT RET95571   PAGE NO. 1

	% TO TOTAL	CURRENT	% TO TOTAL	YEAR TO DATE
SALES	100.00	13,352.41	100.00	31,075.20
COST OF SALES				
OPENING INVENTORY		68,288.80		69,324.80
MERCHANDISE PURCHASES		18,087.75		38,685.20
TOTAL		86,376.55		98,324.60
LESS CLOSING INVENTORY		77,724.13		77,724.13
COST OF SALES	60.98	8,142.06	62.64	19,467.82
COST OF MARKDOWNS	3.82	510.36	3.70	1,150.65
COST OF MERCHANDISE SOLD	64.80	8,652.42	66.35	20,618.47
0810 PLUS FREIGHT IN	.65	86.42	.85	265.50
COST OF SALES	65.45	8,738.82	67.20	20,883.97
GROSS PROFIT	34.55	4,613.59	32.80	10,191.23
OPERATING EXPENSES				
0809 EMPLOYEE DISCOUNTS	.15	20.00	.21	66.80
0811 DISCOUNT EXPENSE	.41	54.24	.57	176.40
0817 ADVERTISING	.44	59.00	.59	186.25
0834 OVER - SHORT	.01	1.11	.01	4.21
0835 BUYING EXPENSE	.36	47.50	.28	87.50
TOTAL OPERATING EXPENSES	31.03	4,143.14	29.46	91,534.40
NET PROFIT	3.52	470.45	3.34	1,037.83
OTHER INCOME				
0803 POSTAGE INCOME	.01	1.75	.01	1.75
0804 ALTERATIONS INCOME	.03	3.50	.03	8.50
0807 SERVICE CHARGE INCOME	.01	1.50	.01	2.65
0853 DISCOUNTS EARNED	.30	40.00	.45	140.00
TOTAL OTHER INCOME	.35	46.75		153.90
NET PROFIT	3.87	517.20	3.85	1,191.73
0994 LESS EST FED INC TAX	1.16	155.16	1.28	398.60
NET PROFIT AFTER INC TAX	2.71	362.04	2.55	793.13

Figure 7.8. An income statement "keeps management informed of their profit picture, monthly."

Source: NCR Corporation, Dayton, Ohio.

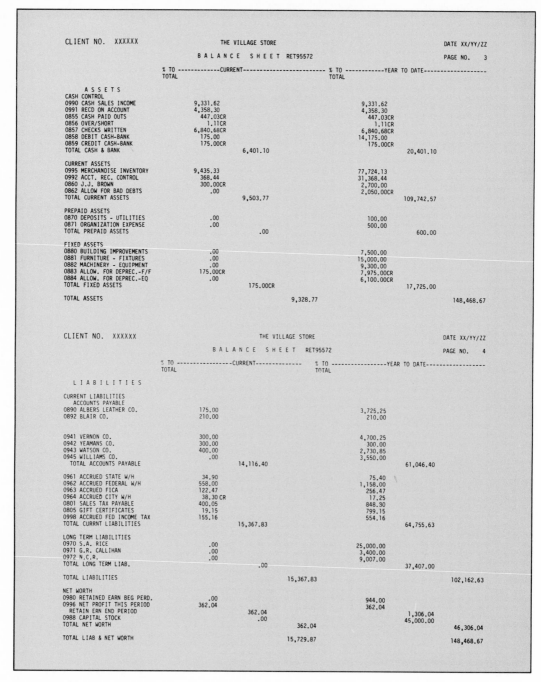

Figure 7.9. A balance sheet "keeps management informed of their financial position on a monthly basis."

Source: NCR Corporation, Dayton, Ohio.

NCR PROFITABLE STORE   SALESPERSON PRODUCTIVITY   STORE NO. 1   (CN123456)   9/30/7-   PAGE   1

CLERK	DEP	GROSS SALES	GROSS RETURN	CURRENT NET SALES	ITEMS	AVG SALE	CALC COMM.	COST FACTOR	%COST /SLS	GROSS SALES	GROSS RETURN	YEAR TO DATE NET SALES	ITEMS	AVG SALE	CALC COMM	CALC COST FACTOR	%COST /SLS
123456	12	453	10	443	4	111	20			15402	310	15092	136	111	755		
	13	252	11	241	22	11	12			8568	341	8227	1088	8	411		
	15	352		352	59	6	11			11968	217	11751	2006	6	353		
	20	905	0	905	181	5	27			30770	155	30615	6154	5	918		
	40	553	4	549	18	31	11			18802	240	18562	612	30	371		
							25								1202		
ALLEN J R		2515	25	2490	284	9	106	150	9.7	121448	1263	120185	9996	12	5212	5850	10.9
1.0 FXD																	
234567	12	547	0	547	5	109	26			18598	220	18378	173	106	873		
	13	416	0	416	43	10	20			14144	75	14069	1563	9	677		
	16	935	12	923	62	15				31790	128	31662	1978	16			
NELSON W P		1898	12	1886	110	17	46	110	8.3	64552	423	64109	3714	.17	1550	4290	9.1
STORE 1		68923	7581	61342	3438	20	2052	925	8.4	559265	27146	532119	29681	18	21633	29250	9.6

Figure 7.10. The salesperson productivity report allows evaluation of each salesperson on the basis of dollar volume, number of customers served and the average sale.

Source: NCR Corporation, Dayton, Ohio.

Summary

For information of a recurring nature, many retailers have turned to electronic data processing. New technology, especially the electronic cash register, is making data capture more complete, accurate, and faster. Computer manufacturers have developed highly specialized programs which can provide the retailer with complete reports for merchandising, accounting, and control.

Computer hardware and business machine manufacturers are working hard to provide both the hardware and the programs that will supply retailers with necessary information. Computers provide an opportunity for retailers to concentrate on the business of retailing.

Questions and Problems

1. *What factors determine the feasibility of a retailer's adapting an EDP system to his operations?*
2. *Why were many retailers slow in adopting EDP systems? What caused the change?*
3. *What role can vendors play in simplifying the retailer's use of EDP?*

Situations and Activities

You are the credit manager in a small junior department store. The store manager is considering installing a computer system and has asked you to develop preliminary plans for its use in your department. You would like to include analysis of accounts receivable, billing procedures, and credit verification. How should you proceed? What information do you need? How might it be obtained?

You are the buyer for a men's wear department. Management is currently reviewing the reports being received from the EDP system. Of particular concern are new and/or improved applications in inventory management. What information will be most valuable to you? How often will you need different kinds of inventory information? If the point-of-sale data system uses prepunched tags, what input information will you want on the tag? Keep in mind the limited space on the tag.

Prepare for the manager of a ladies' ready-to-wear store with $500,000 in annual sales an analysis of the advantages and disadvantages of purchasing "Data Processing Packages" from a computer systems supplier.

Library assignment: Imaginative and creative retail managers will lead the way in finding new applications for the computer in retailing which may cause significant changes in the future. Look for several articles in trade and professional publications which discuss possible changes. Record your findings. Can you think of any other possibilities? Indicate how the changes will affect retailing in the future for small specialty stores, department stores, and chain discount stores.

Bibliography

"Cash Drawers that 'Talk' Computer." *Business Week,* August 29, 1970, pp. 66—67.

Edelman, Bernard. "Retailing Systems: Instant Information Anywhere in the World." *Columbia Journal of World Business,* November-December, 1970, pp. 87—89.

Fleisher, David T. "Poor Marks for Computers in the Merchandising Area." *Retail Overview,* Summer, 1970, pp. 33—41.

National Retail Merchants Association, Retail Research Institute. *1969—1970 Report on Status of Electronic Data Processing in Retailing,* New York.

Smith, Spencer B. "Automated Inventory Management for Staples." *Journal of Retailing,* Vol. 47, No. 1, Spring, 1971, pp. 55—62.

8

Infomation from Research

contents

behavioral objectives

Retailers should understand the sources and uses of information gathered from research. The manager should be alert to the application of research techniques when obtaining information to solve retail problems.

Upon completing this chapter, you will be able to do the following:
☐ Identify the components of a good research design.
☐ Describe the sources of secondary information.
☐ Explain how primary information can be obtained from resondents.

Retailing faces so many dynamic factors, management must increasingly rely on masses of information for help in making intelligent decisions. As we have seen, information provided on a regular basis, evolves from basic store records and more and more frequently the regularly needed information is provided through electronic data processing (EDP).

However, good management decisions also benefit from information that must be sought out and that tends not to recur. Much of this information is obtained through the efforts of research. We will therefore examine what retailing problems require marketing research and how to approach the research process.

Problems That Require Research

Problems that require informational inputs from marketing research are numerous and varied. Figure 8.1 outlines a list of such problem areas in the categories of markets, location, products, promotion, and pricing.

Perhaps the most common use of research is in making a market analysis. For the store, a market analysis might develop customer profiles showing demographic, psychographic, and geographic characteristics such as were discussed in Chapters 2 and 3. Management is more and more trying to understand consumer behavior; therefore, market analyses increasingly emphasize the study of customer buying habits and motives.

Research is needed to provide information for product planning, development, and evaluation. Understanding the needs of the market provides the input necessary for new product ideas such as adding or deleting a line. Every store should know how a suggested product contributes to the total product offering of the firm in terms of both image and profitability. Information from customers may be needed to develop warranty plans, package designs, and service offerings. Advertising and pricing policies may depend on the results of product or service-image studies.

Distribution analysis is another form that research may take. Distribution analysis could include studies on locations for stores, traffic, flows, material handling, store layout, and freight system alternatives.

Pricing is a frequently neglected area of research. Pricing analysis provides information about the nature of the demand curves—the basis on which intelligent pricing can take place. The cost structure of the store, comparable industry and competitor information all require informational input. Information derived from pricing research may be used to establish profit objectives and sales budgets.

1. Research on markets.
   a. Analyzing market potentials for products.
   b. Sales forecasting.
   c. Characteristics of product markets.
   d. Analyzing sales potentials.
   e. Studying trends in markets.

2. Research on products.
   a. Customer acceptance of proposed new products.
   b. Comparative studies of competitive products.
   c. Studying customer dissatisfaction with products.
   d. Product-line research.

3. Research on promotion.
   a. Evaluating advertising effectiveness.
   b. Analyzing advertising and selling practices.
   c. Selecting advertising media.
   d. Motivational studies.
   e. Evaluating present and proposed sales methods.
   f. Analyzing salesperson effectiveness.
   g. Establishing sales quotas.

4. Research on distribution.
   a. Location and design of stores.
   b. Handling and packing merchandise.
   c. Cost analysis of transportation methods.
   d. Supply and storage requirements.

5. Research on pricing.
   a. Studying competitive pricing.
   b. Demand elasticities.
   c. Perceived prices.
   d. Cost analysis.
   e. Margin analysis.

Figure 8.1. Research information can be useful in making many decisions.

Source: Adapted from Richard D. Cripp, *Marketing Research Organization and Operation*, Research Study No. 35, New York: American Management Association, 1958, pp. 39–47.

Communications analyses are almost as frequently conducted as market analyses. A market analysis that yields demographic and psychographic profiles of customers may serve as the basis for determining the theme and content of advertising and sales messages. Media-audience studies ensure that the medium being considered delivers an audience that matches the profile of the target market. Content analyses of broadcast programming and printed media help a store choose a medium that projects the desired image. Measurement of the results of advertising, sales promotion, and personal selling programs is another vital area of communications analysis.

The Research Process

A systematic approach to the research process is illustrated in Figure 8.2. This research process includes a situation analysis; identification of the problem; statement of hypothesis; development of the research design; collection, processing, and interpretation of the data; and preparation and presentation of findings in the form of a report.

The starting point for most research is the situation analysis. The researcher usually recognizes a broad problem, but this may not be the central issue. Therefore, the researcher should investigate the total situation thoroughly before choosing the research direction.

A situation analysis may involve examinations of the general economic condition, new competitors, and competitors' retailing activities, as well as of each element of the store's own activities. After such a broadly varied situation analysis, the researcher may tentatively state a problem. Having formulated a tentative problem, the researcher makes a preliminary study of internal and published information sources to refine the problem statement.

The problem-identification statement must be specific enough to set the direction of the research effort. The problem statement may even be presented as the objective for the study. For example, if the problem were stated as being an incomplete understanding of the buying patterns of potential customers, an appropriate objective would be to conduct a complete behavioral market analysis.

An effective tool for guiding a research project is the establishment of hypotheses.

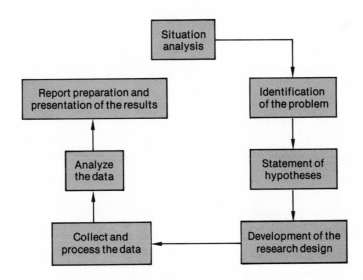

Figure 8.2. The research process.

Hypotheses are tentative statements describing relationships between concepts or possible cause-and-effect relationships. These statements reflect a belief about real-world relationships, but they must be supported or rejected based on evidence gathered from the research effort. For example, one hypothesis might be: "Over 60 percent of the potential shoppers at Jones' Hardware, as determined by the expression of a favorable store image, are over forty-five years of age." Notice the direction that this hypothesis gives the researcher. Information must be obtained from potential buyers (not present buyers), image of store, and age data information must be collected.

The heart of research is the research design. A research design is the overall plan that determines information needed and that specifies how the investigation to obtain it will be conducted. A complete research design would include the following elements:

1. Statement of the evidence necessary to solve a problem and the basic methods whereby the solutions will become revealed or validated.
2. Specification of the evidence—where and how it will be obtained.
3. Anticipation of how the data will be analyzed to produce answers to the problem.
4. Guidelines for the calculation and approval of the feasibility and cost of the project.
5. A plan to guide the carrying out of the work.[1]

Information Sources

A key element in the research design is the specification of the information sources. Information for making decisions may come from either secondary or primary sources. To make effective use of research requires a good working familiarity with gathering both types of information.

Secondary Sources provide information

collected for some purpose other than to solve a current problem. It is information that already exists and of which researchers may avail themselves. There are many secondary sources available to the researcher, either inside or outside of the firm. All levels of government, trade and professional associations, and many private sources are valuable secondary sources for information.

Most information-gathering efforts should begin with a search of secondary sources. The information used to solve a problem can often be found in secondary sources more quickly and inexpensively than from primary sources. Even when the secondary information does not solve the problem, the research results may refine the problem definition, suggest alternative solutions, and help plan the collection of primary data.

Even though secondary information can often be obtained quickly and at relatively low cost, it must be evaluated before use by the researcher. The data must be directly applicable to the identified problem. Because the data was gathered for some other use it may provide useful background information but may not lead to the problem solution. Also, the researcher must evaluate the integrity and bias of the data source. In addition, the data and the source must be evaluated to be sure that the data are accurate and up-to-date.

Many sources of information for retailing decisions are readily available in school, university, and public libraries. A search for information in a published source should begin with the use of an indexing service. Indexes list information sources by topic, title and author. Of the many such services these three are among the most widely used by business students. *Business Periodicals Index* indexes about 160 periodicals in all business areas. *Readers' Guide to Periodical Literature* indexes the contents of general magazines. *The Wall Street Journal* publishes an annual index listing articles that have appeared in the publication during the year.

Much important information will be found in periodical trade publications covering almost every aspect of retailing. Sources for

---

[1] David L. Luck; Hugh G. Wales; and Donald A. Taylor, *Marketing Research.* Englewood Cliffs, N.J.: Prentice-Hall, 1970, p. 85.

locating these include: *Ulrich's International Periodicals Directory* (New York: R. R. Bowker, revised periodically) covers more than 30,000 publications, *N. W. Ayer and Son's Directory of Newspapers and Periodicals* (Philadelphia: Ayer and Son, published annually), *Business Publications Rates and Data* (Skokie, Ill.: Standard Rate and Data Service, monthly supplements).

Examples of retailing-oriented publications are: *Stores, The Department Store Economist, The New York Retailer, Display World, The Merchandiser, Chain Store Age, Discount Merchandiser, Hardware Retailer, Progressive Grocer, Modern Jeweler, National Jeweler, Clothes, Merchandising Weekly, Womens Wear Daily, Mens Wear, Journal of Retailing, Supermarket News,* and *Journal of Franchising.*

Many of the trade periodicals devote one or more issues a year to "statistical issues." These issues provide a wealth of up-to-date information concerning such factors as industry sales, operating results, financial data, growth rates, and trends.

There are also many special trade-association publications. Most publish information on sales, costs, returns and allowances, expenses, profits, stock-turnover rates, accounts receivable, bad-debt losses, and the like. Check for listings in the *Directory of National Trade and Professional Associations of the United States* (Washington, D.C.: Columbia Books, Inc.), and in the *Encyclopedia of Associations* (Detroit: Gale Research Company).

Government documents. The United States Government Printing Office is the world's largest printer. Through the various government agencies, an unbelievable amount of information is published covering almost every conceivable topic. The two agencies that publish the most information directly related to the retailer are the Department of Commerce and the Small Business Administration. The Department of Commerce maintains excellent reference libraries in more than thirty cities, and the Small Business Administration maintains field offices in more than fifty cities. In addition, many university libraries are depositories for most government publications.

The major guide to government documents is the *Monthly Catalog of United States Government Publications* (Washington, D.C.: Superintendent of Documents), which provides a comprehensive list of federal publications.

Department of Commerce. The Bureau of the Census of the Department of Commerce conducts a census of population, housing, and agriculture every ten years. Every five years, a census of business and a census of manufacturers are conducted. All of the publications listed below are published in Washington, D.C., by the Department of Commerce, Bureau of the Census, unless otherwise indicated. An important guide to locating census information is the *Catalog of United States Census Publications.*

The Statistical Abstract of the United States (published annually) provides a summary of statistics from all of the census publications, as well as other important statistics.

The *Census of Population* (published every ten years): Vol. I (Characteristics of the Population) contains general population, social, and economic characteristics. Vol. II (Subject Reports) details cross-relationships on families, material status, education, employment, occupation, income, and the like.

Census Tract Reports contain detailed information on population and housing, and the *County and City Data Book* (published annually) summarizes statistics for small geographical areas.

The *Census of Housing* (published every ten years): Vol. I (Housing Characteristics for States, Cities, and Counties) includes detailed occupancy, structural, and financial characteristics of housing. Vol. II (Metropolitan Housing Characteristics) contains cross-classifications of housing and household characteristics. Vol. III (Block Characteristics) details block statistics on plumbing, size, rent, value, and occupancy. Vol. IV (Components of Change) documents physical changes since the previous census for the larger Metropolitan Housing Characteristics (Vol. II above).

The *Census of Retail Trade* (last published in 1972) has six volumes. Vols. I, III, and V summarize statistics for retail, wholesale, and selected service trades by geographic areas. Vols. II, IV, and VI contain statistics by kind of business for counties, cities, and standard metropolitan statistical areas. The service trade census provides data on receipts, employment, number of units, and organization.

The *Census of Business—Selected Services* (last published in 1972) contains special reports on selected businesses, including motion-picture theaters, gasoline service stations, eating and drinking places, laundry and cleaning establishments, and travel agencies.

County Business Patterns (published jointly by the Department of Commerce and the Department of Health, Education and Welfare) has statistics on number of business units, employment, and payroll figures.

The *Survey of Current Business* (published by the Department of Commerce, Office of Business Economics) regularly brings up-to-date over 2500 statistical series.

The *Monthly Labor Review* (published by the Department of Labor, Bureau of Labor Statistics) reports current labor statistics, including employment, wages, labor turnover, and price indexes.

The *Federal Reserve Bulletin* (published by the Board of Governors of the Federal Reserve System) is a monthly source of financial statistics, including banking, government, business, real estate, and consumer finance. In addition, it provides data in such areas as savings, national product and income, department store sales, prices, and production.

Small Business Administration. The Small Business Administration publishes several hundred "aids." Many of them cover subjects directly applicable to retailing and retail store operations. A list of all of the aids available can be found in the SBA's *Classification of Management Publications.* This list covers the following series and titles: management aids, technical aids, small marketers aids, small

business bibliographies, small business management series, small business research series, and starting and managing series.

Other sources. The *Standard Rate and Data Service* (Skokie, Ill.: Standard Rate and Data Service), in eleven volumes, provides all of the information needed to prepare and place advertising in the media, including coverage, costs, timing, and so on. Consumer market data are included as part of the Spot Television Rates and Data, the Spot Radio Rates and Data, and the Newspaper Rates and Data. Also included are data on population, consumer spendable income, total retail sales, and sales by major classification for states, metropolitan areas, and cities.

The *Rand McNally Commercial Atlas and Marketing Guide* (Chicago: Rand McNally, published annually) contains statistics and maps for every part of the world. There are about 40 statistical items in marketing tables for each county in the United States. *Advertising Age Market Data Issue* (Chicago: Advertising Publications, published annually) is an excellent source guide to privately published data on national, regional, and local markets, industries and products. *Sales Management Survey of Buying Power* (New York: Bill Brothers Publishing Corporation, published annually) contains detailed population, income, and retail sales data for states, counties, metropolitan areas, and cities. *Editor and Publisher Market Guide* (New York: Editor and Publisher, published annually) contains data on transportation, utilities, population, wages, employment, and housing for some 1500 daily newspaper markets.

Primary Sources provide information that is derived from research specifically designed to answer a problem at hand. For retailers the main source of primary information is from respondents, whether they are customers, potential customers, uninterested observers, or knowledgeable employees of the firm. Information is obtained from respondents either by questioning or by observing behavior. Questioning respondents properly helps provide information about their past, current, or intended behavior and helps provide information that may be associated with behavior, such as attitudes and opinions, or psychographic, demographic, and socioeconomic characteristics.

Questioning or interviewing of respondents may be structured or unstructured and may be either direct or indirect. If the questioning is to be structured, a formal questionnaire is prepared, with specific questions to be asked in a specific order. Structured questioning has the advantage of asking for the desired information in a systematic manner. Careful wording of questions helps avoid the possibilities of ambiguities and misunderstandings. However, it is difficult for the researcher to get at motivational factors through structured questioning. If unstructured questioning is used, the wording of the questioning and the question order is adapted to each interview, the only guideline being the type of information being desired. Unstructured questioning is more flexible and allows the interviewer to pursue the motive or cause behind an answer. However, controlling the variances in responses caused by interviewer differences is difficult. Also, with an unstructured format it may be difficult to cover all desired information areas, and the more open-ended responses are sometimes difficult to interpret.

In indirect questioning the purpose for asking the questions is disguised and the questioning is often conducted with what are called projective techniques. Indirect interviews are most useful when the researcher wants to obtain information about deep-seated motivation or values. There are several commonly used projective techniques. One familiar technique involves word-association and sentence-completion tests. In these indirect tests, a respondent is asked to give a spontaneous reaction to a word or sentence, which in turn tells the investigator something about how the respondent is thinking. Less familiar are techniques such as the Thematic Apperception Test (TAT) and the Third Person techniques. The TAT takes the form of a series of cartoons depicting people and the problem situation. The respondent is asked to assume the role of

one of the persons in the situation and to describe what that person is doing or saying. In the Third Person technique, the person is asked for the opinions or views of a third person. This presumably allows the respondent to project her or his own opinions without feeling pressured to give an acceptable answer.

We can see that a researcher desiring information may ask questions in one of four forms: (1) structured-direct, (2) structured-indirect, (3) unstructured-direct, or (4) unstructured-indirect. Which of the four combinations to use largely depends on what situation exists. If the respondent knows the information and is willing to respond if asked, direct, structured or unstructured questioning will provide the information needed. If the respondent knows the information but for some reason is not willing to answer direct questions, some form of indirect questioning may be required. Lastly, if the respondent is unable to verbalize the desired information, projective techniques may be necessary. Obtaining reliable and valid information from respondents is difficult because respondents often (1) just do not know the information; (2) have forgotten information; (3) do not want the researcher to know the information; and (4) want to be nice, so they give an acceptable answer, one they think will make the researcher happy.

Mail Surveys are particularly useful for employing structured-direct questioning. Because mail surveys use questionnnaires, they are economical and make large samples possible. In addition, people are often more willing to anonymously report personal information, such as income, by mail, than by telephone or in person. But mail surveys also have their limitations. One of their weaknesses is the lack of personal communication, which can help explain misunderstandings and help interpret questions. In addition, mail surveys are dependent on the individual's willingness to fill out and return the forms. This can lead to a high degree of nonresponse error. Mail questionnaires also generally need to be short, the questions completely clear, and the nature of the desired answer obvious.

Telephone Interviewing has the advantages

of being quick and of relatively low cost. Telephone interviewers must be well trained to be alert to a respondent's difficulty in understanding the question or a respondent's being offended by the question. The list of questions must be short and the questions carefully worded.

Personal Interviews may be used for any form of questioning. The more unstructured and/or indirect the questions, the more likely personal interviewing will be needed and the better trained the interviewers will have to be. Personal interviewing is slow and expensive but it is often the only way to obtain complete detailed information.

Three questionnaires are illustrated in Figures 8.3—8.5.

Observing the behavior of respondents is sometimes an excellent source of information.

Furthermore, it is often difficult for respondents to verbalize the reasons for their behavior, yet observation may demonstrate those reasons. Observational studies may also be undertaken simply to validate information obtained by questioning. If the research were concerned with store layout designs, some of the most valuable information might be obtained by observing the movement of people in stores.

Other counts (observations) might be used to determine peak selling days and peak time of day for sales and/or customer traffic.

Observational studies may be made to count the foot traffic, measuring number of potential shoppers, the proportion of window lookers or percentage of passers-by entering the store.

Vehicular traffic counts are important in location and site selection decisions.

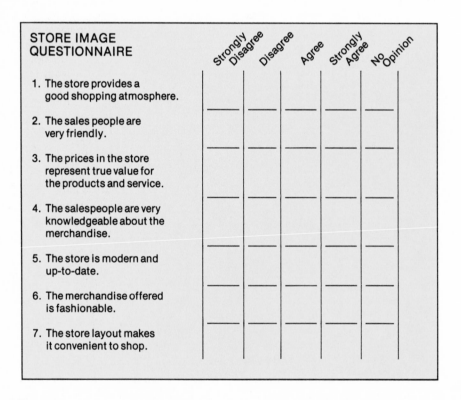

Figure 8.3. A questionnaire administered by telephone in an attempt to measure store image.

SUPERMARKET QUESTIONNAIRE

1. At which store do you or your household presently do the majority of your grocery shopping?

___King's Markets   ___Foothills Market Basket

___National Roberts   ___Mountain Market Basket

___Mulberry Savemore   ___Thrifty Foods

___Prospect Savemore   ___Beavers

___Foothills Mall Savemore

2. How often does the person in your household that does the grocery shopping usually go to the store?

___once a month   ___once a week

___twice a month   ___more than once a week

3. When you do your grocery shopping do you usually also shop at other stores in the area?

_____Yes _____No. If yes, at which of the following:

___Laundromat   ___Drugstore   ___Beauty Salon

___Men's Clothing   ___Bank   ___Discount Store

___Women's Clothing   ___Cafeteria Restaurant   ___Liquor Store

___Hardware   ___Barber Shop   ___Other (please state)

4. Do you feel that Lakewood needs a shopping center?___Yes ___No

5. Following is a list of stores that could be included in a new shopping center in Lakewood. Please rate each type of store in terms of your interest in having it included in the center.

$\checkmark$ = Really would like   O = Some interest   X = Don't really need

___Grocery Store   ___Drugstore   ___Liquor Store

___Laundromat   ___Barber Shop   ___Fabric Store

___Men's Clothing   ___Beauty Shop   ___Other (please state)

___Women's Clothing   ___Bank

___Hardware   ___Cafeteria Restaurant   _____

6. From the three following statements, please check the one that best fits your attitude toward a possible new supermarket in Lakewood.

___I would definitely shop for groceries in a new Lakewood supermarket if the prices were competitive with other stores in the city.

___I would not change from the supermarket where I now shop no matter what the prices are in the new supermarket.

___I would probably shop at a supermarket in my neighborhood even if the prices were slightly higher.

7. Check the words that describe the person filling out the questionnaire.

Does most of the grocery shopping? ___Yes ___No

Sex: ___male ___female

Figure 8.4. A mail questionnaire to determine grocery shopping location and response to possible new shopping center. Instructions provided in a cover letter.

Fashion Mall

This is a customer profile study for the Fashion Mall. Through this study we hope to better know you, our customer, so that all the merchants in the mall can better serve your needs.

Thank you very much for your cooperation.

1. Male _____ Female _____

2. Stage in the Family Life Cycle:
_____ Single, not living at home.
_____ Single, head of household.
_____ Married, no children.
_____ Married couple, with youngest child under six.
_____ Married couple, with dependent children over six.
_____ Married couple, with children living away from home. Household head in labor force.
_____ Married couple, children living away from home. Household head retired.

3. My occupation: _____
Spouses occupation: _____

4. Family Income Bracket:
_____ $5,000-$9,999
_____ $10,000-$14,999
_____ $15,000-$19,999
_____ $20,000-$24,999
_____ $25,000-or over

5. Do you rent _____ or own your own home _____?

6. Where is your place of residence?
_____ Altus
_____ Duncan
_____ Jacksonville
_____ St. Albans
_____ Rutland
_____ Other:

7. Do you have a favorite day to shop? Yes _____, No _____
If yes, what day is it? Monday _____ Tuesday _____ Wednesday _____ Thursday _____ Friday _____
Saturday _____ Sunday _____

8. Are the hours that the Fashion Mall is open: 10:00 a.m.-9:00 p.m. Monday through Saturday, and 12:00-5:00 p.m. Sunday, satisfactory for you? Yes _____, No _____

If No, what hours would be better?

9. How often do you shop at the Fashion Mall?
_____ more than once a week, _____ twice a month, _____ once a month,
_____ other.

9a. Are you shopping in the mall today for an Advertised Sale? Yes _____, No _____

10. How did you hear about the Sale at the Mall?
_____ Mail received at your home?
_____ Radio: What station
_____ Newspaper: Which
_____ TV.: What station.

11. Which of the following newspapers do you read regularly?
(You may check more than one)
_____ Altus Post
_____ Duncan Banner
_____ Second Thursday
_____ Guthrie News
_____ Burlington Review
_____ The Collegian
_____ Other:

Questions 12-19 refer to your feelings toward the mall itself in relation to the various items mentioned. Please place a check-mark in the spot that best expresses your opinion.

	VERY GOOD	ACCEPTABLE	BELOW STANDARD
12. Availability of Fashion or Quality Merchandise	_____	_____	_____
13. Selection and Variety of Merchandise	_____	_____	_____
14. Price Appeal (lower prices, good bargains and good values)	_____	_____	_____
15. Sales Clerk Service	_____	_____	_____
16. Access Routes to the Mall . . .	_____	_____	_____
17. Parking Availability on Arrival	_____	_____	_____
18. Satisfaction with returns and adjustments	_____	_____	_____
19. Mall events	_____	_____	_____

20. What percentage of your purchases for clothes are made at the Fashion Mall?
0-25%, _____ 25-50%, _____ 50-75%, _____ 75-100%.

21. Do you have any comments on anything in particular that you like or dislike about the mall?
_____

22. What have been your favorite mall special events?
_____

Figure 8.5. A personal interview questionnaire to measure attitudes and behavior.

A fashion count might be used periodically in an attempt to recognize trends in the purchase of fashion goods. Observations of potential customers might simply involve the recording of the number (percentage) of customers wearing a particular style or color.

Research firms may use audits and recording devices to observe behavior. Pantry audits of consumer households, to record brands, quantities, and sizes of products, are useful for determining past behavior. Recording devices such as cameras and psychogalvanometers are also used for observation. A psychogalvanometer works like a lie detector and is used to measure stimulation responses to interesting advertisements.

Information from a sample. If a data source to be studied is small, or if there are no limitations of time or money, a census may be conducted. In a census, every member or item in the group is approached to provide data; that is, the entire population of the universe is included in the study. A population or universe refers to all items or elements in a group under study. However, even without the limits of money, time, and/or physical constraints, it is often impossible to locate or obtain the cooperation of everyone in the population or universe. In any case, such an attempt is seldom wise or even necessary. The results obtained from a carefully selected portion of the universe may well present a better picture of that universe than would a census.

Sampling

The process of selecting a limited group to represent a larger group is known as sampling. The purpose of sampling is to obtain measures that approximate the characteristics, or parameters, of the entire universe faster, as accurately, and at lower cost than would be the case with a census. (Parameters are a set of measurements used to describe the universe under study, such as mean, median, mode, range, and standard deviation.) To be able to fulfill its purpose, the sample must be collected by using the principles of simple random sam-

pling, to ensure that every item in the universe has an equal chance of being included in the sample. The basic assumption of random sampling is that the results derived from a sample, when subjected to strict statistical analysis, will allow generalizations that are valid for the entire universe.

Because sampling tries to estimate the parameters of a universe from a limited part of the universe, it is possible for inaccurate results to occur. A major cause of inaccuracy arises from bias, which occurs when certain items have a much greater chance of being included in the sample than others have. Assuming that the researcher is not intentionally trying to influence the results of the study, bias is primarily caused by inadequate planning and improper data collecting, recording, or analyzing. These kinds of errors are not inherent in the sampling process and are referred to as nonsampling errors. Sampling errors are inherent to the process, because sample results may differ from the true characteristics of the universe due to chance selection alone. The effects of the sampling error can be estimated by statistical methods.

Collecting and Processing the Data

The primary and secondary data that have been gathered must be processed before a meaningful analysis of them can be carried out. This processing includes editing, coding, and tabulation. Editing involves preparing the data for tabulation first and inspecting the data-gathering forms for accuracy, completeness, and consistency.

The raw data from a research study generally must be organized to give it meaning. During editing, but before coding and tabulating the data, categories must be established to subdivide the data, summarizing the results and providing the basis for statistical manipulation. For example, in a customer survey the respondents may be grouped by characteristics such as age, income, occupation, number of children, geographical location, and so on. If the study were designed to determine frequency of store visits and if respondents had been asked the date of the last visit, an almost infinite number of different answers could occur. Without organizing the respondents' purchases into categories such as (1) within the last week; (2) within the last month; (3) more than one month ago; and (4) never, it would be almost impossible to get a meaningful picture of the results.

Coding involves preparing individual answers for transference to punch cards or other types of recording systems. Tabulating the results may be done either mechanically or by hand, depending on the quantity of the data, economic and time restraints, and the type of analysis to be performed.

Analyzing and Interpreting the Data

When the processing of the data has been completed, the difficult task of analysis and interpretation begins. Analysis and interpretation involves the reassembly of the data in a form that can be used to test the hypothesis. The methods by which data are to be analyzed should be specified as part of the research design.

Appropriate statistical methods exist to help the research analyst summarize the data, to determine how well sample results present estimates of the characteristics of the entire population; to see if significant differences exist among categories; and to determine if relationships between categories exist that will help explain differences. If the data is drawn from a sample, it is necessary to determine how close the sample results are likely to be to the actual characteristics of the population. Statistical methods allow the researcher to determine the level of confidence that one can have and if the sample result is a good estimate of the population. Certain statistical techniques determine if observed differences between categories are significant or if they could have occurred by chance, because of sampling variations.

One of the most important phases of data analysis is the attempt to determine relation-ships that help explain differences. For example, if there are differences in the frequency of customer store visits it may be important to know if these differences were associated with demographic or socioeconomic characteristics. Facts must be interpreted; they must be placed in the context of the research study, used to test the hypothesis, and compared to other known facts. What if a retailer found out that 20 percent of the households with children under six years of age shop at his store at least four times a year? This fact does not have much meaning until he asks if that is more or less than he expected (hypothesized) or until he compared the fact with past results or with competitors' performance.

The final report on the research findings should be organized and presented in a manner appropriate to the potential users. Reports should include a brief summary of the findings and recommendations—for a fast perusal—as well as a more detailed explanation of the procedures, findings, and conclusions if a thorough study of the results is desired.

Summary

This chapter has focused on some of the problems and solutions retailers face as they try to solve their information needs.

A retailer should be familiar with the sources and uses of research information in order to make good decisions. Using research data requires understanding the basic research processes. Information is vital for analysis of markets, products and services, location, pricing, and promotion. The research process involves many factors. A situation analysis is conducted to provide a basis for identification of the problem. Hypotheses, which are tentative statements describing cause-and-effect relationships or relationships between concepts, help guide research. The research design is the overall plan that specifies information that is needed and how the investigation will be conducted. Information may come from secondary sources, published information collected for some purpose other than the problem at hand, or from primary sources. Primary-source data is collected to solve a particular problem at hand.

Because of time, money, or physical constraints, information may be collected from a sample of the population rather than the whole. Collecting and processing the data requires careful control of the collection effort and strict adherence to the research design plan. The analysis and interpretation of the data involves reassembly of the data in a form that can be used to test the hypotheses. The ultimate value of the research effort depends on the final report, which must organize and present the research findings in a manner appropriate to the potential users.

Questions and Problems

1. *Visit several of your local retail stores. What evidence do you see of the collection of data at point-of-sale?*
2. *What purpose does market information serve?*
3. *As a researcher, would you rather be faced with a need for primary or secondary information? Why?*
4. *What is simple random sampling? How does a researcher use this concept?*
5. *What does interpretation of results involve? Does data analysis end here? Explain your answer.*

Situations and Activities

Discuss with a local retailer the problems she or he has in identifying the characteristics of present and potential customers. Develop a research design to determine their characteristics.

Tax World is a local financial consulting service. The basic objectives of the firm were stated as follows:

●To establish a lasting good relationship between the firm and the business community.
●To improve awareness of the consulting facility.

The basic problem Tax World presently has is determining if they are fulfilling specific financial needs in the business community. Which research design should be used to discover the business community's needs?

Steven Sienkiewicz, a retailing student, is conducting an exploratory study to determine the attitudes held by college students at Western State University toward the neighboring ski resorts. Approximately 100 skiers were interviewed on a Saturday afternoon. The results were tabulated, and the percentage responses to these questions were calculated. Sienkiewicz thought that the area's resorts would be interested in the results. He mailed them a report consisting of the percentage results and the purpose and conclusion of the study. Sienkiewicz hoped that this study would help him land a job in ski marketing. How reliable and valid do you feel such a survey would be? Why?

Bibliography

Boyd, H. W. and Westfall, R. *Marketing Research:* Text and Cases. Homewood, Ill.: Richard D. Irwin, Inc., 1972.

Kress, George. *The Business Research Process.* Fort Collins, Colo.: Kandid Publications, 1974.

five

STARTING A RETAIL STORE

9

Store Location

contents

behavioral objectives

At some time in their career, many retailers consider going into business for themselves. This chapter attempts to take the guesswork out of determining a suitable location for a retail business. When you know how to describe and analyze the factors involved in establishing a new retail business, you will have made significant strides toward going into business for yourself.

Upon completing this chapter, you will be able to do the following:
☐ Assess retail market opportunities in a community.
☐ Weigh the advantages of buying an existing retail business against starting a new one.
☐ Understand the consequences of affiliating with a franchise operation.
☐ Classify and give the significant characteristics of retail shopping centers.
☐ List factors to consider when choosing a location for a store.
☐ Have a basis for evaluating drive-in locations.
☐ Have a basis for evaluating shopping center locations.

The next two chapters could be subtitled "Being Your Own Boss," for they discuss the steps to take in going into a retail business and the pitfalls aspiring owners should avoid. The assumption made in these chapters is that you have decided to start out on your own.

It's a nice feeling to be in business for yourself. There are always pressures, but the pressures are tolerable if the business is successful. Unfortunately, too many retailers have failed in their businesses, and many more remain in business only by the skin of their teeth. These retailers may lack initiative, may not pay attention to business, or may be poor managers. However, many of them are unsuccessful only because they did not make the correct decisions when they started their businesses.

The decisions made prior to opening the store can spell success or failure for the business. If the correct decisions are made, it sometimes doesn't matter too much how poorly retailers subsequently operate the business. By the same token, retailers can be excellent merchants but if they err on the initial decisions, they may be destined for failure. The important decisions that must be made when starting a business are (1) making a proper assessment of market opportunities, (2) locating and selecting the site for the business, (3) making an estimate of the business's potential, and (4) determining the amount of capital necessary for operation.

Acquiring a Retail Business

Buying an existing retail business

A prospective retail owner can either buy an existing business or start one. If one elects to buy an existing one, he or she should be on the lookout for certain favorable factors. First, the merchandise inventory, fixtures, supplies, and equipment should already be on hand. This could save several months of searching time. Second, there should already exist a customer base. Sales volume and profits may already exist from which a new owner can share and meet the cash commitments. Third, an existing business can generally boast of a qualified

and trained sales force. Fourth, buying an existing business generally requires a lower cash outlay than starting an entirely new enterprise. It has been the authors' experience that negotiations for purchase of supplies, fixtures, equipment, merchandise, etc. can be more easily handled with one seller than with many. And fifth, buying an existing business instead of starting a new one cuts the competition by one. In other words the sales volume that can be earned in a given trade area need not be divided by one more entrant.

Let us share with you some examples of small retail businesses that have recently been for sale or are now operating successfully. In describing these situations, our purpose is to give you some preliminary insight into the sales and profit potential of small retail stores and the amount of capital required. In looking at these examples, you should be aware of an unusual situation—all the stores show profits.

Western wear shop. The community has 20,000 people, and this is the only western wear specialty store in a ten-mile radius. Last year sales were $145,000, and gross margin from operations was $58,000. Net profit, before taxes, was $25,000. The proprietor was asking $110,000, plus fixtures. The $110,000 represented total investment in inventory, as shown on the most recent financial statement.

Laundromat. The total price of the business was $38,000. A purchaser could make a down payment of $5000 and finance the remainder through the owner. The laundromat was in an established area and had been operating successfully for six years. It contained twenty-two washing machines and ten dryers. Total sales for last year were $17,000, of which $10,000 was net profit before taxes and after payments to a man who maintained the machines and serviced the building and facilities.

Family restaurant. The restaurant was operated by a man and wife and two employees. Last year's sales were $120,000 earning a net profit, before owners' salaries and taxes, of

$25,000. Owners were prepared to finance 50 percent over three years. The restaurant was open for one meal (lunch) five days a week; it specialized in barbecued foods and homemade pies.

Muffler shop. The shop was run by an owner-manager and three employees. Last year's sales were $100,000, and the gross margin was 70 percent, or $70,000. Expenses were $40,000, leaving a net profit, before owner's salary and taxes, of $30,000. The owner was not interested in selling the business but would consider (for a fee) helping someone else establish a similar business in another town. To do so would require a total investment of $65,000 (for land at $1.50 per square foot, building, equipment, and working capital).

Pet shop. The shop was run by an owner-manager and one part-time sales person. Last year's sales were $32,500 earning a net profit of $8300, before owner's salary and taxes. Total capital required to buy this business was $9100 (for inventory, $5100; fixtures, $1500; and working capital, $2500). The owner wanted nothing for the good will he had established. He would finance one-half of the capital, taking everything in the store as security.

Even though an existing business is bought, it can still be turned into a new and exciting place to shop, given new ideas, fixtures, and so on that a new owner can bring into the business. It is the possibility for profits compared to the investment that must be made that will influence the decision to buy an existing retail operation.

Starting a new retail business

On the other hand, starting a new business also has some advantages. First, you're not paying for someone's mistakes. Poor merchandise, outdated fixtures and equipment, and customer ill will are risks that do not have to be borne. And second, a new owner does not have to pay for the good will of the seller of an existing business. Good will is the difference between the tangible assets of a business and the seller's asking price. For example, the good will being asked below is $10,000.

Assets:

Inventory	$30,000
Equipment and fixtures	20,000
Total Assets	$50,000
Goodwill	10,000
Asking Price	$60,000

Paying a price for good will may be desirable if it can be concluded that the seller's customer following is important to the business. Usually, however, good will is over valued and of uncertain benefit to the new owner.

Affiliating with a franchise

Some prospective retailers choose to acquire a retail business by affiliating themselves with a franchise operation. If properly used, franchising is a way for them to take advantage of the managerial knowledge of others and in some cases to aid them overcome any lack of initial capital. Although franchise operations are not new, they have expanded greatly since the middle of the 1950's. By 1974 some 398,924 franchised retail outlets had sales of $150,891,438. Although franchising is responsible for a major segment of America's retail sales, there is considerable confusion as to what franchising is and what it does.

Franchising defined. A franchising operation is a legal contractual relationship between a franchisor (the company offering the franchise) and a franchisee (the individual who will own the business). The terms and conditions of the contracts vary widely, but usually the franchisor offers to or is obligated to maintain a continuing interest in the business of the franchisee in such areas as site location, management training, financing, marketing, record keeping, and promotion. In addition, the franchisor offers the use of a trade name, standard products and services, store motif, standardized operating procedures, and a prescribed territory. Also, the franchisee can benefit in the area of sales promotion through the aid of national advertising by the franchisor. To complement this national advertising, the individual franchisee may advertise on the local level. Many franchisors will furnish advertising and promotional material to the franchisee for local programs, agree to pay a portion of the advertising expenses, or provide advice on local sales promotion. Given these many benefits, an investor desiring to enter the retail field with less capital and/or experience would have an excellent opportunity to succeed in a self-owned franchise without as much chance for failure due to mis-management.

The franchisee, in return, agrees to operate under the conditions set forth by the franchisor. Such an agreement prevents the quality of services or products from becoming substandard according to the requirements set by the franchisor. Consumers therefore are assured of receiving products or services at uniform prices and of consistent quality, both of which maintain and increase goodwill for the franchisor. For the help and services provided, the franchisee is expected to make a capital investment in the business. In addition, the franchisee agrees to pay a commission on all of the franchisee's sales and/or agrees to buy from the franchisor all product needs. In this way, the franchisor will benefit in expansion through the use of individual investor's (franchisee's) capital; and the franchisee will be able to successfully follow his or her own interest and initiative in establishing an otherwise unobtainable retail outlet.

Franchises have penetrated virtually every retail market, from auto parts, convenient stores, business aids and services, campgrounds, home improvement services, to fast-food restaurants. An example of a typical franchise and its operations is Randall's Formalwear. This franchise specializes in the rental and sale of men's formal wear. The stores carry the best and most stylish lines manufactured for formal weddings, parties, dances, and other social functions. Randall's helps in coordination of wedding attire and relieves the bride and groom of all detail in planning proper dress. Also, all sizes and styles of shirts, cuff links, ties, and so on are available either for sale or rental.

Randall's offers continuous assistance and research in the latest marketing trends, sales techniques, and style changes. Continuous assistance is given franchisees through bulletins, trade journals, sales seminars, and style shows. The initial investment of about $30,000 covers leasehold improvements, furniture and fixtures, training, and an initial inventory valued at $16,000. The inventory should carry the franchisee through the first year of operation, and continued inventory is purchased from the parent company's selection. In addition to the $30,000 initial investment, the company recommends $5,000 working capital. (Table 9.1 shows additional franchise operations.)

Assessing Market Opportunities

Whether buying an existing business or starting a new business, a prospective retailer must make a careful assessment of the market opportunities. It doesn't matter how good the location is or how well the store is operated if people don't want the product. Although this seems obvious, businesses are often begun because a prospective owner who wants to run a particular type of business does not seriously consider whether there is a real need for the business.

It is no small task to determine whether a need exists for a particular type of business, and it is probably even more difficult to gauge the magnitude of the need. The following are some useful approaches that a prospective owner may take in assessing market opportunities:

1. Pay attention to customer complaints and statements that suggest there is a lack of particular retail services in a market.
2. Look for retailers who are making large profits in a particular kind of business; this may mean that there is a need for additional outlets.

Table 9.1. Franchise Operations

Operation	Training	Services Provided	Investment	Other
Kopy Kat				
Printing service Collating Folding Addressing Mailing	Intensive training	Site selection assistance Protected territory Trademark Financial guidance Advertising and promotion program Grand opening kit Idea exchange seminars	Total of $29,900 or $14,900 down with balance financed	Supplies such as bond paper, cover stock chemicals, ink, envelopes purchased from Kopy Kat headquarters
Arnold Palmer Cleaning Center				
Dry cleaning	Training in all phases of package dry cleaning operation Assists with selection and training of personnel	Site selection assistance along with assistance in selecting machinery Package installation supervision Planned advertising programs utilizing materials furnished with franchise	Total from $18,000 to $60,000; $3,600 to $12,000 down with financing available plus enough capital for first few months expenses including rent, freight, wages, supplies, and so on	"Big name umbrella" Store motif of unusual country club decor
7-Eleven Stores				
Convenience food store (2,400 square-foot stores carrying a limited line)	Provided	Complete accounting service Insurance Merchandising Advertising and financial counseling programs	Total of $14,000; franchisor will finance part in some instances (operating capital not included)	Stores are basically franchised to husband and wife teams; no previous grocery experience required
Mr. Steak				
Full menu family restaurant	Four weeks in home office Two weeks in field Continuing	Site selection Advertising programs Equipment for lease Complete computerized accounting	Total of $36,300 Initial cash variable Financing available Variable does not include working capital	Standardized physical plant and menu Supplies purchased from headquarters

Source: Adapted from *Franchise Journal,* Volume 3, Nos. 2, 4, 7, 9, and franchisor materials.

3. Have knowledge of population shifts and spending patterns. For example, in the 1970's there is an explosive growth of young families, an increase in the number of people who do not have children, an increase in the number of senior citizens, and increased spending power among people under thirty.
4. Watch for new businesses based on new ideas, and consider copying them; the second bite of an apple may still be good.
5. Query bankers, Chamber of Commerce officials, real estate people, retailers, and so on for the businessman's view of the market needs in retailing.

Location Selection

Retail stores should locate where the market opportunities seem best. In selecting a location one should try to find those cities, areas, or types of location which seem to offer an adequate amount of traffic. After a general location has been identified as satisfactory, a specific site needs to be chosen. For some retail businesses, such as clothing stores, there may be only one or two desirable sites in the trade area. (A trade area is an area within which a given establishment can economically serve potential buyers of a good or service.) For other types of retail businesses, such as motorcycle shops, there may be a large number of good sites available. In fact, there is less chance of making a mistake when choosing a site for a motorcycle business than for a clothing store because the site is not as important to the success of the motorcycle business. This chapter discusses aspects of choosing a location while the next chapter discusses choosing a specific site within a location.

Guidelines for selecting a location

There are five guidelines which can aid in the intelligent selection of a location.[1] Care

---

[1] William Applehaum, "Guidelines for a Store—Location Strategy Study," *Journal of Marketing*, Vol. 34, No. 4, American Marketing Association, October, 1966, pp. 42—45.

should be exercised by conducting a thorough study before a location is chosen. Because of population shifts, changing competitive conditions, evolving customer spending patterns and habits, and altering transportation influences, retail location evaluations are a must. Nothing is more frustrating to a retailer or harder on the pocketbook than being situated where nobody comes to see you.

Selecting an appropriate location for a retail store is serious business. Every retail store strives for its differential advantage; for some stores it is price, for others it is promotional expertise, and for still others it is the nature of the store's services. But for all retail stores the appropriate location is a unique asset. Once a site has been selected it cannot be occupied by another. A site, if properly chosen, will be an added differential advantage. Other elements of the retailing mix can be copied, but not the location.

1. *Define the Objective.* A suitable location cannot be selected without first determining the firm's objectives. Firms that wish to emphasize price appeal need not command as good a location as firms that emphasize quality. Firms seeking a branch location, have different considerations than those moving into a community for the first time. What constitutes a suitable location may also be influenced by a prospective owner's non-business objectives such as the desire to reside in an area with good schools, selecting a progressive retail community, and availability of cultural and sporting events.

2. *Analyze the Economic Base.* The economy of a given area under consideration for location of a retail business should provide long-range opportunities. The number, type, trends, and stability of industries that might effect business in the market area need to be considered. Employment, income, retail sales and expenditure figures all provide information from which the economic stability of the area can be ascertained.

3. *Study the Population and Its Characteristics.* Factors such as the composition, growth, wealth, mode of living and character of consumers residing in the market area should be studied. Where consumers live, how they get around, and whether their numbers are increasing also suggest some of the dynamic characteristics of the population. Some firms even construct maps to visually portray where certain types of customers reside. City planning commissions can also make these maps available to prospective firms.

4. *Ascertain the Environmental Conditions.* Adequacy of banking facilities, well planned road networks, intelligent land use planning, and the general or overall characteristic of retail business centers say much about the environmental conditions of an area. These can have significant influences that affect customers and business firms.

5. *Make an Inventory of Competition.* Competition exists when more than one of the same type of business compete for the same patronage. In one way a firm might like to be the only one of its type in a given market area, but there are also occasions when good strong competition enhances the overall business potential of a given area. Locations where strong competition exists, but which provide ways for a firm to differentiate itself from its competition, offer a good potential for sales. As mentioned above, maps may also be developed to show retail locations of competitors.

To obtain information important to satisfying these guidelines, a prospective store owner needs to investigate sources and question people who know the community. For example, visits to the local Chamber of Commerce; asking for advice from local industrial development groups; talking to bankers, real estate brokers, newspaper editors, and other businessmen; checking secondary sources, such as government publications, for statistical information; and visiting shopping center developers are all ways of gaining this information.

Kinds of retail locations

There are six basic types of retail locations:

Central business district. This is the downtown area of a shopping district.

Secondary shopping area. This area is similar to the central business district. The same types of stores are found in the secondary shopping area, that are found in the central business district, but they are usually smaller and there are probably fewer of them.

String street development. These are minor shopping districts located along a fairly well-traveled thoroughfare.

Neighborhood area. This area contains a group of convenience stores located close to a residential area.

Free standing location. As the term suggests, this store stands by itself, removed from other retail stores.

Shopping center. A shopping center is a cluster of retail stores located in a suburban residential neighborhood. The stores handle a wide variety of convenience and shopping goods similar to the goods found in the central business district but almost always on a smaller scale.

Each kind of retail location has resulted from the needs of the particular market it was designed to serve. Consumers' needs for convenience and/or comparison in shopping, the extent of the purchasing power in a market area, and the transportation facilities available, all have led to the development of different kinds of retail locations.

Drive-in and Shopping Center Locations

Of particular interest to today's retailers are drive-in locations and shopping center locations.

San Francisco's Embarcadero Center is an example of downtown redevelopment. The three towers hold offices, and the landscaped shopping areas at the base of each tower contain numerous restaurants, shops, and services.
Photo courtesy of Embarcadero Center

An innovative approach to a shopping area. Shopping area layouts which show variations in their design and are attractive make shopping a fun and pleasant experience.

Photo courtesy of the San Francisco Convention & Visitors Bureau

Drive-in locations

Drive-in locations are selected to accommodate the customer who travels by automobile. These locations are usually positioned along or beside a heavy traffic arteries. Drive-ins that are quick-service operations such as Photo-Mat stores, require a smaller amount of space than park-and-shop stores where the customer leaves the car and enters the store. In both cases, however, the total volume of passing traffic is important to the sales potential of drive-in retailers. The greater the density of traffic, the greater the amount of business to be derived from this traffic. An automobile traffic count (as explained in Chapter 10) is therefore absolutely necessary to identify suitable locations for drive-ins.

Traffic flow may be described in terms of why a customer is making the trip, whether it is to or from work, for shopping, or for pleasure or recreation. A work-trip customer may drop off cleaning on the way to work and stop for gas on the way home. In this situation, drive-in cleaners would profit from positions on the inbound side of the street while the service station operators would do better on the outbound side. Since customers do not like crossing lanes of traffic, such positioning would encourage more sales from those customers going to work, and for the other from customers who are going home.

Customers on a shopping trip are more easily stopped if a location is positioned along the righthand side of a thoroughfare. This is particularly true if a drive-in is located between the customer's place of residence and a major shopping area. If there are a number of stores located in the general vicinity where the drive-in is considering locating, it should be on the same side of the street as those stores. This is usually a good indication of the preferred side of the street. To attract recreation or pleasure trip shoppers locations along a heavily traveled artery are best. The location should be convenient to enter and leave, and adjacent to the incoming traffic. (See Table 9.2.)

Shopping centers

Until recently, the central business district was the core for all shopping in an area. Because retail shopping is done fairly near the householder's place of residence, while a community was relatively small the largest proportionate share of shopping was done in the downtown area. Thus, the central business district contained the largest concentration of department stores, clothing stores, jewelry stores, variety stores, and shoe stores within an area. It provided for large-scale comparative shopping, and it offered both convenience goods and exclusive luxury products. The

---

Table 9.2. Useful Points for Evaluating Drive-in Locations

1. Fast traffic or congested areas do not produce drop-in traffic for the drive-in retailer. Traffic averaging 35 to 45 miles an hour is preferable. A feeder location will produce more potential customers than an arterial location consisting of fast, undelayed traffic.
2. A stop sign slows traffic. Thus a drive-in location before or after a stop sign will usually produce more customers at an intersection location.
3. A street where crossover is possible increases the number of directions from which a site may be approached. If the traffic speed or congestion is not great, a location on such a street is preferred. However, the lack of crossover should not be detrimental if there is a high traffic count of desirable traffic.
4. Within the community, sites at the intersection of two or more streets may be classified as far-corner, near-corner, or triangular. An inside location is a site between the corner locations. The sites at the intersection are preferred as the traffic may enter from three or four directions.
5. A far-corner site is preferred over a near-corner site as it provides greater visibility. A near-corner site is preferred when a right-hand turn is made at the intersection.
6. The quicker the customer recognizes a site as that of a drive-in retailer, the greater the chance of his stopping. Thus, a drive-in site should have adequate frontage—from 100 feet for a park-and-shop drive-in to 200 feet for a quick-service drive-in. On a highway location, the frontage should be quite wide—300 feet or more.
7. The site should be deep enough to allow adequate parking for peak customer use. If possible, a drive-around exit should be provided to service the building and allow the customer ease of exit.
8. A drive-in site should be easy to enter and to leave. Ideally, the site should be free from curbs, allowing entry along the complete frontage. Curb cuts of twenty or more feet are desirable if complete cuts are not allowed.
9. Parking space should be sufficient to allow ease of parking, turning around, and backing.
10. Zoning regulations should permit the sign to be seen. It is preferable to have the sign hanging over the lot line. Trees, bushes, and other visual barriers should be removed. Where there is more than one drive-in, the sign should be placed so that it is distinct from the others. If the lot is adequately wide, this is usually possible.
11. Do not locate where traffic congestion may affect the accessibility of the site.
12. Avoid locations adjacent to very fast, undelayed traffic.
13. Avoid locating in a drive-in "jungle," unless the site is adequate from the standpoint of width and depth.
14. Avoid areas that have a great deal of competition for customers from the same flow of traffic.
15. Most drive-ins cannot exist primarily on highway traffic. Locate where the store can also feed on considerable local traffic.
16. Avoid a location on the inside of a curve, especially on a highway. Such a site lacks adequate visibility. Otherwise, a curve location is acceptable, except on a twisting road.
17. Do not locate on a hillside. If such a location is considered, it should be on a slight upgrade lest the drive-in be obscured.
18. Do not locate too close to the road; it may be widened later.
19. To serve transient traffic, the site should be on the right-hand side entering rather than leaving town.

Source: John E. Mertes, "Site Opportunities for the Small Retailer," *Journal of Retailing*, Vol. 39, Fall 1963, p. 39.

downtown area also met the needs of out-of-town shoppers.

Unfortunately, many downtown areas have deteriorated, growing old without being renovated. Traffic congestion has become intense; and the lack of adequate parking facilities has made shopping downtown difficult. Coupled with rising rental costs, satisfactory locations have been increasingly hard to justify. Unless downtown areas have had an aggressive program to cure some of these ills, retailers have begun looking elsewhere to locate their businesses.

Some downtown areas are making significant strides in combating the trend of retailers moving away from downtown locations. Increasing numbers do not allow automobile traffic into the center of the town, but provide ample parking space on the periphery. Others go one step further, plant trees, provide park benches, standardize and modernize store fronts, and generally follow the layout formats of the shopping centers. Still others are encouraging the building of office buildings, condominiums, restaurants, tourist attractions, and similar things which are designed to increase shopping traffic.

On the other hand, as communities have grown in size, and although a great deal of shopping continues to be done in the central business district, as large numbers of people began to move to the suburbs, and as the rental costs for downtown locations began to skyrocket, other shopping districts were developed. These shopping districts, called shopping centers, have drawn trade away from the central business district because of their accessibility, good parking facilities, and bright, clean stores.

Basically, there are four kinds of planned shopping centers.[2]

---

[2] Homer Hoyt, "Classification and Significant Characteristics of Shopping Centers," *The Appraisal Journal,* April, 1958, pp. 214—222. See also Hoyt's article "Appraisal of Shopping Centers," in *Encyclopedia of Real Estate Appraising,* Englewood Cliffs, New Jersey: Prentice-Hall, 1959, pp. 281—295.

1. Large regional centers contain at least one department store of 100,000 square feet or more. This is the principal store, and it is supplemented by numerous women's and men's apparel stores, shoe stores, household appliance stores, furniture stores, drugstores, and supermarkets. Such centers have a total store area of 250,000 to 1,000,000 square feet on a 35 to 100 acre site. A trade area of 200,000 people is required to support this type of center.

2. The community center usually has a junior department store, such as J. C. Penney or Montgomery Wards, as its principal tenant. This main store usually has 25,000 or more square feet of floor space. Supermarkets, drugstores, variety stores, and some apparel stores are found in the center, which has a total store area of 100,000 to 400,000 square feet. The site is 15 to 40 acres. A trade area of around 100,000 people is required to support a center of this type.

3. The large neighborhood center has as its principal unit a variety store, such as Woolworth or Kresge, which takes up an area of 10,000 to 20,000 square feet. The total store area is 50,000 to 100,000 square feet on a site of 10 to 20 acres. A supermarket, a drugstore, and local convenience stores are typical. A trade area of 35,000 people is required to support such a center.

4. The neighborhood center has a supermarket of 20,000 to 30,000 square feet as its largest unit. The total store area is 50,000 square feet or more and usually includes a drugstore and local convenience stores. Such a center can be supported by 5,000 families, or around 17,500 persons.

As we have suggested, accessibility, parking, and pleasant surroundings have contributed to the success of shopping centers. Accessibility is usually measured in terms of driving time. A general rule of thumb suggests that large centers should locate in a market area so as to be in a position to attract customers from a distance of thirty minutes driving time; community centers should attract customers from a distance of twenty minutes driving time; and neighborhood centers should attract customers from a distance of ten to fifteen minutes driving time.

Parking, more than any other factor, has been instrumental in causing the demise of downtown business shopping areas. People will not tolerate the inconvenience of scarce or expensive parking. Shopping center developers have realized this and have been careful to plan for an adequate number of parking spaces. In general, shopping center developers plan for 80 percent of the total land space to be devoted to parking area.

Shopping centers are, in most cases, new and exciting architectural forms. They employ the latest in store design to provide customers with conveniences. Air conditioning, enclosed malls, and the interstore coordination of merchandise offerings are only three of the conveniences that make shopping centers pleasant shopping places. Because of attractive features, the prices in shopping center locations may be somewhat higher than in other retail locations, but they are usually lower than in downtown locations. In general, the annual rent paid in a shopping center location averages $6.00 per square foot of selling area. Even this figure varies with how earnest the leasor is in attracting the leasee to the center, space location within the center, and so on.

In selecting a particular shopping center in which to locate, careful advance planning and studies of customer buying habits and motivations should be undertaken. In particular, will the center attract the type of customers who will buy the kind of merchandise an individual retailer leasee is selling? Is the space one is to occupy in the main flow of traffic? And is the concept of the center appealing enough to draw customers to it? Other things to look for in selecting a shopping center location appear in Table 9.3.

Summary

Retailers need the most advantageous locations for their stores. The problem is finding the best one, for to err is to jeopardize the store's potential for profit. In choosing a location, many factors need to be considered: what types of customers one wants to attract; how many potential customers are there, and what are their buying habits; how progressive is the community and its retail centers; and what are the competitive characteristics of the area.

Of particular prominence in today's retailing scene are drive-in type locations and shopping center locations. Although both depend on traffic flow, drive-ins require high traffic density to succeed. Shopping centers, on the other hand, are usually organized to appeal to certain types of customers. The numbers of these customers are of most concern to retailers in deciding whether to locate in a given shopping center.

Questions and Problems

1. Choose one kind of retail business, and describe the factors that make your town a favorable or unfavorable place in which to locate the business.
2. Describe what you believe to be the significant trends in selecting retail locations.

Situations and Activities

You are considering opening a bridal shop. You hope to offer your customers merchandise offerings including gowns for the bride and bridesmaids, bridal accessories, tux rentals, and wedding invitations. In addition, you will offer free wedding consulting service. You have two sites from which to choose. One is in a regional shopping center located in the popular end of town. It would rent for $10 a square foot for 800 square feet. The other is located at

Table 9.3. Check Points for Evaluating Shopping Center Locations

1. Who is the shopping center developer?
2. How long has he been in the business of developing real estate?
3. What are his financial resources?
4. With whom has he arranged for the financing of the center?
5. What is his reputation for integrity?
6. Who performed the economic analysis? Does the report cover both favorable and unfavorable factors?
7. What experience has the economic consultant had?
8. Has an architectural firm been retained to plan the center?
9. Has the architect designed other centers? Have they been successful from a retailing standpoint?
10. Who will build the center? The developer? An experienced contractor? An inexperienced contractor?
11. Has the developer had experience with other centers?
12. What is, or will be, the quality of management for the center?
13. Will the management have merchandising and promotion experience? (Some developers are large retailers rather than real estate operators.)
14. What per cent of the leases have been signed? Are they on a contingent basis?
15. Has every facet of the lease been carefully studied?
16. Is the ratio of parking area to selling area 3-to-1 or more?
17. Has sufficient space (40 feet) been assigned to each car?
18. Is the parking space designed so that the shopper does not walk more than 300 to 350 feet from the farthest spot to the store?
19. What is the angle of parking space? (Ninety

degrees provides the best capacity and circulation.)
20. What is the planned or actual car turnover? (3.3 cars per parking space per day is the average.)
21. Is the number of total spaces adequate for the planned business volume? (Too many spaces make the center look dead; too few openly invite competition around the center.)
22. Does the parking scheme distribute the cars so as to favor no one area?
23. Is there an adequate number of ingress/egress roads in proper relationship with the arrangement of parking spaces?
24. For the larger centers, a ring road is preferable. Is this the case?
25. Is the site large enough for the type of center?
26. Is the size sufficiently dominant to forestall the construction of similar shopping centers nearby?
27. Is the center of regular shape? If not, does the location of the buildings minimize the disadvantage of the site's shape?
28. Is the site sufficiently deep? (A depth of at least 400 feet is preferred; if less, the center may look like a strip development.)
29. Is the site level? Is it on well-drained land?
30. Does the center face north and/or east?
31. Can the center be seen from a distance?
32. Are any structures, such as a service station, located in the parking area? (If so, do they impede the site's visibility?)
33. Is the site a complete unit? (A road should not pass through the site.)
34. Are the buildings set far enough back on the site that the entire area may be seen?
35. Are all the stores readily accessible to each other, with none having an advantage?

Source: Mertes, "Site Oportunities . . ." p. 44.

the other end of town in a convenience shopping center, in a less populated area renting for $5 a square foot for 800 square feet. With only this information available from which to make a decision, which site would you choose?

You are the owner of a small shop in a college town of about 25,000 population. There are 7,000 students attending the college. Your shop sells only submarine (sometimes called

hoagie) sandwiches. Business has been fairly good, but you feel that because you offer only take-out service, you are missing an opportunity to do more business. Therefore, you are considering expanding your business to take in the vacated store next to yours. Then, you could provide your customers with tables and chairs. What should you take into consideration as you make your decision? What alternative actions might increase business?

Indicate, in order of your preference, four franchise businesses which you feel would have good potential in your community.

Where would each franchise be best located? What things did you take into consideration as you made your selection?

Bibliography

Applehaum, William. "Methods for Determining Store Trade Areas, Market Penetration, and Potential Sales." *Journal of Marketing Research,* Vol. 3, May, 1966, pp. 127—141.

Cohen, Saul B., and Applehaum, William. "Evaluating Store Sites and Determining Rents." *Economic Geography,* Vol. 36, January, 1960, pp. 1—35.

"Food Franchise Study." *Franchise Journal,* Vol. 3, No. 7, July, 1970, p. 42.

Hoyt, Homer. "Classification and Significant Characteristics of Shopping Centers." *The Appraisal Journal* April, 1958, pp. 214—222.

Hoyt, Homer, "Classification and Significant Characteristics of Shopping Centers." *The Appraisal Journal* (April, 1958), pp. 214—222.

Real Estate Research Corporation. *Retail Location Analysis Manual and Retailing in Low-Income Areas.* Chicago: Economic Development Corporation, 1970.

Sales Management: Survey of Buying Power. New York: Bill Brothers Publishing Corporation. Published annually.

Scott, Peter. *Geography and Retailing.* Chicago: Aldine, 1970.

Shulman, David. "Dry Cleaning Franchises." *Franchise Journal,* Vol. 3, No. 4 April, 1970, p. 23.

U.S. Department of Commerce. *Census of Retail Trades.* Washington, D.C.. U.S. Government Printing Office, 1968.

U.S. Department of Commerce. Small Business Administration. *Starting and Managing Series.* Washington, D.C.: U.S. Government Printing Office.

10

Setting Up the Business

contents

behavioral objectives

Financial planning is important to starting and staying in the retail business. Putting together such a financial plan anticipates how many dollar sales you can do, what your costs will be, and how you will finance your business. When you know how to judge the monetary consequences of your decisions, you'll substantially reduce the risk of being in business on your own.

Upon completing this chapter, you will be able to do the following:
☐ Measure market and sales potential for a retail business.
☐ Calculate a break-even point that is useful in evaluating a site.
☐ Determine the capital requirements necessary for a new business or the value of an existing business.
☐ Discuss where a prospective retail store owner can get money to go into business.
☐ Determine one's ability to pay back a business loan.

In Chapter 9 we introduced the topic of going into business for yourself. One requisite for success emphasized was choosing the proper location; choice of an area, selection of a city, or type of location within a city. In this regard guidelines were provided to aid in making a wise decision and descriptions were provided of different types of retail locations.

This chapter takes the process of going into a retail business one step further—selecting a specific site in which to locate. The decision to locate at a specific site is an extremely important one. Because even locating on the wrong side of the street can mean the difference between the success or failure of some businesses. There are two basic considerations important to determining whether a particular site is acceptable. The first involves considering qualitative-type factors. Qualitative factors include the way customers shop for the goods to be handled by the store, the nature and kind of competition near the site, the acceptability of the site facilities, and the general economic climate in the market area. The second involves determining whether a site is acceptable by considering quantitative factors. Quantitative factors include measurements of the market potential and arriving at a sales forecast.

A Case Study in Site Selection

To put site selection into its proper perspective, let us review the efforts of one man to establish a full-line fabric shop. After we have described the situation, we will analyze some of the qualitative factors that he might have considered as he was making his decision to locate his store.

Mr. Royer was a man of about forty years of age. After graduation from college twenty years ago, he had first worked as a management trainee in a fairly large department store; subsequently, he became a buyer and, later, a merchandise manager in the same store. Most of his merchandising activities had been devoted to soft lines. Recently, Mr. Royer had been feeling disenchanted with his job, espe-

cially since a new management group had come into the department store. He felt that if he were ever to go into business for himself, he should do so now. He selected the fabric business, because this seemed to complement his experience, and the present and future in fabric seemed to be good.

Mr. Royer never considered relocating to a new town. He was well established in the small western community in which he was living; his children liked the public schools they attended; and he had a fine, comfortable home. His basic decision, then, involved the selection of sites for his business. Predictably, there were none available that filled all of the requirements he had for his fabric store. Nevertheless, two sites seemed suitable enough for him to conduct a detailed investigation into their applicability. Both of these sites were in the downtown area.

The diagram in Figure 10.1 shows the layout of the downtown area. In essence, the downtown area was composed of a shopping district five blocks long. As one would expect, general merchandise stores as well as selected parasitic stores (retail stores which depend upon other stores to generate traffic for them; for example, shoe stores) were located there. The two sites on the diagram that were available to Mr. Royer are designated "1" and "2." The types of stores surrounding each location are also shown. Most of the stores in the downtown area had been there for some time, were well established, and as yet had experienced no real competitive pressure from the shopping centers being built in the outlying sections of the city.

Site 1 was situated in the heart of the downtown shopping district. The rent was $600 per month or 6 percent of gross sales, whichever was larger, for a space with a 20-foot front and a 72-foot depth. A three year lease was required, and the lease contained an option to rent for another five years. The store had previously been occupied by a successful clothing store, which had recently moved to larger quarters.

The second site was on the edge of the shopping district. Its area was 25 by 30 feet,

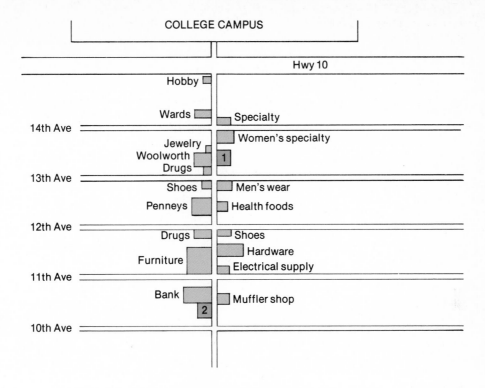

Figure 10.1. A downtown area.

Qualitative factors

Mr. Royer, in selecting a suitable site for his fabric store, should have considered the following questions:

1. How do consumers shop for this kind of merchandise? Who are the consumers, and what or who influences their buying decisions?
2. What is the nature of the stores adjacent to the specific site under consideration?
3. Will there be enough floor space to operate the kind of business desired?
4. What are the lease arrangements for the land and building?
5. Does the site possess ample traffic flow for the kind of business contemplated?
6. Can the business afford the rent?

and it rented for $250 per month. Most recently, the store had been occupied by a custom tailor shop, and the owner had retired early because of ill health. In this site Mr. Royer could obtain a two and one-half year lease, which he could break if his venture did not work out as planned. Although the site was two blocks away from the heart of the downtown area, Mr. Royer felt that he could draw trade to his store by advertising.

Regardless of the site he chose, Mr. Royer planned to emphasize value at low prices. To keep operating costs low, he was going to restrict service offerings. However, he did plan to stock a fairly complete selection of merchandise, consisting primarily of nationally advertised brands of cottons, woolens, and other fabrics, along with domestics. Merchandise was to be of medium and high-medium quality. At the present time, there were no other specialty fabric shops in the downtown area.

Probably the most fundamental consideration in choosing a site is to question customer motivation and customer buying habits. Thus, Mr. Royer should have first considered how customers shop for fabrics. Customers (usually women) buy fabrics to save money, because they want to make original clothes, because they enjoy sewing, and because they want quality products often associated with home sewing. When buying fabrics, consumers will use one of two basic approaches. The first approach is to buy fabrics on an impulse basis. Thus, a woman might buy a fabric on the spur of the moment, because the pattern is exciting, or because she can imagine someone wearing a new blouse made from the fabric, or because the fabric is on sale. In any event, the importance of this from the standpoint of site selection is that stores wishing to get as much of the impulse trade as possible should locate in the busiest area, next to other stores that sell similar goods. In other words impulse purchases of one type of good can take place while the customer is actually shopping for another.

There are other customers who shop for fabrics by going to one store that gives them the highest quality and the most complete selection or the best price. These customers deliberately try to find such a store. If there is ample parking space and if the service is good, they are willing to make the special effort to shop there. Under these conditions, the choice of a site is less important than it was under the conditions of impulse shopping. Customers lost because there is less walk-in traffic are compensated for by more regular, steady customers. Furthermore, there is lower rent for the store in the less central site. Therefore, from the standpoint of customer shopping characteristics, sites 1 and 2 may be equally satisfactory. It depends on which customers Mr. Royer wanted to attract.

The second question concerns the nature of the adjacent stores. Compatible stores are stores that complement one another so that customers of one store are also customers of another. Of course, merchants like to have customers who shop at a neighboring store also shop at their store. In our example this would happen if the stores near the fabric shop were primarily general merchandise stores; it would probably not happen if the neighboring stores were primarily eating establishments.

Thus, for Mr. Royer, Site 1, in which neighboring stores sold shoes, general merchandise lines, and clothing, had compatible stores. Site 2 did not have compatible stores; the neighbors were a bank and a muffler shop. Bank customers are usually hurried businessmen and housewives, who probably would not spend time looking at fabrics on a trip to the bank. A person who needs a muffler is unlikely to be interested in fabrics. Muffler shop customers are usually men who, as a rule, have little interest in fabrics. Furthermore, the smell of grease, the noise of automobiles, and the general appearance of a garage are not compatible with fabric merchandising.

Competition attracts trade. People will make a special effort to shop in an area when they know that several stores handling competitive lines are located near one another. Competitive stores located in the same area may not merely divide up the traffic, but may, in fact, increase the total traffic. Enlightened merchants, for example, choose to locate next to such formidable competitors as Sears and Penney's because these stores draw a large amount of traffic. There is no room in retailing for people who are afraid of competition. In this case, Site 1 has the advantage.

The third question to be answered involves adequacy of floor space. Some retailers mistakenly rent facilities that are too large for them and, as a result, have bare shelves, whereas other retailers rent facilities that are too small and, thus, cannot stock enough merchandise to meet customer expectations. Stores of the first type look dead and unsuccessful. Stores of the second type look cluttered.

Neither of the sites considered by Mr. Royer offered an abundance of floor space. Certainly, at Site 2 it would have been extremely difficult for Mr. Royer to do what he said he wanted to do—offer fabrics, patterns, and sewing notions. Considering the need for service counters and stock areas, a 25 by 30 foot store is small.

The fourth question concerns a lease. Some prospective businessmen rent without a lease because they consider it an advantage. They feel that if their business fails, a no-lease agreement eliminates liability for rental payments. However, the other side of this coin is that if a merchant can break a rental agreement, so can a renter. If a merchant who had bought store equipment, had improved store facilities, and had developed a loyal following were asked to vacate the premises, he would have been well advised to have signed a lease.

There is probably protection for both parties in entering into a formal lease agreement. Site 1 called for such an agreement. It would have been to Mr. Royer's advantage to ask for a lease in Site 2.

The fifth question involves traffic flow. To attract business to an out-of-the-way location, a merchant may have to spend a large amount of money on advertising. Therefore, a satisfactory traffic flow is desirable. What is satisfactory depends on the type of store being operated and the customers the merchant wants to attract.

Traffic flow is measured in terms of foot traffic or automobile traffic. Obviously, stores such as automobile dealers are interested in auto traffic, whereas stores such as clothing stores are interested in foot traffic. Frequently, city planning offices have automobile traffic counts for particular points in cities (see Figure 10.2). These figures are readily made available to retailers.

Foot traffic, or pedestrian counts are usually made by merchants themselves. The usual procedure in making such counts is to count the number of pedestrians who pass a store site for, say, five minutes during each business hour. These counts are totaled and the totals analyzed in terms of the quantity and composition of the traffic. Traffic counts provide a strong indication of the volume of sales to be derived from a site.

Chain stores, often blessed with data experience from their many outlets, can use traffic counts to forecast sales volume. If they have at their disposal the following information, a forecast can be made with reasonable accuracy:

Number of pedestrians (cars) passing location (daily)

Percentage of passers-by who stop and go in

Average dollar sale of those who go in (purchasers and non purchasers)

For example:

No. of daily pedestrians (500) × % who go in (10%) × average sale ($4.70) × no. of working days (307) = annual sales forecast ($72,145).

In measuring traffic flow, it is also important to determine whether the traffic is on "your side" of the street or the "other side." Surprisingly enough, customers will not cross the street to shop at a particular store if ample opportunities exist on the other side of the street. In addition, a site on the "other side" of the street may require the shopper to cross against the traffic.

On balance, it seems better to choose a well-located site even if this means paying a higher rent. Therefore, if Mr. Royer's business were able to support a rent of $600 or more, Site 1 was a better choice. If Mr. Royer had chosen Site 2, he would have had to offer a more complete line than his competitors, more services, lower prices, or any number of other things to attract people to his site.

The sixth, and last, question concerns rent. Although no hard and fast rule exists, most retail stores are ill advised to pay more than 5 percent of sales for rent, and some should pay less (see Table 10.1).

The typical methods of quoting a rent to a prospective renter are by basing the rent on a fixed amount per square foot of floor space or a fixed amount per square foot of floor space plus a percentage of gross sales. In a shopping center location, rent may also include, in addition to the charge per square foot, a charge for parking spaces assigned to the renter and a promotional fee to be used by the center.

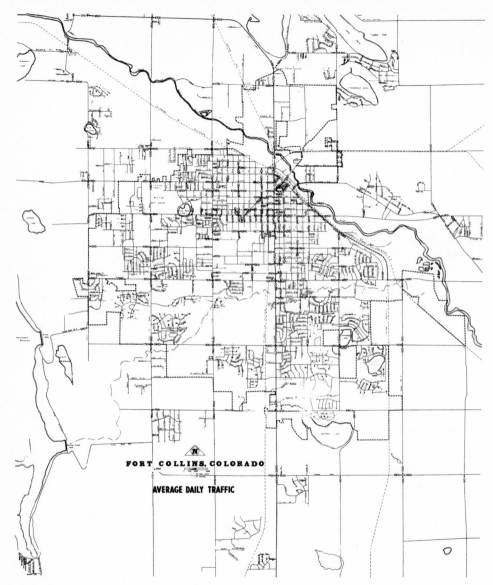

Figure 10.2. Traffic counts.

In Mr. Royer's situation, the rent per square foot for Site 1 was $5.00 per square foot [($600 per month rent times 12 months equals $7,200 per year) divided by (72 feet times 20 feet equals 1440 square feet)]. Site 2 had a rental charge of $4.00 per square foot [($250 per month rent times 12 months equals $3,000 rent per year) divided by (25 feet times 30 feet equals 750 square feet)]. The question is, Can Site 1 pull trade better than Site 2? And, is either $4.00 or $5.00 per square foot an exorbitant amount to pay for rent? The answer to the first question is probably Yes; the answer to the second is probably No.

Mr. Royer's decision. Site 1 seems to be the better site for locating a fabric store. It is near favorable competition; it is compatible with its neighbors; its store size is better adapted to full-line merchandising policies; it is located in the hub of the shopping district and, therefore, can probably generate impulse, as well as shopping, sales; and the rent of $5.00 per square foot is within reason for a downtown location.

Quantitative factors

As you may recall, a trade area is an area within which a given establishment can economically serve potential buyers of a good or service. A trade area is usually defined in terms of geographical boundaries (see Figure 10.3). For example, the trade area of the J. C. Penney store within your city may follow county lines, city limits, or even neighborhoods. The trade area of a liquor store though may extend only five blocks from each side of the store.

Trade areas are useful for considering the quantitative factors involved in selecting a site. Quantitative factors are factors susceptible to measurement. They include the market poten-

tial of a trade area and the sales forecast. Market potential is the total amount of the business (or sales in dollars) that can be obtained by all stores that sell a particular product or product line within a trade area. A sales forecast, by contrast, is the amount of business a particular retailer hopes to obtain within the trade area during a particular period of time, usually a year. Thus, sales forecast is a subset of market potential.

Determining market potential. There are two major determinants of the market potential for a trade area. These determinants include (1) the number of potential consumers within the trade area and (2) the amount of money consumers spend for the product or product line in question. For example, a retailer can determine the market potential by multiplying the number of potential consumers in the trade area times the average amount they spend for the product. Generally, market potential figures are based on yearly estimates. Suppose, for example, that five hundred potential customers reside in the trade area of a retail liquor business. If it were known that each potential customer spends approximately $19.00 per year on wine, beer, and liquor (a

---

Table 10.1. Rent Expenses of Selected Retail Businesses

Type of Business	Percent	Type of Business	Percent
Automobile dealers	.79	Liquor stores	2.10
Auto parts	1.90	Lumber and building materials dealers	.65
Bakeries	3.20	Men's apparel stores	3.75
Beauty shops	5.35	Music stores	3.40
Book stores	4.10	Nursery and garden supply	1.60
Children's and infant wear	4.55	Office supply and equipment dealers	1.89
Cocktail lounges	3.60	Paint and wallpaper dealers	3.50
Confectionery stores	2.44	Photographic studio and supply shops	4.40
Florists	2.55	Service stations	2.60
Furniture stores	1.73	Shoe stores	3.60
Garages	3.25	Specialty food stores (delicatessens)	4.00
Gift and novelty stores	5.60	Sporting goods stores	2.80
Food stores	.93	Taverns	3.25
Hardware stores	3.82	Women's specialty shops	4.70
Jewelry	3.20	Variety stores	5.05

Source: *General Information: Expenses in Retail Business,* November, 1973, The National Cash Register Company, Dayton, Ohio.

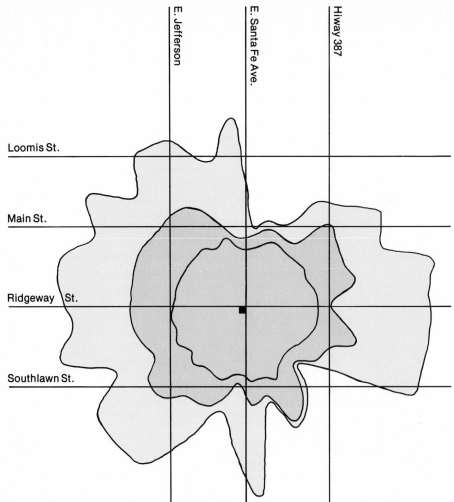

Figure 10.3. Trade area of a retail store. The innermost circle represents the area within which 50% of the store's customers reside; the next circle represents 75%; and the outer circle represents 90%.

figure determined through trade statistics), the total market potential for liquor sales in that trade area would be $9,500.

Population statistics, most commonly used in arriving at market potential, are expressed either on a per capita, a per household, or a per family basis. Sources of population information include the U.S. Government's *Census of Population,* the *Survey of Buying Power* (the special June issue of *Sales Management* magazine), and local government agencies.

Let's stop for a moment and look at census information as an aid in arriving at population information.

Census data provides in addition to nationwide statistics, data for every city, town, and village in the U.S. For cities of 50,000 or more inhabitants, material (called SMSA's) has been tabulated for census tracts and blocks. SMSA stands for the "Standard Metropolitan Statistical Area." This is a geographical designation encompassing a county (or counties) containing a central city of at least 50,000 inhabitants, plus contiguous counties which are socially and economically integrated with the central county. Census tracts are small areas within an SMSA with about 4,000—5,000 population. Blocks are subdivisions of census tracts and generally include populations of around 300 people.

Summary information is available for an entire metropolitan area, census tract, as well as for blocks within a city. Answers to questions such as those below can be found in the census reports. SMSA and census tract data provide fairly comprehensive information whereas block statistics give general characteristics of the population because of their smaller geographical unit.

—How many persons or families are there in the trading area and how has this changed over time?
—Where do they work?
—How many young or old persons are there, how many children or teenagers?

—How many families with small children or with teenagers?
—How many one-person households, how many small or large families?
—What is the income of the families or individuals?
—What do they do for a living?
—Is the area an older established one or one where most residents are newcomers?
—How many families own their homes? How many rent?
—What is the value of the homes? What is the monthly rent?
—What is the age and quality of the homes?
—Do the homes have air conditioning; other appliances?
—How many of the families own an automobile? How many own two or more?

In the census reports, tracts and blocks are portrayed on maps much as appears in Figure 10.4. Therefore if the trade area is defined as

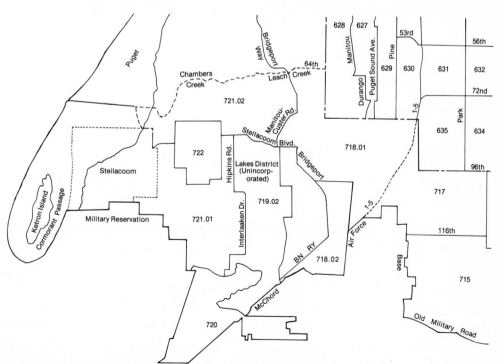

Figure 10.4. Using census block data to select a store site.

shown in the figure to include blocks 719.02, and 718.02, then it is the population characteristics within these blocks (or fractions of blocks) which most interests the retailer. For this information the retailer turns to another page of the census material and locates the relevant population data. A portion of the trade area block statistics is shown in Figure 10.5.

Unfortunately, in using census data, merchants must be aware that the information is usually based on political subdivisions. Obviously, a trading area may have little relationship to a political breakdown. The merchant may be able to get a more detailed breakdown of population by checking (1) with the local Chamber of Commerce for any detailed studies that they may have made, (2) the local newspaper for circulation statistics, (3) the local post office for the number of boxholders on delivery routes, (4) the local public utilities office for information on the number of residential electric or gas meters, and (5) the city planning office, fire department, and police department for information on the number of residents within a trade area. Regardless of the sources used, however, the merchant will probably find it necessary to adjust population information for a trade area by using the information collected in combination with individual judgment about the area.

Up to this point, we have implied that retailers are interested in total population figures, when, in fact, they may be interested only in a segment of the population. This segment could be identified according to age, sex, religion, color, educational level, or a number of other characteristics. Obviously, merchants interested in appealing to a market segment should obtain as much population information as possible concerning that segment.

In addition to population information, the retailer must collect information on the number of dollars being spent by consumers for the product or product line in question. Probably the best sources of such information are established trade associations for the kind of business being started. These associations usually provide information on how much is being spent per capita for the products their members sell. Other sources of information include *Sales Management's Survey of Buying Power* (see Figure 2.7) and the U.S. Government's *Census of Retail Trades* supplied by the Bureau of the Census. The latter source contains retail sales for seventy-two kinds of businesses. The merchant should, however, realize that this information is published at infrequent intervals (usually once every 5 years) and that it may be necessary to adjust county or state figures to meet local conditions.

A merchant interested in arriving at a per capita consumption expenditure figure could use the census data by taking the total retail sales for a particular kind of business and dividing it by the population of the state or area. For example, in the state of California, if all stores selling footwear did a total volume of $580,132,000, in 1975, and if you divided this figure by the number of people in California in 1975 (21,500,000) you would get a per capita footwear expenditure of $26.98.

Determining a sales forecast. As we mentioned earlier, the sales forecast for a firm is the amount of business that it expects to obtain in a particular time period. An accurate appraisal of sales forecast is important because on it depends the amount of inventory that will be purchased, the number of employees that will be needed, the dollars that can be spent for expenses, and the amount of debt capital that the business can comfortably afford.

Unfortunately, for some types of retail businesses, such as restaurants, the sales forecast figure can be elusive. To arrive at such a figure, one must consider (1) the competitive strengths in the market, (2) the amount of business that can be drawn from substitute products, and (3) management's own expertise in operating its business.

To assess the competitive strengths in the market, the retailer starts with an assessment of the total market potential, then assumes that business will obtain at least the average amount of sales being realized by the competi-

Characteristics of Housing Units and Population, by Blocks: 1970

[Data exclude vacant seasonal and vacant migratory housing units. For minimum base for derived figures (percent, average, etc.) and meaning of symbols, see text]

Blocks Within Census Tracts	Total population	Percent of total population — Negro	In group quarters	Under 18 years	62 years and over	Year-round housing units — Total	Lacking some or all plumbing facilities	Units in — One-unit structures	Structures of 10 or more units	Owner — Total	Lacking some or all plumbing facilities	Average number of rooms	Average value (dollars)	Percent Negro	Renter — Total	Lacking some or all plumbing facilities	Average number of rooms	Average contract rent (dollars)	Percent Negro	1.01 or more persons per room — Total	With all plumbing facilities	One-person households	With female head of family	With roomers, boarders or lodgers
625	24	—	—	33	13	7	—	7	—	5	—	5.0	17300	—	2	…	…	…	—	2	2	1	—	—
626	54	—	—	32	6	22	—	15	5	7	—	6.1	21300	—	14	…	2.8	79	—	2	2	4	3	—
627	93	—	—	3	7	55	—	8	44	4	…	4.8	17500	—	49	—	3.0	135	—	1	1	18	—	1
628	12	—	—	25	42	5	—	5	—	4	…	5.2	15000	—	—	…	…	…	—	—	—	—	—	—
629	11	—	—	9	11	5	—	5	—	5	—	6.0	14800	—	—	…	…	…	—	—	—	1	—	—
630	18	—	—	28	—	5	—	7	—	5	—	…	…	—	2	—	…	…	—	—	—	—	—	—
631	2	—	…	—	—	—	—	—	—	—	—	…	…	—	—	…	…	…	—	—	—	1	—	—
632	36	…	—	14	42	24	3	4	—	21	2	2.9	…	—	2	…	…	…	—	1	1	13	1	32
718.02	5649	8	—	32	3	2263	9	898	714	639	6	4.7	15400	7	1451	3	3.7	121	8	163	163	306	213	32
102	36	8	—	33	8	12	1	12	—	9	1	5.4	16000	11	2	—	—	—	—	2	2	2	1	1
103	44	41	—	52	—	11	—	11	—	10	—	6.3	21400	40	1	—	—	—	—	1	1	—	2	1
104	18	6	—	17	28	10	—	6	—	2	—	—	—	—	7	—	3.9	99	14	—	—	3	2	1
105	129	1	—	36	1	44	—	17	1	13	—	6.4	26900	3	31	—	3.6	116	3	2	2	5	9	—
106	36	14	—	31	17	17	—	10	—	9	—	4.2	13800	—	6	—	4.0	102	—	—	—	4	1	5
107	504	14	—	35	5	191	—	67	51	84	—	4.6	13300	18	98	—	3.4	110	18	18	18	31	22	1
108	72	4	—	42	7	20	—	20	—	12	—	5.3	11700	5	7	—	4.4	100	14	3	3	1	3	1
109	85	11	—	46	—	27	—	27	—	15	1	4.3	15200	8	9	—	5.1	101	13	3	3	—	5	—
201	74	46	—	46	4	17	—	16	—	9	—	5.1	11500	20	8	—	4.8	118	11	3	3	—	5	—
202	85	4	—	38	4	29	—	28	—	20	—	5.5	14300	11	8	—	4.8	123	13	3	3	3	6	—
203	10	18	—	30	10	7	—	6	—	—	—	—	14300	—	4	—	4.6	123	—	—	—	2	—	—
204	50	7	—	26	8	18	—	17	1	13	—	4.8	12800	15	5	—	4.6	91	29	2	2	3	1	1
205	59	10	—	42	2	20	—	20	—	10	—	5.2	12800	10	7	—	4.5	98	9	3	3	3	4	1
206	102	16	—	44	—	27	—	26	—	16	—	4.3	12800	13	11	—	4.6	94	22	4	4	3	—	1
207	109	16	—	44	3	37	—	36	—	23	—	4.6	12600	4	9	—	4.6	101	12	6	6	6	4	1
208	176	9	—	49	2	48	—	47	—	22	—	4.8	11600	9	26	—	4.5	121	—	11	11	4	14	1
209	79	9	—	52	5	22	—	21	—	13	1	4.8	12400	8	7	—	4.9	105	20	5	5	1	4	—
210	85	14	—	34	2	25	1	24	—	15	—	4.8	14300	20	10	—	5.0	128	—	3	3	4	3	—
211	73	22	—	49	3	19	—	19	—	13	—	5.8	14300	8	6	—	5.0	…	50	3	3	1	5	—
212	129	12	—	38	3	35	—	34	—	29	—	4.8	13900	14	5	—	5.0	118	20	6	6	1	4	2
213	154	17	—	44	1	43	—	43	—	23	—	4.8	14800	22	16	—	4.8	116	13	8	8	1	6	1
214	91	4	—	47	2	27	—	26	—	16	—	4.9	14300	—	10	—	4.8	103	20	4	4	2	5	—
215	81	17	—	35	2	88	—	27	—	16	—	4.9	15200	13	10	—	4.7	124	5	4	4	2	3	—
	163	3	…	22	2																	15		
	93	5	…	18	1																			

Figure 10.5. Block statistics (as appear on a page of actual census material).

tive businesses in the trade area. If there are five of these businesses (the new retail establishment makes six, in all), each business might be expected to have one-sixth of the business available in the trade area. In other words, given a market potential of $600,000, each business should expect to obtain $100,000. If one store, by virtue of its size, location, merchandising ability, and so on, were capable of achieving a greater sales volume than the average, an adjustment in the sales volume of each business could be made.

Although this approach may not seem as sound as that used in measuring market potential, it does provide an analysis of competitive strength, and the figure derived is usually conservative. This approach can be very useful in particular situations. Suppose, for example, that a new firm came into a five-store trading area in which the market potential was $600,000, and this new firm had to do $400,000 merely to break even. Obviously, the firm's chances of success would be slim. The smaller the market share a firm needs, the greater is its likelihood for success.

It is possible to use other methods to gauge competitive strength. One such method is to obtain an approximation of the square footage, the number of employees, the lineal counter footage, or the number of check-out stands in competitive establishments. Then, by using trade publications or firsthand information of typical productivity ratios, such as sales per square foot, sales per employee, sales per lineal foot of counter space, and sales per check-out counter, one can estimate the amount of business being done by competitors. For example, a fabric shop does, on the average, around $55 per square foot of selling area. If existing fabric shops had a combined selling area of 4,000 square feet, the total volume of business from these shops might be estimated at $220,000. Obviously, it would be possible to compare the total figure calculated for competitive establishments against the market potential figure for the trade area. If the figures are fairly similar, the trade area probably has sufficient stores, and a re-

tailer establishing a business in the area would have difficulty obtaining business. One must, of course, use productivity ratios with considerable judgment.

Break even point. A retailer who is considering buying an existing business or starting a new one must use a sales forecast in two ways. First, as we said earlier, the retailer needs a reliable sales figure to plan accurately to meet inventory, expense, and financial requirements. Second, the retailer must make a quick assessment as to whether to go into the business in the first place. In other words, can the store expect to do enough business to break even?

A quick but useful vehicle for determining the break-even volume is to calculate the expenses needed to operate the business (a fairly easy task) and apply the typical trade ratio of expenses to sales. Then, one can determine the amount of business needed to cover the expenses and leave no profit, that is, to break even. For example, a prospective proprietor of a new paint store might estimate expenses for the first year of operation as $30,000, for rent, salaries, insurance, advertising, heat, and so on. Trade ratios reveal that a paint store's ratio of expenses to sales is usually 40 percent, with no profit. Therefore, the proprietor would need to do $75,000 in business to cover expenses ($30,000 divided by 40 percent equals $75,000). The following is the profit and loss statement at break-even sales volume.

	$	%
Sales	$75,000	100
Cost of goods sold	45,000	− 60
Gross margin	30,000	40
Expenses	− 30,000	− 40
	0	0

Site selection. Once the volume necessary to break even has been determined, the retailer must still decide whether or not to go into the paint business at all, and if so, what location to choose. He or she could make this decision in one of several ways. First, look at the $75,000 figure and subjectively evaluate, based upon previous experience with this kind of business, whether $75,000 seems to be a realistic figure to attain. Second, and this approach is similar to the first, the retailer could take the $75,000 and divide it by the number of working days in the year to arrive at a sales-per-day figure. In this case, the answer is $244 (75,000 ÷ 307). The retailer would then try to determine whether it were possible to obtain $244 of business every day. If the operation were an appliance store, even breaking this down into the number of units the store would have to move on a daily basis. Third, the retailer might compare this figure with the market potential figure obtained and judge whether the differential advantage was good enough to attract that many sales dollars into the store.

Determining Capital Requirements for a New Business

Having identified a location for a store and estimated its potential sales, the prospective retailer must decide how much capital is needed to start the new business. This is of great importance because if there is one cause of business failure, aside from management's lack of ability, it's the lack of equity, or owner's capital, within the business.

We will use "capital" to refer to investment in the business by both owners and creditors. In other words, capital shows up on the liability side of the balance sheet and includes short-term debt, long-term debt, and owners' equity. As you may recall from Chapter 6, when we discussed the balance sheet, all liability items are used to support or finance the assets contained in the business. Therefore, management must determine all of the assets needed in the business so it will know how much capital will be required to start the business.

In a retail business, there are essentially four assets that management must plan for and which appear on the balance sheet as of the opening day of operation. These assets include (1) inventory, (2) accounts receivable, (3) equipment and fixtures, and (4) cash.

Inventory

Inventory is probably the single most important asset that management must plan for. There are essentially three ways for management to arrive at the dollar inventory figure. One way is to use the stock turnover figure. You will recall that merchandise inventory is determined by using typical trade relationships between inventory and sales. In other words, if we plan sales at $100,000, and the typical stock turnover figure for this line of business is five, the merchandise inventory needed to support $100,000 worth of sales is $20,000 at retail. If our gross margin is 40 percent, we use the markup formula to find that the cost of the $20,000 worth of goods is $12,000. Assuming that we stock inventory for one turnover period (a realistic assumption), our dollar investment cost in inventory for the opening day of operations is $12,000:

$$\text{Stock turnover rate} = \frac{\text{planned sales}}{\substack{\text{average inventory} \\ \text{at retail}}}$$

$$\frac{\$100,000}{\$\ 20,000} = 5$$

$$\text{Cost} + \text{markup} = \text{retail price}$$
$$\text{Cost} + .40r = \$20,000$$
$$C + (.40 \times \$20,000) = \$20,000$$
$$C + \$8,000 = \$20,000$$
$$\$12,000 + \$8,000 = \$20,000$$

Cost = $12,000 (beginning inventory at cost) (See Appendix D, Markup Calculations, for aid in the calculation of markup)

Another way inventory requirements may be determined is by arriving at a figure based on customer wants. In this instance, an assortment plan is prepared and translated into inventory dollars. Usually, merchants rely greatly on the advice of their suppliers in developing a beginning inventory for a store.

Accounts receivable

At one time, determining the amount of capital needed to back up the accounts receivable that a store was going to carry was a significant and important consideration in developing capital requirements. Today, however, because of programs such as Master Charge and BankAmericard, many retailers do not carry credit on their books. Instead the accounts are carried by card-issuing agencies.

However, those merchants who wish to have their own credit program may use the following procedure for determining the capital necessary to support the accounts receivable. Assume, for example, that a store's yearly sales are expected to be $100,000 and that 20 percent of these sales will be charge sales, or $20,000 for the year. Because the average collection period for a charge customer is usually about 45 days (which gives a receivable turnover figure of 8—360 days divided by 45 days), the amount of capital needed to finance the accounts receivable is $2,500 ($20,000 divided by 8). In other words, $2,500, on the average, will show on the books. Thus, even though the merchant has sold the goods and even though his expenses continue to accumulate, he doesn't receive money from the credit sales for some time and must, therefore, secure capital to support these sales.

$$\frac{\text{Days in a year}}{\substack{\text{Average number of days} \\ \text{accounts receivable} \\ \text{are outstanding}}}$$

$$= \text{receivable turnover}$$

$$= \frac{360}{45} = 8$$

$$\frac{\text{Planned charge sales}}{\text{Receivable turnover}}$$

$$= \text{average amount of receivables on the books at any one time}$$

$$= \frac{\$20,000}{8} = \$2,500$$

Fixtures and equipment

A merchant must also plan for capital to support the fixtures and equipment in the store. Cash registers, counters, stock bins, requisition baskets, carts, trucks, and other items too numerous to mention must be bought and paid for. Determining the capital requirements for equipment and fixtures is easy; all one has to do is add up the costs of these items.

Cash

A retailer must have cash on hand to pay for opening expenses, such as fees for lawyers, advertising, and licenses. There is also a need to have cash to meet operating expenses, such as salary, heat, light, and rent during the first months of operation.

There is no strict rule to follow to decide how much cash should be on hand at the beginning of operations. However, it is best to have as much cash as possible in case the business doesn't at first do as well as expected. In general, it is necessary to have two to three months cash on hand. Some retailers believe that there should be enough cash on hand to meet expenditures for approximately one turnover period. In other words, if the turnover rate is six times a year, or once every two months, there should be enough cash on hand to meet necessary expenditures for a two-month period.

Determining Capital Requirements for an Existing Business

Some people decide to buy an existing business instead of starting a new one. There are two significant advantages to doing this. The most significant advantage is probably that it is possible to make a more accurate estimate of the profit potential of the business. Existing information gives the size of the volume that has been generated and the amount of profits that have been made. If these figures are considered in light of the former management's strategy, it is possible to make a fairly accurate assessment of the potential of the business. The second advantage to buying an existing business is that the prospective proprietor needs less equity capital than he would if he were to start a new business. This is so because existing owners usually finance a greater portion of the capital requirements than do creditors, such as banks.

The capital requirements for an existing business are evaluated on the basis of the same factors that are used in evaluating capital requirements for a new business. In other words, capital requirements include inventory, accounts receivable, fixtures and equipment, and cash. However, in starting a new business, one assesses the value of the assets on the basis of market prices; for an existing business, one assesses the value of assets that already exist. Thus, it is necessary for the buyer and the purchaser to agree on the value of every asset.

Not all assets can be appraised on the basis of original market price. There will be, for example, some items in inventory that are worthless. And there will be some accounts receivable that obviously will be difficult or impossible to collect. Often, buyers will not purchase existing accounts receivable, and sellers must collect these. When the buyer purchases the receivables, the buyer and the seller must agree on a price.

After all the assets have been evaluated and added together, the total may fall below the asking price. If it does, the seller is asking the buyer to pay for good will, or "blue sky" as it is frequently referred to. There is nothing wrong with purchasing good will as long as the buyer knows how much is being paid for it and as long as there is value in it. The buyer should be willing to pay for good will if the business has enjoyed a substantial and loyal following, if the store is located in a prime location, and/or if higher than average profits have been and are likely to continue to flow from the operation.

Obtaining the Funds and Paying Them Back

After the capital requirements have been determined, the buyer must obtain the necessary funds. The obvious source of funds is the buyer's own savings. In fact, people usually cannot go into business unless they can put some of their own capital into the firm. In general, a buyer should be able to invest 50 percent of total capital needs. This percentage can be higher or lower, depending on the experience of the buyer, the outlook for the business, and the ease with which money can be obtained.

The next most logical source of funds is the local commercial bank. The bank is in the business of lending money and will do so if the venture looks relatively good. Banks require that interest be paid regularly on the loan and that there be an amortization (pay off) of the debt within a fairly short period of time, usually within two or three years. They will help finance equipment and inventory needs and will usually ask that their loans be secured with the assets they are financing.

Other sources of funds include industrial banks, relatives, prospective partners, and the Small Business Administration.

Once the buyer finds ways to accumulate the necessary funds, he or she must determine whether the necessary financial arrangements can be met. If the business is financed entirely by owner's capital, there is, of course, no problem. However, the situation is different if funds must be borrowed. If the money is borrowed from a bank, there will be interest payments as well as repayment of debt. Each of these obligations is a drain on the business because cash must be set aside to meet them.

Assume, for example, that the buyer has developed the following pro forma (forecasted) profit and loss statement.

Sales	$100,000
Costs	− 60,000
Gross margin	40,000
Operating expenses (exclusive of owner's salary)	25,000
Depreciation	1,000
Total expenses	26,000
Profit before taxes	14,000
Taxes at 20 percent (.20 × $14,000)	2,800
Net profit	$ 11,200

Further assume that there is $20,000 available to invest in a business and that the total capital needs are $40,000. The buyer will, therefore, borrow $20,000 from the bank for three years at 7 percent interest on the face amount of the loan, or $4200 ($20,000 times 7 percent times 3 years equals $4200).[1] The total loan is, therefore, $24,200 ($20,000 plus $4200).

The problem is now one of determining whether the business can be expected to earn enough to pay back the loan over the three-year period. The following calculations show how unlikely it is that the business could provide such earnings. What has developed here is that the owner will have $5,200 available cash from which to pay a debt of $8,066.

Loan Agreement
Loan repayment $8,066 per year
($24,200 ÷ 3 years)

Source of Debt Repayment	
Profits	$11,200
Depreciation (a noncash expense)	+ 1,000
Total	$12,200
Owner's salary	− 7,000
Net available funds for debt repayment	$ 5,200

Summary

Starting a retail business or buying an exist-ing business involves some risks. The problem for a new owner, therefore, is one of reducing the risks. This requires a systematic study of the new venture. In conducting the study, the buyer should concentrate on three main considerations. First, look at the location and site of the proposed business to determine (1) whether the business is situated in a place where consumers are likely to shop for the goods being sold, and (2) whether enough sales volume can be generated to make the business profitable. Second, the buyer should determine how much money will be required to establish the business in the manner necessary for successful operation. Third, the buyer should determine the type of financing that would best fit the business.

Questions and Problems

1. If you were asked to suggest ways of revitalizing your downtown shopping district, what would you propose?
2. What are the various ways that a prospective retail store owner can get into trouble when starting a new business?
3. Should a person twenty-one years of age who has completed two years of college go into business on his or her own? Examine this question in terms of advantages, disadvantages, and alternatives.

Situations and Activities

You are given the opportunity to buy a small confectionery store. This store makes its own candy and also sells candy purchased through national manufacturers. The business is located in the downtown area of a town with a population of 40,000. Currently, downtown retail sales are equal to those of a shopping center located at the edge of town. Within the next two years another major shopping center—a regional shopping center—will come into the community. It is expected that this center will have a substantial impact on the retail sales of the downtown area and on the sales of the other shopping center. The confectionery store has enjoyed profitable trade for twenty-five years in its present location. The owners will sell the business for $25,000. Last

---

[1] Interest is a before tax expense. However, to simplify our calculations we have treated it as a payment to be made on the principal of the loan. Although not strictly correct, this treatment, if anything, is a conservative approach to the cash flow position.

year, they netted $17,000, exclusive of the owner's salary. Would you buy this business? Explain.

Develop a market potential figure for liquor sales in your community. Use as your source of information the Census of Retail Trade and population statistics (market potential = population units times amount spent on the product).

List, in order of their potential, the sources of capital available in your community. What is the cost of using each source; what demands are placed upon you, the user of the funds?

Often treated incidentally but always crucial to establishing a retail business are considerations relating to (1) taxes; (2) insurance coverage; (3) making a will; and (4) retirement plans.

Plan a program to meet the needs of each. Interview the appropriate professional people in your community to solicit their ideas.

Bibliography

The Economic Effects of Franchising. Washington, D.C.: U.S. Government Printing Office, 1971.

Gist, Ronald R. *Retailing: Concepts and Decisions.* New York: John Wiley and Sons, 1968, pp. 219—221.

"Survey: of Buying Power." *Sales Management.* July 23, 1973, pp. 13—24.

Weiss, E. B. "New Store Locations in the Core City." *Stores,* May, 1972, pp. 43—44.

11

Store Design and Layout

contents

behavioral objectives

All retailers should have a clear understanding of store design and layout. This understanding helps them to merchandise so they achieve the level of sales of which the store is capable. As you study this chapter, pay particular attention to (1) the aspects of store design that are helpful to retailers, and (2) the requirements for achieving good management of store layout.

Upon completing this chapter, you will be able to do the following:
- ☐ Describe the decisions that must be made to develop a comprehensive store layout plan, and provide some implications of these decisions.
- ☐ Develop a customer traffic flow pattern for a retail store.
- ☐ Analyze a store layout based on some generally accepted rules.

In the preceding two chapters we examined the problems of store location, and we looked at methods for establishing a retail store. The next step is to explore aspects of store design and layout. We want to examine ways in which one can effectively sell the image of the store and at the same time provide for a smooth-running operation by developing the store's interior and exterior. This chapter provides insights into the factors that should be considered in planning a new store, or remodeling an old one, and it provides ideas for using store design and layout as a merchandising tool.

A Comprehensive Store Layout Plan

The first step in designing or providing for the proper layout of any store is to develop a comprehensive plan for the overall requirements of the store. To this end, merchants must study (1) the needs, habits, and buying potential of the shoppers in their area, (2) the amount of dollars received per square foot of selling area for the kind of business that they are operating, (3) the need for storage as well as selling space, (4) the need for store service and overall general customer comfort, (5) the need for proper amount of lighting and temperature control, (6) the need for achieving the best traffic circulation possible throughout the store, (7) the need for fixtures. A careful study of these factors helps merchants make their stores attractive, conducive to shopping, and as operationally efficient as possible.

In developing a comprehensive store layout plan, there are several agencies to which the retailer can go to get specialized assistance. For most retailers, getting specialized assistance makes a great deal of sense. Usually, retailers lack expertise and familiarity with the latest developments in store design and layout. Furthermore, they rarely have the time to check building codes, work with contractors, and shop for store equipment.

Some of the agencies that help in store planning include merchandise suppliers, local architects and engineers oriented to store planning, store equipment firms, and consulting firms specializing in store planning. Contact can be made with the consulting firm nearest the store through the Institute of Store Planners, a national organization. In general, the cost of using professional store planners approximates 7 percent of the construction costs. Some of this cost can be offset by discounts that are made available to the store planners by suppliers and that may not be available to retailers acting on their own behalf.

Store Design

Store design is, by definition, the architectural character or decorative style of a store. As such, it conveys to the customer "what the store is all about." Merchants planning a store's design must take into consideration their own retail strategy while planning their fixture, window, lighting, color, and store entrance requirements.

Stores vary so much in kind, size, and geographical location that it is difficult to generalize about store design. However, one generalization may be made: Today, retail stores are assuming a new look. First, they are becoming larger. Then, new approaches are being used in designing display fixtures and cabinets, and new lighting techniques are being tried. Color is playing a new role in store design. And new efforts are being made to achieve a professional approach to merchandising activities.

Store match

A store's design should match the store's character. This means that in store design consideration should be given to the type of store image the merchant hopes to project. In addition, the design should also match with the other stores surrounding it; it should enhance the salability of the merchandise within the store; be in good taste; and it should, in general, match the personality of the store's owner.

A uniquely created interior display arrangement by Joseph Magnin Co., Inc. for the Christmas selling season.
Photo courtesy of Joseph Magnin, Co., Inc.

Display windows

Open back windows rival closed back windows in the frequency of their use and are now an acceptable type of store design. The open back, as opposed to the closed back, is a window through which the interior of the store is seen. The idea is that the store itself becomes the display case. When open back windows are used, the store doesn't have valuable selling floor space tied up in window space, management need not concern itself with planning window displays, and the problems of keeping windows clean and timely are usually avoided. However, the open back window has caused some new display problems and has exaggerated some old ones. The most significant of these problems concern reflection, sun glare, sun control, artificial lighting for both day and night, and the necessity for a general reorgani-

zation of merchandise within the completely exposed store.

Awnings

Awnings pose a particular problem for retailers. Retailers who are located on the shady side of the street and who do not have to worry about faded merchandise or the daily raising and lowering of awnings are fortunate.

Most awnings are made of fabric and are of the old scissors or outrigger style. In recent years, however, one sees more and more fabric awnings that can be fastened into a recessed box at the end of the building. Another type of awning is one that is a structural part of the building.

Awnings come in many assorted sizes, colors, and styles. In a way, this is unfortunate for the consumer, because each merchant may

Today's "modern" store fronts often make use of existing structures to dramatize the warmth and friendliness to be encountered by all who enter.
Photo courtesy of The San Francisco Convention & Visitors Bureau

attempt to attract customer attention by using a special type of awning. Competing awnings can be almost as distracting, obtrusive, and unattractive as competing neon signs. When selecting an awning, merchants should find one that is interesting and that is also compatible with the building and the nature of the business.

One way in which merchants have attempted to overcome objections over the awning has been to do away with it completely. Because glare would still be much in evidence, the alternative was to install a new type of glass. The glass panes that have been available have had a yellowish hue, a bluish cast, a grayish or greenish tone, and some were even pink in shading. Unfortunately, if such glass did succeed in reducing the glare, it usually had the attendant disagreeable feature of darkening

the interior of the window and making it difficult to distinguish the color of the merchandise inside. Also, it did very little to reduce the susceptibility of merchandise in the window to fading.

The store entrance

One of the first and most meaningful impressions customers get of a store is the impression they receive as they go through the front door. An entrance should be more than a device to keep people out of the store or to encourage them to come into the store. It should be more than something to protect against the elements. An entrance should have character; it should say to a prospective customer, "Please come through the door and you will be treated with courtesy and friendliness and will be served to the best of our ability." To this end, the entrance should be more than a door with glass. It should reflect grace; it should be compatible with the store design; and it should provide an easy way to enter the store.

Today's retailers are increasingly using textured building materials (brick, rough-sawn wood, and so on) at the store's entrance to give a pleasant feeling to the store's front. In recent years merchants have also been experimenting with means by which customers might more easily enter their stores. These experiments have resulted in "doorless" stores, which have a curtain of air separating the interior of the store from the outside. Sliding panels make the entire front of the store open to the street. This curtain of air, which is barely noticeable to the customer, keeps out the cold in the winter and the heat in the summer; it also keeps bugs and dirt from entering the store.

Multiple-level stores

Today's retailers are increasingly accepting the multiple-level store as an appropriate store design. Because of the need for increased parking space in relation to shopping area in suburban stores and shopping centers, the multiple-level store is especially appealing to retailers. Even supermarkets have experimented with this type of store design. Properly carried out, a multi-level design offers the merchant both a means of expanding the selling area and segregating these areas from one another. It also gives an overall feeling of unity to the store.

Fixtures

Another consideration to be made by the retailer in developing an appropriate store design involves the use of fixtures. Probably the best fixture is no fixture at all. In other words, the sole purpose of a fixture is to sell merchandise. If the merchandise can be sold without the use of fixtures, fixtures are unnecessary. Today, merchants buy fixtures that are light in appearance and flexible in use. They have interchangeable parts and can be used in different parts of the store. They will permit the merchant to easily adjust to seasons, sales volume,

and buying trends. Figure 11.1 illustrates some of the "new" in fixture design.

Temperature control equipment

No store, regardless of its type, size, or financial condition, should be without air conditioning. Because so many of today's customers have air conditioning in their own homes, they almost demand it of a business. People will simply not shop in an overly warm atmosphere. Competitors probably possess air conditioning. A retailer who has an up-to-date store design cannot afford to provide less.

If cool temperatures are important to the customer in the summer, warm temperatures are equally important in the winter. Unfortunately, some merchants economize by cutting back on the amount of heat in the store. Shopping center developers who recognize this tendency on the part of merchants will often use a central control device which governs the amount of heat that each store must provide its customers. To turn back the temperature or invest in heating equipment that is under capacity is to provoke the wrath of customers and sales people alike.

Lighting

Proper store lighting is one of the more important considerations in store design. Whereas at one time the function of lighting was to provide customers with a means of feeling their way through the store, today's lighting has become a viable display media. It is an integral part of the store's design characteristics. Lighting should match the mood that the retailer attempted to create with rest of the store decor.

Store lighting should complement rather than detract from the merchandise being presented. Too much or too little lighting, or even the wrong type of lighting, can create false impressions about the merchandise on display. Incandescent lighting used alone, for example, accents yellow and red. Frequently, fluorescent lights build up blues and purples. (Imagine the use of fluorescent lighting on meats!) Therefore, retailers are concerned with finding

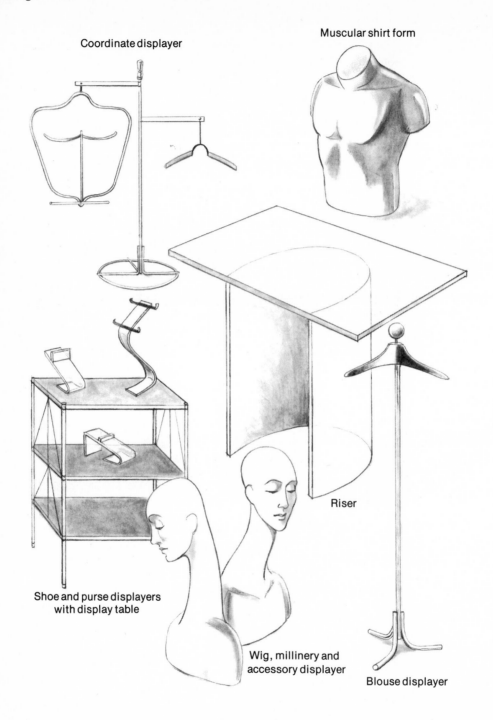

Coordinate displayer

Muscular shirt form

Riser

Shoe and purse displayers
with display table

Wig, millinery and
accessory displayer

Blouse displayer

Figure 11.1. Fixture designs.

a combination of lighting that gives a correct impression of the merchandise while it de-emphasizes the source of the light itself.

Color

Today's retail stores should be color-oriented. The psychological effects of color and the integration of color with lighting and display are gaining new significance for retailers. Retailers are becoming especially appreciative of the fact that color, probably more than any other factor except price, is the "stopper" that catches the customer's attention. Therefore, intelligent use of color is important in store design.

Storage of stock

There are three accepted ways to handle storage of stock in designing a retail store. The first way is to use direct selling storage—storage that exposes stock in showcases, counters, drawers, and storage that is behind cabinet doors. The second way to provide for storage is through stock rooms directly behind the selling area and perimeter stock areas. The third way to provide for storage is through a central storage location. In general, central storage is best located next to receiving and marking areas and as close as practical to selling areas.

The trend today is to have as little merchandise in concealed stock as possible. Nothing is sold that is located in a box or in a corner in the basement. Furthermore, stocking time and stock maintenance time are reduced by having little concealed stock. For these reasons, exposed merchandise has great appeal. In addition, the trend toward self-service selection has made it practical to display most of the stock in the store.

Store name

Although not strictly a problem associated with store design, the choosing of a store name does reflect on store design. The favorable or unfavorable image generated by the use of a name can help to enhance or negate the style characteristics engendered by approaches to store design.

At first glance, choosing a name for the business may seem to be a rather easy task in which there is little chance for error. Unfortunately, this is not the case. The retailer who thought of the name Equ-ulus (the name of a local gift shop) certainly made a mistake. This name is not pronounceable, and it has little meaning for the majority of the customers to which the store is appealing. Some guidelines to use in choosing a name for a store are as follows:

1. The Mod Shop, Men's Toggery, and The Hub are the kinds of names given to specialty men's shops. As such, they are immediately meaningful to the shopper.
2. Don't choose a name that is too difficult or complicated for customers to remember or pronounce. Cute names have their place only if they can be remembered by the customer.
3. In naming your store, consider using your name. Although some people may accuse you of egoism, using your own name enables you to identify with your business. As people begin to know you, they begin to know your store. Don't use a name that is offensive, negative, or that has a disagreeable sound.
4. Use a name that will not become dated. As your business expands or as it changes character to meet changing conditions, a name that is always timely has distinct benefits over one that is not.

Store Layout

Layout is actually a subset of store design. It is the allocation of space to each selling and nonselling department of a store. The primary considerations in developing an effective store layout are (1) providing for good customer traffic flow throughout the store, (2) achieving maximum profit per square foot of selling space, and (3) maintaining a productive and efficient work environment for employees and their merchandise handling activities.

Store layout is not a one-time problem for the retailer. It is true that a complete layout of a store must be planned during the opening, expanding, or remodeling of a store. However, equally true and of probably more significance to retailers is the realization that every day brings problems associated with store layout. Promotional, seasonal, clearance, and new stock merchandise must be properly positioned in the store.

Ideas for layout management

The goal of layout management is to obtain the maximum benefits from the available space, both in terms of sales and profits and in terms of satisfying customer needs. To do this, provisions must be made to accommodate all the functions the store hopes to perform. Thus, retailers rely on definite ways of planning the store so they achieve the best possible utilization of space. Department stores and chain stores were probably among the first to use and experiment with these ideas, but today they are used by all types of retail stores.

For our purposes, there are nine basic layout ideas that retail managers should remember when they make layout decisions. Ideally, all of these ideas come into play each time the retailer chooses the location of a particular department or a particular kind of merchandise. This is sometimes not practical, however. Therefore, the retailer's goal should be to implement as many of them as possible. Layout decisions often represent an exercise in compromises.

Value in space. The first idea, and perhaps the most significant in planning store layout, is that store space varies in value. Some parts of the store are visited by more people than are other parts. Therefore, it is easier to make sales along the routes traveled by customers. This means that the value of the space is higher along the more highly traveled routes.

As one would expect, the area that is closest to the store's entrance, and is easiest to reach, is the most valuable part. The space nearest to the front ranks second in value, and so on, back through the store. If there is more than one entrance—for example, one in front and one in back of the store—the least valuable space tends to be somewhere around the middle of the store.

By the same line of reasoning, store space is less valuable at parts of the store that are hard to reach, and one would expect variations of sales and profits on different floors. As the height from the ground floor increases, the difficulty of attracting customers to the upper floors becomes greater. Therefore, space on the upper floors or in the basement has less value than space on the main floor.

In general, what this means is that there is a problem in obtaining proper customer circulation throughout all parts of the store. Knowing this, retailers should assign space to departments in such a way that the sales volume per square foot of selling area is maximized for the total store space.

Customer traffic flow. Stores, like cities, should be laid out so that customers can get to various parts conveniently and with little effort. For this reason, some aisles (or streets in the case of cities) are made larger and are designed to accommodate larger traffic segments than are others. In general, aisle widths should be wide if (1) the merchandise adjoining the aisle is the type of merchandise that customers like to look at for a long time before purchasing, (2) there tends to be large concentrations of customers, such as at entrances and escalators and before promotional merchandise displays, and/or (3) the merchant is attempting to control the traffic to maximize customer exposure to the various merchandise departments.

One way of gauging the effectiveness of one's store layout is to "map" the flow of customers as they move throughout the store. In developing a customer flow map, the exact path, each customer's movements, are charted on store layout replicas. A separate store layout sheet is used for each customer. As selected customers move unaware throughout the store their movements are recorded. The information on each layout sheet is then recorded on a single master sheet.

The master sheet representing the layout of a pharmacy is presented in Figure 11.2 as an example. Observations of the density of customer traffic throughout different parts of the store reveal that customer flow is unequal. Management would certainly wish to correct this situation. Alternatives open to them might be to relocate merchandise, improve positions of displays and signs, and reposition counters. The results would hopefully be to improve customer flow and thereby generate greater sales per customer. Customers can't buy what they don't see.

In addition to recording customer traffic flow, observations could also be made of:

1. Sex of customer
2. Estimated age of customer
3. Time spent in the store
4. Amount spent (as appears in cash register)
5. Purchases.

There are two basic types of layout patterns

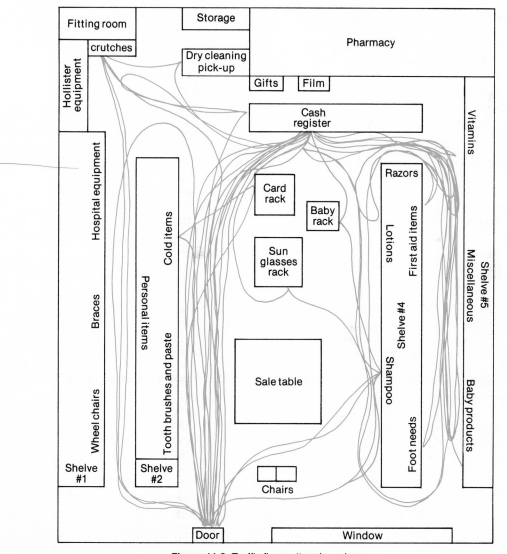

Figure 11.2. Traffic flow pattern in a pharmacy.

that merchants use to control traffic flow in a store. One type is known as the grid pattern, and the other, the free flow pattern. The grid arrangement has main, secondary, and tertiary aisles. Its advantages are savings on costs because of the possibility of standardizing construction and fixture requirements.

The free flow arrangement differs in that it provides for flexibility in store layout. It reduces to a minimum the structural elements that form the fixed shell of the building, such as columns and fixed partitions. Counters are arranged to give maximum visual interest and customer attention to each merchandise department. Counters can be positioned so their angles will literally capture customers in a department.

The "shoppe" or boutique concept has been a natural extension of the free flow layout arrangement. The basic idea behind the "shoppe" is to create departments that sell merchandise that is related in use. A ski shoppe, for example, sells merchandise traditionally carried by the shoe department (ski boots), the sweater department (ski sweaters), the sporting goods department (skis), and so on. "Shoppes" must be presented to the public so they stand out from other departments, and in fact, so they become small, intimate specialty stores within themselves. The free flow layout pattern makes it easy to accomplish this.

Impulse goods versus demand goods. Impulse goods are goods that customers buy on the spur of the moment. Demand goods, sometimes called generative goods, are goods for which customers have a preconceived need and for which they make a specific effort to come to the store. Impulse goods benefit by being located in high traffic areas where customers, as they pass by the displays, are likely to pick up an item for purchase. Demand goods, on the other hand, because of the preconceived need, may be situated in more remote areas of the store.

Related merchandise departments. Related merchandise departments are departments in which the merchandise is complementary so a sale of an item in one department prompts a sale of another item in another department. For example, a sale of a shirt could logically lead to a sale of a tie, which in turn, could lead to a sale of a tie pin. Because of these additional sale possibilities, it is, therefore, appropriate to place related merchandise departments close to one another.

Good-looking and action-related merchandise. Some merchandise has better display potential than other merchandise and is capable of making higher sales per square foot. A leather goods department, for example, lends itself to both an interesting and a dramatic display. Therefore, departments with such capabilities should receive choice locations on the floor.

High gross margin and high sales volume departments. Some departments command a higher gross margin and/or higher sales volume per square foot than other departments. Because departments such as jewelry, candy, and toys can pay their way in the high value locations of the store, they can be placed in the most valuable store areas.

Store image. When customers enter a store, they want the store's displays and departments to tell them what the store is all about. The image that the store is attempting to project should be immediately obvious to them. If the store wants price as the predominant image departments emphasizing this aspect should be placed up near the entrance. If fashion is the image that the store wants to portray, the fashion department should be placed near the entrance. Therefore, the store should give the best space to those departments that best say to the customer, "This is what I am."

Seasonal departments. Some departments need considerable space during particular times of the year. Seasonal departments such as toys, lawn and garden supplies, hardware, and stationery are examples of such departments. Because these departments must be expanded during certain times of the year, provisions must be made to accommodate their expansion. To accomplish this, departments with off-setting seasonal peaks in sales should be placed next to one another (toys, for example, next to lawn and garden).

Other considerations. Other considerations that may be important in developing a workable layout plan for the store but that do not need any elaboration include the following:

1. Use the least desirable space in the store for employee areas, stock areas, and customer service areas.
2. Place departments which require extensive stock requirements close to stock areas (such as a shoe department).
3. Place departments which require refrigeration, cooking facilities, heavy fixturing, and which sell large bulky items, on the perimeter of the store.

Sunset variety store

Now that we have reviewed some of the factors involved in store layout decisions, let us take a look at one firm's efforts to come up with an effective layout arrangement. As this layout arrangement is discussed remember that although good layout decisions are developed from the ideas which we present, the experience that the retailers accumulate with their customers is what makes the ideas work.

Background. The Sunset Variety is located in the downtown shopping area of a large metropolitan area in the East. The store boasted of 90,000 square feet of selling area. Figure 11.3 shows the layout of the selling area for both the main sales level and the lower sales level.

When this store was first engineered, it was done so with a background of information on space/sales relationships from previous experience within the industry and a knowledge of the buying patterns of the customers shopping variety stores. The data at the bottom of the page show the space/sales relationships that the store worked with.

It was the intent of the owners to present an image that was, basically, variety yet to reflect in many departments an image of being a junior department store. The store hoped to attract people through advertising and employ to the fullest extent the use of advertised specials. The customers of this downtown location represented the office and retail workers from the surrounding stores, shoppers from the outlying suburban districts, and those customers who lived within a fairly close radius of the store.

Decisions made. Some of the ideas inherent

	% Gross Margin	$ Per Sq. Ft.	% of Profit Contributions
Notions & small wares	45.3	51.3	8.2
Drugs	38.7	37.8	5.4
Stationery	46.0	32.9	9.8
Toys, books, games	42.0	36.0	9.2
Housewares & furnishings	39.8	37.8	11.6
Hardware, paint, electrics	39.6	37.8	6.2
Dry gds., domestics, yd. gds.	33.2	40.4	5.6
Apparel, accessories	36.5	44.2	23.6
Jewelry	45.0	42.8	2.6
Confectionery	35.5	35.9	4.8
Fountain and food service	64.0		13.0

in the decisions that surrounded the layout of the store were as follows:

1. Sunset relied heavily on the concept of related selling. Looking to Figure 11.3, we can see the results of this type of thinking by witnessing the grouping of certain departments. For example, variety piece goods are located next to the sewing notions department, ladies' wear next to lingerie, jewelry next to nylons and purses, and artificial flowers, frame pictures, and gifts and glassware located next to one another to build upon the gift nature of each of these departments.

2. Sunset tended to put merchandise or de-

Main Sales Level

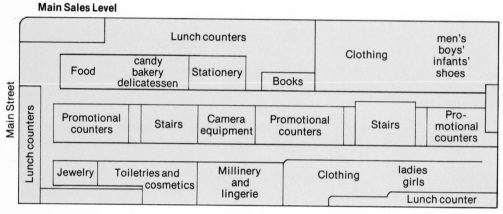

Hogan Street

Lower Sales Level

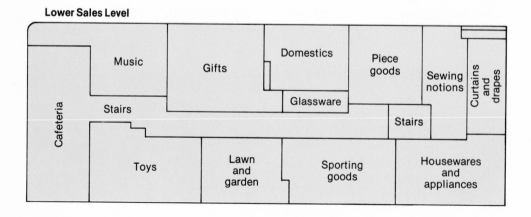

Figure 11.3. Layout of selling areas in Sunset Variety.

partments selling impulse goods predominantly in high traffic areas. Conversely, they placed demand or "generative" merchandise departments in more out of the way locations. For this reason the candy department, jewelry department, and seasonal merchandise were placed on counters positioned close to the entrances and in the most valuable store space available. Customers interested in shopping for clothing items, housewares, and domestics will make the effort to walk to the store's perimeter or basement, and consequently the owners felt comfortable in placing these departments in less easily accessible sections of the store.

3. One of the better locations in the store, from the point of view of traffic exposure, is the spot immediately off the stairway leading to the basement. Toys were placed in this strategic spot. Probably two things influence the selection of this department. First, toys would be considered to be an action department. Something always seems to be going on in the toy department. It has an interesting appeal to customers young and old alike. Customers will go out of their way, even go downstairs just to search out the toy department. It may be that customers who might not otherwise have gone downstairs will be pulled downstairs because of their interest in the toys or the interest that their youngsters express in looking at the toy department. And second, toys are also a fairly high gross margin department. To this extent, the toy department can support the more valuable space which it occupies.

4. Another high gross margin department is the food service operation. The high gross margin of 64% and the high percent of profit contribution, 13%, are substantial reasons why so much space might be given to the food operation. In addition, the fact that it is a downtown store and a need exists to service downtown shoppers as well as office workers with convenient yet inexpensive meals, suggests why a total of 14,000 square feet or 15% of its total selling area is devoted to the food facilities. In fact, the store can serve about 1,800 people an hour at peak times. The positioning of the food facilities on the perimeter of the store is largely due to management consideration. With the type of equipment necessary to operate a food operation, it becomes impractical to place food facilities in the middle of the selling floor. However, because of the profit potentials of the food business, they are given choice locations next to the entrances into the store. The candy, bakery, and delicatessen departments, representing largely impulse merchandise, are given locations in high traffic areas.

5. One of the best locations in the store is located in the corner of the Hogan Street and the Main Street entrance. Toiletries, drugs, and jewelry obtained these high-traffic locations because of their impulse nature, because of their relatively high gross margin, and just because of the nature of the departments that they represent. These departments are in a prime position to catch the lunch-hour shoppers. In addition, these departments offer a substantial advantage to give the promotional punch, such as mass stacked hair spray islands, required of a price store. And finally, these departments represent traditional merchandise that variety stores typically handle. To this extent, then, a person walking through the front door and noticing these goods gets the whole picture of the variety image that the store is attempting to portray. The hair notions are displayed next to hair toiletries for maximum related sales.

6. Housewares and home furnishings departments account for about 48% of the lower sales level. These departments were carefully grouped from the standpoint of customer logic and from the standpoint of grouping related departments.

Observations of Layout Patterns for Different Retail Stores

Cafeterias

At most cafeterias, the serving lines are arranged to tempt customers. The salads are displayed first; next the soups and vegetables; then the meats, desserts, and finally the beverages. This is the most common and profitable layout for a cafeteria. Salads and pastries pay the largest gross margin so they are offered first to tempt one who feels hungry. Once salads and pastries have been selected, one must still select a meat with a dish of vegetables. A beverage, too, is usually selected. When people reach the end of the counter, they have picked out more food than they are capable of eating. Proprietors know this, so they lay out their counters accordingly.

Hardware stores

A hardware store stocks a variety of merchandise besides hardware. A person entering this type of store usually does so to buy some type of hardware. Therefore, it is not necessary to give the most valuable space in the store to hardware items. Nonhardwares, such as sporting goods, are a better choice for the more valuable space. This merchandise is often bought on impulse, and, therefore, needs good display space.

Bulky, heavy, or unattractive items are kept in the rear of the store. Nails, hinges, wire, and wood are examples of such items. Some items such as stoves, linoleum, and ashcans are not displayed but are shown only as samples. The middle of the store is usually devoted to items such as electrical appliances, kitchenware, and silverware. If there is a paint department, it is in the back portion of the store. Novelties, new lines, high priced items, and small bulk hardware are usually found on the counters and are given good locations.

Drug stores

The common drug store presents layout problems because of the wide variety of goods that it handles. Tobacco and candies are found near the front of the store because of their impulse nature and because they are frequently purchased. If they are placed next to each other, tobacco is placed nearer the entrance and the candy can be spread out along some of the aisles, where bargains can be offered on boxes of candy. If a soda fountain exists in the store, it is usually found against one of the walls. The departments bordering the opposite side from the fountain consist of toilet articles, dental supplies, and colognes (impulse merchandises). In the center aisles are magazines, stationery, and specially priced articles such as alarm clocks, car waxes, and leather novelties. In the rear of the drug store are medicines, hospital supplies, and the prescription counter. These are set in the back of the store because customers will make the special effort to go to the rear of the store to seek them out.

Summary

We have taken you through some of the ideas useful to good store design and good layout planning. Each of these ideas had as its objective the development of customer goodwill, the arrangement of merchandise in a manner convenient for customer shopping, and the production of profitable sales.

Questions and Problems

1. In your opinion should space be allocated to products on the basis of sales, gross margin, or on some other basis? Would your answer vary according to the product under discussion? Support your position.
2. In store layout how do you resolve the dilemma of finding the right location for a department when today's stores have many entrances?
3. Store design and layout result as much from management considerations as from customer considerations. Comment.
4. What do you think are the current and future trends in store design and layout?

Situations and Activities

You are the manager of a surplus store. Your store handles everything from sporting goods to clothing items and from paint to hardware. It is located in an old section of town and occupies an old building. Your store has enjoyed phenomenal success. It is the type of store that people like to come into and browse around in; many spend a half hour to an hour merely walking through the aisles. Recently, a new discount house has come into town, and you are already beginning to suffer decreased sales. Consequently, you are evaluating your total operation, especially layout, to determine whether improvements can be made. It has been your philosophy that a store such as yours should carry a great deal of merchandise and should have a cluttered appearance, for this conveys the image of a surplus store. One of the things you have attempted to do is to keep people moving slowly through the store because this promotes sales. To accomplish this objective you have made the aisles narrow; you have merchandise, such as sporting goods, located in four or five different locations in the store; you have made the counters high, reaching up to about six feet; and you have staggered the counters throughout the store so there is no one continuous aisle. Will you make any changes in this layout?

You are the manager of a gift shop. In recent months you have become aware of how old and drab your store seems to be in comparison with the new stores coming into town. You especially notice your store has high ceilings, high windows, drab colors, and old fixtures. In fact, your store has the appearance of deterioration. You wish to remodel with an absolute minimum of expense, and yet you want to create a new look. What can you do?

Select a store of your choosing. Prepare a revised layout plan using graph paper and give an explanation for your recommended changes. Show it to the store manager for his comments. Write an explanation of your recommended changes.

Select a store of your choosing. Sketch a layout of the store and trace the movement of 50 customers who enter the store. Chart the direction each one goes, record how much they spend (or don't spend), and how much time each customer spent in the store. Analyze the customer traffic plan within the store. What conclusions would you draw? What recommendations would you make?

Bibliography

"Checkouts Call for a Revolution." *Women's Wear Daily,* January 19, 1970, pp. 1—13.

"Customer Traffic Patterns: Key to Selling Efficiency." *Progressive Grocer,* January, 1966.

Markin, R. J. "The Supermarket Today and Tomorrow." *Atlanta Economic Review,* October, 1972, pp. 20—24.

Moore, Plasco G. *Principles of Merchandise Display.* Austin, Texas: University of Texas, Division of Extension.

Mulhern, Helen. "Looks, Shops, and Fixtures." *Stores,* April 1972, pp. 10—12.

Salmon, Walter J., Buzzell, Robert D., and Cort, Stanton D. "Today the Shopping Center, Tomorrow the Superstore." *Harvard Business Review,* January—February, 1974, p. 89—98.

six

OPERATING A RETAIL STORE

12

Knowing How Much to Buy

contents

behavioral objectives

All retail managers need to understand and be able to develop some kind of merchandise plan. Their plans for a selling season should include predictions of the items that will be bought and the amount of money that will be spent on them. When you master merchandise planning, you will possess one of the most important assets of a retail manager.

Upon completing this chapter, you will be able to do the following:
☐ Develop and know when to use an open-to-buy and an assortment plan.
☐ Understand the importance of merchandise classifications in running a department.
☐ Plan beginning and ending inventories within a budget period.
☐ Know how to adjust inventories in order to achieve a planned stock turnover.
☐ Develop a basic stock list and a model stock plan.

What makes you think you're a buyer? We heard an angry manager make that remark to his assistant after the manager reviewed the inventory position of the assistant's department at the end of selling season. The assistant just didn't seem to know what he was doing—the job had gotten away from him. Markdowns were much too high, there was too much merchandise in stock, and there was too much out-of-season stock. Each of these problems took its toll on profits.

Curiously enough, the assistant had always felt that buying merchandise was his bag. He felt he had the knack. But successful buying results from more than merely possessing a knack. Buying merchandise is hard work. It requires constant attention to details; a thorough knowledge of one's customers, including a knowledge of their likes and dislikes; familiarity with the thousands of old and new products offered for sale; the testing, evaluating, and retesting of products that have been purchased; and careful buying that results in a sufficient amount of the right stock but does not result in overstocking, with too much of the investment tied up in inventory. Buying merchandise involves working with resources in a way that benefits the store. It requires more than a knack; it is a demanding, critical job requiring knowledge, an innovative spirit, and an analytical mind.

It is true that some people are said to have a flair for buying. They seem to be able to distinguish significant fashion trends; they are creative enough to assemble a stock of merchandise that is balanced and appeals to customers; and they can predict the merchandising potential of various items offered for sale. Buyers who possess this flair, however, are the first to say that it is mainly the result of experience and hard work.

The aspects of the buying function that most directly affect retail managers are shown in Figure 12.1. Essentially, they include (1) knowing how much to buy, (2) knowing what to buy, and (3) knowing how to place the order. In this and the following chapter, these aspects of the buying function are examined.

Preparing to Buy

We said that successful buyers work hard at their job, know their customers, and master the many details accompanying the buying function. One requirement of working with the details of buying is a system for getting the most out of trips to the market, that is, the place where merchandise is bought. Whether one buys from a firm across town or on the other side of the world, a buyer must be well prepared before embarking on a buying trip. To be unprepared is to end up lost in the corridors and a prey for all passersby.

Buyers preparing to buy do so either in their stores or make visits to the market (locations where merchandise is offered for sale). For most merchandise, the biggest part of the buying is done on these "trips to the market." The number of visits made depends upon (1) the buyers' nearness to the market, (2) departmental sales volume, (3) market conditions, (4) whether the store enjoys buying assistance, e.g. resident buyers (agents permanently located at the market), and (5) store policy. It is the purpose of these trips to purchase merchandise and/or to obtain information on what suppliers are offering, compare ideas with other retailers, and generally get a feel for trends in fashion.

Basic to all buying preparations are answers to the following questions:

1. What do our customers want? How much will they buy?
2. What is our rate of sale on what we're buying?
3. How long does it take to replenish stock?
4. How large an assortment will we need?
5. Who supplies the best selling merchandise for our situation?
6. Which styles, prices will move the best for us?
7. How will we promote the merchandise we buy?

The answers to these questions say a great deal relative to how much money to

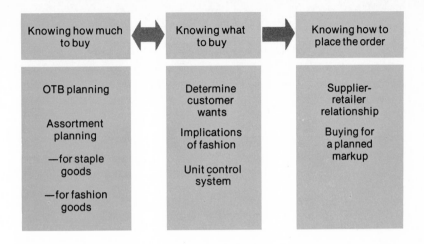

Figure 12.1. Selected aspects of the buying function.

spend and on what merchandise to spend it. It will be our job to first determine how much money to spend on inventory and what items to buy. Some retailers make this decision either by spending the money they have available or by spending until they no longer see merchandise they want to stock. The two methods described in this chapter are based on more scientific principles than these two approaches and require intelligent planning.

A Top-Down Versus a Bottom-up Approach

There are two methods of determining how much to buy. To ignore or default on either one is to court disaster. The first of these is planning the *open-to-buy* (OTB), or planning the amount of purchases (in dollars) to make for an upcoming selling season. The second method is *assortment planning,* or planning the proper stock balance (in dollars *and* in units) for an upcoming selling season.

At first glance, OTB and assortment planning seem essentially the same, because both involve planning for future dollar purchases. To a large extent, they do duplicate each other, except for one very important difference—the

method by which one arrives at planned dollar purchases.

The procedure in OTB planning is essentially a top-down approach: A dollar purchase figure is the end product. This figure is obtained by determining how much merchandise (in dollars) is needed. Merchandise needs are planned by broad categories such as by departments and by classifications.

The weakness in OTB planning is its lack of a systematic way of determining how many items in a category or department should be purchased. Since customers buy in units—one golf bag, one scarf, one pair of sunglasses—then buying plans should also reflect unit purchases. To overcome this weakness assortment plans are developed.

The procedure in assortment planning is essentially a bottom-up approach: Plans call for dollar and unit purchases of items or groups of items. Merchandise needs are classified in narrow categories, such as guns in a sporting goods department and wide-brim hats in a millinery department.

As an example of the difference between the two procedures, let us suppose you are the buyer for the accessories department. You have broken down your merchandise offerings into three groups: jewelry, handbags, and scarves. Using the OTB planning procedure, you would arrive at planned purchases by saying to yourself, for example, "Last year I sold $20,000 worth of goods in this department, and this year I expect to sell $22,000 worth, so I'll plan purchases for this year at $22,000." In other words, under the OTB procedure, you, as the buyer, would work with broad departmental figures to plan purchases. Under the assortment planning procedure, you would determine how many dollars to spend on purchases in each category of merchandise. Your plans would, again, be based on last year's sales. Your assortment plan for this year, for example, might call for purchases of

12 dz.	floral scarves
2 dz.	hand knit scarves
1 ea.	grandfather clock

—and so on—

until all needed merchandise units had been planned for the upcoming season. In the ideal situation the summation of the dollars representative of the unit plan would approximate the $22,000[1] arrived at through the dollar plan.

A buyer is delighted when the two procedures produce the same results. If the figures aren't alike or similar, the buyer must reconcile them by reevaluating the plans. One procedure is, then, a check on the other procedure.

To place all this into perspective from management's standpoint, OTB planning is useful as an overall, master control of the dollar purchases to be made within a broad merchandise category. It doesn't aid management in planning how many dollars should be purchased for particular items or small groups of items in a department. Assortment planning, on the other hand, fulfills this function. Assortment planning begins with particular items and small groups of items and builds up to a total purchase figure. An advantage of assortment planning is that early in the planning process,

particularly before going to market, a buyer must think in terms of a balanced assortment of items (in units).

Both OTB planning and assortment planning involve the establishment of merchandise plans called budgets. A merchandise budget is a guide that details a merchandising unit's investment in inventory. It is difficult to imagine how any successful retailer could operate without such planning. Merchandise goes in and out of the store rapidly, and there are hundreds of items from which to buy. Furthermore, there are sometimes long lead times from the time the order is placed and the time merchandise is received. In addition, in today's market, fashion plays such a prominent role in all merchandising activities that some kind of merchandise plan is necessary. The owner of a small retail store may make merchandise plans only in his mind. If he or she is a skillful merchant and carries a limited number of items, this kind of planning may be all that is required. However, for a large retail operation, formal, systematic methods of planning (OTB and assortment planning) are necessary. Conceptually, these formal methods are useful to the small independent retailer as well as to the large chain retailer.

Merchandise Classifications

Before OTB and assortment planning can be discussed further, it is necessary to explore a topic of importance to both methods—merchandise classifications. The preceding chapter emphasized the importance of maintaining sales records on a departmental basis, so merchants can keep abreast of a department's performance. Departmental breakdowns are also relevant to buying. Because departments are built around a homogeneous grouping of merchandise, departmental breakdowns give buyers the opportunity to (1) be efficient in locating resources, (2) provide a coordinated assortment of goods, and (3) maintain inventory control. If a store is small and has limited merchandise, a departmental

---

[1]The $22,000 is expressed in terms of retail prices. At some time you would have to determine the cost figure equivalent to $22,000 at retail prices. In the next chapter, when we talk about the actual buying of merchandise, we'll explain how to convert the retail price to a cost price.

breakdown is both necessary and adequate. However, as stores increase in size, more merchandise is offered for sale, and departmental breakdowns may not be sufficient to provide feedback for effective inventory management and buying. An alternative way of grouping merchandise may, then, be required.

One kind of merchandise breakdown currently in favor is merchandise classification. Merchandise classification is an extension of the merchandise breakdown exercised through the departmental structure. Merchandise within a department is classified according to a segment of customer demand, for example, brand, size, color, material, and price. As such, merchandise classifications contain homogeneous items reasonably interchangeable in the eyes of the customer (see Table 12.1). In other words, merchandise classifications are based on the way customers shop for merchandise.

As shown in Table 12.1, there may be several levels of merchandise classifications. The number of levels that management decides to establish depends on (1) the amount of control that management feels is necessary to the successful performance of a department and (2) the number of merchandise breakdowns necessary to describe a balanced assortment of goods.

It is not necessary for all merchandise within a department to be included in some classification. Classifications of merchandise will evolve when and if management is faced with merchandise groups that represent significant volumes of business or pose particular problems related to timing of purchases, shortages, stock balance, and others, or when different buying responsibility exists across merchandise lines. Although it is difficult to know for certain how merchandise classification helps a store alleviate some of these problems, the improvements in control and buying that result from such a system may increase net profits by 35 percent. A merchandise classification may not be useful to all retailers, but it may help managers who find it difficult to keep track of their merchandise inventory.

OTB Planning

Open-to-buy planning was described as a master control plan based on a top-down approach. As such, it is a control on the number of retail dollars (called dollar control) that will be spent for merchandise inventory within a given period. The objective is not to have too much money tied up in inventory, which requires a large amount of capital and subjects the merchandise to possible risks, nor to have too little merchandise, which leads to out-of-stock conditions and lost sales. OTB planning operates on a broad dollar scale rather than on individual items or even on small groups of items to prevent such occurrences.

Table 12.1. Merchandise Classifications		
Level 1 classification	**Level 2 classification**	**Level 3 classification**
1. men's	high heels	straps
2. women's	medium heels	pumps
3. children's	low heels	
4. boots	flats	
5. house slippers	wedges	
6. boys'		
7. growing girls'		
8. rubber footwear		

Basically, OTB planning involves a given budget period and three predictions:

1. Planned sales
2. Planned ending inventory
3. Planned beginning inventory.

It is illustrated in Table 12.2. In this table the buyer thinks she will need $75,000 worth of inventory for the period to meet the sales projections. She expects to have $50,000 in inventory on hand at the end of the budget period and $40,000 available and on hand at the beginning of the budget period. Orders for $10,000 worth of inventory have already been placed for delivery during the budget period, called stock on order. Therefore, $75,000 worth of merchandise will have to be bought during the period.

Table 12.2. OTB Budget

Needed
Planned sales	$ 75,000
Planned end of period inventory (at retail)	50,000
	$125,000

Available
Planned beginning of period inventory (at retail)	$40,000
Stock on order	10,000
	$50,000

OTB = $125,000 − 50,000 = $75,000 (at retail)

Planned sales

Fundamental to any kind of planning in retailing is planning for sales volume in the upcoming budget period. No store or department within a store should ever proceed without having first made an estimate of the sales it expects to obtain. Without this figure, intelligent planning of promotion expenditures, personnel requirements, and supplies cannot be done. OTB planning is no different; the first step is to plan sales.

There are probably as many different methods of planning for a store's sales volume as there are retailers. However, most of these methods contain one or all of the following considerations:

> Last year's sales volume
> Last month's sales volume
> Local and national economic conditions
> Fashion trends
> An assessment of competitive forces
> Sales promotions planned for the store
> Wholesale and retail price changes
> Local employment conditions
> Changes in store policy.

Using each of these considerations would be a difficult task for most retailers. Therefore, retail businesses that have been in operation for some time are likely to use the sales figure for the last two months of operation to forecast sales for the forthcoming period. The assumption is that sales in the forthcoming period will follow fairly closely recent sales. In other words, if the store has recently experienced a 10 percent increase in sales, it is reasonable to assume that in the forthcoming period there will be an increase of 10 percent over the same period a year ago.

A retailer who can assess the impact of economic conditions, employment, and fashion trends on retail sales will modify the planned sales figures accordingly. Most likely, he or she will make assessments in qualitative terms rather than attempting to assign numerical values to them. If numerical values are desired, the retailer should use such sources as *Business Week, Department Store Economist, Survey of Current Business, Federal Reserve Bulletin,* the local newspapers, and the many trade publications that carry articles on predictions for the economy and their implications for the retail industry.

Planned inventories

Having established planned sales for the OTB budget period, the retailer should plan how much stock should be in inventory at the beginning and end of the budget period. A retail store must have inventory on hand so it can sell merchandise at the beginning of each new selling season. It must also have inventory on hand at the end of the budget period so it can sell merchandise at the beginning of the next budget period. It is management's responsibility to plan for each of these inventory situations.

In OTB planning, beginning of the period inventory has been bought during a prior budget period and, therefore, represents inventory available for sale. It is not necessary to buy this inventory for the current OTB period. On the other hand, end of the period inventories are inventories that must be on hand at the end of the current budget period, and therefore, must be bought during this period. Look again at the sample OTB budget, Table 12.2. It should now be clear why end of the period inventories were included under the "Needed" column and beginning of the period inventories under the "Available" column.

Last year's stock. You may wonder how management arrives at a planned retail inventory level. Plans are formulated several months before the OTB period. How, then, can management know how many dollars of inventory will be on hand at the beginning and at the end of the upcoming budget period? Actually, management cannot be sure of its exact dollar position, but it should try to make estimates that hopefully will not be wide of the mark.

One obvious way to arrive at planned inventory positions is to use last year's stock position at the same point in time and project current needs from that figure. For example, if the beginning of the open-to-buy period last year showed a $100,000 stock inventory, it is reasonable to assume that this year stock will amount to $100,000, plus or minus any projected increase or decrease in sales.

Stock-sales ratios. Another way to arrive at planned stock figures is to establish a ratio of stock to sales. Usually, this relationship will vary, depending on the size of the store, the nature of the goods being carried, whether the goods are seasonal, staple, or fashion items, and the stock turnover rate representative of the kind of store in operation. The relationship is usually established by dividing the planned sales for the month or period into the beginning of the month's or period's stock:

Stock-sales ratio

$$= \frac{\text{beginning of the month stock}}{\text{sales for the month}}$$

or

$$= \frac{\text{beginning of the period stock}}{\text{sales for the period}}$$

For example, suppose management has determined that for a particular month (January) a department had sales of $20,000 last year and had a beginning of the month (January) inventory of $100,000. This information suggests that it took $5.00 in backup stock to generate $1.00 in sales. If management plans to do $30,000 worth of business for the same month this year and the stock-sales ratio has been 5, management must plan for a beginning inventory of $150,000 in order to generate $30,000 in sales.

Stock-sales ratio
$$= \frac{\$100,000 \text{ (beginning of month)}}{\$20,000 \text{ (sales)}} = 5{:}1$$

Using this kind of analysis, management can establish its stock levels on a basis consistent with the amount of sales anticipated for the department. Obviously, more refined planning can be accomplished by averaging several years' stock-sales ratios.

Stock turnover. A well-run store or department maintains a satisfactory stock turnover rate (remember that stock turnover rate is determined by dividing average inventory at retail into the net sales). A satisfactory stock turnover rate is important because too much inventory on hand ties up capital, and therefore, unnecessarily increases the cost of doing business. Also, merchandise that is kept in a store for a long time may deteriorate or become obsolete. Too much inventory also gives a store a junky appearance, makes it difficult for shoppers to find merchandise, and yields a mass of old, slow moving merchandise that is not in demand. On the other hand, having too little inventory on hand leads to being out of stock on merchandise needed by customers and lost sales.

Retailers should remember that capital is a commodity and costs money like any other commodity. For example, for a retailer who borrows from a bank, an investment of $100,000 in inventory costs approximately $11,000 a year in interest (11 percent interest × $100,000). Consequently, if reductions in inventory can be made, say from $100,000 to $60,000, without losing sales, the cost of doing business can decrease from $11,000, to $6,600 (11 percent × $60,000). This happens even before the doors are opened for business. Is it any wonder that management should be extremely interested in stock turnover rates?

Unfortunately, even though department managers know that they are being evaluated on a particular stock turnover performance, they often do not know how to plan for satisfactory stock turnover. To do so, however, is not difficult. Take, for example, the open-to-buy illustration previously presented (Table 12.2). Let us assume that this OTB budget is for the period August 1—January 31. (See Table 12.3.)

Table 12.3. OTB Budget (August 1- January 31)

Needed	
Planned sales	$ 75,000
Planned end of season inventory (Jan. 31)	50,000
	$125,000
Available	
Planned beginning of season inventory (Aug. 1)	$40,000
Stock on order	10,000
	$50,000

We have already learned that stock turnover is derived by dividing average inventory at retail into the net sales. Using the figures in the illustration, one can determine the average inventory at retail for the period—the first step in solving for stock turnover rate. Because average inventory is found by adding the beginning and ending inventory figures and dividing by their number, it is possible to add $50,000 and $40,000 and then divide by two to arrive at an average inventory at retail of $45,000. Subsequently, if the average inventory figure ($45,000) is divided into the planned sales figure ($75,000), the stock turnover can be derived for the budget period. The stock turnover figure is 1.67.

Average inventory at retail

$$= \frac{\text{beginning} + \text{ending inventories}}{2}$$

$$= \frac{\$50,000 + \$40,000}{2}$$

$$= \$45,000$$

Stock turnover rate

$$= \frac{\text{net sales}}{\text{average inventory at retail}}$$

$$= \frac{\$75,000}{\$45,000} = 1.67$$

Now let us assume for the moment that a stock turnover rate of 1.67 is unsatisfactory and that, in fact, management has decreed that a satisfactory level of performance for a department for the upcoming OTB period will be a stock turnover of 2. The manager of the department will have to make adjustments in the plan in order to realize a stock turnover of 2.

To realize a particular stock turnover rate, department managers may either adjust the planned sales figure or the average inventory figure. If department managers have done an acceptable job of determining customer wants, it is unrealistic for them to adjust planned sales figures merely to obtain a given stock turnover rate. Therefore, they usually achieve a given stock turnover rate by making adjustments in their planned stock levels. The following calculations show how department managers may plan for a given stock turnover rate:

Step 1. $\dfrac{\$50,000 + \$40,000}{2} = \$45,000$

$\dfrac{\$75,000}{\$45,000} = 1.67$ stock turnover

Step 2. Divide the buyer's stock turnover by management's decreed stock turnover as the basis for adjusting beginning and ending inventories:

$$\frac{\text{Buyer's stock turnover}}{\text{Management's stock turnover}} \quad \frac{1.67}{2.00} = 83.5\% \quad \text{inventory adjustment factor}$$

Step 3. Adjust the buyer's beginning and ending planned inventories in the OTB:

$50,000
× 83.5%
$41,750 new end of season inventory

$40,000
× 83.5%
$33,400 new beginning of season inventory

OTB with stock turnover of 2.0 (see Table 12.4)

New stock turnover

$$\$41,750 + \$33,400 = \frac{\$75,150}{2} = \$37,575$$

$$\frac{\$75,000}{\$37,575} = 2.0 \text{ (rounded)}$$

To pull our discussion of open-to-buy planning together, let's look at what we have accomplished so far.

1. We have planned for sales (in the "Needed" column).
2. We have planned for beginning inventory (in the "Available" column).
3. We have planned for ending inventory (in the "Needed" column).

Be advised also that sometimes markdowns, employee discounts, and shortages (called retail reductions) are also included in the "Needed" column after planned sales. These have the same effect as sales since they reduce the value of the stock on hand.

The only remaining element to consider in our OTB is stock on order, and this is treated very simply by adding the stock on order to the "Available" column.

Most OTB plans (also called merchandise budgets or plans) are prepared on a semiannual basis. Their ultimate objective is to guide the day-to-day operations of a department or store toward the seasonal goals. Generally, the plans are built around selling seasons. In clothing, for example, the Fall season begins in August and ends in January. Planning for the Fall season is usually completed by the preceding February. With the time lag which exists between the time plans are prepared and the actual selling season begins, you can well imagine that the figures which are planned for in February may not materialize by August. Generally, management expects this, but hopefully the two sets of figures will not be too far apart. If they are, an adjustment in plans may have to be made.

For example, let us assume that our plans called for an OTB of $73,350 as shown above. Let us further assume that right after the buyer prepared her plan in February, she went to market and bought 80% of her OTB to ensure delivery by August 1 or $58,680. Again let us assume that new competition came into the buyer's trading area and it became apparent to her about July 15 that her planned sales for the upcoming budget period would have to be revised downward by 20% or $15,000. Finally, let us assume that inventory levels can be held constant (probably an unrealistic assumption). Adjustments are clearly in order as demonstrated in Table 12.5.

As you can see, the buyer is already in an overbought position by $330. This is not particularly serious, because management never adheres rigidly to the figure; flexibility within limits in budgeting is an acceptable practice. On the other hand, if planned inventories were also to be decreased causing a much greater overbought position, serious problems would exist in the department. The buyer would be faced with expensive hand-to-mouth buying, many promotional expenses, and/or taking costly markdowns in order to get her inventory in line. Other things which could affect the OTB plans include employee or community strikes, an environmental disaster, economic downturn, and poor sales planning.

Table 12.4. OTB With Stock Turnover of 2.0

Needed		Available	
Planned sales	$ 75,000	Planned beginning of season inventory	$33,400
Planned end of season inventory	41,750	Stock on order	10,000
	$116,750		$43,400

OTB (given new inventory positions) = $116,750 − $43,400 = $73,350

Table 12.5. Revised OTB August 1 - January 1

Needed		Available	
Planned sales 75,000 - 15,000	$ 60,000	Planned beginning of season	
Planned end of season inventory	41,750	inventories	$ 33,400
	$101,750	Received or stock on order merchandise,	
		58,680 + 10,000	68,680
			$102,080

OTB (given updated information) = $101,750 − $102,080 = (330)

One more point needs to be made. Buyers continually examine their OTB position—not just under the situations mentioned above. Every time a vendor approaches the buyer for the purpose of making a sale, the buyer must determine whether she is OTB. The technique for doing so is quite simple. Using the equation *Open to buy = Stock to be provided (STP)— Stock already provided (SAP)* determines how much more (if any) a buyer can purchase. For example, going back to our example when the buyer was OTB $73,350, and assuming the buyer wanted to know her OTB as of November 10, if the buyer had ordered (but not received) $8,000 worth of merchandise and had received the $10,000 merchandise listed as "stock on order" at the beginning of the budget period, her OTB as of November 10 would be $55,350.

OTB   =   STP   −   SAP
$55,350 = $73,350 − ($8,000 + $10,000)

Assortment Planning

Assortment planning helps the buyer in two ways. First, it forces a plan of attack, the thrust of which is to ensure a balanced stock in terms of units and retail dollars. In achieving this stock balance, the buyer is influenced by (1) the kinds of goods typically carried in the department or store, (2) the space available for inventory, and (3) the sales and profit potential of the merchandise. Intermingled with these considerations, and in fact crucial to all operational decisions made in the business, is the need to achieve stock balance in the context of

a well-defined store image. If there is no well-conceived, systematic approach to planning the appropriate assortment of merchandise, a store is not entirely satisfactory to anyone. Usually, it is in business in a halfhearted way: carrying a little of this and a little of that.

Second, assortment planning provides a comparison with the open-to-buy plan. Since both the OTB and assortment plans yield a projected total dollar purchase figure, each serves as a check on the other. The difference between the two is that OTB is a top-down approach, assortment planning a bottom-up approach: OTB gives planning information in dollars; assortment planning gives planning in dollars and units.

In planning a good assortment of merchandise, the buyer must be fully informed of the various customer types the department serves. In this regard the buying function is dynamic. Customers whose business once may have been important may have dwindled in numbers while others may have increased. Changing customer interests and buying habits and motivations must also be given consideration. These things as well as others will more nearly assure that the department will achieve both balanced and adequate assortments.

Basic stock lists

Basic stocks in a retail store are staple merchandise. They represent merchandise for which there is a fairly constant demand and for which fashion plays a relatively unimportant role. The demand for cigarettes, toothpaste, girls' white bobby socks, and many other items is constant—it does not vary significantly from season to season.

A basic stock list is usually developed for goods of this kind. Such a list is a precise statement of the items to be carried in stock. It includes the name of each item, its description by style number, size, price, color, weight, brand, and so on. Sometimes a picture of the item is listed for easy identification. In addition, many basic stock lists contain room for the buyer to record the inventory position on each item (see Table 12.6).

Typically, chain operations send to their stores a basic stock list in notebook style. This notebook contains a listing of all staple merchandise that must be carried by the store. To be out of stock on even 5 percent of the items listed in the notebook is to invite the wrath of management.

Small independent stores maintain a basic stock list by accumulating product information sheets and filing them in systematic order. These sheets originate at the manufacturer's plant and/or with suppliers selling to the retail store. Once a merchant prepares a basic stock list, it should continually be updated.

A basic stock list serves as the assortment plan for staple merchandise. As such, it provides a plan to ensure a balanced stock of staple merchandise; the merchandise is expressed in terms of specific units and the dollars to be invested in these units. Following through on the information provided in Table 12.6, the buyer has apparently decided to

have the department covered for the forthcoming budget period in the following way:

1. Toothpaste will be carried in two brands (Crest and Gleem); Crest will be carried in two sizes, economy and regular, and Gleem in one size, regular (see Column 1).
2. Minimum packing units are 1 dozen (see Column 2).
3. From last year's unit sales, this year's sales can be projected (Column 3).
4. Given the retail price of the item (Column 3) and projected unit sales (Column 3), total dollar sales can be projected (Column 4).
5. Column 5 shows projections for each month of the budget period. As is probably obvious by now, the total dollar sales built via a bottom-up approach (assortment planning) should yield the same number of dollars achieved by using the top-down approach (OTB planning). They both tell the buyer how much to spend on inventory for the budget period.

Model stock plans

Model stock is an assortment of goods that seems to best fit the needs of the store's cutomers. Model stock is expressed in terms of the salient features of the assortment: price lines, styles, colors, materials, sizes, and so on.

A model stock plan is a breakdown of the merchandise that a store plans to stock. Once

Table 12.6   Basic Stock List

Column 1	Column 2	Column 3				Column 4	Column 5					
		price		sales		project	jan. sales		feb. sales		mar. sales	
merchandise description and stock number	packing	cost	retail	last year	this year	dollar sales	last year	this year	last year	this year	last year	this year
287 Crest toothpaste economy size	1dz											
288 Crest toothpaste regular size	1dz											
289 Crest toothpaste regular size mint flavored	1dz											
293 Gleem toothpaste regular size	1dz											

the plan is developed, the store buys the appropriate quantities. These quantities are determined on the basis of planned sales.

Recall that the basic stock list also gave a breakdown of expected stock. However, in the basic stock list, the breakdown was definitive; that is, it described each item to be carried. A model stock plan also describes the stock to be carried, but items are identified by general characteristics, not by specific details.

In assortment planning the model stock plan is used for normal stocking of fashion items. Among staple items, individual articles can be clearly identified, but identification of individual fashion items is more difficult. Therefore, plans are made to buy by common characteristics, such as sizes and price lines. In other words, when drug buyers go to market they know, for example, that they will buy sixteen cases of Crest toothpaste, regular size. Dress buyers, on the other hand, know only that they can buy so many dozen dresses at the $10.95 price, in assorted sizes. They have no way of knowing the style number they will purchase until they see the suppliers' offerings.

Illustrative of a model stock plan is one developed by a department manager prior to making her buys for the six-month selling season beginning in February and ending in July. The department was men's shirts; the merchandise classification for which she was currently planning purchases was men's sport shirts. In planning to purchase sport shirts, the department manager worked from a model stock plan, because each season and each year the merchandise was different and the styles were new. On the other hand, the department manager set up an assortment plan for men's dress and men's work shirts (a merchandise classification in which her department also stocked) through the use of basic stock lists. Dress and work shirts were staple items with style numbers that were carried from season to season.

In working up the model stock plan for sport shirts, the buyer was influenced by the following facts:

1. The general characteristics of sport shirts:
   a. Long and short sleeves
   b. Plain and fancy styles
   c. Small to extra-large sizes
   d. Regular and tall lengths
2. The department currently carried $4.50, $6.50, and $10.50 price lines. (Retail stores often stock according to a limited number of price groupings, called price lines.)

The buyer's model stock plan is shown in Figure 12.2. As you can see, it is designed to enable her to buy according to (1) price line, (2) type of shirt, (3) sizes, and (4) the "Remarks" given on the form.

The percentages of price lines were based on percentages the buyer had found to be satisfactory in past years. After an analysis of last year's sales of sport shirts, the buyer had found that the following percentages prevailed:

Price lines	Average of last year's sales	Average percentages of last year's sales in price lines
$ 4.50	$ 3,000	30%
$ 6.50	4,000	40%
$10.50	3,000	30%
	$10,000	100%

Because she believed that last year's assortment of each price line was adequate, she based her assortment plan on this information. The same rationale was used for further breaking down the assortments into plain and fancy styles and lengths.

Carefully follow with us the steps the buyer went through to arrive at the other figures in Figure 12.2:

Step 1. The buyer arrived at the total dollar retail value of inventory that she should stock in men's sport shirts for the budget period. Figure 12.2 shows this amount to be $9,000 (top of the right-hand column). This figure was arrived at by taking last year's sales in men's sport shirts and projecting this year's sales.

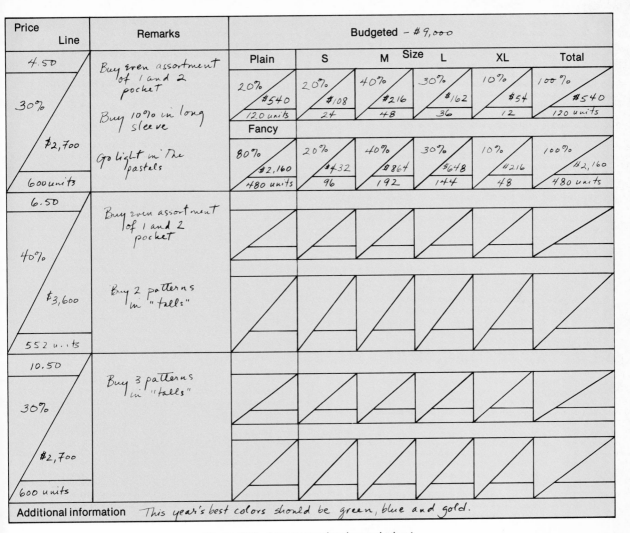

Price Line	Remarks	Budgeted – $9,000					
		Plain	S	M	Size L	XL	Total
4.50 / 30% / $2,700 / 600 units	Buy even assortment of 1 and 2 pocket	20% / $540 / 120 units	20% / $108 / 24	40% / $216 / 48	30% / $162 / 36	10% / $54 / 12	100% / $540 / 120 units
	Buy 10% in long sleeve	Fancy					
	Go light in the pastels	80% / $2,160 / 480 units	20% / $432 / 96	40% / $864 / 192	30% / $648 / 144	10% / $216 / 48	100% / $2,160 / 480 units
6.50 / 40% / $3,600 / 552 units	Buy even assortment of 1 and 2 pocket						
	Buy 2 patterns in "talls"						
10.50 / 30% / $2,700 / 600 units	Buy 3 patterns in "talls"						

Additional information   This year's best colors should be green, blue and gold.

Figure 12.2. Assortment planning work sheet.

Step 2. The buyer selected the general characteristics that might be used to describe men's sport shirts—characteristics she will look for when she makes her buys. As we said, these characteristics are usually determined by the way customers buy the merchandise. It is important to have enough but not too much detail (characteristics). The buyer can't afford and doesn't need to plan for every purchase eventuality. Therefore, the buyer selected *major* characteristics that showed a balanced assortment. Then she planned for coverage of these characteristics, taking into account the many other characteristics that she might have used to balance out the line. Figure 12.2 shows that the buyer decided to plan to stock men's sport shirts by price lines, kind (plain and fancy), and sizes. She alerted herself to other characteristics by writing inserts in the "Remarks" column.

Step 3. The buyer planned how many units and dollars to stock in the price lines, kinds, and sizes chosen to represent the assortment. By checking last year's sales and the assortments needed to back up these sales, she arrived at the percentages. Then she established proportional relationships for the current totals. This is exactly what we did earlier, when we calculated the proportion of last year's sales realized in each of the three price lines.

Step 4. The buyer arrived at the dollar and unit amounts in the following way:

(a) She calculated the amount of stock to be carried at the $4.50 price line as $2,700 ($9,000 × 30 percent). The dollar values of the $6.50 and the $10.50 price line were derived in the same way.

(b) Using the percentages on the assortments to be carried in the plain and fancy shirts at the $4.50 price line, the buyer calculated $540 should be carried in the plain shirts ($2,700 × 20 percent) and $2,160 should be carried in the fancy ones ($2,700 × 80 percent). Again, the same method was used for the plain and fancy shirts at both the $6.50 and $10.50 price lines.

(c) The percentage figures given for size distributions were applied against the dollar value of the types of shirts by price line. In other words, in the $4.50 plain shirts, small size, the firm would stock $108 (20 percent × $540).

(d) Finally, the buyer calculated the number of units to be carried in stock by dividing the dollar totals by their price lines. The buyer, for example, planned to spend $2,700 on the $4.50 shirts; therefore, she planned to buy 600 shirts ($2,700 divided by $4.50 = 600). The same procedure was used to derive the remaining stock (in units).

Buyers may not inventory all the merchandise at the beginning of the selling season, but may initially commit themselves only to a percentage of their buy. This permits them to buy fill-ins and specials when they are needed and available.

The necessity of planning for a balanced stock assortment cannot be emphasized too strongly. A buyer who doesn't plan finds gaping holes in the inventory (unless the buyer is more astute than most). This is not the way for a store to win customer approval.

The procedure most commonly used in assortment planning provides results similar to those found in Figure 12.2. Although other formats may be used, all provide the same kind of information.

As previously indicated, any assortment plan must provide for balanced and adequate stocks, including items which are in continuous demand, as built into basic stock lists, as well as seasonal goods as built into model stock plans. On the other hand, in certain retail circles such terms as basic and model stocks have lost their meanings as being considered outmoded approaches to developing today's assortment plans. Some argue that a more comprehensive attitude to merchandise assortments should be used. No distinctions should be made between staple and fashion merchandise when setting up an assortment, but instead buyers should think in terms of all merchandise, regardless of the frequency of demand. Operationally, this means establishing an assortment plan by listing every item currently in stock, all other items stocked over the past twelve months, and those which are expected to be stocked. Next, through a classification system one establishes unit requirements. As you can see, this approach is not particularly at odds with the more traditional approach, but it does serve to emphasize a more comprehensive attitude toward merchandise assortments.

How Much Stock Is Enough?

Obviously, it is necessary to have enough stock to accommodate the needs of customers. This doesn't mean, however, that a store should attempt to satisfy all needs. It would require an abnormal investment in inventory which would not be consistent with expected profits.

Take, for example, men's dress shirts. It is possible to stock men's dress shirts from a size 14 neck to a size 27 neck. It is also possible to stock them in sleeve lengths from 29 to 36. The bulk of sales will be made in and around the 15½ neck, 33 length sleeve. The distribution of sales and sizes shown in Table 12.7 demonstrates that 12 percent of all dress shirt sales will probably be in 15½ neck, 33 sleeve. Only one shirt will probably be sold in 14½ neck, 29 sleeve.

Shirts are bought in lots of three. A buyer who stocks 14½ neck, 29 sleeve with the expectation of selling only one shirt would have an overstock of two shirts. As you already know, overstocking leads to the tying up of funds in investment and the risk of having to take markdowns on inventory because of slow movement, possible deterioration, and obsolescence. The natural reaction, then, would be not to stock for this one sale, and, in fact, be out of business in the 14½ neck, 29 sleeve shirts.

This returns us to the original question, How much stock is enough? The answer is, Large enough to serve *most* potential customers. The following are guidelines for maintaining a satisfactory stock turnover rate by keeping a stock small, but ample:

1. Carry a few brand styles and price lines for which there is a steady demand.

2. Carry a complete assortment of these brand styles and price lines.

3. Carry the items you know will sell in your store and beware of putting too much emphasis on what goes well in someone else's store.

4. Do not buy all the unusual lines that some vendors would like to sell you.

5. Do not be hoodwinked into purchasing excessive quantities by the lure of extra discounts.

6. Order only items that are needed rather than placing orders across the board, which leads to duplication of similar items already in stock.

Summary

This chapter has emphasized an important aspect of buying—knowing how much to buy. To buy proper amounts of merchandise, managers must pay attention to details and must plan. Two formal plans used by retailers before making their buys are open-to-buy and assortment plans. The purpose of OTB plans is to develop dollar figures the retailer can use to plan purchases so there is neither too little nor too much stock on hand for the expected amount of business. The purpose of assortment plans is to develop dollar and unit figures with which to plan purchases to provide for a balanced assortment of merchandise. All plans must be tailored to a planned stock turnover rate.

Table 12.7. Distribution of Expected Sales of One Hundred Shirts by Size

	14	14½	15	15½	16	16½	17	17½	18
29	—	1	1	2	—	—	—	—	—
30	1	2	2	3	—	—	—	—	—
31	2	3	3	3	—	—	—	—	—
32	2	4	5	7	2	—	—	—	—
33	1	3	8	12	6	5	3	—	—
34	—	—	2	4	3	1	1	—	—
35	—	—	—	1	2	1	1	—	—
36	—	—	—	—	1	1	1	1	—
37	—	—	—	—	—	—	—	—	—

Questions and Problems

1. *Managers often suffer more severely from their own ignorance than from their competitors' actions. Of what value are merchandise planning and control in overcoming ignorance?*
2. *Why is inventory turnover of great importance to retail managers? How can managers achieve a planned inventory turnover?*
3. *Suppose that stock for January 1 is planned at $15,000 at retail, and sales for January are planned at $2,000, with retail reductions planned at 2 percent. Stock for February 1 is planned at $12,000. What is the open-to-buy figure for January? Would proper merchandise planning permit an alteration of this open-to-buy figure? Explain.*
4. *Give the characteristics of an assortment plan for men's hats. Give the characteristics for power hand tools.*

Situations and Activities

You have recently been hired to manage a western wear shop doing $120,000 of sales a year. Because your experience has been with a large chain operation, you feel that the store needs to improve its merchandise planning and control. Specifically, you want to initiate open-to-buy planning and assortment planning. Before implementing your ideas, you ask the owner of the store for his opinion. To your surprise, he is against your ideas, feeling that your system is unnecessarily elaborate for a store of this size. You can now try to convince him that your procedure is appropriate in this situation, or you can modify your system to make it acceptable to the owner. Which course of action is best? Detail the merchandise plan that you feel is appropriate for this store.

You are the buyer for a bedspread department. Use the following information to determine your assortment plan for the coming season.

Planned purchases: $30,000
Average sale: $15

		By Price Line		
Last year's sales	Total	$5–16	$20–29	$36–60
Quilted	41	14%	73%	13%
Nonquilted	36	63%	21%	16%
Chenille	8	100%		
Youth	15	100%		
	100%			

Remarks:	Size distribution:	Twin	Full	Queen
		30%	50%	20%

Develop a six months' merchandise budget (January through June) given the following information. Answer the questions opposite.

Department total *annual* sales	$200,000
Markdowns (January-June planned)	2%
Shortages (January-June planned)	2%

Stock on order for April delivery $3,000
Gross margin (January-June
   planned) $40,000

Percentage Sales Distribution by Month

J	F	M	A	M	J	J	A	S	O	N	D
6	5	8	10	9	5	4	7	10	10	12	14

Stock/Sales Ratios

J	F	M	A	M	J	J	A	S
2.5	2.4	2.8	2.9	2.6	2.6	3.0	3.2	3.5

O	N	D
3.6	3.3	3.0

a. What is the open-to-buy at retail? At cost?
b. Adjust the beginning and ending inventories in a. to satisfy a stock-turnover rate of 2 for the six months' budget period.
c. Given as of February 20:
   Actual sales to date, $30,000
   Stock on order, $3,000
   Merchandise received to date, $20,000
   Retail reductions taken to date, $2,000

Find open-to-buy for the remainder of the budget period.
d. Given that you purchased 40% of your January through June open-to-buy at a 30% cumulative markup, what average markup would you have to realize on the remaining purchases?

Choose any mail order catalogue (for instance, Sears or Wards) and turn to the pages of a merchandise line which would be considered a fashion line (millinery, purses, suits, etc.). Develop an assortment plan for the line assuming that you are the buyer for a small department and that the mail order catalogue represents the market from which you can make your selection. In developing your assortment plan: (1) make any assumption about your retail customers that you wish, (2) assume that this year's sales volume in your department is forecasted at $10,000, and (3) plan on developing a balanced assortment which will give you coverage across four or five characteristics of the line (for instance, bedspreads might be broken down into the following characteristics: material, price, size, color, general style).

Bibliography

"Computer and Buyer." *Stores,* March 1969, pp. 41—42.

Goldenthal, Irving. "Stock Management in Small Stores." Small Business Administration, Small Marketers Aids, No. 26. Washington, D.C.: U.S. Government Printing Office, August, 1957.

McConanghy, David. "An Appraisal of Computers in Department Store Inventory Control." *Journal of Retailing,* Spring, 1970.

The National Cash Register Company. *Merchandise Planning and Open-to-Buy.* Dayton, Ohio.

National Retail Merchants Association. *Arithmetic for Retail Training.* New York, 1960.

National Retail Merchants Association, *The Buyer's Manual.* New York, 1965.

National Retail Merchants Association. *Merchandise Control and Budgeting.* New York, 1965.

Smith, Spencer B. "Automated Inventory Management for Staples." *Journal of Retailing,* Spring, 1971.

Weir, June. "Sears—New Fashion Face." *Women's Wear Daily,* July 14, 1969, pp. 8—9.

Wingate, John W., and Friedlauder, J. S. *The Management of Retail Buying.* Englewood Cliffs, N.J.: Prentice-Hall, 1963.

13
Knowing What to Buy

contents

behavioral objectives

Knowing what to buy requires insight into customer shopping habits and motives. This insight comes with a basic understanding of consumer behavior and a knowledge of methods of determining customer wants. After mastering the contents of this chapter, you should be able to approach buying decisions in an enlightened way by systematically taking into account the means of determining customer wants. You should also be able to make an actual buy in an intelligent manner.

Upon completing this chapter, you will be able to do the following:
☐ Formalize your approach to determining customer wants.
☐ Discuss alternative concepts of fashion and ways of managing fashion buying.
☐ Distinguish between two different kinds of unit control systems and determine the conditions under which each might be used.
☐ Reorder merchandise.
☐ Understand the working relationships that should exist between vendors and their suppliers.
☐ Buy toward a planned markup.

Knowing how much to buy and knowing what to buy are inseparable concepts. As a retail store plans to purchase, it must simultaneously consider what merchandise will fit customer needs and how many dollars it can best afford to spend. As a consumer, you do essentially the same thing as you consider your pocket-book in relation to all those things you've been wanting. Chapter 12 described the various methods retailers may use to exercise prudence in spending money for inventory. This chapter describes methods retailers may use to determine on what to spend money. The last part of the chapter concludes the discussion of buying by highlighting some of the mechanics of making the buy.

What to Buy

Knowing what to buy requires knowledge of the wants and needs of the market. It sounds simple enough, but in execution difficulties arise.

Consider a retailer who owns a clothing store. The market represents everyone because everyone wears clothing. All of us know that defining one's business in such general terms is unrealistic, if for no other reason than that it is impossible to satisfy everyone. A more realistic approach is to satisfy the needs of those one expects to serve. This means carving out a segment of the market that offers sales potential. It means stocking merchandise that earns day-in and day-out customer acceptance. And it means that one deals with customers in a way that eliminates doubt about what the store stands for and to whom it appeals.

Determining customer wants

Once a retailer has decided how he wants to be in business—that is, once he knows whom he wants to serve—he must thoroughly understand his customers. He must know who they are, where they came from, what their shopping habits are, what motivates them to buy, and how, when, where, and how much they will buy. The material covered in Chapters 2 and 3 provides a foundation for the analysis and understanding of retail shoppers. This chapter, however, contains explicit suggestions that help one gain additional understanding of customers.

Soliciting opinions from customers. Although the obvious way to find out what customers expect a store to handle is to ask them, few firms do this. There are, however, several ways to obtain customer feedback. One is to distribute a questionnaire to people as they shop in the store (see Figure 13.1). In this case, the questionnaire asks what kinds of merchandise customers think they will want in the forthcoming season. Similarly, a store may send a questionnaire to its credit customers, asking them what kinds of goods and services they would like the store to handle.

Another way to find out what the customer wants is through use of a consumer panel. Businesses of all sizes can organize a small group of customers who advise management on new products, styles, store policies, and other issues. For example, stores selling primarily to teenagers have successfully used panels of young people to keep management aware of teenage wishes.

Consumers, however, cannot always give objective evaluations. They may be in too much of a hurry to think over their answers, or they may say what they think someone wants to hear. Retailers, then, should not rely solely on questionnaires.

Information from store records. A store's records can aid it in its buying. Records give dollar and unit sales of merchandise by color, style, price, and so on. Records of inventory counts show product movement. Other records list markdowns and sales returns, both of which indicate unsuccessful products. Studying one or all these records can help retailers determine the rate of sales and the acceptability of items. Such information is also invaluable in determining merchandise trends.

Want slips are another kind of record that

TEEN FAD QUESTIONNAIRE

Girls
Softline

Please circle those characteristics of the merchandise listed which you think you will be most interested in buying for fall.

Sweaters

CARDIGAN
a. solid b. print c. bulky d. light material

CREW NECK
a. long sleeve b. short sleeve c. solid d. print

MOCK TURTLE NECK
a. long sleeve b. short sleeve c. solid d. print

V NECK
a. long sleeve b. short sleeve c. solid d. print

Skirts

A-LINE	STRAIGHT
a. solid b. print c. belt d. leather	a. solid b. print c. belt d. leather
DIRNDL	COULOTTES
a. solid b. print c. belt d. leather	a. solid b. print c. belt d. leather
KILT	PLEATED
a. solid b. print c. belt d. leather	a. solid b. print c. belt d. leather

Jackets

NYLON SHELL
a. snap b. zipper c. hood d. without hood e. solid f. print

NYLON TYPE SKI PARKA
a. print b. floral c. hood d. without hood e. fur trim f. reversible

JACKETS
a. suede b. hood c. without hood d. fur trim e. leather f. pile g. wool

Coats

MATERIAL
a. wool b. leather c. pile d. fur trim

Hosiery

STYLE
a. panty b. regular

COLOR
a. cinnamon b. coffee c. tan d. black

Dresses

STYLE
a. short sleeve b. long sleeve c. fitted waist d. shift e. nehru

LENGTH
a. mini b. just above the knee c. below the knee

Figure 13.1. Sample teen fad questionnaire which could be used by a retail store to determine customer wants.

can help retailers make buying decisions. Many retailers, both large and small, have employees fill out a form for each item of merchandise that is requested but is either currently out of stock or not carried. Such forms are called want slips. When buyers plan their buys for the upcoming season, they review the want slips. Most want slips include (1) the name of the article requested and a description of it by style, price, and color, (2) the quantity requested, (3) information on whether the sale was lost or whether the customer accepted a substitute, and (4) comments or suggestions made by the customer or the sales person. A simplified version of this type of want slip is shown in Figure 13.2.

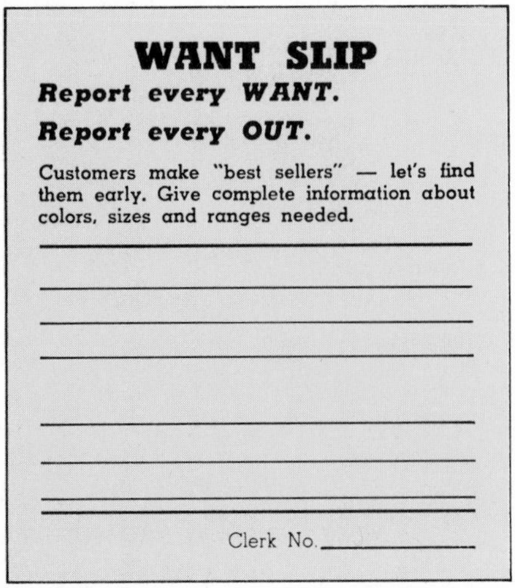

WANT SLIP
Report every WANT.
Report every OUT.

Customers make "best sellers" — let's find them early. Give complete information about colors, sizes and ranges needed.

Clerk No.

Figure 13.2. Want slip.

Finally, stores may use records of comparison shopping activities. Because retailing is highly competitive, retailers should know at all times exactly what the competition is doing. Information on product offerings, pricing, and sales promotions of competitive stores is important to the retailer. Retailers obtain this information by shopping (making visits to) competitive stores. Shopping is done either by buyers or by employees who are fulltime comparison shoppers. The written reports of the shoppers are made available to buyers. Comparison shopping information ·should, however, be used in conjunction with other information. There is no reason to stock an item merely because the competitor has it.

Information from the trade. The trade—suppliers, trade publications, and the store's sales staff—can provide valuable input for the buyer. These sources of information, probably more than any of those already mentioned, can be invaluable in foretelling merchandise needs. They are in the unique position of both appraising and influencing trends.

In deciding what to purchase, retailers should consider their suppliers to be important sources of information. Even though suppliers obviously have a vested interest, they are farsighted enough to know that their customers' best interests are also their own. Suppliers have worked hard to find the best available merchandise. As they have visited buyers in other retail stores, they have seen what is being purchased and, in many cases, have obtained information on customer responses to individual items. Although a supplier's total line may not be appropriate for a store, the manager should listen to him and welcome his advice and suggestions.

Trade publications provide a wealth of material. For example, trade association magazines and company newspapers, called house organs, provide current, factual information. Wholesale houses issue "hot item" releases. Resident buying offices supply special reports to their clients concerning items that seem to be good buys. There are special buying reports, such as the Tobi Fashion Report (see Figure 13.3). In fact, there is so much material that buyers cannot absorb all of it. It would be foolish of them to ignore it completely, however.

Retailers should never make a buy without first soliciting ideas from sales people. First, sales people are buyers' first line of defense (or offense, as the case may be) because they are in a position to know what merchandise the

THE PERFECTIONIST SHOP
FOR DRESSES
conservative; upper prices

NEW RESOURCES FOR THE PERFECTIONIST DRESS SHOP MAY HELP SAVE THE DAY!

1. The put-together for the dress customer who can't do it alone: dark-green double-knit wool pull-on pants with a dark-green-ground small-leaf-printed acrylic challis shirt and a dark-green V-necked ribbed pullover with white/red edges picking up the colors of the print. <u>Ms. Arkin</u>, #93, 49.75.

2. Simply super casual long spare-time dress with a ribbed black sweater top featuring striped edging that picks up the colors of the very flared black-ground lilac/brown giant-floral-printed acrylic challis skirt. <u>Ms. Arkin</u>, #60, 39.75.

3. A great little package whose parts can go separately in lots of ways. Black-ground art-deco bright geometric-printed poly-ester jersey for soft pajama pants, a sashed tunic top and a self-banded cardigan that can also look just as great over a slinky black dress. <u>Teal</u>, #4060. 59.75.

4. Put this all together and it looks fine; take it apart and each component has another life. These Clothes That Work are a small-patterned red/camel double-knit polyester cardigan edged with a more complex companion pattern and a pleated skirt which matches the main pattern. The shiny jersey ascot shirt is camel colored, too. <u>Teal</u>, #4085, 75.75.

Figure 13.3. Tobi fashion report.
Source: Copyright 1974, Tobé Associates, Inc.

<u>A BRAND-NEW GROUP OF MANUFACTURERS MAY HELP SAVE THE DAY FOR PERFECTIONIST SHOPS</u>

The decline in recent seasons of the dress business per se and total business in dress departments (that sell, as you know, clothes other than just dresses) is due to many factors that you all know about--factors we won't dwell on repetitiously here. Instead, we want to tell you about the major ingredients that can help pull this one segment of the dress business out of the doldrums for fall. One is realistic prices. Perfectionist dress departments are meant to serve the so-called better-dress customer who is conservative but not entirely "dumb" in her fashion outlook. She is a customer that by her very nature and her position in the economic squeeze has become very conservative about her money. Therefore, we are delighted to find at least six resources that are either entirely new or oldies that have changed their outlooks so completely as to be considered new. They start at the magic price of 29.75 and go no higher than $150 (usually for several put-together outfits). The 29.75 to 49.75 price range has already been proved as a key to dress-business success by the phenomenal business being done by Kiva, so the groundwork has been laid.

Although it has never been a retailing policy to trade down, today is not the time to trade up, and we are delighted that this segment of the market has developed to such a degree that there is a viable group from which you can choose clothes that give your customers enough fashion at prices that are realistic.

The makers we have chosen to report on these pages are as follows.

Ms. Arkin, 530 Seventh Avenue, is a new division at Arkin. It is a very small collection with enough news and good fashion. With more development and more adventurous design leadership, it may eventually qualify as a Designer's Showcase resource. This plus Ilka at Arkin, an all-knit collection, show that the Arkins have awakened to the current needs of stores and customers.

Teal, 550 Seventh Avenue, is a new business that combines the selling and design talents of the Teal Traina organization with the manufacturing and distribution know-how of Gay Gibson. This collection of put-together clothes has enough news at good prices for any dress department in the medium to better price range.

Bob Papell, 550 Seventh Avenue, has just opened his doors on his own after years with such biggies as Jerry Silverman. He has come up with a mini-collection that has some outstanding fashions at excellent prices. Watch this one, too, as a future Designer's Showcase possibility.

Dalani and Adele Martin, 498 Seventh Avenue. Forget everything you ever knew about these two collections and look at them as if they'd just gone into business. We don't want anyone telling us in June, "We haven't done well with them in the last few seasons." If they would have changed their names the very same person would be breaking down the doors.

Figure 13.3. Continued

customer is talking about and buying. Second, merchandise is sold by sales people; if they don't like it, it may go unsold. Soliciting their ideas about merchandise before it is purchased can aid in selling it on the floor.

In addition to sales personnel, buyers may seek advice from fashion coordinators, display personnel, their own superiors and fellow buyers. Display personnel, for example, may realize that a good display window could not be built around an item of merchandise under consideration. This knowledge would be invaluable to the buyer.

The implications of fashion

Today, retailers are preoccupied with fashion. They frequently say that if they could only gauge the fashion picture correctly, success would be certain. To some extent, this is an accurate picture of the importance of fashion in retailing. However, this may also be an exaggeration of the realities of merchandise buying.

Before fashion is discussed, it is necessary to define two frequently used words. "Fashion" and "style" are often used interchangeably. In the fashion world, however, there is an important distinction. Style is a characteristic or distinctive mode or method of expression, presentation, or conception in the field of art. Fashion is the currently accepted, or popular, style in a given field. In other words, a V-necked cardigan sweater, because of its distinctive characteristic, is a style. It may not be a fashion if few people are willing to buy it. Whether a style becomes fashionable will depend on its ability to satisfy consumers' desire for change.

Explanations of fashion. Two theories are used to explain the phenomenon of fashion. The first theory is the more traditional view of the two. It is founded in a concept known as the fashion cycle. The fashion cycle refers to the rise, culmination, and decline of popular acceptance of a style. According to the concept of the fashion cycle, a fashion begins with a group of innovators who tend to have high social and economic status. Innovators have both the social daring and the financial re-

sources to wear designer originals to social functions. If a particular style catches on, clothing manufacturers, developing some confidence in the still new fashion, may decide to produce it. It soon appears in store windows and dress racks. The general public becomes attracted to it, and it sells in increasing numbers and at increasing rates. (See Figure 13.4.) As the fashion becomes more and more popular, it becomes less attractive to the innovators who introduced it, and they begin once again to look for the new and different. The fashion cycle, then, may be partly described by the well-known phrase "keeping up with the Joneses."

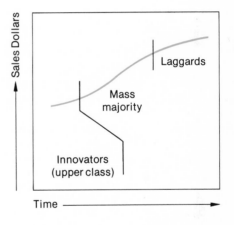

Figure 13.4. Fashion trends.

The same concept was expressed by one student of fashion as a trickle-down theory of fashion. In essence, the trickle-down theory suggests that fashion represents a vertical flow, which begins in the upper socioeconomic levels, where fashions are first adopted (see Figure 13.5). As the flow gains momentum, other consumers, who also want to "keep up with the Joneses" but who are either not courageous enough to introduce new styles or who have less money to experiment with begin to adopt the style introduced by pacesetters. Thus, impetus is added to the vertical flow.

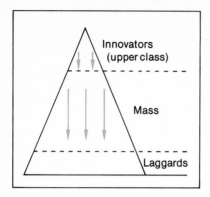

Figure 13.5. The trickle-down theory.

When the style has become generally adopted—when the great mass of consumers have tried to conform—the style has become a fashion.

The traditional view of the fashion adoption process, known as the fashion cycle or the trickle-down theory, has been frequently challenged. Most challenges are directed at two aspects of the theory. First, some people feel that innovators need not belong to high socioeconomic levels. An innovator may be anyone who has the daring to try something different. An innovator might be a popular singer or a member of a singing group, a teen-age girl on a California beach, an office girl in Chicago, or a character in a popular movie. In other words, the masses may emulate some-one or some group of people who do not necessarily have high economic and social status. The second argument concerns the speed at which the fashion cycle moves. Some people feel that it occurs so fast that it is a blur, and is, therefore, a meaningless concept. Un-doubtedly, factors such as the affluence of to-day's consumers, the leveling process among classes, the impact of mass media such as TV, women's magazines, fashion seminars, radio news reports, and so on have increased the rate at which new fashions are adopted. For today's affluent consumers, the financial con-sequences of wrong decisions are simply not as

great as they once were. Furthermore, the chances of consumers making a wrong deci-sion are minimal, owing to the large reservoir of information they can draw upon and the great purchasing sophistication they possess.

These arguments against the fashion cycle, or the trickle-down theory, lead to what may be called a trickle-across theory of fashion. Proponents of this theory suggest that no longer are the Joneses the symbolic innovators found only in the upper classes. Innovators try out new styles in their own groups—at church, on the job, and in the community. They are independent, resourceful, intelligent, and gen-erally more sophisticated. In other words, the trickle-across theory suggests that there may be Mrs. Joneses in all walks of life, who serve as innovators for their particular groups (see Fig-ure 13.6). Fashions begin with them and trickle across to imitators within the group. The trickle-across theory provides an explanation for the speed with which fashions are adopted by defining the innovator base in broader terms.

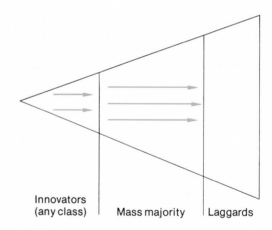

Figure 13.6. The trickle-across theory.

Buying fashion merchandise. How are theories of fashion related to buying? First, they confirm what is already known: The con-sumer market is made up of many segments.

In some of these segments are people searching for the daring and the unusual. Other segments are made up of more traditional, conservative elements. Retailers must decide what merchandise is appropriate for the segment to which they are appealing.

Second, theories of fashion suggest that fashion changes rapidly. In some lines, particularly soft lines, fashion may change as rapidly as every several weeks, whereas changes in other lines may occur over a period of months. In both cases, however, purchases must be timed so that merchandise moves quickly; this is critical to making a reasonable profit.

Far too many retailers become nervous when they think of buying fashion merchandise. True, the elements of timing and proper selection pose risks. However, buying fashion merchandise is not significantly different from buying staple merchandise. *Major* fashion changes (for example, short length skirts to long lengths) do not occur that rapidly. Retailers are rarely expected to choose untried merchandise that is very different in style from the current fashion. Instead, retailers must choose styles from a particular fashion trend. In this respect, the problems associated with fashion buying are no different from the problems associated with buying other kinds of merchandise.

Furthermore, there are safeguards in fashion buying. Today, merchandise moves in and out of stores so rapidly that even if a poor selection of fashion merchandise is made, a new shipment of merchandise will probably arrive the following week. Then, too, buyers of fashion merchandise do not operate in a vacuum. They have information from past sales; they have been soliciting their customers' opinions; and probably most importantly, they have information from their vendors on purchases by other merchants and on trends, in general. Smart retailers rely on this information. Of course, they use the same kind of information when buying staple merchandise. In the final analysis, then, the difference between buying staple and fashion merchandise is the element of timing, complicated partly by the rapidity

with which fashions change. Because of this difference, the secret in buying fashion merchandise is alertness.

Unit control systems

Before concluding our discussion of how to know what to buy, we want to look at one more aspect of the subject. We have examined ways of determining customer wants, and we have explored the implications of fashion. Successful merchants must also have some knowledge of unit control.

Unit control is a system of recording units of stock on hand, on order, and sold in a given period. It indicates the degree of customer acceptance of a particular item of merchandise. Unlike dollar control (OTB planning), which is used to control the financial investment in inventory, unit control is used to keep track of the number of items and pieces in inventory. Like dollar control, however, unit control provides information that helps buyers know how much to buy.

One kind of unit control system, called a periodic control system, involves actually counting inventories periodically.

Another kind of unit control system, called a perpetual control system, involves keeping track of inventory changes through accurate bookkeeping records.

Periodic control system. Periodic control is the basic system for control of staple, low value merchandise. Because staple merchandise enjoys a continuous demand, there is less necessity to take markdowns on it than there is on other merchandise.

Periodic control of staple items is accomplished by monthly, weekly, or even daily inventory counts. Counting too often is time-consuming and expensive; failure to count often enough may not achieve the level of control desired. A happy medium has been found when a merchant finds he can use the system (1) to make certain that merchandise is ordered as needed, (2) to find out about the speed with which different items are selling,

	Month																			Dec.			
Dept.	Jan.				Feb.				March					April						Dec.			
Week	1	2	3	4	1	2	3	4	1	2	3	4	5	1	2	3	4			1	2	3	4
1	X				X				X					X						X			
2		X							X														
3	X		X		X		X		X					X		X				X		X	
4		X				X																	
5	X										X									X			
6		X				X					X				X						X		
54	X				X				X					X						X			

Figure 13.7. Inventory master count schedule.

and (3) to plan the length of time required to correct stock levels.

Merchants should plan a year in advance for inventory counts. One merchant set up a schedule like the one in Figure 13.7. To do this, he had to take the following into consideration:

1. Counts should be scheduled so that not all of them come due at once.
2. Intervals between counts vary according to the type of merchandise being controlled.

The rotated control suggested in Figure 13.7 works only if it is strictly followed. Inventory must be counted on the days shown on the schedule. If a count is late by a week, the merchandise will probably be out of stock for that period of time—unless a good reserve stock is always kept on hand. However, we already know that too high a stock level, which includes reserve stock, increases the investment in inventory and reduces stock turnover. Therefore, if merchants don't make their counts on time, they run the risk of either being out of stock or reducing turnover. If these are the alternatives, it's best to make the counts when scheduled.

A less formal way of making periodic counts is an inspection. The inspection system involves looking over the stock from time to time, noting the quantities on hand, and ordering as needed. Some stores place labels on the front of the shelves or on top of counter boards; these labels show the minimum quantities of stock that should be on hand (see Figure 13.8). If an inspection reveals that the count is at or below the minimum, a buy is made to bring the stock up to the maximum.

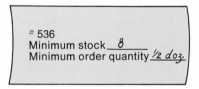

Figure 13.8. Ordering information.

The inspection system is used by hardware stores, shoe stores, grocery stores, and many self-service operations. It is simple to administer and easy to set up, but the following considerations are important when using it:

1. Place merchandise on the shelves proportional to the quantities to be stocked.
2. Stock shelves so the number of items sold may be easily determined.

In this system, as in the more formal one, schedules should be established to guarantee that stock will be inspected periodically.

Perpetual control system. The other kind of unit control system is the perpetual inventory system. Perpetual controls are used for merchandise that is (1) of high unit value, (2) sold in a short selling season, and (3) extremely vulnerable to obsolescence. In these cases, merchandise markdowns are more frequent because quick action must be taken to liquidate slow sellers. Just as important, quick action is needed to reorder best sellers.

Under perpetual control, merchants receive continuous feedback on how the merchandise is moving. Because they receive this information on a weekly or even daily basis, they can adjust inventory levels when necessary. To get this information, stores must establish a method of recording all sales, receipts of merchandise, and merchandise returns by units.

One of the most highly developed forms of maintaining a perpetual unit control is that used to keep track of women's ready-to-wear. Ready-to-wear merchandise is worth the cost of obtaining additional information because errors in handling it are very costly. Most perpetual unit control systems for ready-to-wear have these characteristics:

1. All unit control recordings are performed at a central location by an office staff specialized in recording changes in stock levels.

2. Information on the units in stock is kept on unit control cards. Typically, information contained on the card includes sales, stock on order and on hand, style number, size, color, price, merchandise received, and any other characteristic of the merchandise that the store wishes to follow (see Figures 13.9 and 13.10).

3. Merchandise is tagged or sales are recorded so the data required on the control cards may be recorded. When tickets are used, they are made of two pieces so half of a ticket can be detached at the time of sale; the half that is detached is sent to the unit control office, and the other half remains with the garment (see Figure 13.11).

4. Frequently, summary reports are developed from individual unit control cards. These reports may be developed weekly, monthly, or by the selling season. They tell the merchant how much was sold and how much is on order and on hand; major categories such as price lines, colors, materials, classification, and sizes are used (see Table 13.1).

Merchandise reorders

Reorders of merchandise depend heavily

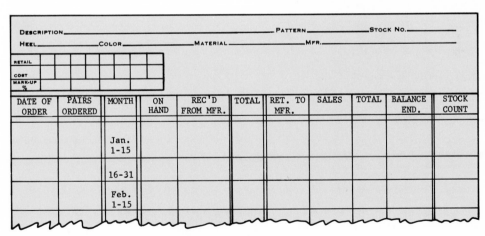

Unit Control Card — Side A

Figure 13.9. Unit control card, side A.

WIDTH	0	1	–	2	–	3	–	4	–	5	–	6	–	7	–	8	–	9	–	10	–	11	–	12	–	13	–
AAAA																											
AAA																											
AA																											
A																											
B																											
C																											
D																											
E																											
EE																											
EEE																											

PAIRS ON HAND

RECEIVED

Unit Control Card – Side B

Figure 13.10. Unit control card, side B.

upon unit control information. Buyers are posed with the problem of reordering merchandise frequently. Especially in the case of basic stocks, buyers forecast sales based on information from unit control records and current records give information on stock in inventory. In figuring the amount of merchandise to be reordered, buyers start with the notion of *maximum operating stocks.*

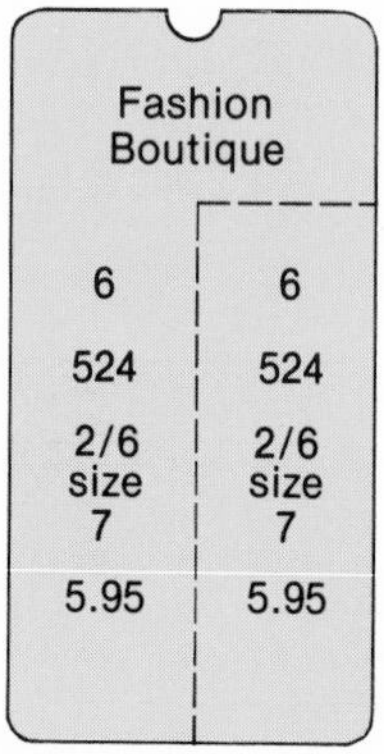

Fashion
Boutique

6 | 6

524 | 524

2/6 | 2/6
size | size
7 | 7

5.95 | 5.95

Key to coded information

6 — Dept. no.
524 — Style no.
2/6 — Date received
7 — Size
5.95 — Price

Figure 13.11. Sale tag.

In other words, it is the stock represented by a minimum selection stock (basic low stock and a cushion) plus the stock needed to cover the buying period (reorder interval and the delivery time) otherwise called maximum operating stock. Between deliveries, stock on hand should fluctuate between minimum selection stock and maximum operating stock. After maximum operating stock has been determined, stock in inventory should be subtracted to arrive at the OTB in units that can be purchased.

Before giving an illustration of how to compute reorder stocks, the following terms should be understood:

basic low stock—lowest level of stock permissible without losing sales due to an out of stock condition
cushion or reserve stock—protection stock as a hedge against unanticipated surge in demand
minimum selection stock—quantity of a given item below which inventory would ordinarily not be permitted to drop (basic low stock plus cushion)
reorder interval—elapsed time between two conservative reviews of an item (or the stock needed to cover this period of time)
delivery or lead time—the stock needed to cover normal time between executing an order and receipt of the merchandise

Table 13.1. Summary Report—Unit Control

Summary of Unit Sales
Department No. 524
Merchandise Classification   Misses' shoes

	Aug.	Sept.	Oct.	Nov.	Dec.	Jan.	Total
Color							
Black	110	284	203				
Navy	53	49	101				
Coral	6	22	66				
White	42	84	21				
Brown	268	131	260				
Red	21	139	148				
Purple	16	65	158				
Gold	11	128	213	—	—	—	—
Total	526	902	1170				
Size							
10	28	26	35				
12	168	223	257				
14	116	206	267				
16	127	252	266				
18	87	195	345	—	—	—	—
Total	526	902	1170				
Price							
6.95	66	. . .	. . .				
8.95	98	131	107				
10.95	166	281	346				
12.95	18	52	118				
14.95	71	200	288				
17.95	107	238	311	—	—	—	—
Total	526	902	1170				

buying period—equal to reorder period and delivery time

maximum operating stock—sum of minimum selection stock and the stock needed to cover the buying period.

An example might be the situation where a buyer needs to reorder a certain style of women's key chain. Stock control records show that the item sells on the average of 10 units a week and that sales are generally stable throughout the year. Periodic stock counts on this item are taken every four weeks with deliveries received within three weeks of placing the order. The buyer tries to provide a safety allowance (cushion) of one week's sales and maintain a basic low stock of 12 units. Assuming that this period's stock count equaled 20 units and stock on order was 15 units, what amount should the buyer reorder? In other words, what is she open to buy?

Minimum selection stock

Basic low stock		12
Cushion (sales for one week)		10
		22 units

Stock needed during buying period

Reorder interval (4 week sales)		40
Delivery time (3 week sales)		30
Maximum operating stock		70 units

Total stock available

Stock count	20	
Stock on order	5	
		25 units
OTB		67 units

In our situation if the stock on hand had exceeded the maximum operating stock, the buyer would have been overbought and would not have needed to reorder.

What to buy—a summary

To know what to buy, a retailer must make a detailed analysis of customer wants by getting information from many different sources. These sources should, at least, include the customers themselves, store records, and the trade. Each of these sources helps buyers decide what kinds of staple and fashion merchandise to purchase. Additional knowledge of what to buy comes from unit control systems. Unit control systems help merchants decide how much and what kind of merchandise to stock; they also help isolate trouble spots.

Making the Buy

In addition to knowing how much and what to buy, retailers must have some knowledge of how to make a buy. It is important to remember, however, that not all retailers go to market to make their purchases. Small store retailers often purchase their goods right in their own stores from supplier salesmen, rather than traveling someplace to make purchases. Large store retailers sometimes do the same particularly when they buy for reorders and fill-ins. In some cases, both small and large store retailers make purchases locally through cooperative buying arrangements with other retailers and through wholesaler arrangements. The decision to make purchases locally usually results from one or all of the following circumstances. Often, merchants don't have the money to finance the trip to market. Often, too, merchants don't wish or can't afford the time to go to market. Then, too, merchants

who sell primarily staple goods have less need to go to market.

Market Influences on Buying

Retail buyers are confronted by conditions in the market that often are not under their control. If circumstances were always the same, any changes would be reasonably predictable and their job certainly would be simplified. Unfortunately, such is not the case and the buyer must be prepared to adjust to the changing supply and demand conditions that exist in the marketplace.

Smart buyers have repeatedly emphasized the need for flexibility in the buying function. If the economic picture begins to show a downtrend, if important merchandise cannot be purchased, or for whatever other reasons, buyers must be prepared to enter into or get out of the market in a short time. Armed with this information plus knowing in general terms how to enter a market and how much merchandise to commit oneself to is important to intelligent buying.

Markets may be described in terms of a consumer's market (supply of goods exceeds the demand) or a retailer's market (the demand for goods exceed supply). Under a consumer's market, the trading advantage goes to the consumer; whereas under a retailer's market, the retailer predominates.

Consumer's market

In a consumer's market, the retailer enters the market with a preseason plan. In the early stages of the season he or she is basically concerned with two types of stocks—basic stocks and test stocks. The basic stocks are those for which the retailer can anticipate fairly accurately needs for the forthcoming season. To this extent, the initial orders reflect seasonal needs. The test stocks are those stocks which are purchased for the purpose of gauging customer reactions to merchandise before large orders are placed. Retailers may be uncertain as to which fashions their customers will respond to during the season; they must be particularly alert to hot items. Usually, however, if an item proves to be hot in one store, it is likely to receive similar responses in other stores. By that time, manufacturers may be hard pressed to supply the onrush of orders which they receive. Obviously, it is important for the retailer to detect these trends as early as possible so as to assure delivery at the peak of the selling season rather than as sales begin to trail off.

Once the season has begun, retailers must commit themselves to stocking merchandise in depth so as to assure that inventory will be adequate at the height of consumer buying. One thing that retailers particularly want to avoid is getting caught with fad merchandise. Fad merchandise is represented by items which enjoy a very short sales experience, such as recently when pet rocks came onto the market. In this situation, retailers are competing with other retailers for this popular merchandise and may have to wait for deliveries. Unfortunately,. after a fad runs its course this merchandise is extremely difficult to move off the shelf. Retailers are best advised to run short on fad inventory rather than put themselves in an overbought position, and consequently be forced to take substantial markdowns on these items.

Late season planning dictates that conscious effort be made to work stocks down before demand for products slackens. To be unprepared for this will result in an overstock position late in the season. Sometimes, to support demand late in the season, retailers will offer special promotions to stimulate customer interest. Markdowns can also serve to keep interest alive. Substantial markdowns and clearance sales are often used to move merchandise out of stock, at the end of the season.

Retailer's market

A retailer's market situation occurs where the seller can sell all the products available. Usually prices are rising in a seller's market. This makes sense if we understand that prices tend to rise in a period of a shortage. In this situation, retailers attempt to cover needs before the prices go still higher. To do this, they will engage in more forward buying—that is buying ahead of needs, constantly checking with resources, and generally, looking for goods or substitutable items that can be counted on for delivery. It is at this time that the retailer's supplier relationships that have been established over the past go a long way in assuring that the retailer receives preferential treatment. Relationships which in the past have been mutually beneficial will be important to the retailer at this time.

Regardless of where a buy is made, three aspects of the process are of great importance: working the market, working with suppliers, and buying for a planned markup.

Working the market

Retail department store buyers often have representation in a market through resident buying offices through whom they can work. These are wholesalers who are permanently located in major market areas. They advise on the best sources of merchandise, keep constant contact with the market, buy when requested by their client, follow up on orders, handle complaints, and generally work with the store's buyers when they come to market by setting up appointments with vendors and providing work space. Large retailers are serviced by their own offices or through a syndicate. A syndicate is a co-op of stores which are generally centrally managed. In this situation the stores usually enjoy the use of cooperatively owned resident buying offices which are usually referred to as association offices.

The smaller retailer, on the other hand, usually becomes affiliated with an independent buying office. Privately owned and operated, these buying offices, called merchandise brokerage offices, service clients by either charging a set fee, or working on a commission. Firms charging a fee generally work under a one year contract and receive 1/2 to 1 percent of a store's yearly sales volume, payable monthly. If the retailer conducts very little business as a result of the activities of the buying office, a monthly fee may be all that is required. Some brokers do not charge fees, but instead, operate on a commission of 2 to 7 percent on the cost price of the merchandise for which they have helped initiate a sale.

When going to market, buyers are well advised to first contact their resident buyer to expedite their buying. He or she has been preparing for your visit and probably has identified key resources which are worth investigating and may even have established a clinic where buyers can exchange opinions relative to fashion, merchandise, and markets. Resident buyers will be on call to schedule appointments with suppliers in the order most beneficial to a buyer. Some buyers like to see their major suppliers first, some like to see their top-of-the-line merchandise first to better gauge fashion trends, while others may visit suppliers on a geographically systematic basis to conserve time.

There is no one right way to "see a line." Much depends on a buyer's preference and the type of merchandise being purchased. There are, however, some basic guidelines which may prove useful: 1. Try to have the line shown in the sequence one prefers—price lines, brands, etc. 2. Go through the line quickly and have potentially desirable items set aside; then go through this selection to narrow it down. 3. Now, begin to take notes; later on one will write an order after she or he has seen all the lines; in the meantime, notes might include some of the following as suggested in *The Fashion Buyer's Job:*

- list the best numbers first, so that you can drop the bottom ones if you have taken too many for your needs
- set down complete details of prices, fabrics, size ranges, etc.
- include full information about terms: discounts, shipping points, transportation, cooperative advertising, etc.
- note available "dealer aids": display fixtures, glossy photos, material for distribution to sales people or customers, statement stuffers, etc.
- identify each resource fully: name, address, telephone, salesman who served you
- get answers to customer questions that are frequently asked on the selling floor—about washability, hems that can be let down, reasons for variations in price, etc.

Some suppliers provide buyers with a visual printed breakdown of their whole line, such as appears in Figure 13.12. In this instance, style number, price, sizes, invoice terms, and descriptions are shown. Buyers can refer back to this later for merchandise recall when they get ready to place their orders as well as making it convenient for them to see the line.

Working with suppliers

Probably no one is more important to the operations of retailers than the supplier. Yet many retailers are disdainful of their suppliers, particularly supplier salesmen. Too often retailers treat these salesmen in an ill-mannered fashion, acting as if the salesmen purposely try to interfere with the daily work routine.

While shopping in a shoe store recently, we observed an encounter that illustrates our point. One of the store's regular supply representatives came into the store. Retailers are expected to treat all people coming into their stores graciously, much as one treats invited guests in his home. In this case, the representative was totally ignored by the store manager for at least twenty minutes, and when he was finally acknowledged, the manager said, "Joe, don't bother me today. Can't you see I'm busy?"

Imagine what kind of impression that made on Joe. As we indicated earlier, imagine the type of service Joe might one day give to this store manager if a request were made for special help in obtaining a hot item.

Obviously, there are two sides to the story. It is equally important that suppliers act responsibly toward retailers. Unnecessary demands on the retailers' time and failure to follow through on promises may cause poor retailer-supplier relationships. Both parties must exist; each party depends on the other, and both

FALL '77
SPORTSWEAR NO. 4

ACCT.
NO.

NAME

ADDRESS

FOR SALESMAN'S USE ONLY

DEPT.

SALESMAN'S NO. AND NAME.   SRCE

SIG. OF BUYER

DELIVERY DATE   TOTAL $

START   COMPLETION

DATE OF ORDER   CUSTOMER ORDER NO.

PLATE HERE

CAMEL CLASSICS

*6981 85% Wool 15% Mohair Glen Pld.
Button Front A Line Skirt 2 Pkts - 17" Length

COLOR	TOT	5	7	9	11	13	15
CmlComb 25							

EXTENSION   SUGGESTED RETAIL $14.00 $7.40

6982 85% Wool 15% Mohair Glen Plaid
Circle Skirt 22" Length

COLOR	TOT	5	7	9	11	13	15
CmlComb 25							

EXTENSION   SUGGESTED RETAIL $15.00 $7.80

6983 85% Wool 15% Mohair Glen Plaid
Cuffed Short 16" Length

COLOR	TOT	3	5	7	9	11	13
CmlComb 25							

EXTENSION   SUGGESTED RETAIL $13.00 $6.25

PLAID BOTTOMS

GROUP MAT 90751

*6984 85% Wool 15% Mohair Glen Plaid
Fly Frnt. Fit & Flare Hipstr. Pant - 26" Leg

COLOR	TOT	5	7	9	11	13	15
CmlComb 25							

EXTENSION   SUGGESTED RETAIL $17.00 $9.00

National Ad

6999 85% Wool 15% Nylon Glen Plaid
Cuffed Hipster Pant

COLOR	TOT	5	7	9	11	13	15
CmlComb 25							

EXTENSION   SUGGESTED RETAIL $19.00 $9.75

*6986 85% Wool 15% Mohair Check
8 Gore Flip Skirt 17" Length

COLOR	TOT	5	7	9	11	13	15
Cml/Red 25							

EXTENSION   SUGGESTED RETAIL $12.00 $7.40

CHECK BOTTOMS

6987 85% Wool 15% Mohair Check
Pleat Front Skirt 17" Length

COLOR	TOT	3	5	7	9	11	13	15
Cml/Red 25								

EXTENSION   SUGGESTED RETAIL $15.00 $7.80

6988 85% Wool 15% Mohair Check
Cuffed Wide Straight Leg Pant w/Waistband 27" Leg

COLOR	TOT	5	7	9	11	13	15
Cml/Red 25							

EXTENSION   SUGGESTED RETAIL $20.00 $10.40

National Ad

*6998 85% Wool 15% Nylon Check
Low Rise Hipster Pant - 36" Leg

COLOR	TOT	5	7	9	11	13	15
Cml/Red 25							

EXTENSION   SUGGESTED RETAIL $19.00 $8.75

SOLID

*6990 85% Wool, 15% Mohair Solid
8 Gore Flip Skirt with Narrow Belt - 17" Length

COLOR	TOT	3	5	7	9	11	13	15
Cml 25								

EXTENSION   SUGGESTED RETAIL $14.00 $7.25

*6991 85% Wool 15% Mohair Solid
Button Front Pleat Skirt 25" Length

COLOR	TOT	5	7	9	11	13	15
Camel 25							

EXTENSION   SUGGESTED RETAIL $16.00 $8.40

6992 85% Wool 15% Mohair Solid
Cffd. Wide Straight Leg Pant - Wstbnd - Narrow Belt

COLOR	TOT	5	7	9	11	13	15
Camel 25							

EXTENSION   SUGGESTED RETAIL $20.00 $10.75

Figure 13.12. Buying form.

benefit from sound, honest, and fair dealings in their relationships with each other.

Using key suppliers. Many retailers have found it advantageous to do the bulk of their business with one or two key suppliers. There are several reasons for doing this. First, because there is a large number of suppliers in the market and each supplier handles a large number of lines, it is confusing to work through many suppliers. Second, retailers who purchase from only a few suppliers reduce the amount of time they must devote to buying. Using few suppliers reduces the number of contacts retailers must make; not only do they spend less time actually making buys but they also spend less time making adjustments that arise from shipping errors. Third, consolidating orders may bring advantages in credit terms, delivery, price breaks, and service arrangements, such as liberal adjustment policies. Fourth, suppliers are usually able to give considerable attention to retailers who account for a significant portion of their business.

On the other hand, buyers would be derelict in their duties if they did not attempt to get acquainted with resources new to them. Buyers need to be continually looking for new merchandise. Small firms are particularly useful in producing that unusual item that can give distinction to a department. In addition, looking at potentially new suppliers gives the buyer an opportunity to assess the rightness of the buying decisions that she has made or is about to make.

Evaluating suppliers. Some retailers attempt to evaluate their suppliers in a systematic fashion. This evaluation may take the form of periodically assessing the supplier's performance by determining the average markup obtained on goods purchased through this source, the markdowns taken, customer complaints, store returns and adjustments, speed and dependability of delivery, and other services and/or concessions supplied. To make such an evaluation, retailers must establish a system for collecting the necessary informa-

tion. Having collected the information, they may judge their suppliers and decide whether to continue doing business with them. They may also decide on what bases it is best to use different suppliers. A sample resource evaluation form is found in Figure 13.13.

Buying to a planned markup

Before leaving the topic of making the buy, let's turn to one more extremely important aspect of buying: buying to a planned markup. What this means is that retailers, before going to the market and making any purchases, should plan what markup, on the average, they want to take on the goods they buy. This will help them decide to buy some goods and to ignore others. Markups, of course, are the basis of profits.

There are several ways retailers can plan for a profit figure. They may steer their operations toward a particular profit level. They may use last year's profit level as a base, accepting that figure or trying to improve on it. They may forecast sales and apply a percentage that is reasonable for profit. They may establish a profit figure based on some target return on investment. In the last situation, a planned profit figure is arrived at by obtaining a percentage return (for example, 20 percent) on an investment (for example, $20,000). The method for doing this is to multiply $20,000 × 20% = $4,000 planned profit.

$$\frac{?}{\$20,000} = 20\% \qquad \frac{\$4,000}{\$20,000} = 20\%$$

Mechanics of figuring for a planned markup. As was indicated earlier, once the open-to-buy-at-retail has been calculated, the retail figure must be adjusted to a cost figure, because merchandise is purchased at cost. To arrive at the cost value, it is necessary to use some markup figure. The markup figure chosen should, of course, be based on the profit one wants to make. In other words, the markup figure will provide the basis for buying and, ultimately, for pricing merchandise. Not all goods purchased must be consistent with the planned

---

RESOURCE EVALUATION

Manufacturer/jobber _____ Dept. No. _____

Address _____ Date _____

History of the Line:

Buyer Contacts—State peculiarities or special handling required by
   a. Sales Office
   b. Factory

Rating—Dun & Bradstreet

Manufacturer's Ethics

Position in Industry

Vendor Importance to Store

Store Importance to Vendor

Record of All Arrangements (Terms, Trade Discounts, Cash Discounts, etc.)

Markdowns

Adjustments History

Customer Credits, Complaints and Adjustments

Speed and Dependability of Delivery of Goods

Cooperative Advertising, Demonstrators, Pre-packaging

Other Services

Remarks (Additional information that will guide any member of our organization who may have to deal with this resource)

                                  Evaluator _____

Figure 13.13. Resource evaluation form.

markup figure, but if merchandise is consistently bought to be priced below the planned markup, the desired gross margin will not be met. On the average, then, it is necessary to plan a merchandise mix with markups that will yield the planned markup.

In establishing a planned markup figure for a department, it is necessary to follow four procedures:

1. Establish a planned sales volume for the period. Because the planned sales figure has already been used in other ways in the management of the business, this figure is readily available.
2. Determine the operating expenses for the period. This figure is forecast from last year's figures. It is not difficult for management to determine how much money will be spent in the forthcoming period on rent, salaries, heat, and so on.
3. Determine the retail reductions, that is, the markdowns, discounts to employees, and stock shortages, that are expected for the upcoming period. Again, figures for previous years yield a reliable approximation of the reductions expected.
4. Establish a net profit goal. This figure may be based on an attempt to equal last year's performance, to better last year's performance, to obtain a particular rate of return on investment, and/or to equal the competition's profits.

In other words, retailers should average out markups on the goods purchased for the period so they can (1) meet expenses, (2) take necessary retail reductions, (3) achieve a particular profit level, and (4) accomplish all these in light of the desired sales volume. Business operating performance does not simply happen—it is planned.

A formula for the relationships indicated above may be expressed as follows: Planned markup equals expenses plus profit plus retail reductions divided by net sales plus retail reductions. (Expenses + profit = gross margin.)

Planned sales	$100
Planned expenses	$ 20
Planned profits	$ 10
Planned retail reduction	$ 10

Planned markup
$$= \frac{\text{gross margin} + \text{retail reductions}}{\text{sales} + \text{retail reductions}}$$

Planned markup
$$= \frac{\$30 + \$10}{\$100 + \$10} = 36\% \text{ (rounded)}$$

Making multiple purchases. Before leaving the subject of buying against a planned markup, let's go one step further. Suppose that you had gone to market with an OTB of $75,000 at retail and that you were going to spend it all on this buying trip. Suppose also that you had done some preliminary planning before going to market and you decided that you would have to buy merchandise that, on the average, would yield a planned markup of 36 percent. Assume that with the first vendor you approached, you placed an order of $10,000 at retail prices that would yield you a markup of 25 percent. The vendor's merchandise was good, and you felt that you could move it easily; but unfortunately, you felt that sales would be jeopardized if you priced the goods to give more than a 25 percent markup.

Obviously, your problem now becomes one of buying the remaining $65,000 so that the overall markup obtained on all goods purchased averages out to 36 percent. Intuitively, you know that the remaining $65,000 must be spent on merchandise that will give more than a 36 percent markup. Table 13.2 shows the solution for finding the markup percentage on the remaining goods.

Table 13.2. Markup Percentage on Remaining Goods

	cost	+ markup on retail =	retail
OTB	$48,000 (64%)	+ $27,000 (36%)	= $75,000 (100%)
Bought	7,500 (75%)	+ 2,500 (25%)	= 10,000 (100%)
Left to buy	$40,500 (62.3%)	+ $24,500 (37.7%)	= $65,000 (100%)

To determine the markup percentage to be obtained on the goods yet to be purchased, divide the dollar markup required of the goods left to be bought by the retail value of the goods left to be bought:

$$\frac{\$24{,}500}{\$65{,}000} = 37.7\%$$

In other words, because the first order yielded a 25 percent markup, if you purchase the remaining goods to yield a 37.7% markup total purchases should permit you to achieve the planned markup of 36 percent. Subsequently, you will realize your planned gross margin figure.

In reality, everything may not come out as perfectly as we have shown. It is important, however, to do a thorough job of controlling buys. Some retailers may not feel that it is necessary to figure out markups on paper. If they don't, they should use essentially the same methods and make calculations in their heads.

Summary

In this chapter we were concerned with the factors managers must consider when determining what merchandise to buy and how to go about making the buy. Like the preceding chapter, which dealt with knowing how much to buy, this chapter emphasized the planning and control aspects of the buying function. Proficiency in buying comes, in part, through actual experience in timing and selecting of purchases. However, proficiency also depends on proper planning and control; these are best learned through formal approaches. Thus, in this and the preceding chapter, we have emphasized the importance of OTB and assortment planning, methods for determining customer wants, unit control, selection of suppliers, and buying for a planned markup.

The following appendix, "Discounts and Invoice Terms," contains some of the buying terms and discount arrangements most frequently used in retailing. If you are not already familiar with these terms, a knowledge of them will aid you in negotiating for purchases and in reading invoices.

Questions and Problems

1. Evaluate this statement: It seems as if retail stores are attempting to buy to please everyone. What implications does this statement have for buying?
2. Show how you might use a fashion adoption theory to aid you in buying and merchandising swimwear during the forthcoming season.
3. Some merchants shun the use of any type of unit control system. Under what conditions, if any, do you think this is justified? Which type of unit control system best fits which retail inventory situation (for example, millinery, nuts and bolts, stoves, dresses, and so on)?

Situations and Activities

You have listened patiently to the store manager for the last fifteen minutes as he talked about the importance of the store's "fashion image." Among other things, the store manager said that to maintain a fashion image it may be necessary to sacrifice quality when purchasing. He said that this is especially true when the store finds it necessary to get "the look" or that "hot item" fast. Then, it cannot wait for quality merchandise. The store manager suggested that, to a large extent, consumers choose fashion over quality anyway. What do you think of these ideas?

You have recently been hired to manage a hardware store doing approximately $400,000 of business a year. This store, in addition to handling the typical items found in a hardware store, carries appliances, TV's, an extensive line of work clothes, and has a rather large gift department. When you assumed your responsibilities, you inherited a unit control procedure which seemed to you to be time-consuming. This unit control system could best be described as a perpetual inventory control system. Every time a sale was made, whether it was a TV set or a nut, a can of paint or a lawn mower, the item was recorded and later transferred to inventory books. In this way, the store had information on how many units of an item were in stock, and the information was available daily. Would you continue to use this system? If not, what changes would you make?

You have recently been hired to manage a medium-size furniture store. You have worked there for only several weeks, but you have talked to a large number of sales representatives. When you check back through the company's invoices, you notice that orders have been dispersed to thirty different companies. You check with the office staff and learn that the previous manager's policy was to order from as many different sources as possible. The manager argued that this policy enabled the store to offer a wide choice of mer-

chandise. The manager also argued that if supplies ran short, he was always able to find merchandise for his store. Will you follow the same buying policy in selecting vendors? Explain.

Assume that you are the buyer of ladies' sportswear (or men's sportswear) for a fashionable specialty store and that you are preparing to make your selections for the upcoming selling season. Which general styles will you buy? From what sources did you collect information with which you have made your decision? What did each of these sources tell you? How confident are you in the decision that you have made?

What do you consider to be a workable merchandise control system for a hardware store; a toy and hobby store; or an infants' wear store?

Select three different kinds of retail stores. Interview the store managers to obtain information on what merchandise is on an automatic reorder system and how their stores buy to meet competition.

Bibliography

Buzzell, Robert D., Salmon, Walter J., Vancil, Richard D. *Product Profitability Measurement and Merchandising Decisions.* Howard University, Division of Research, Graduate School of Business, Boston, 1965.

King, Charles W. "Fashion Adoption: A Rebuttal to the 'Trickle-down' Theory." In *Toward Scientific Marketing.* Edited by Stephen A. Greyser. Chicago: Proceedings of the Winter Conference of the American Marketing Association, 1964, pp. 108—125.

King, Charles W. "The Innovator in the Fashion Adoption Process." In *Reflections on Progress in Marketing.* Edited by L. George Smith. Chicago: Proceedings of the American Marketing Association Fall Conference, 1964, pp. 324—339.

The National Cash Register Company. *Buying to Sell Profitably.* Dayton, Ohio.

The National Cash Register Company. *Controlling Merchandise: A Chapter of Better Retailing.* Dayton, Ohio, 1958.

National Retail Merchants Association. *The Buyer's Manual.* New York, 1965.

"The Purchasing Executive's Adaptation to the Product Life Cycle." *The Journal of Purchasing,* Vol. 3, Number 2, May, 1967, pp. 62—68.

Rich's Department Store. *Rich's Buyers' Manual.* Atlanta, Georgia.

Rosenthal, Richard. "Sexual Expression: How Far Does the Retailer Go?" *Stores,* September, 1969, p. 16.

Wasson, Chester R. "How Predictable are Fashion and Other Product Life Cycles?" *Journal of Marketing,* Vol. 32, July, 1968, pp. 36—43.

Appendix C
Discounts and Invoice Terms

To administer prices, retailers should understand something about discounts and invoice terms. A *discount* is a reduction in price given to retailers by their suppliers. An *invoice* is a bill sent by suppliers; it calls for payment for merchandise delivered. Information on discounts and invoice terms helps retailers bargain effectively for price allowances, and calculate how much to pay their suppliers when they receive bills.

Our treatment of discounts and invoice terms is divided into two parts: terms of sale and terms of payment. Terms of sale are the conditions under which merchandise is sold. The terms specify the trade, quantity, and seasonal discounts offered retailers. Terms of payment are the conditions under which retailers must make payment. They indicate the permissible cash discount and describe the circumstances under which payment must be made.

Terms of Sale

Trade discounts

A trade discount is a reduction in price available to some classes of buyers, such as wholesalers and retailers. Trade discounts are usually quoted in a series and are expressed as a percentage reduction from a supplier's list price: "Less 40%—10%." (List price is the same as suggested retail price. Only in trade discounts is the retail price listed on the invoice. All other invoices show the cost price to retailers.) The rate of discount is determined by operating expenses in the trade. For example, some toy manufacturers give discounts of 12, 6, and 4 percent to their wholesale customers;

the 12 percent is for handling and credit costs, the 6 percent for selling effort, and the 4 percent for profit. Footwear manufacturers give 40 percent and 10 percent discounts to their retailer customers; the 40 percent is for the retailer's operating expenses and profit, and the 10 percent if the retailer assumes the functions of a middleman (this occurs when merchandise goes directly from the manufacturer to the retailer and, therefore, bypasses the wholesaler).

There are two reasons why suppliers use trade discounts. First, a trade discount may be a simple way of adjusting prices on a rising or falling market. When suppliers increase or decrease their prices, they may merely publish a change in the discount rate, rather than change the price on each individual item. Second, trade discounts enable suppliers to exert some control over the suggested retail price. Suppliers specify the suggested retail price on the invoice and then set up a series of discounts so that retailers can make a given margin.

In calculating a trade discount, assume that you have an invoice similar to the one shown in Table 13.3. Notice that this invoice carries a total list price of $749.90 with trade discounts of less 40—10. The percentages should be applied to the list price in the order they appear. Thus, 40 percent is taken off the list price, and 10 percent is taken off the balance:

$749.90
× .40 (discount)
$299.96

$449.94
× .10 (discount)
$ 44.99

$749.90
−299.96 (discount)
$449.94

$449.94
− 44.99 (discount)
$404.95

Table 13.3. Invoice: Johnson's Footwear, Inc.

Sold to: City Bootery   Invoice No: 0246591
            Fort Collins, Colorado   80521   Your Order No: 25892
Terms: 2/10 n/30   Shipped: F.O.B. store via Air Freight   Date: 5/6/77

Style	Quantity	Description	Price	Extension
497	50 pr.	House slippers	$4.98	$248.20
563	10 pr.	" "	6.98	69.80
201	10 pr.	" "	6.98	69.80
781	10 pr.	" "	4.98	49.80
98	75 pr.	" "	3.50	262.50
158	10 pr.	" "	4.98	49.80
			Total	$749.90

Less: 40–10

Prices Subject to Change
Without Notice

Quantity Discounts Allowed

$100–$1000 -   5%
$1000–$5000 -   7%
$5000–over - 10%

If no other discounts are given, the cost price to the retailer is, then, $404.95.

Quantity discounts

A quantity discount is a discount allowed retailers who buy a given quantity. Table 13.3 shows that a 5-percent quantity discount was earned by the retailer. As you can see, the retailer met the qualifications for the discount by making a total dollar purchase between $100–$1000 ($404.95). The quantity discount is figured after the trade discount has been calculated. In this case, the cost of the merchandise (after the trade discount was taken) was $404.95; an additional 5 percent discount yields a revised cost that is calculated in the following manner:

$$\begin{array}{l} \$404.95 \\ \underline{\times\ .05} \\ \$\ 20.25 \end{array} \text{(quantity discount)} \qquad \begin{array}{l} \$404.95 \\ \underline{-\ 20.25} \\ \$384.70 \end{array} \text{(discount)}$$

Seasonal discounts

A seasonal, or early order, discount is one retailers earn by ordering or taking delivery of merchandise before the normal selling period has begun. It is the suppliers' inducement to encourage retailers to buy early, and it helps suppliers obtain business during slack periods.

For example, ski supply retailers may not need an inventory of skis until early October; because they don't want to tie up dollars in inventory prior to the time they begin to sell skis, they may be reluctant to buy until the fall. Ski manufacturers, on the other hand, may have completed production of skis by mid-July; because they want to use their storage facilities for other purposes, they may wish to get the skis out of their plants as soon as possible. As an inducement to retailers to buy skis early, they may give a seasonal discount of, for example, 10 percent. In addition, they may not require payment on the goods until mid-December. Seasonal discounts, then, give retailers a reduction in price and time in which to receive money from sales before they must make payment on goods.

Terms of Payment

Terms of payment—terms that show the conditions under which retailers must make payment—reflect the cash discounts allowed and the circumstances under which payment must be made.

Cash discounts

Cash discounts are a reduction in price

given by suppliers in return for prompt payment of the invoice. Cash discounts, perhaps the oldest kind of discount, benefit both suppliers and retailers. In the past, suppliers offered cash discounts for early payment of bills in order to reduce credit risks and losses from bad debts. Today, cash discounts not only serve these purposes but they also permit suppliers to reinvest the money that is paid promptly or to use it to pay their own bills.

Look back at Table 13.2. On this invoice, the retailer was offered a 2 percent discount, which is shown as 2/10, n/30. The 2 represents the amount of the discount, and the 10 represents the deadline for taking the discount. The 30 represents the number of days within which the retailer must make payment. If the retailer had cash available, he should pay within ten days of the invoice date, or May 16 (May 6 plus 10 days). At that time, he would write a check for $377.01. If he paid the bill after the ten days, he would have to pay $384.70 by June 6.

$384.70
× .02   (cash discount)
$ 7.69

$384.70
−   7.69   (cash discount)
$377.01

Payment requirements

Some terms establish the conditions under which invoices must be paid. They may be classified as either ordinary terms or advanced dating.

Ordinary terms. 1. *Net.* Terms such as net 30 mean that payment of the invoice must be made within thirty days of the invoice date.

2. *F.O.B. (free on board).* This means that merchandise is placed free on board a truck, a railroad car, or an airplane. The merchandise is the responsibility of the supplier until it reaches a point designated by the supplier as the place at which he will no longer assume responsibility. For example, in the case of F.O.B. factory,

the supplier ceases to assume responsibility after the merchandise leaves his dock. In the case of F.O.B. destination, the supplier assumes responsibility until the merchandise reaches the docking point of the retailer.

3. *C.O.D. (cash on delivery).* These terms may be used when the supplier is unfamiliar with the retailer or when the retailer may be a poor credit risk. In essence, the supplier is saying to the retailer that he is taking no chances—first the payment, then the goods.

Advanced dating. 1. *Extra dating.* One type of extra dating is expressed as 2/10—60x n30 (x stands for extra). In this case, the retailer has 70 days from the date of the invoice in which to take the discount (10 days + 60 days) or 90 days in total in which to pay the bill. Notice that the retailer has 60 extra days before the ordinary dating of 2/10, n/30 begins. If in Table 13.2 2/10—60x n30 appeared in place of 2/10, n/30, *then for the purpose of taking the discount,* the invoice date would change from May 6 to July 6.

2. *E.O.M. (end of month) dating.* Under E.O.M. dating, the ordinary dating period does not begin until the end of the month of the date shown on the invoice. For example, an invoice dated September 2, with terms of 2/10 E.O.M. n30, would mean that the cash discount could be taken through October 10. In other words, for purposes of taking the discount, the new invoice date becomes September 30 (E.O.M.), and the retailer is given another ten days beyond September 30. Because the net date calls for 30 days, the bill would have to be paid by October 30.

3. *R.O.G. (receipt of goods) dating.* Under R.O.G. dating, the terms of the discount do not begin until the goods are received in the store. For example, if an invoice were dated September 2, showing 2/10 R.O.G. n30, and if the goods were received by September 10, the store could take the discount if it paid any time before September 20. If the retailer chose not to take the discount, the bill would have to be paid by October 5, because the net period is measured from the date of the invoice.

14

Retail Pricing

contents

behavioral objectives

Pricing depends in large measure on judgment. It is both an art and a science. The art of pricing comes with experience; the science of pricing can be learned through study. After reading this chapter, you will have learned the essentials of pricing if you can (1) plan for pricing, (2) set prices, and (3) analyze the consequences of setting prices.

Upon completing this chapter, you will be able to do the following:
- ☐ Distinguish among original markup, additional markup, markup cancellation, markdown, markdown cancellation, planned markup, and cumulative markup.
- ☐ Explain why the percentage markup on cost is always greater than the percentage markup on retail for a given dollar cost, dollar markup, and dollar retail.
- ☐ Understand the benefits of applying a standard markup percentage in pricing.
- ☐ Distinguish between the cost-plus approach and the dollar margin approach to pricing.
- ☐ Know how retailers use psychology in pricing.
- ☐ Know how to use price lining to advantage and understand some of its attendant problems.
- ☐ Know what makes good "sale" merchandise.
- ☐ Manage markdown pricing.

Pricing is a major decision area in retail management. By definition, price is the value assigned to something bought, sold, or offered for sale. In retail establishments, price is usually expressed in terms of monetary units, although other units may also be used. The 15 cents you paid for the last candy bar you bought was the price of that bar. On the other hand, when you take an apple from your lunch pail and trade it for an orange, the price of the orange is one apple.

In pricing merchandise, retailers must price goods so they sell at a satisfactory rate. They must also set prices so (1) inventory costs and expenses are covered, (2) a predetermined profit is made, and (3) customers are treated fairly. Unfortunately, in attempting this, retailers cannot depend on specific formulas and rules. Pricing decisions are made mainly on the basis of judgment; retailers rely on their knowledge of customers and their previous experience in pricing merchandise.

This chapter focuses on the pragmatic aspects of retail pricing. It lays the groundwork for the discussion of pricing by presenting pricing definitions, then explores price and price policies in the past. This exploration is followed by a discussion of setting prices. The chapter concludes with an examination of some pricing practices.

Markup and Markdown Definitions

Students of retailing are often confused by two groups of terms used in pricing. The terms in the first group concern the marking up and marking down of merchandise and the actual setting of prices. These terms include original markup, additional markup, markup cancellation, and net markdown. The terms in the second group also concern markup but they are used specifically in planning for and analyzing markup performance. These terms include planned markup and cumulative markup. (See Table 14.1.)

Table 14.1. Terms Used in Pricing and Planning Pricing	
Group 1 (Used in Pricing)	**Group 2 (Used in Planning Pricing)**
Original markup	Planned markup
Additional markup	Cumulative markup
Markup cancellation	
Markdown	
Markdown cancellation	

Markups and markdowns used in setting prices

The markups and markdowns that appear in Group 1 in Table 14.1 are used in pricing. The first of these is original markup.

Original markup. By definition, markup is the difference between the price of an article and the cost of that article. In other words, if merchants buy scarves at a cost of 25 cents and price the scarves at 35 cents, they are pricing at a markup of 10 cents:

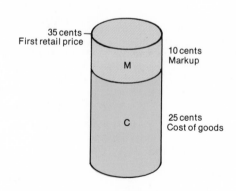

Figure 14.1. Original markup.

This markup is frequently called original markup. Original markup is the markup placed on goods when they are first priced for sale (see Figure 14.1).

Original markup may be expressed in percentages, as well as in dollars and cents. It may be expressed either as a percentage of retail or

Table 14.2. Frequently Employed Markups, Based on Retail and Cost

Markup Percentage on Selling Price (Retail)	is equiva-lent to	Markup Percentage on Cost	Markup Percentage on Selling Price (Retail)	is equiva-lent to	Markup Percentage on Cost
20.0		25.0	34.0		51.5
21.0		26.6	35.0		53.9
22.0		28.2	35.5		55.0
22.5		29.0	36.0		56.3
23.0		29.9	37.0		58.8
23.1		30.0	37.5		60.0
24.0		31.6	38.0		61.3
25.0		33.3	39.0		64.0
26.0		35.0	39.5		65.5
27.0		37.0	40.0		66.7
27.3		37.5	41.0		70.0
28.0		39.0	42.0		72.4
28.5		40.0	42.8		75.0
29.0		40.9	44.4		80.0
30.0		42.9	46.1		85.0
31.0		45.0	47.5		90.0
32.0		47.1	48.7		95.0
33.3		50.0	50.0		100.0

a percentage of cost. The following method is used to show markup as a percentage of retail:

$$Cost + markup = retail price$$
$$25¢ + 10¢ = 35¢$$
$$\frac{Markup}{Retail} = \frac{10¢}{35¢} = 28.6\%$$

In a similar manner, markup may be shown as a percentage of cost:

$$\frac{Markup}{Cost} = \frac{10¢}{25¢} = 40\%$$

Most retailers express markup as a percentage of retail to make their markup percentages comparable to other percentage calculations, such as percentage of profit, percentage of gross margin, and percentage of expenses. All of these calculations are based on retail, rather than on cost, figures.

Table 14.2 shows some markup percentages based on retail with equivalent markup percentages based on cost. Do you understand why the markup percentage on retail is always smaller than the equivalent markup

percentage on cost? Is it possible to have a 200 percent markup on retail? on cost?

Additional markup. An additional markup is a price increase made in addition to the original markup. If an article were originally priced at 35 cents and an increase made the price 45 cents, an additional markup of 10 cents was taken. The selling price of goods is increased for different reasons: (1) A higher price may make an article more attractive to customers (not outside the realm of possibility); (2) A retailer whose inventory costs have gone up wants to take an inventory profit;[1] (3) A retailer must meet competitors' prices; or (4) An article has become scarce.

Markup cancellation. A markup cancellation is a price reduction in any additional markup

[1] Inventory profits are sometimes made when the cost of an item is raised by the manufacturer. The retailer then raises the retail price. However, the retailer may have items in stock paid for at the original cost. On the items already paid for at the lower cost, the retailer makes an inventory profit.

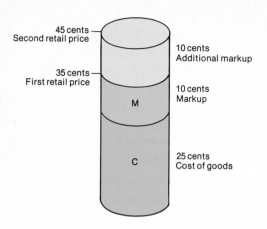

Figure 14.2. Additional markup.

already taken. If the article in Figure 14.2 were to be repriced downward from 45 cents to 40 cents, a markup cancellation would have to be made.

A markup cancellation is made because of a change in the situation that caused the additional markup.

In this situation a markup cancellation of 5 cents going from 45 cents to 40 cents was taken as shown in Figure 14.3. Net additional markup is additional markup minus markup cancellations. Thus in Figure 14.3 the net additional markup would be 10 − 5 or 5 cents.

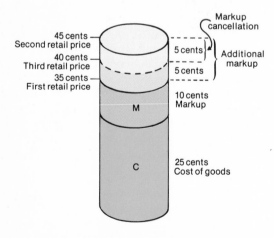

Figure 14.3. Markup cancellation.

Markdown. A markdown is a reduction in the original retail price of an article. Markdowns occur as a result of (1) special sale events, (2) the desire to meet the competition, or (3) the need to clear out merchandise that has deteriorated, become obsolete, or is part of broken assortments. A markdown of 5 cents is illustrated in Figure 14.4.

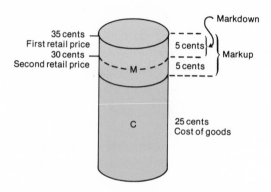

Figure 14.4. Markdown.

Like markups, markdowns can be expressed in percentage terms. The markdown percentage is derived by dividing the original price into the markdown taken:

$$\frac{\text{Markdown}}{\text{Original price}} = \frac{5¢}{35¢} = 14.3\%$$

Markdown cancellation. A markdown cancellation is a price increase in any markdown already taken. If the article in Figure 14.4 were to be repriced anywhere from 30 cents to 35 cents (the original price), a markdown cancellation would have to be made. Markdown cancellations are usually made to restore the price of goods that have been temporarily marked down (see Figure 14.5).

Net markdown is the difference between markdowns and markdown cancellations. Thus, in Figure 14.5 the net markdown is 5 − 5, or 0.

Markups used in planning prices

Two other kinds of markups are planned and cumulative markups. Each of these markups is used not in setting prices on individual items but in planning for pricing or analyzing the prices set on all items. These markups are usually expressed in terms of percentages.

Planned markup. Planned markups were discussed previously in connection with buying merchandise. Retailers should attempt to buy merchandise that may be sold at a price consistent with a planned gross margin. To achieve a specific gross margin, retailers must price their goods so all expenses, profits, and expected retail reductions are covered:

Planned markup
$$= \frac{\text{expenses} + \text{profit} + \text{retail reductions}}{\text{sales} + \text{retail reductions}}$$

Cumulative markup. Cumulative markup, often called purchase markup, is the difference between total merchandise handled at cost and total merchandise handled at retail. It shows merchants whether their goods have, on the average, been priced to yield a given markup. You may recall that when we discussed the retail method of inventory (in Chapter 6), we mentioned cumulative markups. The cumulative markup is the average markup on all goods in stock; the cost complement of cumulative markup (percentage) is used to calculate the ending inventory at cost.

Aside from its use in the retail method of inventory, the cumulative markup serves as a yardstick for measuring whether a store is moving smoothly toward its gross margin objective. Any erosion of the cumulative markup should be of concern to a retailer. Obviously, a retailer whose planned markup was 40 percent would stand a slim chance of achieving the planned gross margin if the cumulative markup were running at 30 percent. If retailers could, for example, receive cumulative markup information monthly, they might be able to adjust their buying and/or pricing, when necessary.

Retail Pricing in the Past and the Present

In the past retailers did not consider pricing decisions to be as important as other major decisions. Buying, advertising, and administrative and control decisions were given high priority and overshadowed pricing. This reluctance to give price its proper due resulted, in part, from retailers' inability to understand the role of price. If, for example, retailers did a more effective job of advertising than their competitors, they knew that they could anticipate increased sales volume. Expertise in advertising was a talent that competitors could not easily copy.

The markup percentage in retail pricing

Retailers, however, were not sure that they could increase sales by using the same kind of decision making in pricing. They found that it was very easy for competitors to respond to price changes in a way that often had adverse effects on their own businesses. When competitors responded by meeting price changes, nobody had an advantage and, if price changes resulted in retail price wars, all retailers suffered.

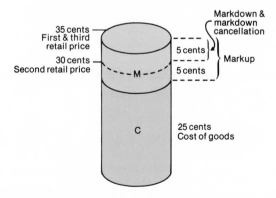

Figure 14.5. Markdown cancellation.

For these reasons, retailers began to rely on standard markup percentages for pricing their goods (see Table 14.3). The markup on electric appliances, for example, was usually 33-1/3 percent; on shoes, 40 percent; and on clothing, 50 percent. Thus, when retailers bought goods at a standard cost and used a standard markup, they could expect that other retailers, buying the same goods and using the same markup, would arrive at the same retail price. The effect, of course, was to reduce the role that price played in retail management.

Table 14.3. Sample Markups on Selected Merchandise in a Supermarket	
Meats	22%
Produce	35
Dairy	18
Ice cream	27
Frozen foods	21
Bakery	70
Grocery	16
Baby foods	8
Household supplies	30
Pet foods	1
Vegetables, canned	18
Health and Beauty Aids/	
General merchandise	26

Suppliers also helped standardize prices when they began to price their goods so retailers could apply standard markup percentages and arrive at a sound retail price. For example, a shoe supplier might offer one line of children's rubber footwear at $2.90 so retailers could apply the standard 40 percent markup and charge $4.95—a reasonable price for the shoes. Suppliers also encouraged price standardization by providing suggested retail prices.

Retail pricing today

Today, retail pricing is significantly different from what it was in the past. For retailers, the situation is more volatile and more dangerous. To understand that price is assuming new dimensions for retailers, one has only to observe the number of ads giving prices before, during, and after a season, or witness the significant inroads made by discount merchandisers. Furthermore, when one adds actual price reductions to profit reductions caused by promotional giveaways, increased services, and trading stamps, one understands even better why retailing is as competitive as it is. Obviously, modern retailers can no longer ignore the importance of pricing.

Pricing has a new role as an important variable in decision making partly because today's consumers are bargain-conscious. Even though people have more money than they have had at any time in their lives, they look for good buys. Something in human nature motivates consumers to look for bargains; interestingly enough, this seems to hold true for the rich, as well as for people of lesser means. In fact, bargain-conscious behavior seems to be acceptable at all income levels. Bargain-consciousness, together with increases in mobility, shopping time, sophistication, and education have produced such price-discriminating consumers that list prices may already be obsolete.

Setting Prices

Obviously, not everyone buys by price. Furthermore, some kinds of merchandise are more susceptible to being purchased on the basis of price than are other kinds of merchandise. The point, however, is that retailers should no longer set prices in the traditional way; today, a manager cannot afford to adopt a passive attitude toward price and concentrate only on promotion, services, displays, and layouts. Careful attention should be given to price, and retailers must define its role and decide how best to set and implement price decisions.

The role of price

Most merchants have preconceived ideas of the role of price. Some use price to encourage customers to come into their stores. In other words, they appeal to bargain-conscious shoppers by pricing their products *under the market*. Furthermore, they advertise prices and promote their stores on the basis of price.

There are two ways that merchants convey the image of a price store. One involves pricing goods for a lower than usual markup. This is the traditional method of discounters, who accept low markups and deal in great volume. Another way to convey the same image is to run many sales before, during, and after selling seasons. The managers of stores run in this way often offer leader merchandise— merchandise that is appealing enough to attract customers to the store. Retailers take a low markup on leader merchandise to generate business.

Other merchants consistently price their merchandise *above the market.* Stores that do this appeal to people who want to buy exclusive types of merchandise and who can pay high prices. Because there are greater markdowns on this kind of merchandise than there are on other kinds, because the goods are of high quality, and because expanded services are usually necessary to sell the goods, merchants can justify the high prices they charge.

Many merchants set prices in the middle of these two extremes. Merchants who price *at the market* believe that a significant number of customers neither look for the lowest prices nor are willing to pay the highest prices. When making a purchase, these customers consider the convenience and attractiveness of the store, the expertise and attitude of the sales personnel, and the number and kind of services offered, as well as the price of merchandise. Retailers who price at the market, then, appeal to the majority.

It is clear that to set prices a retailer must determine the role that price will play in the business. A retailer who does not have clear expectations for pricing policies continually fights shadows. A policy of reacting to other stores' price strategies causes a retailer to lose money and confuses customers who are unable to obtain a clear picture of store policies.

Pricing policies

Before they make day-to-day pricing decisions, managers should think through the kinds of pricing decisions they will have to make. They should establish some guidelines or policies that help make pricing decisions easy and routine. Some common kinds of policy considerations include the following:

1. Whether to price to cover full costs
2. Whether to retaliate on a competitor's special sale
3. Whether to sell at one price
4. Whether to use psychological pricing
5. Whether to use price lines.

Pricing to cover full costs. All retailers hope to set prices high enough to cover costs and make a reasonable profit. Two common ways of accomplishing this objective are (1) the cost-plus approach and (2) the dollar margin approach.

The cost-plus approach is designed to provide a floor beneath which prices cannot fall. Because an article has its cost and its expenses, any price set below the sum of the two outlays causes a loss on each item of the article sold. To cover these costs, the standard markup percentage is usually applied.

In the past a standard markup percentage seemed justifiable and gave retailers the security of knowing that if they used the standard markup percentage correctly, they could at least cover costs and expenses and would, in fact, probably make a profit. However, in recent years increasing competition from all forms of discount operations has led retailers to begin to question this method of pricing.

Some retailers now believe that strict adherence to a standard markup percentage forces them to rely unduly on making a definite percentage profit on each item sold. They argue that this is an inflexible approach to pricing, which leaves them vulnerable to price competitors. Especially vulnerable are retailers who deal in small volumes but handle the kind of merchandise that can be sold in mass quantities, and those who handle big ticket items. Competitors of the first kind of retailer can justify slim percentage margins because of volume. Competitors of the second kind can justify slim percentage margins because each sale still makes a significant dollar contribution.

An alternative to the standard percentage markup is the dollar margin concept. Retailers who use this concept do not price to achieve a given profit on each item. Instead, they price on the basis of demand, appeal, and competition. They consider cost only when deciding whether they will buy an item. As disagreeable as this may sound to some people, then, price is set on the basis of "what the market will bear."

To retailers, "what the market will bear" means simply that a given item has some value to customers. Sometimes this value permits retailers to make a profit; sometimes it doesn't. From a pricing standpoint, whether retailers do or do not make a profit on a particular item is immaterial. Their sole concern is to price the item so that it moves out of the store in a reasonable period of time. They carry some items that don't make money to offer customers a complete merchandise selection; this develops their goodwill. Of course, for every item that doesn't make money, there are fifty other items that do.

Probably the best way to price to cover full costs is to follow the practice of most leading retail chains. Chains operate on both a standard markup percentage and a dollar margin basis; management is required to achieve both a planned percentage profit goal and a dollar profit goal. Keeping a watchful eye on the monthly cumulative markup percentage (an indication of the success of achieving a planned percentage profit) *and* the dollar gross margin (an indication of the success of achieving a planned dollar profit) helps management compete realistically. It makes prices consistent with the competition's prices, customer needs, and the economics of running a business.

Retaliation to a special sale. In today's competitive world retailers are constantly emphasizing price in newspapers, handouts, on radio, and other media. Almost every week, a retailer can see a competitor advertising a special sale in which there is a price reduction on merchandise identical to his own. The problem facing the retailer is to decide whether to retaliate by meeting or bettering the advertised price.

As a matter of policy, most retailers are inclined to permit competitors to have their sales and hope that competitors will permit them to have theirs. There is some justification for doing business this way, considering the disadvantages of price retaliation: (1) Retailers must decide against which competitors they will retaliate, and (2) many bothersome, costly price adjustments are involved in meeting price changes. Furthermore, most customers shop for individual sale items at all stores offering them but usually give continued patronage to a store on the basis of overall strategies relative to price, buying, and promotions.

Selling at one price. Selling at one price is the practice of selling to all customers at the same price. This is different from selling policies in some markets (for example, pawnshops, auto dealerships, and auctions) and in some countries (for example, Mexico and Morocco). In some kinds of stores and in some countries, retailers pursue variable pricing policies, as opposed to policies of offering merchandise essentially at a take-it-or-leave-it price.

Most retail firms in the United States today follow a one-price policy. From an operational standpoint, this practice saves retailers money. Imagine the extra amount of time salespeople would have to spend in bargaining with customers. Imagine, too, the extra training that would be required to teach salespeople to be effective bargainers. Looking at it from the consumer standpoint, consumers probably don't save an appreciable amount of money when they have the chance to bargain. In general, stores that use variable pricing are ones that accept trade-ins, sell high ticket items, or offer variable price as the normal way of doing business.

Psychological pricing. Many retailers feel that consumers can be influenced to buy by the way prices are quoted. Common attempts at using psychology in pricing revolve around policies associated with the price-quality relationship, odd-number pricing, multiple unit pricing, and oddball pricing.

Some consumers decide that a product is superior or inferior solely on the basis of price. Such customers are suspicious of low prices, and therefore, presume that high prices necessarily indicate high quality. Retailers must be aware of the possibility of consumers associating quality with price. Retailers in particular kinds of businesses should be especially aware of this, for customers tend to rely on price when they are unable to judge the quality of the goods they are purchasing (for example, carpets and jewelry) or when fashion is an important consideration (clothing).

It is also important to remember that there is a bottom price for some merchandise, and no price should be set below it. If, for example, hair spray usually sells at 69 cents a can and a retailer purchases hair spray that can sell at 24 cents a can, customers may react with disbelief. They may feel that the 24 cent hair spray cannot be as effective as other hair sprays. A price closer to 69 cents may, in fact, generate a greater number of sales.

Another form of psychological pricing is odd-number pricing. Odd pricing is the practice of ending a price in an odd number. For example, 99 cents is an odd price; $1.00 is not—it is an even price. Retailers first began to use odd prices for two reasons. First, they felt that consumers were more likely to buy an item at, for example, $4.99 than they were for $5.00, because the first price *seems* much less than the second. Second, merchants wanted to force their sales people to use the cash register to make change, therefore limiting their opportunity to avoid ringing up a sale in order to pocket the money. Today, neither argument in favor of using odd prices seems very convincing, although the practice is still in general use. There is no conclusive evidence that customers are more likely to purchase goods because of odd prices. Today, the argument for using odd pricing to force sales people to make change from the cash register is weakened because of the practice of collecting sales taxes and the use of checkout counters.

Multiple unit pricing is the practice of combining two units of a product and selling them as one; for example, two tubes of toothpaste, each retailing at 49 cents, may be packaged together and sold for 98 cents. Oddball pricing is the practice of selling an assortment (related merchandise) at the same price—a so-called oddball price. For example, several different gift items may be placed on a table and priced at 88 cents each. The price is oddball, because it bears no direct relationship to cost, desired markup, or traditional selling price of any of the items.

Both these pricing policies give the illusion of low prices, and consequently, sell merchandise. If as some people think, bargain-conscious customers look at the average price that they spend for items rather than at the price of each item, merchants can put a full line of related items together to sell at the same oddball price.

Price line pricing. Another policy used by many retailers in setting retail prices is that of pricing merchandise by price lines. Price lines, as you may recall, enable retailers to offer merchandise at a limited number of prices. For example, fishing lures could be offered to sell at 69 cents, 79 cents, 89 cents, 98 cents, $1.00, $1.09, $1.25, $1.29, $1.39, $1.50, $2.00, $2.98, $3.19, $3.49, $3.50, and so on. A retailer who chose to carry an inventory of fishing lures at each of these prices would face two problems: (1) Too much capital could be tied up in inventory with not the necessary depth of stock; and (2) sales people could not logically justify the difference in the quality of a 98 cent and a $1.00 lure. Merchandise that lends itself to price lining is merchandise that offers an adequate assortment and yet allows for significant differences in price. Clothing and furniture, for example, are frequently sold by price lines.

For purposes of practicality, most retailers use price line zones. Men's sport coats may, for example, fall within these price line zones: an $18.00 to $25.00 zone, a $35.00 to $50.00 zone, and an $80.00 to $100.00 zone. These three zones represent good, better, and best. Using price line zones permits merchants to reap the advantages of price lining and still gives consumers alternatives by providing depth in assortments.

There are two disadvantages of price lining: (1) Strains are placed on the gross margin during periods of rising wholesale prices, and (2) it is difficult to take markdowns. The first disadvantage becomes apparent when suppliers increase their prices. To live with price increases while maintaining stable prices, merchants must accept decreases in their gross margins. The other alternatives open to merchants are to lower the quality of merchandise offered while maintaining gross margin and prices or to adjust price lines upward. Obviously, the latter move is possible only at infrequent intervals. Changing price lines too often creates confusion among customers, who no longer know what price level is used by the store. Merchants who use price line zones avoid some of the problems associated with wholesale price increases. For example, assume that a price zone of $20 to $30 exists and a price of $20 was originally placed on an article. If subsequent purchases of this article by the retailer required that he or she price the article at say $25 (because of a wholesale price increase) to get the same markup as earned on the original purchase, such a markup could be taken without destroying the price zone.

The second disadvantage of price lining concerns markdowns. Suppose, for example, that a merchant sets one price line at $6.50 but feels that a 10 percent markdown would move a $6.50 item out of the store at a satisfactory rate. If the next lowest price line is $5.00, the merchant is posed with a problem created by price lining. The alternatives are to segregate all sale merchandise from regular stock and price the merchandise so it moves, run the stock in with regular merchandise and clearly indicate on the price ticket that a particular article is sale merchandise, or mark down to the next lowest price line. The problem of markdowns, like that of rising wholesale prices, can be minimized by using price line zones.

Pricing Practices

Even though it is important to consider all pricing factors, pricing mainly involves decisions based on judgment. Pricing involves trial and error and knowing one's customers, the competition, and one's costs and profit goals.

Up to this point, we have discussed the role of price and pricing policies, but the rest of this chapter is devoted to the way retailers actually set prices. First, we discuss pricing decisions made on incoming merchandise—both new regular merchandise and new sale merchandise. Then, we discuss pricing decisions made as adjustments on merchandise in stock. The latter decisions are implemented through markdowns, markdown cancellations, additional markups, and markup cancellations. ditional markups, and markup cancellations. Because markdown cancellations, additional markups, and markup cancellations have already been covered, they will not be discussed again. However, it is necessary to say more about markdowns. Thus, price adjustments involving markdowns are given further treatment.

Pricing incoming merchandise

New regular merchandise. It seems as if regular price decisions should be made routinely and, to a large extent, they are. A variety store manager who has thousands of items to price cannot devote too much time to any one item. Therefore, he or she depends on a routine procedure such as the standard markup percentage.

In using the standard markup percentage, retailers first look at costs. Gross margin percentage performance is so integral to pricing that retailers start with the cost of an article and then apply an average markup to arrive at the retail price. In other words, if a furniture retailer purchases some case goods at a cost of $30.00 and usually receives a 40 percent markup, the goods would be retailed at $50.00. Realistically, the retailer might decrease or increase the price slightly to conform to established price lines or standard industry prices.

Some retailers are unwilling to routinize the pricing procedure. Among such retailers are those who work from a planned markup; those who sell high priced, highly competitive, fashion-oriented goods; and those who operate small stores. Such retailers are likely to base price on their knowledge of the value customers will place on the goods.

Actually, it is unlikely that any retailers price all goods in a routine manner or price all goods in a completely random manner. Most retailers use both techniques to determine price. What usually happens is that once retailers have used the standard markup percentage to give them an estimate of the price, they generally rely on their judgment and evaluate that price against these factors: (1) The prices of the same or similar merchandise offered by competitors, (2) the effect of price differences on demand, (3) the merchandise's appeal to consumers, (4) the manufacturer's suggested retail price, (5) the price history of the merchandise, and (6) the kind of image they want their store to maintain.

Sale merchandise. Many stores bring in new merchandise to sell at sale prices. The intent is to stimulate sales by attracting customers to the store. Once there, the customers may buy regular merchandise at nonsale prices. Legitimate retailers offering bona fide sale merchandise will usually price the merchandise so they realize decreased margins and give customers greater than usual value. One retail store that one of the authors worked at bought sport shirts and placed them on sale with only a 7 percent markup. This was hardly enough markup to cover the expenses of selling the shirts, but the bargain attracted many customers to the store.

Some kinds of merchandise make better sale, or promotional, merchandise than do others. You have probably noticed that the same kinds of merchandise are offered in ads run by a retailer. In fact, the merchandise run in last year's ads is probably being run again this year.

Merchandise that is currently selling well makes the best sale merchandise. Seasonal goods also make good sale items. Items that are well-known and/or well-advertised brands and items which are price sensitive or are bought frequently also make attractive sale merchandise. Retailers try to find such traffic builders in every department of their stores.

Taking markdowns

Because merchandise is not always bought correctly, markdowns are common. Furthermore, new merchandise arrives frequently from manufacturers, and retailers must move old stocks out, via markdowns, to make room for incoming merchandise.

In taking markdowns, retailers must consider both the timing and the amount of the markdown. Timing is important because minimal markdowns may be sufficient if they are taken at an appropriate time. Early markdowns also usually protect the gross margin better than do markdowns taken later.

Markdowns should be taken when customer interest begins to wane, that is, when sales have peaked out and appear to be softening. At this time, there is probably still enough demand for the item to move well with only a slight markdown. That is why markdowns in summer ready-to-wear clothing are taken as early as mid-July—at a time when most of us feel summer is only beginning. Retailers know that consumers have already bought a substantial portion of their summer clothes by then, so they offer new or promotional merchandise and begin to prepare for the fall season.

Anyone in retailing knows that toward the end of a selling season old merchandise hangs heavy on one's hands. For example, imagine that you are in women's shoes and have been selling light colors and whites during the last few months. Around the first of July, the store receives its first fall offerings, which are suedes, in rich oranges, browns, and blues. You find this merchandise exciting, new, and clean. Your customer's reaction to the shoes will probably be the same as your own. Suddenly, the light colors and whites seem less attractive, and you stop showing them to customers, who are beginning to demand the new merchandise. Retailers must be alert to this eventuality and begin moving merchandise early by taking slight markdowns and whatever promotional methods are necessary. When merchandise movement has lost substantial momentum and consumers are uninterested in buying it, only large markdowns will generate sales.

Obviously, timing is closely associated with the amount of the markdown. There is no standard rule that one can apply to decide how much of a markdown to take. In general, however, retailers feel that to activate demand the first markdown should be at least 10 percent. They also feel that reductions greater than 25 percent unnecessarily eat into profits.

Equally important to recognizing when to take markdowns and in what amount is finding ways to control them. To control markdowns means first understanding why markdowns occur. Figure 14.6 is the analysis of ways that markdowns can be controlled made by Bullock's, a department store in Los Angeles. It is reproduced in card summary form for their buyers to keep with them for ready reference.

Summary

This chapter began with markup and markdown definitions. These aspects of pricing show retailers what they are doing (markups and markdowns), what they have done (cumulative markup), and what they should do (planned markup). Markup and markdown definitions were followed by a discussion of the role of price in retail operations. Once this role was established, consideration was given to ways of simplifying pricing decisions. To make pricing decisions retailers must understand the difference between the standard percentage markup and the dollar margin concept. Finally, the chapter suggested ways of setting prices for incoming merchandise and for making price adjustments.

The following appendix is designed to take you through the basic calculations used to arrive at price.

Questions and Problems

1. Do discount stores charge lower prices than other stores? Explain.
2. Pricing is more of an art than a science. Do you agree? Why or why not?
3. One method of pricing is based on the ability to exchange markup for gross margin. Explain.
4. Suppose that you, as a retailer, bought a style of shoes to retail at $8.95, giving you a gross margin of 43 percent. Suppose, too, that after you received the shoes, you believed that you could charge $10.50. Would you do this? Describe the consequences of your decision.

Situations and Activities

You are the manager of a small automotive parts store in a small town. The practice of most automotive parts stores is to not mark prices on displayed merchandise. The main reason for this is that the automotive replacement parts business sets different price levels for different customers. In other words, retail customers pay one price, machine shop customers pay another price, highway construction customers another price, and schools, hospitals, and other institutions pay yet another price. You have been following this practice. Recently, however, you have noticed that many of your retail customers are reluctant to purchase merchandise because they cannot readily determine the price. Should you do anything about the situation? If so, what alternatives do you have?

You are the manager of a women's wear boutique shop. You are preparing to go to market to do your semiannual buying. During

1. Balanced Buying
    Do you:
    Strive to maintain an open-to-buy position in all classifications?
    Know what your customers want?
    Consult manufacturers?
    Watch classification reports?
    Know best styles, colors, prices, fabrics, and patterns?
    Know stock on hand and on order?
    Study information on rate of sale?
    Watch other stores?
    Determine markdown record for each resource?
    Select top resources?
2. Careful Promotional Buying
    Check the following:
    Is it a tested item or style?
    Is it in the best selling price line or below?
    Is it in the best selling sizes?
    Is it in the best selling colors and styles?
    Is it from a reliable manufacturer?
    Is it made of proven materials?
    Is the quality right?
    Is the timing for promotion correct?
    After the sale, will the merchandise fit into regular stock?
3. Experimental Buying
    Do you:
    Test customer acceptance of high fashion and extreme styles?
4. Well-Timed Deliveries
    Do you:
    Check delivery dates?
    Work closely with manufacturers?
    Buy early enough to insure merchandise arrival when needed?
    Know selling season for each item?
    Know when to stop re-orders?
5. Good Selling
    Do you:
    Check to see items are on the selling floor?
    Keep salespeople well informed through weekly meetings?
    Check location of merchandise and its presentation by salespeople?
6. Good Receiving and Stockkeeping
    Do you:
    Inspect merchandise on arrival?
    Instruct salespeople on proper care of stock?
    Buy prepackaged items if possible?
    Provide cleaning and repairing equipment?
    Take action on any soiled or damaged merchandise?
7. Clerical Mistakes
    Do you:
    Check to see that all orders and invoices are correctly and legibly retailed?
    Spot check salespeople's classification and stock control records?

Figure 14.6. Bullock's markdown reminder card—avoid wasteful markdowns.

Source: Adaptation of *Bullock's Markdown Reminder Card* from *198 Ways of Controlling Markdowns,* National Retail Merchants Association, New York, N.Y. 1957, pp. 57–59.

the preceding buying season, you bought, among other things, head scarfs that were to retail at 98 cents, $1.19, $1.29, $1.98, $2.50, $2.98, $4.50, $5.00, $7.50, $8.50, $10.00, $10.50, and $12.98. Unfortunately, this head scarf merchandise has not moved as satisfactorily as you had hoped it would. What steps should you take to buy more satisfactorily than you did the last time? What kinds of problems should you have anticipated before you bought the head scarfs?

Draft a pricing policy for a store of your choosing. How would you set prices for different items?

Select a small retail store in your community and check its prices across a given product line (for instance, shoes, millinery). Using the concept of price lines or price zones, develop prices for the merchandise contained in the line. What things did you take into consideration as you did this? What were some of the problems you faced?

Bibliography

Carmon, James M. "A Summary of Empirical Research on Unit Pricing in Supermarkets." *Journal of Retailing,* Winter, 1973, pp. 63—70.

Fatt, Arthur C. "Price Policies: Why They Should Be Based on Dollars Instead of Percents." *Printers Ink,* March 28, 1958, p. 64.

Green, Mark R. "Market Risk—An Analytical Framework." *Journal of Marketing,* Vol. 32, April, 1968, pp. 49—56.

Harper, Donald V. *Price Policy and Procedure.* New York: Harcourt, Brace, and World, Inc., 1966, pp. 247—249.

Hollander, Stanley C. *Retail Price Policies.* East Lansing, Michigan: Michigan State University, Bureau of Research, 1958.

Jones, Robert I. "Objectives and Basic Principles of M.M.A." *Journal of Retailing,* Spring, 1958, pp. 2—15.

Knox, Robert L. "Competitive Ogligopolistic Pricing." *Journal of Marketing,* Vol. 30, July, 1966, pp. 47—51.

Leavitt, Harold J. "A Note on Some Experimental Findings About the Meaning of Price." *Journal of Business,* 1954, p. 205.

McNair, Malcolm P., and May, Eleanor G. "Pricing for Profits." *Harvard Business Review,* May—June, 1957, p. 106.

Moyer, Reed and Bolwadt, Robert J. "The Pricing of Industrial Goods." *Business Horizons,* June, 1971, pp. 27—34.

National Retail Merchants Association. *Arithmetic for Retail Training.* New York.

National Retail Merchants Association. *Markdowns: Their Causes, Their Preventions, Their Correction.* New York, 1957.

"Odd-ball Pricing." *Chain Store Age,* December, 1960, p. 18.

Sevin, Charles H. *Marketing Productivity Analysis.* New York: McGraw-Hill, 1965, pp. 43—48.

Appendix D
Markup Calculation

This appendix is designed to give you an understanding of markup calculations. A retailer who doesn't understand the mechanics of making these calculations could price himself out of business.

Markup, as we have already said, is the difference between the retail price of an article and the cost of that article. In making all markup calculations, one must know only one formula:

$$cost + markup = retail$$

Markup as a Percentage of Retail

Markups may be expressed either as a percentage of retail or as a percentage of cost. To determine markup as a percentage of retail, we divide the markup (in dollars) by the retail price. In so doing, we determine what percentage of the retail price is represented by the markup. For example, if the cost of an article is 25 cents, the markup 10 cents, and the retail price 35 cents, we find the markup as a percentage of retail in the following manner:

$$cost + markup = retail$$

$$\frac{markup}{retail} = \frac{10¢}{35¢} = 28.5\% \text{ of the retail price}$$

Now we can express the formula in percentages if we wish. We have already determined that the markup percentage based on retail is 28.5 percent. The retail price is the base figure, or 100 percent. To complete the formula, we find the cost percentage by subtracting 28.5 percent from 100 percent. We obtain 71.5 percent. We then look at the total formula and verify the results by adding 71.5 and 28.5:

$$cost + markup = retail$$
$$71.5\% + 28.5\% = 100\%$$

Markup as a Percentage of Cost

As we said earlier, it is also possible to express markup as a percentage of cost. To do this, we divide the markup by the cost. Using the previous example, we divide 10 cents by 25 cents:

$$\frac{markup}{cost} = \frac{10¢}{25¢} = 40\% \text{ of the cost price}$$

Note that the only difference in determining markup percentage based on retail and markup percentage based on cost is that in the latter cost replaces retail in the divisor.

It is also possible to show this formula in percentages. We have already arrived at a markup percentage of 40 percent. We know that our cost figure is 100 percent because in this example we are working with a markup based on cost. Thus, we incorporate these two percentages in our formula:

$$cost + markup = retail$$
$$100\% + 40\% = 140\%$$

Sometimes you hear the statement that there is

a 200-percent markup on jewelry. Is this mark-up percentage based on cost or on retail?

Different Markup Situations

There are six situations in which you might be asked to work with markups. You have already encountered two of them:

1. Cost is 25 cents and retail is 35 cents. Find the markup, in dollars.
2. Cost is 25 cents and retail is 35 cents. Find the markup percentage based on retail and the markup percentage based on cost.

The remaining ways in which you may have to work with markups are these:

3. Cost is 25 cents and markup is 28.5 percent of retail. Find retail.
4. Retail is 35 cents and markup is 28.5 percent of retail. Find cost.
5. Retail is 35 cents and markup is 40 percent of cost. Find cost.
6. Cost is 25 cents and markup is 40 percent of cost. Find retail.

Situation 3. There is only one formula with which to work. Thus, we substitute the known figures in the formula:

$$cost + markup = retail$$
$$25\text{¢} + 28.5\%r = r$$

We also know that retail is a 100 percent, because we were told that markup is a percentage of retail. Therefore, we can substitute further, using the decimal equivalents of 28.5 percent and 100 percent:

$$cost + markup = retail$$
$$25\text{¢} + .285r = 1.00r$$

Since we have like unknowns, r, on both sides of the equation, we must transfer them to the same side. The algebraic procedure, you may recall, is to subtract the unknown that we wish to move from both sides of the equation:

$$25\text{¢} + .285r - .285r = 1.00r - .285r$$
$$25\text{¢} = .715r$$
$$r = 35\text{¢}$$

To find r, we divided 25¢ by .715.

Situation 4. Again, we substitute our known information into the formula:

$$cost + markup = retail$$
$$c + .285r = 35\text{¢}$$

We know that the markup is 28.5 percent of the retail price. From elementary algebra, you may recall that 28.5 percent is interpreted as 28.5 percent times r, or, in decimals, as .285 times r. We know r to be 35 cents. Thus, the markup (in dollars) is calculated as follows:

$$.285 \times 35\text{¢} = 10\text{¢ markup}$$

To find the cost, we simply subtract the markup from the retail:

$$r - m = c$$
$$35\text{¢} - 10\text{¢} = 25\text{¢}$$

Situation 5. Again, we substitute the knowns into the formula:

$$cost + markup = retail$$
$$c + .40c = 35\text{¢}$$

We also know that cost is 100 percent because we were told that markup is a percentage of cost. Therefore, we can substitute further:

$$1.00c + .40c = 35\text{¢}$$

Next, we simply solve for c:

$$c + m = r$$
$$1.00c + .40c = 35\text{¢}$$
$$1.4c = 35\text{¢}$$
$$c = \frac{35\text{¢}}{1.4}$$
$$c = 25\text{¢}$$

Situation 6. We follow the same procedure of substituting the knowns into the equation:

$$\text{cost} + \text{markup} = \text{retail}$$
$$25¢ + .40c = r$$
$$25¢ + .40(25¢) = r$$

In this situation, we must determine only the markup in dollars and add it to cost to find re-tail. Markup in dollars is determined simply by multiplying out the markup term:

$$.40 \times 25¢ = 10¢$$

We then add cost to markup to arrive at an answer for retail:

$$\text{cost} + \text{markup} = \text{retail}$$
$$25¢ + 10¢ = 35¢$$

15

Retail Advertising and Sales Promotion

contents

behavioral objectives

No retailer can realize the full potential from a business without understanding how to communicate with the retail customer. This chapter provides you with the insights necessary to make promotional decisions. Specifically, it covers the subjects of advertising and sales promotion.

Upon completing this chapter, you will be able to do the following:

☐ Discuss why it is important for retailers to use promotion, and how it can influence retail customers.

☐ Define advertising and sales promotion.

☐ Know the seven questions retailers must ask themselves before beginning any advertising effort.

☐ Discuss the importance of matching product analysis with market analysis in advertising.

☐ Describe different ways of setting up an advertising budget.

☐ Explain the types and uses of sales promotion devices.

Retailers try very hard to provide a facility that will be attractive to and convenient for customers. They develop a combination of products and services with features that they believe will appeal to potential purchasers. They price products at a level that they hope potential customers will see as reflecting true value. Furthermore, they seek to devise messages that portray perceptions of price, products, and store image to encourage prospects to purchase from them. This chapter and the one following show how retail managers use messages that aid them in managing their stores. This chapter explores considerations retailers should take into account in managing advertising and sales promotion. The following chapter examines the role of personal selling.

The Role of Retail Communications

To communicate effectively, retailers devise messages that tell customers what they want them to know. These messages are sent to customers in the form of words and pictures. Words and pictures serve as symbols, which, in turn, represent objects and ideas. The symbols are selected and arranged in a way that makes them meaningful to customers. When the messages are received, customers try to create meaning by relating the messages to their established thought patterns and their experiences. This communication process is illustrated in Figure 15.1.

If they are to influence customers to take a desired action, messages must contain a proper balance of *information* and *persuasion*. Customers need and desire a constant flow of factual information to use as a basis for making purchasing decisions. It is necessary for them to know what the store hours are, what specials are being run, what styles are in fashion, what features a particular product has, and a host of other things. Information alone, however, is seldom sufficient to motivate customers to purchase. Communications must contain an element of persuasion.

Retailers should never apologize for using persuasion in their messages to customers. Persuasion is an appeal to reason or emotion that causes customers to like this, buy that, or otherwise react favorably. In other words, persuasion induces or influences the customer to *want*. The power of persuasion has been effectively used by retailers to cause their customers to desire more and, thus, in effect, to increase their standards of living.

The job, then, is to communicate information about a store to potential customers and, thus, affect their behavior. Communication stimulates and creates demand. In addition, it determines how potential customers perceive the prices, products, and services a retailer is offering.

Communication Devices

The primary communication devices used by retailers, and the ones over which they have direct control include advertising, sales promotion, and personal selling. The secondary devices used by retailers and the ones over which they have little control include word-of-mouth communications, packaging, and publicity. These devices are often defined and studied as a series of specific activities. From a management point of view, they should be viewed as channels through which the retailer's message is communicated to customers (see Figure 15.2).

Advertising

Advertising comprises a set of activities that involve the presentation of a mass message, called an advertisement, about a product, a service, or an idea; the message is paid for by an identified sponsor. Note the key words in the definition. Mass message implies that a large group is reached, usually through TV, radio, magazines, newspapers, and direct mail. The message is not limited to information about products; services and ideas may be the major subjects of messages. The message is paid for, which distinguishes advertising from

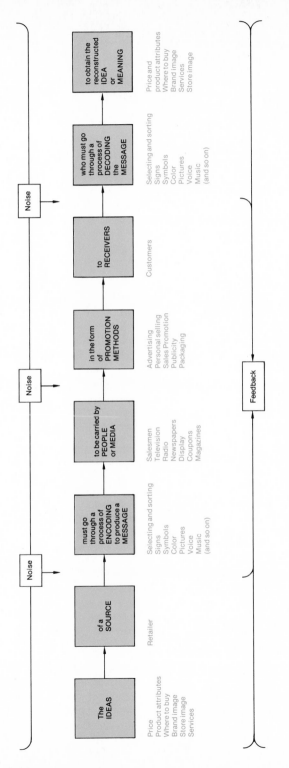

Figure 15.1. The retail communications process.

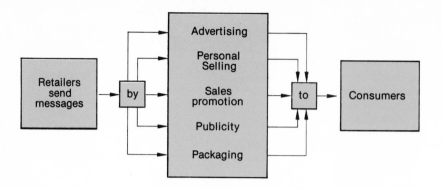

Figure 15.2. Communication channels.

publicity. Because the advertiser is identified, consumers may judge the validity of the message—at least to the extent that they know the advertiser.

Sales promotions

Sales promotions are different from advertising in that they do not involve the use of mass media. Many sales promotions are designed to encourage the immediate sale of goods, while others have longer-run goals of keeping customers loyal to the store, aiding salespeople, or attracting customers into the store. Later in this chapter we will discuss such sales promotions as displays, fashion shows, coupons, price reductions, trading stamps, and other sales promotion devices.

The term *promotion* is used to refer to all communication efforts made on an impersonal basis, including sales promotions, publicity, and advertising.

Personal selling

Personal selling involves individual, face-to-face communication, in contrast to the impersonal mass communication involved in advertising. Effective personal selling is often the most important element in retail communications. The next chapter is devoted to the topic of retail selling.

Publicity

Two factors distinguish publicity from advertising: cost and control. When a newspaper, magazine, TV or radio station features a retailer's store, personnel, products, or events and the retailer does not have to pay for that feature, he receives publicity. The retailer cannot, however, control the time, direction, or content of the message.

Word-of-mouth

One channel by which messages reach customers is by word-of-mouth publicity. In other words, customers talk to one another about stores and products. Retailers cannot directly control what customers say to their friends about their stores, services, and products. However, they should be aware of this channel of information because potential customers often rely on what customers of a store say about it. Unfair treatment of *one* customer can create an ever widening web, as more and more people are told about the customer's experience. Fortunately, fair treatment and real value are also discussed among customers, although positive aspects may not have as much influence as negative ones do.

Packaging

Proper product packaging should protect the product as well as provide a message that facilitates its sale. Unfortunately, in most cases, retailers purchase their product already packaged and, therefore, have little control over the communication on the package as it comes from the manufacturer. However, the retailer should always consider the image and message projected by packaging as a part of the total communications mix.

The retailer does "package" many goods with paper and plastic bags, boxes, and wrapping paper. Such packaging, carefully designed, can be an effective yet inexpensive extra in the total communication program.

The Use of Advertising

When a retailer considers the use of advertising, a number of questions are raised and must be answered. The answers to these questions will, in the final analysis, tell the retailer whether any advertising should be done and, if so, in what manner it should be carried out. The questions are as follows:

1. To whom will you direct your advertising?
2. What do you want to accomplish?
3. What will you advertise?
4. What will you say?
5. Where will you place your advertisement?
6. How often will you advertise?
7. How much will you spend?

These questions must be answered by retailers who are developing a total advertising program for the store, working up a promotional campaign, or considering running a single ad. Although more effort is spent on developing an advertising program than is spent on the running of a single ad, the same considerations apply. Because some retailers do a great deal of advertising each week, they may answer the questions only subconsciously; nevertheless, they are answering them. Our discussion of these questions will be appropriate whether planning an advertising campaign or the running of a single ad.

To whom will you direct your advertising?

In making any advertising decision, one must first analyze a retail market and the demand within it. As suggested in previous chapters, a retail market is analyzed in terms of population, income characteristics, and the motivating influences that form the basis for purchasing behavior. Without such an analysis, store policies concerning merchandise offerings, pricing, and advertising will miss the mark.

Most retailers like to think that they do a fairly good job of defining their market and then tailoring their retail mix to best hit that market; and by and large, this is true. However, there is one element of the mix that is given less attention than others. This concerns identification of the people toward whom advertising is directed. Retailers will, for example, direct ads for household furnishings toward particular consumer segments. In planning their ads, however, they often do not determine who does the buying, who makes purchasing decisions, who reads or listens to the advertisements, and who influences purchases. The answers to these questions identify a market and determine toward whom advertising will be directed. If you look at yesterday's newspaper, you can't help noticing the lack of true market identification revealed in many ads.

What are you trying to accomplish?

After carefully analyzing and defining the market, a retailer must define his or her main advertising objective. A knowledge of the objective helps retailers choose among alternatives and provides a standard against which performance can be measured. In developing an advertising objective, retailers should consider two things. First, they must consider how far along consumers are toward making a purchasing decision. Second, they must determine whether the objective provides a method of quantitatively measuring performance.

Possible advertising objectives. Consumers may be in one of four situations as far as *making a purchasing decision is concerned.* Naturally, the advertising objective is influenced by the number of consumers in each situation.

Situation 1. Consumers may not know the store exists or the nature of its products and

Now, how about something for us, Elf?
I tell you what, this year let's put off
our nap for an extra day.
I want to see what we can select
from Macy's Year End Sales.
The big 24-page tabloid will be
in this newspaper tomorrow.
We can read it early on Sunday and then
shop from 10 to 7. (Sacramento,
Stockton and Monterey 11 to 7.)
Yes, Elf, we did our best. But I think,
this year, maybe Macy's has outdone us.

macys

All Macy's closed Christmas Day.

An example of institutional advertising, used to promote
the store itself, rather than a specific product.
Courtesy of Macys

Should you
buy a CB radio
now?

Maybe you're wondering about buying a 23-channel Citizen's Band radio. Will it be obsolete when the 40-channel sets are available Jan. 1st? On the contrary. A 23-channel CB is all you need to be a big Apple (CB enthusiast), and buying a unit now at a **sale price** could be the biggest bargain of the season. **Here's why.** A 23-channel unit is a solid nugget of communication. Whether you're a housewife, rancher, trucker or outdoor sportsman; whether you derive information or entertainment from CB, you'll continue to enjoy all of its inherent advantages. **Highway safety.** The main channels used for highway safety and by truckers still will be available on a 23-channel unit. **Practicality.** With a CB, you're always conveniently in touch, even in the most remote regions. **Pleasure.** In effect, a CB radio owner joins a club of more than 15 million fans when he buys a unit. There's a whole language and life style that revolve around CB. Enjoy them now at bargain prices from Macy's. CB Radios - all Macy's

Save 20% to 50%
on every CB radio in
Macy's great selection

HERE'S JUST A SAMPLE

79.00 YOUR CHOICE   **99.00** YOUR CHOICE

COBRA 19
Orig. **130.00.** The Cobra 19 AM mobile super-compact is small enough to mount anywhere, yet carries the maximum legal power! Other features: •Built-in speaker and automatic noise limiter •Plug-in mike and bracket for convenience.

JOHNSON 123A
Orig. **160.00.** This 23-channel mobile unit has a 100% solid-state chassis for reliability, and electronic speech compression on transmit for extra range. Also: •Illuminated metering gives relative transmitter output, received signal strength readings.

ROYCE 1-601
Orig. **160.00.** Royce's mobile 23-channel CB transceiver has large S-RF meter with built-in transmit light. •High clarity reading with continuous receiver fine tuning •Pushbutton high/low tone switch and automatic noise limiter to reduce static.

JOHNSON 123SJ
Orig. **170.00.** Bright red LED read-outs display both received signal strength and relative RF output •Instant changeover from negative to positive ground at the flip of a switch •Plus all the quality features of the Messenger 123A.

macys

Sale includes all 23-channel mobiles, base stations and single sideband units. Sale is limited to stock on hand, floor samples included. All models are subject to prior sale, and all models are not in all stores. Shop early for best selection. Sorry, no mail or phone orders. Shop at Macy's 'til 9:30 Monday thorugh Saturday, Sunday 11 to 6.

A price advertisement, usually associated with a sale,
is shown above.

Focus in on
Vivitar savings

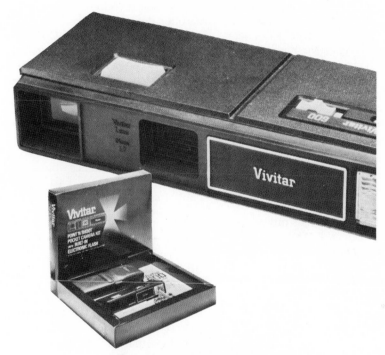

Sale 39.50
Regularly 45.00

The Vivitar 600 Point'n Shoot© camera is a slim, portable wonder that slips into pocket or purse and is incredibly easy to use. To load film, just pop in a cartridge. To take a flash picture, just press a button and the electronic flash is ready to go. Comes with carrying case, film, batteries — everything you need to catch the holiday action! Sale ends 12/26.

Cameras — all Macy's except San Rafael.

macys

 Shop all Macy's late Monday through Saturday, Sunday 10 a.m. to 7 p.m. Order 24 hours a day. In San Francisco dial 468-4444. Elsewhere in N. CA. 800-792-0800. Macy's can promise delivery in the Bay Area if you order by December 17.

A product advertisement promotes one specific brand name which the customer can purchase at a particular store.

Courtesy of Macys

services. The advertising objective might then be to *stimulate awareness.*

Situation 2. Consumers are in the initial stages of the purchase decision and are beginning to obtain market information; only now they are becoming aware of various merchandise offerings. The advertising objective might be to *increase the disposition to buy.*

Situation 3. Consumers have made a tentative decision to purchase and have begun to search in earnest for the right product or service. The advertising objective might be to provide both information and persuasion. Its intent would be to *gain an immediate sale.*

Situation 4. Consumers are buying merchandise routinely, out of habit. The advertising objective might be to remind or reinforce an existing preference, and therefore, *retain patronage.*

Advertising objectives may also be developed for other situations such as the following:

Situation 5. When special sales promotion events are planned such as a "red tag" sale, the advertising objective may simply be to provide an *announcement.*

Situation 6. Rather than advertisements for a particular product or event, the emphasis may be on brands, services, or other patronage advantages designed to *create or enhance a store image.*

Situation 7. Much retail advertising is tied to manufacturer advertising for a particular brand. In this case the retailer's advertisement seeks to *direct the traffic to this store.*

What we have said, then, is that a well-defined advertising objective (for a total advertising program, a campaign, or a single insert) depends on the retailer's knowledge of what should be communicated to consumers. Fundamental to this understanding is a knowledge of where consumers stand in making a purchase decision. Retailers selling some products (for example, facial soap) would find that few of their customers would ever be in the first two situations; instead, most would be in the third and fourth situations. On the other hand, re-

tailers selling other products (for example, microwave ovens) would find that most of their customers are, at the beginning, in the first situation. Thus, retailers must consider the kinds of products they sell when they are developing their advertising objective.

Advertising objectives and performance measurement. After an advertising objective has been defined in terms of how far along the consumer is in making the purchasing decision, the objective should be stated in precise terms that can serve as a point of reference against which performance can be judged.

Suppose, for example, that a store carries the Botany 500 line of men's suits. The advertising objective might be stated as follows: To communicate to the maximum number of customers that we carry a complete line of Botany 500 men's suits. Notice three flaws in this statement of objectives. First, no market segment is specified and, therefore, there is no way to select a communication channel that would best reach the market. Second, there is no indication of the number of potential customers who are already aware that this line is carried. Third, there is no standard by which advertising effectiveness could be measured after implementation.

The objective might have been stated as follows: To communicate to an additional 10 percent of the market that the Botany 500 line of men's suits is carried by the store; this 10 percent is made up of white-collar workers, aged 25 to 35, who earn over $10,000 a year and live in suburban areas. Because the market is precisely defined, the retailer can decide what media might best reach it. Furthermore, the nature of the advertising message is indicated by the *awareness objective* implied by the statement. The reference to "an additional 10 percent" shows that some of the market is already aware that the line is carried and that management wants the awareness level to increase by 10 percent.

What will you advertise?

Decisions about what to advertise are partially made when objectives are defined. Retailers may, however, use definite criteria when deciding what to advertise.

First, *it is a good idea to promote best sellers* or, at the very least, advertise those products that have the potential of being best sellers. Too often retailers try to use promotion to rectify mistakes in buying. Promotion, however, can't make customers buy what they don't want.

When deciding whether a product will be a best seller, retailers should take several factors into consideration. The wants of people in the market have a bearing on what will sell and what won't. Seasonal occurrences such as holidays, leisure activities, and school sessions influence what sells. Products that are heavily promoted by manufacturers and suppliers may be best sellers. Products that attract immediate interest and that may be easily illustrated and written about often make best sellers. Best sellers, too, are often products that represent true value.

Advertising at particular times of the year and for special occasions is effective because custom and tradition have made some occasions and times major shopping periods for Americans. The event should coincide with and attempt to accelerate the customers' mood to buy. Retailers can use Mother's Day, Back-to-School, Easter, Special Purchase, Anniversary Sale, End-of-the-Month Clearance, Preseason Sale, or any kind of special attraction to encourage people to buy.

When retailers decide what to advertise, they should also consider telling something about the store. This enhances its reputation and contributes to its image.

What will you say?

After defining the market, stating precise objectives, and choosing what to advertise, a retailer must consider the structure of the appeal. An appeal matches customer motives with the features of the products, store, and service offerings. The matching process is done by someone—usually a copywriter—who can look at the offering from both the seller's and the buyer's point of view.

Because customer motivation was discussed in Chapter 3, we will not discuss it further here. It is important, however, to remember that motives such as recognition and security must be considered when an appeal is made.

Facts about the product, as well as motives, must be considered in structuring an appeal. Facts are obtained through a product analysis that asks questions like these:

1. What is it made of?
2. How well is it made?
3. What does it do?
4. How does it compare with the competition's product?
5. How much does it cost?
6. How can it be identified?[1]

From the many product facts, it is necessary to select those few that will be of real interest to the customer. From the seller's point of view, these facts become the features, or the selling points, of the product. Typically, they will be facts that make the product unique, a special value, or fill a clearly defined need. From the buyer's point of view, they become benefits.

The concept of customer benefits is important to retailers. Customers buy benefits, not products. If a benefit satisfies a need, the retailer can make a successful appeal. To pinpoint the features that may be considered benefits, the retailer must question those aspects of the product (derived from the product analysis) that he thinks will be most important to consumers. By expressing product facts in terms of their features, the retailer narrows in on the benefits desired by the consumer. One way to focus on customer benefits is to raise these kinds of questions about the product.

What product features will
make the buyer feel more important?
make the buyer happier?
make the buyer more comfortable?

[1] Charles L. Whitter, *Creative Advertising*, Holt, Rinehart and Winston, Inc., New York, 1955, pp. 56—60.

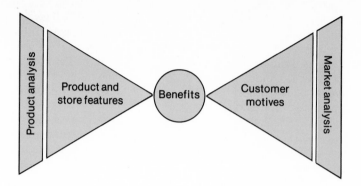

Figure 15.3. The advertising message should focus on customer benefits.

make the buyer more prosperous?
make work easier for the buyer?
give the buyer more security?
make the buyer more attractive or better liked?
give the buyer some distinction?
improve, protect, or maintain the buyer's health?[2]

In summary, then, retailers decide what to say in their ads by bringing together a product analysis and a market analysis (see Figure 15.3). The appeal—what is said—results from a matching of product features to customer motives. It is this matching that highlights the benefits, which should be the basis of an advertisement.

Figure 15.4 illustrates a worksheet a retailer might use to develop the appeal to be used in an advertisement. The appendices, "Designing the Newspaper Advertisement" and "Radio Advertisements" following this chapter discuss implementing the advertising appeal.

Where will you place your ad?

The function of media is to provide means for transmitting advertising messages to the market. Therefore, one cannot develop an effective appeal without understanding the medium that is going to carry it. At the same time, the nature of the message influences the choice of a medium.

There are three primary kinds of media:

1. Printed media
   a. Direct mail
   b. Leaflets, handbills, etc.
   c. Newspapers
   d. Magazines
2. Broadcast media
   a. Radio
   b. Television
3. Traffic media
   a. Outdoor advertising—billboards
   b. Signs

Although it is difficult to choose which medium to use, The National Cash Register Company[3] has provided a list of questions that can help managers make selections. Note that in answering the questions a manager must have already made decisions about the market, objectives, and appeal.

1. Does the medium reach the largest number of prospects at the lowest cost per prospect?
2. Does the medium provide an opportunity

---

[2]Whitter, *Creative Advertising*, p. 62.

[3]*Advertise . . . to Promote Your Business, to Sell Your Goods,* © Copyright 1960, by The National Cash Register Company, Dayton, Ohio.

Product: Hand Sanitizer   **Brand:** A-1   **Price:** $18.95   **Sale:** $14.00

Product Analysis	Product Features	Benefits	Customer Motives	Market Analysis
Key components and manufacturing details: *800 watt heating element 2-speed blower*	Unique features: *See Comparison*	*Fast drying, but won't burn hair*	**Primary Motives:** ✓ food and drink ✓ comfort ✓ freedom from fear and danger __ to be superior ✓ to attract opposite sex ✓ welfare of loved ones ✓ social approval __ to live longer	**Demographic:** *adult* age *female* sex __ family *no* married __ other
		Looks great quick		
Competition comparison: *More power for the money; 3- heat setting compared to 1*	Special value features: *Sale price*	*Last minute touch up*	**Learned Motives:** __ cleanliness ✓ convenience ✓ dependability, quality ✓ style, beauty __ curiosity ✓ economy, bargains ✓ information, knowledge ✓ efficiency	**Socio-Economic:** *adult* income *student* social class __ occupation __ area of town *parents* spouse employer __ reference group __ other
Construction quality: *Comparable*	Special need features: *Four attachments*	*Multiple use, function oriented*		**Psycho graphics:** *yes* home importance *no* quality conscious *yes* brand conscious __ price conscious __ family oriented __ religion importance __ other
Materials: *New; non-breakable plastic exterior*	Store advantages: *Stock on hand*	*Save money now*	**Patronage Motives:** ✓ good values, price ✓ location, convenience __ parking, accessibility __ friendly salespeople __ merchandise, assortment, variety, brands __ atmosphere, store image __ services	
Price: *Competitive*		*Own salon-type can replicate use*		
		Only way to get new style		

Figure 15.4. Worksheet for identifying benefits.

for an adequate selling message, or does it make possible only the briefest of copy?

3. Does the medium provide opportunity to illustrate the products or services being sold?

4. Does advertising in the medium present any difficult, time-consuming, or creative problems?

5. Does the medium actually *sell* products or services or merely announce them?

6. What is the medium's flexibility—can the message be changed easily?

7. Does the medium provide opportunities to repeat the selling message?

8. Does the medium provide excitement for special promotions?

9. Does the medium fit my type of store in prestige and distinction?

10. Does the medium cover my entire market area with minimum waste coverage of areas outside my trading zone?

11. Does the medium have any characteristics that might annoy people and give my business poor public relations?

12. Is the total cost of advertising in the medium within my financial capacity? Can I afford it?

Obviously, no one medium is going to provide perfect solutions to all the problems raised. Retailers have to find the media mix through which they can best communicate. However, it is important for retailers to understand the strengths and weaknesses of each medium, as shown in Table 15.1.

How often will you advertise?

It is possible for customers to be exposed to hundreds of commercial messages every day. Each successive message tends to make customers forget messages received earlier. Therefore, it is essential that advertising be done on a regular basis. The frequency with which a retailer advertises depends on how often customers should be reminded and informed about the store's image, products, prices, and services. Because many retailers have only a limited amount of money to spend

on advertising, they advertise with small, frequent insertions rather than spending all their advertising funds on one big ad.

Major events and sales benefit from the practice of advertising regularly. Thus, they will not be isolated events but will seem part of the day-to-day business of the store. Continuity and consistency in communication, then, are necessary to convey an image and to capture and retain the interest of customers.

How much will you spend?

Many retailers try to spend as little as possible on advertising. These retailers probably consider advertising expenditures an expense. However, it is more realistic, and much more positive to consider advertising expenditures an investment in sales and customer goodwill.

How much, then, should be spent on advertising?

The advertising budget. There are two methods that may be used to provide for an adequate advertising budget: the percentage of sales method and the task and objective method.

To make up a budget based on a percentage of sales, one can use (1) last year's sales, (2) anticipated sales, or (3) average industry percentages. Although some retailers base their advertising budgets on last year's sales, this is not a realistic way of making a budget. At the very least, it doesn't allow for changing conditions; no manager should base future action only on past results.

Many retailers estimate the next year's sales and allocate a percentage of those sales for the advertising budget. Basing a budget on anticipated sales often leads to an inflexible budget. Furthermore, it seems an odd procedure—sales are estimated first and *then* the advertising expenditures that generate those sales are determined.

Another way to make up a budget based on a percentage of sales is to use average industry percentages. These percentages are easily obtained through trade associations that serve

Table 15.1. Strong and Weak Points of the Various Media

	Strong Points	Weak Points
Newspaper	Permits product illustration Frequent publication Some flexibility in responding to sudden change Regularly used as a shopping guide Some geographical selectivity Immediacy Traditional advertising medium	Poor color reproduction Short life of individual issues Poor qualitative selectivity—everyone reads the paper Many competing ads
Radio	Personal—human voice can often be more persuasive than print Flexible—permits sudden change in message Particular stations may appeal to selective audience because of program content Relatively inexpensive	Audio only—may make less impact than visual media Can't use illustrations Short life of message Needs consistant use to be most valuable in achieving recognition
Television	Combines sound, sight, and motion to convey the message Some flexibility in responding to sudden change Gives a sense of immediacy	Expensive for small- or middle-sized retailer Message is short-lived Time and production costs are high Complexity of production
Outdoor Advertising	Costs are low per person reached Low cost per impression delivered Frequent repetition of the message Good reinforcement media Good geographical selectivity	Poor qualitative selectivity Extreme copy limitations, message must be simple
Direct Mail	Reaches a select market with precision Can be used on a limited budget Flexible in timing and message Can add a personal touch	High cost per person per message
Throwaway Flyers	Allows specific geographic market coverage Easily prepared Low cost, easy distribution Allows immediate response	High non-readership

the retailing industry (see Table 15.2). Some retailers take the average percentage of net sales spent for advertising and apply the figure to past or anticipated sales. Even with its disadvantages, the percentage of sales method is practical and easy to use, especially for smaller retailers. In every case the unique aspects of a particular store must be considered. Modifications in industry average or store-experience percentages can be made on the basis of several factors:

1. Location—more promotion for a store in a less favorable location.
2. Competition—new or strong competition may require additional expenditures.
3. New stores require additional expenditures until awareness is created and a trade developed.

Table 15.2. Percentages of Net Sales Spent for Advertising

Kind of Business	Percentage of Net Sales	Kind of Business	Percentage of Net Sales
Automobile dealers (all dealers)	0.8	Jewelry stores (cont'd)	
Barber and beauty shops	2.98	Sales $50,000 to $100,000	3.5
Camera and photographic supply		Sales $100,000 to $300,000	4.6
stores	2.06	Sales $300,000 to $500,000	4.2
Confectionery stores	0.50	Sales over $500,000	3.7
Delicatessens	1.03	Lumber and building materials	
Department stores		dealers	0.45
Sales $1,000,000 to $2,000,000	3.73	Men's wear stores (all stores)	2.9
Sales $2,000,000 to $5,000,000	3.91	Sales under $100,000	2.9
Sales $5,000,000 to $10,000,000	3.90	Sales $100,000 to $200,000	2.6
Sales $10,000,000 to		Sales $200,000 to $500,000	2.8
$20,000,000	3.93	Sales $500,000 to $1,000,000	3.6
Sales $20,000,000 to		Sales over $1,000,000	3.3
$50,000,000	3.78	Paint and wallpaper stores	
Sales over $50,000,000	3.55	Sales to $100,000	1.56
Drugstores		Sales $100,000 to $250,000	2.01
Sales under $50,000	0.8	Sales $250,000 to $500,000	1.55
Sales $50,000 to $120,000	1.3	Sales over $500,000	.96
Sales $120,000 to $250,000	1.5	Prescription pharmacies	1.3
Sales $250,000 to $300,000	1.7	Service Stations (all stations)	0.75
Sales over $300,000	1.9	Sales under $25,000	0.76
Electrical appliance stores		Sales $25,000 to $50,000	0.78
(all stores)	2.45	Sales $50,000 to $100,000	0.74
Sales under $250,000	2.27	Sales $100,000 to $200,000	0.63
Sales $250,000 to $500,000	2.94	Shoe stores	
Sales over $500,000	2.33	Sales under $50,000	2.3
Furniture stores		Sales $50,000 to $100,000	2.8
Sales under $250,000	3.52	Sales $100,000 to $150,000	3.0
Sales $250,000 to $500,000	5.88	Sales over $150,000	3.0
Sales over $1,000,000	6.56	Specialty stores	
Grocery stores (all stores)	0.65	Sales $1,000,000 to $5,000,000	4.2
Sales under $50,000	0.52	Sales over $5,000,000	4.27
Sales $50,000 to $100,000	0.61	Sporting good stores (all stores)	2.0
Sales $100,000 to $200,000	0.76	Sales under $75,000	3.0
Hardware stores	1.45	Sales $75,000 to $150,000	2.2
Jewelry stores (all stores)	3.5	Sales $150,000 to $250,000	1.9
Sales under $50,000	2.5	Sales over $500,000	2.2

Source: *Advertise . . . to Promote Your Business, to Sell Your Goods*, © Copyright 1960, by The National Cash Register Company, Dayton, Ohio.

4. Stores with a strong price appeal usually require above average levels of promotion.
5. Addition of special dates and events that offer sales opportunities may require additional expenditures.

An alternative or supplement to the percentage of sales method is provided by the task and objective method. This method is based on the premise that advertising should be budgeted to accomplish specific goals. In practice, the retailer sets a dollar sales objective for the store for the forthcoming period (usually one year) and budgets the amount to be spent on the advertising that will accomplish the sales objective. In developing the budget, the retailer makes an estimate of how much will be needed to promote shopping events and how much will be needed for regular advertising. In addition to making estimates for the store as a whole, the retailer may estimate for merchandise lines, departments, etc.

During the budget period, the sales picture is reviewed at regular intervals. Such reviews provide an opportunity to adjust the advertising budget if sales objectives are not being met or are being exceeded. Some retailers find the careful figuring, the constant watching, and the necessity to make changes a great burden and, therefore, do not use the task and objective method. It is, however, a logical and effective method to use in planning advertising expenditures.

Those retailers who do use the task and objective method also rely, to some extent, on the percentage of sales method. The percentage of sales method is a useful control device. It provides a check on the task and objective method by alerting managers who plan advertising budgets that are significantly smaller or larger than those used by competitive stores. Using average industry percentages in the percentage of sales methods can, then, provide management with a warning device.

Cooperative advertising

Manufacturers often are willing to pay for part of the store's advertising and promotional expenses for the manufacturer's brands. Funds are made available to the retailer to advertise the manufacturer's product with the advantage, of course, that the total promotional budget is increased without the store's actually spending more money. This *cooperative advertising* has other advantages for the retailer. The manufacturer often supplies creative help in the form of a prepared advertisement or a mat that may be submitted directly to the newspaper. These mats are made up by an advertising agency or the manufacturer's ad staff and may be better than what the retailer could produce alone. All the retailer has to do is add the store's name and address to the prepared advertisement in the appropriate place. The manufacturer gains in having national advertising for the brand focused at the local level and identified with a particular store. For the manufacturer, the cooperative advertising becomes an effort in directing the traffic to the stores where his brands of goods are offered for sale. Cooperative advertising is a significant advantage as long as retailers are careful in selecting the cooperative advertising opportunities. They should make sure that the items fit the store's image, that they are timely, and that the products being advertised will actually sell.

Evaluating Advertising Effectiveness

The retailer's efforts in establishing a budget are guided by the amount that accrues when the cost of promotion is weighed against the expected return. And this is no different than the decision-making process used in building a new parking lot, window display or investing more merchandise in inventory. The retailer is going to spend money on advertising because he or she feels the expenditure will be more than offset by additional sales, and ultimately, profits. Whether the decision is one that affects the store image, immediate sales, number of customers, or whatever, the alternatives to advertising or promotion are as difficult to evaluate as difficulty of evaluating advertising effectiveness. Ideally, the retailer would spend money on advertising so that sales were increased and the additional profits generated exceed the expenditure on the advertising effort.

To spend money on advertising so profits are maximized, one must know (1) how sales are related to advertising expenditures and (2) how profits are related to sales. Measurement problems make it difficult to understand these relationships. Finding the relationship between sales and advertising is difficult because the way people have responded to a particular piece of advertising can never be definitely known. They may have responded to a message, or to the medium presenting the message, or because of the number of times they were exposed to the message. Retailers never know for certain what caused a particular sale. Finding the profit generated by sales that may have been produced by advertising poses the same kind of problem. A customer who has been persuaded by advertising to purchase a sale item may become a regular customer and make many purchases in the future. In this case, which profits should be measured against which sales? To measure what is sold by advertising, when it will be sold, and how much profit can be attributed to sales caused by advertising is, once again, very difficult to do.

As an alternative to measuring sales relationships directly, a retailer may attempt to measure through survey research such factors as attitudes toward the store or recall of the store's name and products. Most often, particularly for advertisements designed to stimulate immediate sales response, retailers rely on a simple tool to help them find out what sales were generated through the advertising. Salespeople keep track of the number of units they sell during the time the ad is in effect. Then, managers compute the retail value of these units and divide it by the advertising cost of the item advertised. This gives them an idea of how many dollars of sales they received from each dollar spent on advertising. For example, say a nursery ran the ad shown in Figure 15.5. This ad produced $300 in sales of roses. If the total cost of the ad were $20, the retailer would divide $300 by 20 to find that this ad produced $15.00 for every dollar of advertising spent.

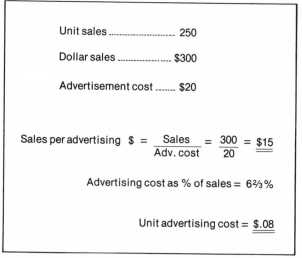

Figure 15.5. Checking sales from a newspaper advertisement.

The retailer compares the rose offering with the results of merchandise and has a basis for (1) deciding whether to run a similar ad again and/or (2) determining whether more or less money should be spent if roses were to be repeated in an ad.

Sales Promotion

Sales promotion refers to a set of communication devices other than personal selling, advertising, and publicity. In this section we will discuss some of the more common ones. Each has unique advantages in the way it can accomplish one or more of the following: (1) generate immediate sales, (2) attract customers into a store, (3) build customer loyalty, (4) increase customer knowledge and information and, thus, bring customers closer to making actual purchases, and (5) promote goodwill.

Most retailers consider sales promotion an important part of the total communication effort. If sales promotion is to be effective, decisions should be made on the basis of the nature of the market and with specific objectives established just as we discussed in the previous section. After these factors have been considered, management may select the most appropriate particular sales promotion device.

Price reduction sales promotions

Price reduction promotions or sales may be designed to:

1. Accelerate sales of slow-moving items. Markdowns should be taken as soon as it becomes apparent that an item is not selling as planned.
2. Generate immediate increased sales with a higher volume making up for the decreased unit gross margin.
3. Generate store traffic with the hope that customers will make additional unplanned purchases.
4. Create or sustain a "price store" image.

It is very important that customers see the price reduction as significant or it will not draw new customers. Slight price reductions will probably only cause customers who would have purchased anyway to purchase sooner.

Displays

Although most retailers use both window and interior displays, few retailers examine the relationship between the costs of such displays and the benefits derived from them. In every display there are, obviously, costs of building and maintenance. However, an investment cost is also involved, because displays occupy valuable floor space that might otherwise be used for selling and merchandise. To determine the value obtained from display costs, retailers must understand the benefits they obtain from different kinds of displays.

The use of displays varies significantly among stores. Window displays, for example, may be used to project the image of a quality store. Other stores may use window displays to project a price or value image. Still other stores may use them merely to attract customers; the displays show customers the kind of merchandise carried by the store.

On the other hand, in-store, or interior, displays are usually designed to encourage customers to try a product; they do this by providing facts and information. Interior displays are very effective in creating product awareness and stimulating unplanned purchasing. In addition, many stores use interior displays to create or enhance the atmosphere.

Manufacturers frequently supply retailers with display, or point-of-purchase, material. Some of it is elaborate and complete. If retailers are tempted to use these materials because they are free, they should remember the costs associated with the use of floor space in addition to those of building or assembling and maintaining a display.

Appendix G, "Display Windows," at the end of this chapter, will provide additional information about this important sales promotion device.

Trading stamps

Many retailers offer the customer trading

Two exciting window display treatments. Displays do an effective job of promoting a store image and selling merchandise.

Photos courtesy of Gump's, San Francisco

stamps as a premium for shopping in their stores. Customers receive trading stamps in proportion to the dollar amount of their purchases and then redeem the stamps for merchandise or for, in some cases, cash.

Trading stamps have been a part of retailing since the late 1800's, but not until after World War II did their use become widespread. By the middle of the 1960's stamp sales to retailers were more than $700 million. In the late 1960's, a period marked by increased consumerism and high inflation, the importance of trading stamps declined. In this period many retailers were successful in dropping stamps and emphasizing low prices. Critics of trading stamps felt that stores added the cost of the stamps (2 to 3 percent of sales) to their prices.

It is difficult to determine what effects retailers may expect from the use of trading stamps. If trading stamps do succeed in building store loyalty, and therefore, lead to increased volume, perhaps the increased volume will cover the cost of the stamps and prices will not have to be raised to maintain margins. If trading stamps do not increase volume, retailers must reduce margins or raise prices. In either case retailers may be satisfied to offer stamps to keep their stores competitive. Maybe the real issue facing retailers, however, involves a decision about whether the 2 to 3 percent sales cost of stamps might be better spent on other forms of promotion, lower prices, or increased services.

Coupons

Store coupons, distributed in advertisements, newspapers, or handouts, are used to build volume and traffic as well as to sell particular products. Manufacturers often use coupons to introduce new products or to stimulate sales. It is hoped that the price reduction given by the coupon will induce customers to try the product and become regular users.

Special events

Many retailers use special events to promote goodwill and increase customer education, as well as to stimulate sales. The nature and extent of the special events used by stores depends on the kind of store and the size of its operations.

Fashion shows are a popular device used by both large and small clothing and department stores. Retailers use fashion shows primarily to obtain goodwill. Only incidentally do fashion shows produce immediate business.

Some products require instruction if customers are to acquire skill in using them. When this is so, retailers provide schools and classes in which present and future customers are taught to use the product. Stores that do this reap obvious benefits: Customers buy associated merchandise, and goodwill and traffic may be substantially increased.

Although other special events such as parades, art exhibits, and lecture series may be tied to specific merchandise sales, most such programs are intended to attract people to the store and create goodwill.

Other devices

The number of sales promotion devices available to the retailer is almost infinite. In addition to those already mentioned, commonly used devices include premiums, contests, and games. In using these and all other sales promotion devices, retailers must evaluate alternatives in terms of the total cost compared to the success of the device in accomplishing the stated objectives.

Summary

Retailers must communicate to customers about their store, products, services, and prices. The channels through which information and persuasion are communicated are advertising, sales promotion, personal selling, publicity, and packaging. Word-of-mouth communication also occurs, but retailers have little control over it.

To advertise effectively, retailers should know the following:

1. Toward whom the advertising is directed
2. What they want to accomplish

3. What to advertise
4. What to say in the advertisement
5. Where to place the ad
6. How often to promote
7. How much to spend.

Answers to these questions provide the foundation on which retailers can base decisions when developing the store's advertising program or when running single ads.

Sales promotions may be designed to:
1. Sell goods immediately.
2. Keep customers loyal to the store.
3. Aid salespeople.
4. Attract customers into the store.

Questions and Problems

1. Is the role played by advertising in manufacturing different from the role played by advertising in retailing? Why or why not?
2. Does the relative importance of advertising, personal selling, and sales promotion vary among a supermarket, a discount store, and a specialty store? What factors cause the difference?
3. Explain why the choice of the media influences the nature of the advertising message, and vice versa.
4. From your local newspaper, select an advertisement for men's or women's wear. Can you identify the target market? Can you determine what the retailer was trying to accomplish?
5. Why do retailers usually employ several media in their advertising programs?
6. A local supermarket is considering the elimination of trading stamps after using them for twelve years. What factors must be considered in making the decision?
7. Explain why it is important that all elements of the promotion effort be coordinated. Select a newspaper advertisement placed by a local discount store. Visit the store. Do you see evidence of coordinated effort?
8. How should you decide whether to use a display piece supplied by a manufacturer?

Situations and Activities

You are the promotion manager in a large metropolitan department store. Last week you attended a meeting between consumers and retailers sponsored by the Downtown Merchants' Association. You were surprised by the ferocity of the outcry against advertising directed toward small children—particularly advertising associated with toys and food products. Because your firm has been sponsoring a clown show on Saturday morning television, you initiated a check of your firm's letters of complaint. Criticism of this type of promotion activity seems to have been increasing dramatically. These are selected quotations:

1. "I deplore your firm's callous manipulation of children for your own profit-oriented purposes."
2. "Who do you think you are? Have you no conscience, morals, or sense of decency?"

3. "Our organization opposes commercial exploitation of small children. Because industry has been unable to clean up its own house, we will concentrate our efforts on passage of strict laws prohibiting this activity. We believe that this is a sensitive political issue. Victory is expected."
4. "Because of your advertising program, our family will no longer buy your products."

What kind of response will you make to consumer groups who are concerned because you are advertising children's toys on TV?

You are a department manager in men's and women's wear in a small department store in the community in which you are attending school. You would like to run a series of advertisements in the local newspaper featuring casual suits. You have been instructed to plan the advertising effort on the basis of the decision questions in the text.

You are the manager of a local supermarket. You think manufacturer coupons are valuable for stimulating initial purchase activity, and you have tried very hard to cooperate with your suppliers when they are running a coupon campaign. Recently, however, several of your competitors have started giving customers the "cents off" on their order even when the couponed product is not purchased. You know that this action violates the manufacturer's agreement with the stores. What should you do? What can you do? What problems are involved?

Develop and execute two different newspaper advertisements for a local appliance store selling black-and-white portable television sets. Make one of the advertisements oriented to college students and one to moderate income families with several children.

a. State what you might want to accomplish with each advertisement.
b. Develop a planning guide for each of your advertisements. Use the following as headings for your planning guides: Description of Potential Customer; Possible Buying Motives; Benefits; Key Product Features; Complete Product Description.
c. Explain how you will get the benefit message across for the two advertisements.
   (1) How much copy? Why?
   (2) What will be illustrated? Why?
   (3) What will the headline be? Why?
   (4) Where do you want your two advertisements located in the newspaper? Why?
   (5) How large do you want each to be? Why?
d. What would each of the advertisements cost in your local newspaper? What would be the cost per subscriber? Cost per prospect?
e. Write your copy and headline, sketch your illustration and do a thumbnail layout of the advertisements.

Select three newspaper advertisements for each of two stores. Show them to a sample of your friends and ask them to tell you what they consider the image of the store to be. Probe for key phrases and words such as: "good place to get a bargain," "high style," "dependable family store," "reliable," "fashion conscious," "progressive," "honest," etc. Does the image projected vary from person to person? What factors in the advertisements caused what image description?

Ask your local district attorney to explain or provide you with copies of any state and/or local regulations covering fraudulent advertising.
a. What are the key points of the law?
b. Examine the advertisements in your newspaper. Do any appear to be in violation?

Make a comparison of radio and newspaper advertisements being run by the same store for the same product. Are different appeals used? If so, why? Are the two ads complementary?

Obtain several examples of "institutional" advertisements from a metropolitan newspaper. Are there similar characteristics about the stores that place institutional advertisements?

Go window shopping in the downtown area of your community. Select what you believe to be the best and worst window displays.
   Sketch the display and analyze the reasons for your choice. Indicate the strong and weak points of each window.

Build (on paper) a unit display (typically found in specialty stores) and a mass display (typically found in mass merchandising stores) using the same merchandise. Do not violate any of the principles of good display.

Bibliography

Jacobs, Laurence W. *Advertising and Promotion for Retailing: Text and Cases.* Glenview, Illinois: Scott, Foresman, 1972.

Nylen, David W. *Advertising: Planning, Implementation and Control.* Cincinnati: South-Western Publishing Company, 1975.

Ocko, Judy Young. *Retail Advertising Copy: The How, The What, The Why.* New York: National Retail Merchants Association, 1971.

Padley, Martin. *A Handbook to Radio Advertising.* New York: National Retail Merchants Association, 1969.

Appendix E
Designing the
Newspaper Advertisement

In this chapter we discussed the decisions that should be made when planning an advertising program. These decisions include knowing (1) what market we are trying to reach, (2) what our objectives are, (3) what we are going to advertise, (4) what the basic appeal should be, (5) where the advertisement should be placed, (6) when and how often the advertisement should be run, and (7) how much to spend. After these decisions are made, the actual advertisement can be designed.

General Guidelines

As retailers consider the elements of the advertisement and the layout of those elements, they should keep several things in mind. First, the advertisement must communicate *with* the customer, not talk *to* the customer. As you design the ad, then, imagine that you are in a two-way conversation with someone you know. Second, the advertiser should remember the guidelines set up during the planning process, with a clear idea of the market, the product, and the appeal. Third, the advertisement must have emotional, practical, and artistic appeal. The total message should be simple and clear. There should be no misunderstanding about information. Fourth, the message should be presented honestly and realistically. An advertiser shouldn't try to be cute or entertaining; the purpose of advertising is to sell products and services through information and persuasion. Finally, the advertiser should always keep in mind the function of the advertisement. It must attract attention, gain

and hold the interest of the reader, create a desire to purchase the product or visit the store, and invite or stimulate action. This is often referred to as AIDA—Attention, Interest, Desire, Action.

The Elements of an Advertisement

A newspaper advertisement usually contains four elements:

1. The headline
2. The body copy
3. The illustration
4. The store signature cut (the signature is the store name and is called a logotype; or logo).

The layout is the model, or plan, for combining the elements into a unified whole. The layout specifies the size and shape of the advertisement, the arrangement of and the space for the illustration, copy, headline, and logotype. The layout also specifies the type sizes and kinds of typeface to be used, the medium to be used, the timing of the advertisement, and the store name (see Figure 15.6).

The headline
The headline must carry a major part of the burden of attracting attention to the advertisement. Many more people will read the headline than will read the body copy. Therefore, the headline must do more than merely attract attention. It must present a message that will make the prospective buyer want to read more.

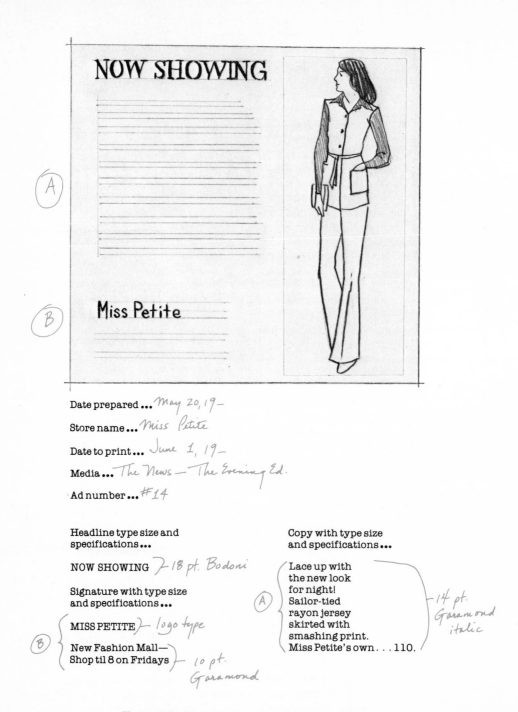

Figure 15.6. Rough sketch of an advertisement layout.

One of the best ways to write an effective headline is to refer to the product's strongest benefit to the customer. For example, references might be made to the pleasure the product gives or to its value. Another way to encourage people to read more is to use a headline similar to ones used for news. Such a headline presents a message that is concise and yet has meaning.

The copy

The copy follows the headline and is directly related to it. The copy should stress product benefits and give reasons for purchasing the product. It should also supply information that helps customers make a decision. The copy should be as brief and as informative as possible. Advertisers should ask themselves whether the copy has an appeal that will create desire and motivate people to act. The benefit approach to developing an appeal was discussed in the text.

The illustration

The illustration is a powerful selling tool. Words permit us only to create our own mental picture, but an illustration creates the picture for us. A good illustration not only works with the headline to gain attention and create interest, but if it is effectively done, it can present the entire selling message. An effectively used illustration can create a mood or an image, explain product uses, and present benefits, as well as simply identify the product.

An illustration should be chosen to complement the advertisement; an advertisement should not be built around the illustration. An advertiser should ask himself whether the illustration presents the message clearly and effectively. When appropriate, a caption should be used.

The logotype

The store's signature cut, or logotype, should provide recognition, individuality, and identification. A distinctive, well-chosen logotype becomes the trademark that projects the image of the store.

The Layout

The first step in designing the actual advertisement is to prepare a preliminary layout. This sketch, which may be only a thumbnail drawing, permits the designer to put ideas down on paper. An improved drawing, called a visual, is made from this thumbnail sketch. Ideas are added and subtracted to the visual until the rough size and shape of the advertisement's parts are formed; at this point, the layout is called a semicomprehensive layout. When the draft is in the final stages, it is called a comprehensive layout.

The size and shape of the layout should be in the same proportions as the final advertisement. The headlines, subheads, illustrations, copy lines, and name plate are sketched or pasted. The copy should be typed on separate sheets and should not appear on the layout.

Early in the preparation of the advertisement layout, space must be proportioned. Proper proportioning is necessary for balance. The proportioning of the advertisement may follow six basic layout plans. These six plans are illustrated below. (See Figure 15.7.)

The main objective of a design is to direct the eye flow smoothly from the top of the advertisement to the bottom. To achieve this objective, techniques are used to form white space, lines, illustrations, and copy blocks into a pattern for eye flow to follow. The three basic designs shown below may be reversed to achieve the same effect. (See Figure 15.8.)

Useful ideas for ad layout design

Designers who lay out advertisements must have a feeling for balance, proportion, and design flow. These are the criteria for an effective advertising design. Figure 15.7 shows the ways in which ads may be divided to obtain balance and proportion. To obtain balance and proportion among the elements, the designer must look carefully at the relative size of each element.

Common deisgn flow arrangements are shown in Figure 15.8. Design flow is intended to lead eye movement logically through the

Sample Layouts Designed to
Achieve Balance and Proportion

Early in the preparation of the advertisement layout, the proportioning of the space must be made. The proportioning of the advertisement may follow six basic layout plans. These six plans are illustrated below: Proper proportioning is necessary for balance.

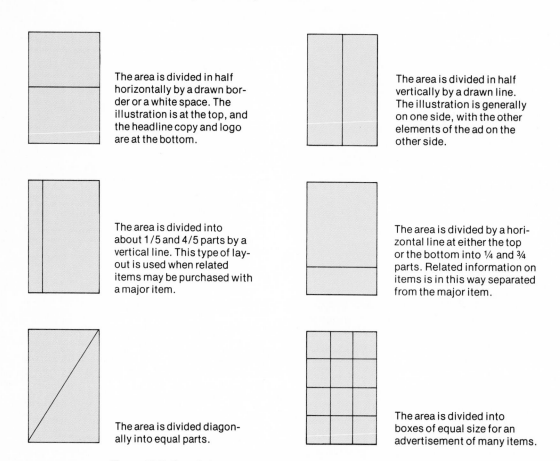

The area is divided in half horizontally by a drawn border or a white space. The illustration is at the top, and the headline copy and logo are at the bottom.

The area is divided in half vertically by a drawn line. The illustration is generally on one side, with the other elements of the ad on the other side.

The area is divided into about 1/5 and 4/5 parts by a vertical line. This type of layout is used when related items may be purchased with a major item.

The area is divided by a horizontal line at either the top or the bottom into ¼ and ¾ parts. Related information on items is in this way separated from the major item.

The area is divided diagonally into equal parts.

The area is divided into boxes of equal size for an advertisement of many items.

Figure 15.7. Sample layouts designed to achieve balance and proportion.

elements of the advertisement. Proper use of white space can be used to stimulate movement and interest. Design flow is often achieved by placing the most important element in what is called the optical center of the advertisement. The optical center is located slightly to the left and above the center of the ad.

The placing of price in the layout of an ad is particularly important. The prominence given to the price should be directly related to its strength as a motive or benefit in the particular situation.

We mentioned previously that selection of type size and face is also a part of layout. Not only must type sizes be in sensible proportions,

Basic Advertising Layout Design

The main objective of a design is to direct the eye flow
smoothly from the top of the advertisement to the bottom.
This objective is accomplished by certain techniques of
forming white space, lines, illustrations, and copy blocks
into a pattern for the eye flow to follow. The three basic
designs shown below may be reversed to achieve the
same effect.

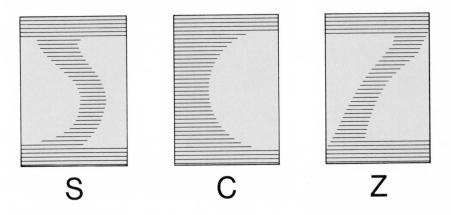

S   **C**   **Z**

Figure 15.8. Basic advertising layout design.

but the typeface (roman, italics, etc.) is important in projecting the desired image.

Some do's and don'ts

The Bureau of Advertising of the American
Newspaper Publishers Association suggest the
following do's and don'ts for each newspaper
advertisement:

1. Do make the ad easily recognizable.
2. Do use a simple layout.
3. Do use a prominent benefit headline.
4. Do let the white space work in the ad.
5. Do make copy complete.
6. Do list price or range of prices.
7. Do specify branded merchandise.
8. Do include related items.
9. Do urge the reader to buy now.
10. Don't forget the store name and address.
11. Don't be too clever.
12. Don't use difficult or unusual words.
13. Don't generalize.

14. Don't make excessive claims.

A check list to apply to an ad layout

Before placing a stamp of approval on an
ad, the retailer should ask these questions
about the finished advertisement:

1. Will people see my advertisement in relation to other ads?
   a. Is the headline big enough?
   b. Is the illustration prominent?
   c. Is the logotype clear and distinctive?
   d. If the advertisement is small, does it
   stand out as well as larger ads?
2. Can the price be easily understood? Is it set
   off in proportion to its effectiveness as a
   motivation for buying?
3. Is the product illustrated well?
4. Does the advertisement have a focusing
   point? Is there something that catches the
   reader's eye?
5. Does the advertisement make use of eye

flow and the optical center?

a. Does the eye flow go from top to bottom?

b. Is the most important element placed slightly above and to the left of the center?

c. Are there any breaks in eye movement?

6. Are the elements in reasonable proportion to one another?

7. Will the layout attract maximum readership? Is the copy short and meaningful?

If the ad satisfactorily passes this test, the retailer can forward the layout design for print.

Appendix F
Writing the Radio Advertisement

Writing an *effective* radio commercial is no more complicated than writing an effective newspaper ad, and can be done easily by adapting the technique. The writer must realize that the listening audience will have only one opportunity to hear and understand the spoken message. Listeners cannot go back and reread the advertisement as is possible with newspaper ads. Radio commercials are aimed at people whose attention is not entirely focused upon the message. Thus, they must be clear, almost as though a picture were being painted with words.

Consideration must be given to the type of audience the radio commercial will be heard by and written in accordance with these differences. Some radio stations may appeal to a young set, while another station's listeners are more sophisticated. This variation is similar to that found in the newspaper audience; different types of readers concentrate their interests in different sections of the paper.

Realizing that differences exist between radio and newspaper ads, a writer should follow the following nine points in writing a commercial for radio suggested by the National Retail Merchants Association.[1]

1. There is no stopper, no big headline or art. *You must get the listener's attention with words.*
2. The ear is less attentive than the eye. Reading takes full concentration, but you can listen with half an ear. That's why you must *repeat, repeat, repeat.*
3. Listeners can't go back to figure out what you mean. So keep your *sentences simple, brief, uncomplicated.*
4. There's no logotype to identify your store. Don't leave them wondering where they can get it. *Tell them again and again.*
5. You have no picture to support your prose. If there are important facts, *you must give word pictures.*
6. Words that look right don't always sound right, and some combinations or words make for stumbling. *Read your commercials out loud.*
7. *Your audience can't absorb and remember a lot of numbers.* Don't try to give three prices, a phone number, and an extension in 30 seconds.
8. The announcer is not a spokesman for the store, but a third party. When he talks about your store, it's "they," not "we."
9. You have only one chance to *attract an audience. .with your lead-in.* If you don't catch them then, they'll turn off their ears.

Radio time is usually sold as 10 second spots (called ID's or identifications), 30 seconds, and full minutes. Depending upon the words themselves, an average of 30 words is possible per ID, 75 words per 30 seconds, and 120 to 150 words in a one minute spot.

Most radio commercials are of the "straight announcement" form. They are read "live" by the station announcer without any additional sound effects. As well as being flexible, this type of ad is less costly since production costs are eliminated.

[1] Judy Young Ocko, *Retail Advertising Copy: The How, The What, The Why,* National Retail Merchants Association, New York, New York, 1975, pp. 74—75.

Other forms are used less frequently. One is the dramatization which is in the form of a playlet utilizing more than one voice, music, and/or sound effects. Also useful is the dialogue. This is a conversation between two people, less elaborate than the dramatization. Finally, part or all of a radio ad may be in the form of a jingle or singing commercial.

Before writing a radio commercial, the writer must collect all of the facts. Knowledge of whether the ad is aimed at immediate sales or improving the store image is necessary, as well as the type of audience, the features of the product, the most important selling points, and the conditions under which the commercial will be heard. Next, the writer must follow the previously mentioned nine points in writing the ad.

Lead-ins must be written to intrigue the listener, always in conversational language. Indirect lead-ins can be used and the ad should include news or customer benefits that will relate to the listeners personally.

Care must be taken to increase memorability of an ad. The more different and diverse the ideas in an ad are, the less memorable each is. A writer should repeat the name of the store and product several times to help create store identification with the sales message. Another memory aid is the jingle or spoken slogan. A slogan is a short, catchy phrase that is repeated in every ad, is based upon the major selling feature and includes the store's name.

To avoid pronunciation problems for the announcer, letter and word combinations that can become tongue twisters should be eliminated. Always reading the ad aloud first is essential.

End radio commercials with a short summary and a call for action. Since the commercial will be heard and not seen, strive to make it logical, clear and concise.

Appendix G
Display Windows

Displays play an important role in a retail store. An attractive and informative display can help sell goods or services. This appendix highlights the key considerations in building displays. The discussion will be built around the topic of trimming windows, although the same comments apply equally well to all kinds of display.

Rules to Follow in Building a Display

In building a display there are some fundamental rules that should be followed:

Achieve balance. In building a display, it is important to make sure that the display appears balanced to the viewer. This is achieved by arranging products (and props) in particular ways. A display may have formal balance or informal balance. Formal balance is achieved by balancing on each side of the center one or more similar items. Informal balance is achieved by balancing on opposite sides of the center dissimilar items. The effects produced by informal balance are less peaceful and less obvious but many times are more interesting than the effects produced by formal balance.

An easy way to understand balance is to visualize a teeter-totter. One way to have the teeter-totter in balance is to place two identically weighted individuals equally distanced from the center (called fulcrum) as seen below. This is a formal balance arrangement.

Another way to achieve balance (in this case informal balance) would be to position unequally weighted individuals, unequally distanced from the center as below. In these situations the heavier object is always closer to the center than the lighter object.

In display fashions a formally and informally balanced display might appear as shown.

Provide for a point of dominance. All displays should have a central point that will first attract the viewer's eyes. This point may be established by using a prominent piece of merchandise, dramatic color, streamers arranged to center on an object. A point of dominance acts as a focal point upon which the viewer's eyes rest and from which the eyes move to other parts of the display.

Provide for proper eye movement. Too many displays do not direct the eyes in a systematic fashion but permit them to jump from one end of the display to the other. If her eyes move indiscriminately around the display, the viewer will not see some of the merchandise in the display and will not understand the display's intended message. To achieve proper eye movement, merchandise should be displayed in such a way that the eyes move from one part of the display to another. Sometimes the use of streamers facilitates this objective.

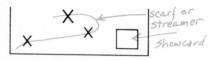

Provide for gradation. Gradation is the sequence in which items are arranged. For example, small items are usually placed at the front of the display, medium-sized items farther back, and large-sized items at the rear. This provides harmony and creates an appealing illusion.

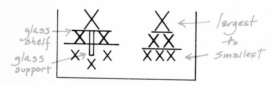

Place at eye level that merchandise designed to have the greatest impact. Because viewers tend to look straight ahead, merchandise placed at eye level is most likely to be seen.

Group merchandise. Too many merchants place one item after another in a long row. Shoe stores, jewelry stores, and mass merchandisers, especially, tend to do this. Stores with large amounts of one item (antifreeze) or with one line of goods (shoes or jewelry) are likely to build displays in this manner. Merchandise should be grouped, so the cus-

tomer's eyes travel from group to group. If this isn't done, the window has a junky appearance, and the customer has difficulty picking out the merchandise being displayed.

Give merchandise sales appeal. All windows should display their best merchandise. Displays take up valuable space and to use slow selling items for display merchandise is to waste the potential in a display. One way to generate sales appeal is to choose the most important feature of the merchandise being displayed and then emphasize it. Another way is to have the display tell a story. In other words, build the display around a theme, such as a Back-to-School or Valentine theme. Customers relate best when they can grasp the total picture; they imagine themselves in the situation and are able to understand the role that the merchandise might play.

Keep displays clean. Merchants who permit dust to accumulate on a display, who leave dead moths lying around, who do not dust display merchandise and props, who do not wash glass display fixtures and windows to eliminate the blue film that frequently collects on them, who do not replace burnt-out light bulbs, and who do not replace merchandise that has been taken out are guilty of poor display maintenance.

Use color properly. Don't use colors in an offensive way. Different colors are appropriate for displays of women's wear and displays of men's wear. Pinks and greens are less appropriate for men than they are for women. The featured items should be in the brightest colors. Light colors deepen a display space, seemingly increasing its size. Dark colors do the opposite.

Use name cards and show cards. Every window should have the name of the store either on a name card or printed on the window. Too many times customers must step back from the window and look up to find out which store is running the display. Show cards are informative and give the sales message, so they should be used to act as sales agents.

LACE TRIMMED

SLIPS

STRAIGHT CUT
BIAS BACK PANEL
WHITE OR PINK

B-2 PEN
1 99
B-0 PEN

RAYON BRIEF 44¢

Don't clutter up a display. Many merchants put too much merchandise in a small area. Keep displays orderly.

Plan displays in advance. The proper procedure is to sketch out a display prior to constructing it. This facilitates the gathering of the merchandise to be used in the display and the collecting of fixtures for the display. Planning should also include attention to show cards; make sure they are ready to be placed in the display. (See Figure 15.9.) Then build the display in the least amount of time possible.

Trimming Display Windows

Now, let's take a look at some specific examples of displays. Figure 15.10 shows a window display in a women's fashion store. The window, as you can see, has a semiopen back. The decorating of the window shows some serious shortcomings. First, there seems to be no focal point (point of dominance) for the eyes to rest on. Thus, it is extremely difficult for the eyes to move systematically from one piece of merchandise to another. They tend to jump all over the window. Second, the merchandise and props have not been well placed. The mannequins are too far back in the window to be viewed; merchandise has been placed flat on the floor, without elevation; a dress is in the corner of the window, in back of the mannequins (as is the rattan prop), causing the eyes to travel to the corners of the window and then possibly leave the window space altogether. Third, there is a weakness in the use of gradation. Merchandise and props move from the floor, to a middle height, to a higher height, then back down to a middle height. Fourth, the show card is positioned so far back in the window that it is difficult to read. Also, the name of the store does not appear either on the window or on the show card. Fifth, the window seems to lack significant sales appeal; the use of related merchandise is weak and no theme seems to run throughout the display.

Figure 15.11, on the other hand, shows a much better treatment of display space. First, there is a focal point to which the eyes are drawn. This focal point is on the left body form. From the body form there seems to be good eye movement to the sign, down to the other body form, and on down to the floor of the display. Second, the display is knit together. Part of this has been accomplished by the grouping of merchandise into a tightly knit display, and part of it has been accomplished by using the black material in which the total display rests. Third, the display has sales appeal. The merchandise is well chosen; related merchandise is displayed; and the show card tells what the display is attempting to do. Fourth, the store name appears in the window. Fifth, the display is artistically sound from the vantage point of balance and gradation.

Fixtures and equip. needed	Inventory needed	Special effects
Namecards Red flocked paper (from Wallorama) special 'pen' lights	Teal Traina dress and accessories	Fall Fashion sign

Figure 15.9. Window display planning guide.

Figure 15.10. A poorly planned window display.

Figure 15.11. A well planned window display.

16

Retail Selling

contents

Personal Selling
The Retail Selling Process
Salesperson Motivation
Summary
Questions and Problems
Situations and Activities
Bibliography

behavioral objectives

Part of personal selling is the art of communicating with customers. To use this communication device successfully, you must
understand when to use it and how to obtain the best results
from its use. After studying this chapter, you will have the foundation necessary for making personal selling decisions.

Upon completing this chapter, you will be able to do the
following:
☐ Define personal selling.
☐ Explain how feedback is received by salespeople from
customers and by customers from retail salespeople.
☐ Describe some job responsibilities of salespeople.
☐ Distinguish among these approaches to selling: the
stimulus-response approach, the formula approach, and the
problem solving-need approach.
☐ Identify the variables that help determine the number of retail
salespeople needed on a selling floor.
☐ Explain how a retail salesperson's performance can be
measured.

Personal Selling

The selling that occurs when a consumer and a salesperson come face to face in a store is the heart and soul of all retailing. All store activities such as financing, accounting, buying, advertising, inventory control, and display have a single justification—a contribution to profitable sales. Although all these activities are important, it is the salesperson who reaches customers by selling and servicing products.

It is unfortunate that salespeople are often held in low esteem—that they are considered clerks and stockers of shelves. Effective retail salespeople are communicators, interpreting product and service features by talking in terms of benefits to the customer. When customers must make decisions about brand, style, quality, price, color, and size, salespeople are the key figures in the retail situation. But salespeople are more than communicators. To customers they are the permanent representatives of the store. Customers judge a store, in large measure, by the impressions given by salespeople. When customers make a purchase, they buy not only the product but also a set of psychological satisfactions provided by the salesperson, the retailer, and the manufacturer. Therefore, every firm and individual in the marketing system is ultimately at the mercy of the salespeople on the floor.

Because there are an increasing number of self-service stores and because manufacturers are attempting to presell merchandise through extensive advertising, it might be argued that personal selling is losing some of its importance. Even in these situations, however, the people on the floor are important to sales because they are asked for information and advice. Supermarkets, for example, are models of self-service. Yet, many people ask for help in the bakery, produce, and meat departments.

Personal selling and communication

Personal selling is a very important part of a store's efforts to communicate with customers. One essential part of effective communication is feedback. Only in personal selling does the potential for a clear feedback channel exist.

As salespeople talk with customers they not only hear verbal reactions to their questions and statements but also see smiles, frowns, and nods. The verbal responses and the nonverbal reactions provide feedback. Together, these responses help salespeople tailor the sales message to the specific needs of the customer. They also help salespeople provide additional information of the kind most likely to reduce customer uncertainty.

Customers also receive feedback from salespeople. As customers receive nonverbal reactions from the salesperson—a helpful manner, pride in the products and the store, and friendliness—their receptivity to the salesperson's verbal messages may increase.

Unquestionably, advertising can call attention to products, create interest in them, and, in many cases, even convince customers to buy them. However, only in the face-to-face communication that takes place in the personal selling situation can retailers (1) clearly identify the individual customer's problems, (2) pinpoint the customer's uncertainties of purchasing and provide knowledge and information to reduce these uncertainties, and (3) provide specific rational and psychological reasons that help the customer make a purchasing decision.

What does a salesperson do?

Salespeople are expected to sell. Through effective face-to-face communication, salespeople translate product features into benefits and satisfactions that solve customers' problems and fill their needs. To do this effectively, salespeople must know their merchandise, find out what their customers want and why they want it, and use selling techniques designed to produce satisfied customers.

All too often retail salespersons seem to think of their customers as a potential sale instead of a person. But the individual in retail selling who sees the customer as a person rather than a sale is the successful salesperson, primarily because retail selling is a very personal type of selling. Why? Because most retail

Eleven Commandments of good business . . .

A Customer is the most important person in any business.

A Customer is not dependent on us—we are dependent on her.

A Customer is not an interruption of our work—she is the purpose of it.

A Customer does us a favor when she calls—we are not doing her a favor by serving her.

A Customer is part of our business—not an outsider.

A Customer is not a cold statistic—she is a flesh and blood human being with feelings and emotions like our own.

A Customer is not someone to argue with but to help.

A Customer is a person who brings us her needs and it is our job to fill those needs.

A Customer is deserving of the most courteous and attentive treatment we can give her.

A Customer is the person who makes it possible for us to earn our salary.

A Customer is the life-blood of our business.

Figure 16.1. The eleven commandments of good business.
Courtesy: Saks Fifth Avenue

customers buy products or services for their own use or for the use of those close to them, such as their family, relatives, and friends.

Retail selling is a difficult job that involves long hours of standing and working with customers who may not always be the most pleasant and can get on ones' nerves. And sometimes working with a hard to please boss isn't easy. The retail salesperson has to keep up with what is new in an environment today where there are more and more items, and where sales features of each product are more varied or many of the items are becoming more technically complicated.

The retail salesperson must perform a number of different functions, including customer contact, stockwork, housekeeping, and security.

Customer contact. Once the retail salesperson has greeted the shopper promptly and courteously, she or he may first be involved in simply making a transaction. In this case, the customer has a specific product purchase in mind and the salesperson's job is simply to complete the transaction, which may involve writing a sales ticket, arranging for payment or credit and possibly wrapping and delivering. Accuracy is very important in handling these transaction functions. The second element of customer contact involves the creative selling element. Identifying the customers' problems, responding to questions, answering objections, showing how a particular product may meet the customer's needs are typical. The third element of customer contact may involve handling complaints. There are times when service is unsatisfactory or products do not work and it is these times when the salesperson must encounter the irrate or unhappy customer. The salesperson must start with the premise that the customer is always right and do whatever is possible in line with store policies to make sure that an unhappy customer is not turned into a permanently lost one; but rather, a customer who is more loyal to the store than before because a complaint has been satisfactorily handled. Salespeople are also responsible for providing after-sale service such as product operating instructions or information about when the product should be serviced, as well as handling returns and exchanges.

Finally, salespeople have responsibilities to the customer. They are responsible for seeing that customers make the best possible product decision in light of their needs and financial resources. It is the responsibility of salespeople to help educate consumers to be wiser shoppers.

Housekeeping and stockwork. Some of the salesperson's time must be involved in housekeeping. Keeping the store and the selling areas clean, merchandise arranged and displayed as it should be is essential. Another area involves that of working the stock. As goods are sold the shelves must be replenished whether the goods are taken from the storeroom or from below counter stocks. They must be put in their proper places on the shelves. This is a continuous task in nature.

Security. The store's best protection against the shoplifter, the bad check artist, as well as the fellow employees' theft, is the retail salesperson. The salesperson has a responsibility to the store to be vigilant and aware of the possibilities and opportunities that shoplifters may use.

How should a salesperson sell?

Almost all views of the selling process fall into one of three categories: (1) the stimulus-response approach, (2) the selling formula approach, or (3) the problem solving—need satisfaction approach.

The stimulus-response approach. The stimulus-response approach is based on the premise that for a given stimulus there is a particular response. You may be familiar with the Russian scientist Pavlov who conditioned dogs to salivate (response) at the sound of a bell (stimulus). This approach suggests that if sales people have a series of things to do or say

(stimuli), and if they say and do them correctly, they will obtain the desired response (buying). However, customers differ. What pleases one customer may or may not please another one.

The formula approach. The formula approach to selling is based upon a standard sales presentation containing statements that lead the customer through stages of thought processes. A frequently seen formula is AIDA: attract *attention;* arouse *interest;* create *desire;* and obtain *action.* Like the stimulus-response approach, the formula selling approach is based on the assumption that all customers can be persuaded by the same message. The approach does not take into consideration customer questions and individual customer needs.

Problem solving—need satisfaction approach. Throughout this book we have stressed the importance of being genuinely concerned about individual customer needs. The stimulus-response and the formula approach show little consideration for such needs. In both cases salespeople dominate the conversation, presenting a message designed to persuade the customer. The problem solving —need satisfaction approach is oriented toward the customer.

In the initial phase of the selling situation salespeople are encouraged to ask questions designed to clarify or define the customer's problem. Careful questioning, with the customer doing most of the talking, helps the salesperson find out what the customer's needs are and how he or she will use the product. Once the salesperson has pinpointed the customer's needs, he or she can select the appropriate combination of features of the product or service. The salesperson's role then, is one of translating the product's features into benefits and advantages. Notice that this process is no different from that used in constructing a good advertising message, except that in personal selling the message can be tailored to the needs of the individual customer.

The problem solving—need satisfaction

WHY SALES ARE LOST

Very often sales are lost through carelessness or indifference on the salesperson's part. Here are some reasons why:

1. Disinterest—Don't conduct a conversation with a fellow employee or another customer while waiting on someone. Give the customer your complete attention. Deadpan expressions, daydreaming, or "take it or leave it" attitudes leave unsold merchandise.

2. Mistakes—If you show the wrong item or make a mistake in change, acknowledge it and make the customer feel you are genuinely sorry.

3. Appearing too anxious—Show customers you want to serve their interests. Overinsistence and high-pressure tactics are objectionable to customers.

4. Talking down other brands—Talk up the brand you want to sell. Do not make unfair remarks about a competitive brand.

5. Arguing—Never argue with a customer. If it appears that an argument might develop, shift the conversation to another topic. There's little profit in winning an argument and losing the customer. If a customer makes an absurd statement, don't laugh or argue. You may anger the customer, and an angry customer is a lost customer.

6. Being too long-winded—A flood of words doesn't make many sales. Some people take time to make up their minds, and silence at the right time allows the customer to think and decide. Being a good listener often makes more sales than being a fast talker.

7. Lack of courtesy—Discourteous salespeople rarely last long on a job; they lose too many customers.

8. Showing favoritism—Never wait on your friends or favorite customers before taking care of customers who were there first.

9. Being too hurried—Take time to find out what a customer wants and then take time to show the merchandise properly.

10. Embarrassing the customer—Never laugh at a person who speaks with a foreign accent or correct a person who mispronounces words or product names.

11. Misrepresenting merchandise—Never guarantee any cures or make any claims for products that cannot be backed up by facts.

12. Lack of product information—Salespeople who are not well informed cannot expect to build a steady clientele for their store.

13. Wasting customers' time—When a customer is in a hurry, finish the sale as quickly as possible.

14. Getting too personal—Assume a professional attitude. Be sincere and friendly, but keep a touch of dignity and formality in all customer contacts. Never let familiarity creep into the conversation, for it is usually resented.

Figure 16.2. Why sales are lost.

approach requires that salespeople have a thorough knowledge of merchandise, stock, store policies, services, promotion, and competition. They must be able to take cues from the customer, to listen well, and to talk about merchandise in specific terms—that is, in terms of how it will help the customer.

The Retail Selling Process

The retail selling process cannot, in practice, be divided into separate actions, but there are at least four parts in the process: (1) approaching the customer, (2) determining customer needs and wants, (3) the selling presentation and (4) closing the sale.

Approaching the customer. Many retail sales are made in the first few moments after the customer arrives in the sales area. If the salesperson displays a courteous, helpful attitude, an excellent start is made. However, the sale will be difficult if the customer is neglected and treated in an unfriendly manner.

The initial greeting to the customer is very important. Many salespersons repeat the worn phrases, "May I help you?" or "Can I help you?" This is an overworked and ineffective approach because the standard response is "No, thank you" or "Thanks, but I'm just looking." Once the customer says this, the salesperson must either leave or possibly make the customer uncomfortable by staying nearby.

Questioning phrases that do not allow for a "No, thank you" are better to use. Ask: "What size are you looking for?", "What size (color, style, etc.) of refrigerator did you have in mind?", or "May I show you the sale merchandise featured in today's newspaper advertisement?" The retail salesperson who uses this approach offers assistance without the customer having to request it and does not invite the negative reply. The key is for the salesperson to show concern for the customers' interests, be willing to provide information, and give customer assistance while making the individual customer feel important.

Determining customer needs/wants. In order to make an effective sales presentation, the salesperson must strive to identify the individual's wants. As was pointed out in the two chapters on understanding the retail customer, this is a difficult task because of the variety of customer tastes and interests. To determine customer needs the salesperson first must learn to listen. If the salesperson will stop talking long enough, the customer may well tell what she wants. But, concentrating on what the customer is trying to say is important, because some customers may have difficulty in expressing their needs in terms of specific product characteristics.

Complementary to listening is learning to ask questions designed to help the customer formulate and express specific needs. Questions such as who will use the merchandise, how it will be used, is it a gift, are there preferred sizes or colors, or methods of payment, all may guide the salesperson in identifying needs. If there is any doubt, ask the customer.

Finally the salesperson must be alert. Observing the customer's behavior, manner of dress, and facial expressions, can provide necessary clues.

The selling presentation. The selling presentation may involve a number of elements. The basis of the salesperson's presentation to the customer is an *explanation* of the product and its benefits as they are related to the needs, wants and problems that the customer may have. An actual *demonstration* of the product always adds impact to the selling presentation. Stimulating the senses through feeling the texture or weight of a fabric, smelling an aftershave lotion, seeing how the shoes look on the feet, or whatever, may well take the customer a major step closer to purchase.

In cases where the exact product or brand is not carried, or if another item may well fit, or clearly offers a better satisfaction to the customer needs, *substitute selling* may be used by the retail salesperson, as they suggest another brand of the same item or an alternative product for the customer. There is sometimes the opportunity for the salesperson to *"trade up"* the customer to buy a more expensive or larger quantity of the product than the customer had originally intended to buy. Both trading up and substitute selling should be approached with caution. Ill will for the store will obviously result if the customer is dissatisfied with the alternative merchandise, or feels that she has been pressured by the seller into accepting an unsatisfactory merchandise alternative. It is obviously better to have the customer not unhappy with your store, even if she gets her merchandise from a competitor.

During the sales presentation, the salesperson may use *suggestion selling* to encourage customers to buy additional items or larger quantities. Often there is an opportunity for suggesting new merchandise. For a buyer of a tennis racket, a salesperson might show her a new fashionable tennis outfit. In another case, complementary items such as matching pants or a coordinating blouse and skirt are examples that might be suggested. Additional seasonal or holiday merchandise, such as ski goggles for the skier or candy for Christmas, is always appropriate. And finally, one should always suggest sale merchandise. Customers are often unaware of special promotions in a department, and a suggestion to look may increase sales, as well as give the customer a more favorable image of the salesperson and the store.

Retailers may do several things to help salespeople improve their ability to sell by suggestion. Developing lists of related items in other departments is very important. A program to ensure that salespeople are knowledgeable about all special promotions within the department and throughout the entire store should be instituted. And, within the department, coordinated and related items should be outlined for each product category.

Very often the selling presentation will require *handling objections*. Salespeople often feel that customers raise objections to buying because they do not want to purchase the merchandise. This is seldom the case. Customers who do not want to buy, or who do not see what they want, usually just leave the store. Customers who raise objections are typically interested in the merchandise but have doubts about buying it. Usually they are concerned about cost, product features, or whether to purchase now or later. Sometimes the customer just needs additional reassurance to convince themselves.

Objections are best handled by anticipating them and providing the information necessary to answer the objection before the customer can raise it. For example, if it appears the customer is concerned about the high price, the salesperson can demonstrate and emphasize the value by comparing quality of a lower priced good during the initial sales presentation. If the salesperson knows the merchandise and can explain its benefits in terms of buyer wants, then objections can usually be handled satisfactorily.

Closing the sale. Closing the retail sale may occur almost as soon as the customer walks into the store. The customer knows exactly what she wants, what brand, and the price she expects to pay. In this case, the salesperson's job, in terms of closing, is simply to complete the transaction. But, many times the retail selling process requires a creative closing effort by the salesperson in order to bring the customer to the actual decision to buy.

Without the close there is no sale, so it is important for the salesperson to learn when to close and how to do it. The close is the process by which the salesperson gets the customer to make a commitment. The first job that the salesperson has to do is to learn when the customer appears to be ready, and as we have suggested, the close may come very early in the selling process. Obviously, the salesperson who attempts to close very quickly will appear overly aggressive. By the same token, the customer who is ready to buy does not want to hear much additional selling information. There are a number of closing techniques that the good salesperson can learn to use. Many are variations on questions such as, "What particular features are you looking for in a chair?'' to obtain responses that will determine how far the customer is in making up his mind about what he wants and to obtain a commitment. If the customer replies with an answer identifying features similar to those the salesperson has iterated, then it's time for another question such as: "Will that be cash or charge?" or "Do you want us to deliver it?" or "Do you want to take it with you?" All of the questions should be designed to determine if the customer has all the information needed and has made a decision.

Salesperson Motivation

The most important jobs managers have are communicating with and motivating their salespersons.

Motivation of salespersons has the dual role of retaining them and stimulating improvement in their work. Most people can be positively motivated if they are given good reasons for doing good work. Among these reasons, the following have been suggested. Many salespeople will work better and harder in anticipation of *money rewards*. They are motivated by money rewards for seniority and for above average performance in sales and service. They may be stimulated to greater effort by quota bonuses and by commissions, provided the rewards are substantial, attainable, and promptly paid. An effective management tool to motivate salespersons is to offer them *sales incentives*. These incentives may run from contests to premiums to gifts—special allowances for the salesperson who achieves or exceeds a sales target figure. One traditional way of motivating a salesperson to sell a particular item is through what is called push-money or a "spiff." Push-money involves a cash bonus received by the salesperson for selling particular goods. The customer assumes that the item is being sold because of the enthusiasm the salesperson has for the product and not necessarily because he or she has been offered an extra sales incentive in the terms of a money reward. Of course, the push-money does create administrative problems in record keeping, determination of which specific items the salesperson has sold, and of course problems can be created where the salesperson makes misrepresented claims because of the extra incentive for selling a particular good or brand.

A job system that furnishes the opportunity for *promotion* within the sales force can be an effective motivator. Promotion to supervisory or executive jobs should also be possible; potential among all employees should be recognized and cultivated.

Everyone needs spoken approval for good performance. Many salespeople need *praise* so much that they completely lose interest in their job when praise is not given.

People will work hard at a job they *like for its content* or *respect for its purpose*. The goals of a store should be consistently presented to employees in terms of consumer benefits whose importance they can recognize. It is especially important to fit job assignments to employees' special interests if possible.

People will *meet standards* and *observe rules* when they are known, reasonable, and enforced. Most people are better motivated in a disciplined work environment. They work good-humoredly and productively in such an environment when they know for a certainty that departures from the rules will be enforced equitably and consistently.

Special considerations

If there are too many salespeople, there is idle time and wage costs are misspent. If there are too few salespeople, customers must wait and customer service is inadequate. Either of these situations results from an uneven flow of customers into the store.

Staffing. Because the salaries paid salespeople are one of the largest expenses for most retail stores, it is important to keep the number of salespeople at a level consistent with demand and customer service requirements. This, however, is not easy to do, because several variables must be taken into consideration:

1. Customer arrival time and frequency
2. The number of contacts made with customers
3. The number and length of actual sales transactions
4. Store expense constraints.

Obviously, it would take a complex mathematical formula to optimize the number of salespeople on the floor at a given time. Frequently, managers simply set an upper limit on sales expenses, expressed as a percentage of sales. They obtain a dollar amount for sales expenses, based on a projected level of sales. Then, they hire as many salespeople as they consider necessary until they exceed their dollar limit. This procedure does not indicate the mix of part-time and full-time employees, nor does it indicate how many employees should be working at any given time of day. However, many managers, by using their experience and by considering the variables previously listed, seem to do a satisfactory job of meeting customer requirements while keeping sales expenses in line.

Training. Every store, large or small, should have a planned training program for new salespeople and a continuing training program for all salespeople. Most large stores have special training staffs that conduct continuing in-store training programs. Such stores usually have their own training manuals, materials, and visual aids. Small stores that do not have specialists to plan and direct their training can rely on experienced salespeople and can use training materials provided by manufacturers and suppliers.

The basic purpose of training is to increase employee productivity by providing product information and knowledge of sales techniques.

Before salespersons can begin to effectively do their job they must have product knowledge. Product knowledge allows the salesperson to translate product features to customer benefits. Knowledge about the customer provides answers to product objectives, but without product knowledge there cannot be the self-confidence that is necessary to convince the customer of the solution to the problem. Training for effective creative salesmanship involves teaching techniques for the approach, how to determine customer needs, the basis of the sales presentation, and how to overcome objections and close a sale. The approach to the customer must gain the customer's attention and make him/her interested in hearing more about what is to be said. By listening to the customer and asking questions, noticing the customer's interest and respecting the customer's preference, effective salespersons focus on the needs of their particular customers. Only then is a salesperson in a position to make a presentation of merchandise, selecting the quality and quantity and price range for the customer to examine. Explaining the values of the goods and demonstrating them may be necessary. To increase salespersons' effectiveness, they may be taught to identify objections, whether the objections are due to the product, price, value or lack of need. Lastly, the salesperson should be trained to know when and how to close a sale.

As knowledge and skills increase, salespeople increase both their confidence and their earnings. Employees know that increased productivity provides additional job security and improves the opportunities for advancement.

Control of employee performance. Control of the personal selling function involves (1) establishing performance standards, (2) measuring and evaluating performance, and (3) taking corrective action when performance falls below the standard. In Chapter 6 we emphasized the necessity of keeping adequate sales records for each salesperson. These records become the bases for measuring and evaluating sales performance. However, not all of a salesperson's time is spent in selling. In fact, it is estimated that as little as 25 percent of the time may be spent in this way. Another 25 percent may be spent on stock work and other activities associated with selling. As much as 50 percent of a salesperson's time may be spent awaiting customer arrivals.

Standards for performance may be established on the basis of several factors:

1. Dollar volume of sales
2. Units sold
3. Number of completed transactions
4. Gross margin contributed.

By measuring such factors as number of contacts and store traffic, retailers may calculate ratios that can be used to set standards of performance as well as to analyze the factors influencing performance. For example, dividing the number of customer contacts by the number of transactions gives the percentage of customers who bought merchandise. Dividing the units sold by the number of customers produces a traffic productivity ratio.

Regardless of the standards set for evaluating sales performance, it is vitally necessary that they be thoroughly understood by every salesperson and that they be fair and reasonably easy to measure and calculate.

Compensation. Salespeople are usually compensated by one of four methods: (1) straight salary, (2) straight commission, (3) salary plus commission, or (4) salary plus quota bonus.

The *straight salary* is the most commonly used method of compensation for salespeople. A specified amount is paid for each period. Similar to the straight salary is the hourly wage, according to which the amount paid varies only by the number of hours worked.

In the *straight commission* method salespeople are paid only on the basis of the total number of sales they make. At the end of the pay period total sales are multiplied by a commission rate to determine earnings. A straight commission is often used in conjunction with a drawing account. Payments are made to employees at a regular interval and are then charged against commissions earned at the end of the month.

A *straight salary plus a small commission* on all sales provides an incentive to make sales. This is a compromise that attempts to combine the best features of the straight salary and the straight commission plans.

The *salary plus quota bonus* is another compromise between the straight salary and the straight commission methods. In the salary plus quota bonus method salespeople are paid a fixed amount for the pay period. In addition, a period sales quota is established. At the end of the period a bonus is paid on the amount by which sales exceed the quota.

In addition to the regularly scheduled paycheck, store personnel are provided with a program of fringe benefits that greatly supplement the dollars received in their paychecks. The fringe benefit programs of many firms cost up to 40 percent of the actual salaries, wages, and commissions paid. All or part of the following may make up fringe benefit programs:

1. Employee discounts for merchandise purchased in the store
2. Social security and unemployment insurance contributions
3. Medical and life insurance
4. Savings plans
5. Profit sharing.

Summary

This chapter is the second of two chapters on communicating with the retail customer. Each chapter was designed to provide you with a frame of reference to use in making communication decisions.

This chapter was concerned with personal selling. Customers are constantly engaged in a search for satisfaction. Their success depends largely on the buying help they receive from retail salespeople. In large part, the success of a store depends on how well this communication device helps customers find satisfaction. Of all retailing activities designed to stimulate buying and serve customers, the most important may be the activities that take place on the sales floor. The role of salespeople is, therefore, a very important one in a retail store.

Questions and Problems

1. Frequently, each of two salespeople may consider the same customer to be his "personal trade." When salespeople are paid on commission, this can create considerable animosity. What problems does a department manager face in trying to handle this situation?

2. What problems does a department manager face in trying to reduce the nonselling time of salespeople?

3. Does the relative importance of advertising, personal selling, and sales promotion vary among a supermarket, a discount store, and a specialty store? What factors cause the difference?

Situations and Activities

You are the owner of a small variety store. You have been considering shifting your operation to self-service. Your preliminary analysis indicates that, today, consumers may not require selling service, at least for your type of product. You think the lower selling expense would permit you to be competitive on a price basis. On what basis should you proceed, if at all? What trade-offs do you face? What provision will you make for your present sales employees?

Go on a shopping trip. Select a product that you might reasonably be in the market for, such as a stereo, radio, or sportswear. Visit four stores carrying the product. *Following* each shopping stop record the following regarding the experience. Plan ahead to have several objections. Example: Too expensive, don't like that brand, color, etc.—YOU DON'T HAVE TO BUY!

a. How did the salesperson greet you? How long did you wait for a salesperson?

b. What questions did the salesperson ask you to determine your needs?

c. Did the salesperson find out how much you were willing/able to pay?

d. How did the salesperson answer your objections?

e. Did the salesperson ask for the sale? How did she or he try to close the sale?

Select the method of compensation that you would use in paying the following types of retail workers. Justify your answer.

salesperson in a high fashion department
appliance salesperson
stockroom checker-marker
bookkeeper
display decorator
department manager
truck driver

Visit department managers of 2 or 3 stores and interview them to find out what they consider to be important characteristics of good retail salespeople.

Bibliography

Baker, Richard M. Jr., and Phifer, Gregory. *Salesmanship: Communication, Persuasion, and Perception.* Boston: Allyn and Bacon, 1966, pp. 335—336.

Buskirk, Richard H. *Retail Selling.* San Francisco: Canfield Press, 1975.

Helfant, Seymour. *Person-to-Person Selling.* New York: National Retail Merchants Association, 1969.

Helfant, Seymour. *Training and Motivating Retail Sales People.* New York: National Retail Merchants Association, 1969.

Kurtz, David L., Dodge, H. Robert, and Klompmaker, Jay E. *Professional Selling.* Dallas: Business Publications, 1976, pp. 265—283.

Mazze, Edward M. *Personal Selling: Choice Against Chance.* St. Paul: West Publishing Company, 1976.

17

Retail Services

contents

behavioral objectives

Service offerings are a source of competition among retailers. Managers should know which services their customers expect them to offer and under what conditions services should be offered. Managers must also know how to manage the service function. After reading this chapter, you should be able to describe the scope of retail services and make suggestions for sound procedures in managing services.

Upon completing this chapter, you will be able to do the following:
☐ Discuss different types of retail services.
☐ Decide what nongoods services might be offered in a particular retail store and know how to manage the offering of them.
☐ Understand the methods a manager might use in organizing for and handling customer complaints.
☐ Describe different types of credit arrangements.
☐ Develop basic procedures for making credit decisions.

Service is the goal of business. All businesses exist to serve customers by helping them satisfy their needs. For retail stores, service entails the provision of shopping conveniences, pleasant shopping surroundings, enlightened sales presentations, product information, and product value.

This chapter explores services offered by retail stores. It begins by describing the types of services that may be offered. It then raises questions retailers must face in dealing with services: Should services be offered? If so, which ones? Under which conditions should they be offered? The chapter next examines the problem of implementing services. Finally it discusses two kinds of retail services: complaint and adjustment services and credit services.

Types of Services

The many services offered by retail stores may be classified in three categories:

Rental goods. Customers rent goods such as lawn mowers, dishes, hospital beds, cement mixers, and horse trailers from some retail firms. Hardware stores, service stations, general rental agencies, and automobile and trailer rental agencies are only some of the businesses that provide rental goods. Renting goods is one type of service.

Owned goods. Repair services are most closely associated with this type of service. Firms that repair TV sets, dishwashers, lawn mowers, and so on provide services for goods owned by customers.

Nongoods services. These are services that retailers provide for customers who buy goods in their stores. Providing these services is not the main function of a store, which is the selling of goods, but the services may be necessary to fulfill that function. Such services include delivery, credit, baby-sitting, wrapping, check

cashing, and so on. Almost all retailers provide one or more of these services.

This chapter addresses itself only to nongoods services. Services involving rental goods and owned goods are marketed in a manner similar to the marketing of products, and consequently, the aspects of merchandising discussed in previous chapters can be applied to the marketing of these types of services. Because nongoods services are significantly different, special attention is given to them.

Nongoods Services

A list of the services that retail stores offer their customers would be very long indeed. It would be of small benefit to a manager, however, to attempt to develop such a list. Most retailers cannot, and should not, attempt to provide for all possible customer needs. Retailers must decide which services they will offer.

The bases for decision

Although it is expensive to provide services, retailers must offer those services customers expect to find in stores. Some retail stores, such as supermarkets, offer few services. Discount houses offer, in place of services, low prices and the advantages of one-stop shopping. On the other hand, department stores usually offer a wide range of services. Stores dealing in, for example, quality men's wear offer many services, too. They must, for customers would avoid a quality men's wear store in which the services did not meet their expectations.

The problem for the retailer is, of course, to determine what services his customers expect him to offer. In making this decision the retailer may classify services into a hierarchy based on customer needs.

Services that provide convenience. These services are basic to the operation of any retail store. They make shopping convenient and are used by all of a store's shoppers. Such services include convenient shopping hours, attractive displays, adequate parking, effective personal selling, pleasing and effective store layout and appearance, convenient store location, and so on.

Services that facilitate sales. These services are used by some shoppers and are tied directly to the kind and the amount of merchandise purchased. Such services include credit, installation, engraving, and delivery. Frequently, sales cannot be made if these services are not offered.

Auxiliary services. These services are usually promotional in nature and are auxiliary to the successful operation of the store. They include gift certificates, lay away, gift wrapping, check cashing, special orders, mail orders, telephone orders, baby-sitting, fashion consulting, and many others.

It should be obvious that the areas in which retailers can decide whether or not to offer services are the second and third categories: services that facilitate sales and auxiliary services. Convenience services must be offered; only in the nature of the offering is there room for decision making. In general, a firm decides whether it will offer services that facilitate sales and auxiliary services on the basis of five factors: customer need, type of merchandise sold, store image, competitive climate, and cost.

Issues in implementation

Charging for services. All customers do not use all services offered by a store. Some customers need delivery service. Others do not. Credit is important to some customers, whereas others prefer to use cash. If the cost of the service is included in the price of the merchandise, those customers who do not use the service are charged for something they neither need nor want. Therefore, retailers must decide whether to implement services free of charge, to charge all customers for services, or to charge only those customers who use the services.

An argument can be made for retailers charging customers for only the services they use. This means that all customers would pay for convenience services (directly or indirectly), whereas only those customers using the other two types of services would pay for them. As a practical matter, however, this approach is unrealistic. Most customers would probably accept charges for convenience and facilitating services. However, many customers would be angry if they were charged for auxiliary services.

It seems best, then, for retailers to provide all services free, even though this increases prices. A retailer who feels that customers may be more interested in a low price than in a particular service offering, may choose to dispense with or not offer a service.

Selling the service package. One of the basic principles of good merchandising is to inform customers about store benefits over and over again. Unfortunately, nowhere is this principle more grossly violated than in the area of services. Customers should know about the efforts the store is making in their behalf.

Services are readily duplicated by one's competitors, and, in fact, it is not unusual for all stores to offer essentially the same package of services. Thus, retailers must sell their services as they do all other products in their stores.

An operating philosophy of one large retail chain is to inform customers of the salient features of its products even though the features may be obvious and the same products may be sold in other outlets. A Winchester shotgun, for example, may be displayed in a window with the sales show card reading, "Variable choke, ventilated rib, automatic disconnecting trigger, and selected American walnut stock." The same item may appear in a window at another store down the street without the benefit of selling information on a show card. However, customers who have seen the window display and the show card in the first store may purchase it at that store because they remember which retailer gave them information that, although it was obvious, was needed.

THE PROFESSIONALS

They're a new breed and a good breed. They are the seasoned veterans of snow, wind and sun—here at the Alpine Haus to help you into their world.

They talk straight and knowingly, your purchase is no joke to them. Rather it is an investment in something they themselves love—the world of skiing.

Come to them with your questions, they care enough to answer because they love skiing and helping skiers.

You will find them at the Professional Ski Shop.

THE ALPINE HAUS
628 So. College
482-2043

Figure 17.1. The selling of services.
Source: Courtesy of the Alpine Haus, Fort Collins, Colorado

Good merchandising requires that retail stores give customers information (product information *and* service information) that is important to the purchasing decision (Figure 17.1).

Unfortunately, in most stores top managers do not concern themselves with service offerings but leave this aspect of the operation to mid-managers. Top managers should plan and budget for innovations in the area of services, and they should help establish control procedures. Costly services that do not fulfill customer needs affect profits and do not contribute to business.

Customer Complaints and Adjustments

In all retail stores customer complaints are inevitable. The number of complaints can be minimized by enlightened store policies, but when there is a complaint, the customer must be satisfied.

A store's image is very important. Many dollars are spent in advertising, displays, sales training programs, and the buying of merchandise to develop the desired image for a store. This money can be wasted if the quality of service, of which the handling of complaints is one very important ingredient, is deficient. Therefore, a firm should go to great lengths to make sure that every dissatisfied customer receives gracious attention and that previously planned adjustment procedures are implemented without delay.

Types of complaints

Most customer complaints fall into one of eight categories:

1. Poor product
2. Bad installation, fit, or adjustment
3. Slow delivery
4. Wrong merchandise
5. Damaged merchandise
6. Errors in billing
7. Resentment of credit collection methods
8. Unhappy with salespeople.

Systems for handling complaints

Complaints are usually handled in one of two ways: on a centralized or decentralized basis. When complaints are handled on a centralized basis, complaints encountered by each department are dealt with a central office. These stores, then, maintain a complaint and adjustment department to which the customer may go. The advantage to handling complaints on this basis is that there is uniformity in the way complaints are handled. A centralized system also provides a store with a useful source of information—a way of finding out about customer preferences and the quality of the goods and services that are offered.

Complaints handled on a decentralized basis are handled on the sales floor by the person who originally made the sale. Most small stores use this system because the volume of complaints is not great enough to warrant a special complaint office. There are two advantages to the decentralized system. First, customers like to talk to the salesperson from whom they made the purchase. The personal contact encourages them to identify with the store on an intimate basis. Second, when the

complaint is handled on the sales floor, it is easier for the customer to exchange merchandise. The centralized system encourages cash refunds, a policy not altogether in the best interests of the customer or the store.

There are, however, disadvantages to the decentralized system. Complaints handled on the sales floor may be dealt with in very different ways, because different employees are involved in each complaint. Furthermore, it is difficult to use complaints as a source of information because the salesperson who handled the merchandise and made the sale also deals with the complaint; if his or her performance is at issue, management will probably not learn this.

Methods of handling complaints

Fundamental to the handling of any complaint is the possession of the right attitude on the part of the store. All customers have a right, and even an obligation, to tell the store about anything that dissatisfies them. Retailers should graciously accept this philosophy and realize that in the long run it will enhance their reputation and their profits. Customers know when a retailer resents making adjustments, and such an attitude necessarily harms the reputation of the store.

When handling complaints, retailers should observe several rules:[1]

Do:

1. Let customers express their complaint before saying anything at all.
2. Suggest early that you will try to correct the situation.
3. Show that you recognize the customer's rights and opinions.
4. Be fair.
5. Handle the complaint in a cooperative spirit.
6. Handle all adjustments promptly.

---

[1] Gerald D. Grosner, *Turning Complaints Into Profits*, Small Marketing Aids, Small Business Administration, Annual #1, U.S. Department of Commerce, Washington, D.C., pp. 57–63.

Don't:

1. Make disparaging remarks about customers or ridicule them.
2. Blame customers or argue with them.
3. Try to satisfy the customer by using halfway measures.

Granting cash refunds. Some retail managers believe the best way to make an adjustment is to encourage the customer to exchange the merchandise or accept a slip that is valid for three to six months from the purchase date. There are several reasons why merchants prefer these alternatives to cash refunds.

First, cash refunds lose customers for the store. A cash refund may end all contact between the store and the customer, and the customer may never learn how effective the store can be in meeting her needs. Second, cash refunds can encourage shoplifting because shoplifters attempt to exchange stolen merchandise for cash. Third, giving a cash refund to a customer who is exchanging a gift may be contrary to the wishes of the donor. The donor who had wanted to give cash would have done so in the first place. Fourth, merchandise that is returned and is soiled or out of its original package may be difficult to resell at the regular retail price. Fifth, asking the customer to accept an exchange instead of a cash refund has the advantage of keeping the profit made on the original purchase.

On the other hand, some retail managers argue that is is best to give cash refunds on all adjustments. They believe that customers are satisfied if they are immediately given their money, without arguments or red tape. Furthermore, giving the customer a cash refund relieves store personnel for productive activities. Some stores, such as discount houses, feel compelled to give cash refunds to prove to their customers that they want to offer low prices without reducing important services.

Handling unreasonable customers. Stores do get their share of unreasonable customers. Fortunately, these customers represent a very small segment of their total clientele. Unreasonable customers should be handled no differently than are other customers with complaints. The store should try to produce a satisfied customer. However, some customers will remain dissatisfied despite any amount of enlightened handling. They may be chronic complainers or may be trying to see how much the store will tolerate.

Retailers must decide whether attempts to please unreasonable customers are worth the effort involved. Retailers can do without customers who are extremely nasty and may want to discourage them from shopping in their stores. Even chronic complainers may not be worth the trouble and effort they create. One store operator reportedly handled unreasonable customers by instructing all salesmen to be tactful but to be out of the merchandise the customers ask for. Employees are told not to sell to such customers if they can avoid it. Customers can, then, complain only that they can never find what they want in the store—not that they have been mistreated.

Credit

Today customers rely on charge accounts, installment buying, and credit cards. "Buy now—pay later" is an accepted form of consumer behavior. The offering of credit has posed some problems for retailers, however. They must decide (1) whether to offer credit, (2) who may receive credit, (3) what credit limit to give each customer, and (4) how to follow up on bad debts.

Deciding whether to offer credit

Whether or not a firm decides to offer credit will depend on several considerations: customer expectations, credit privileges offered by the competition, the cost of credit services measured against expected returns, and, for firms wishing to carry their own accounts, the amount of capital in the business. These considerations should be examined in the light of the obvious advantages of offering credit: increased sales volume, increased sales of expensive merchandise, and leveling the daily sales volume throughout the month. All these variables considered singly and in combination with another form the basis for the retailer's decision.

Types of retail credit

If retailers decide to offer credit, they must choose among different types. What they choose depends on the size of their store, their customers, and the kind of merchandise they offer.

The thirty-day open account. Customers who have thirty-day open accounts may charge merchandise in almost any amount. Only for very expensive items will the customer's charge request be reviewed by a credit authority. In exchange for the privilege of charging almost unlimited amounts, the customer is asked to pay the account in full within thirty days after the billing date. When payment is not made, a slight penalty is levied. However, stores do expect payment to be made within the time limit, and customers should do so if they want to continue to enjoy open account privileges.

Revolving credit. Another type of charge account is the revolving credit account. In revolving credit accounts the unpaid balance is divided into equal monthly repayments based on the highest credit balance. Unlike the open account in which there is no interest charge, the revolving credit account usually involves a percentage charge levied against the unpaid balance. Most stores presently use a one and a half percent per month interest charge. In revolving credit systems there is a credit limit beyond which the customer cannot charge. The credit limit is based on the store's judgment of the customer's ability and willingness to pay. Today, most department and specialty stores use some form of revolving credit.

Deferred payments. Deferred payment plans

are designed to accommodate customers who buy big ticket items. When purchases are made, an agreement is entered into between the retailer and the customer. According to the agreement, the customer makes equal monthly payments for the merchandise purchased. In return for this privilege, the customer pays a service or carrying charge. The credit privilege is applicable only to the particular purchase. Separate agreements must be made for additional purchases.

A special form of a deferred payment contract is the installment contract. Although the installment contract can take several forms, it usually contains these provisions: (1) title to the merchandise remains in the hands of the seller until all the provisions of the contract have been met, and (2) payments are set up on a monthly basis so that the remaining payments always amount to less than the depreciated value of the merchandise. The installment contract gives some security to retailers if customers default on the contract, because it enables merchants to repossess their merchandise.

Bank credit plans. One type of credit arrangement that is becoming increasingly popular with consumers is offered by financial institutions. The BankAmericard and Master Charge credit programs are two examples. In these programs customers maintain a credit account with a local bank affiliated with the BankAmericard or Master Charge program. Customers are permitted to charge merchandise at the establishment of any participating merchant. Purchases are subsequently billed through the local bank. Such a program offers some advantages to retailers. First, they receive cash for the purchase as soon as the charge slip is deposited with the local bank. Second, retailers do not have to maintain their own credit departments, which may cost them as much as 6 percent of sales. Third, retailers are not responsible for collecting unpaid bills, and they assume no liability for them.

The programs offered by financial institutions cost retailers 2 percent to 6 percent of sales, depending on the type of merchandise sold. Grocery stores may pay 2 percent, whereas specialty stores pay approximately 5 percent. The charge is levied against a retailer by deducting the appropriate amount from the charge ticket, and the rest of the money is deposited in the store's bank account.

Granting credit

When offering credit privileges, management must decide which customers will be granted credit. In bank plans, such as Bank-Americard, this decision is the financial institution's and is of small concern to retailers. However, retailers who offer their own credit arrangements must make wise decisions about granting credit.

No retailer would think of offering credit without first investigating the applicant. He must know who the applicant is, where he lives, whether he can pay promptly, whether he will pay promptly, and whether he can be made to pay, if necessary. To obtain this information retailers ask the customer to fill out a formal application blank. This application blank asks for information on income, assets, monthly expenditures, and other charge accounts.

After the application has been filled out, retailers usually check the applicant with retail credit bureaus. Retail credit bureaus have information on most residents in a trading area. The information they give a retail store includes data on open balances of accounts with other firms, the manner in which these accounts are paid (agreed, slow, or very slow), and any evidence of unfavorable credit behavior. To use the services of a retail credit bureau the store makes a monthly payment and additional payments for each file sent them. Both large and small retailers depend greatly on this service.

Credit limits

When a store grants credit to an applicant, it must decide what credit limit the applicant will have. It must also decide the terms of payment (the interest charge, if any) and the payment due date. It is important that the store make the terms clear to the customer and obtain his agreement that he will pay according to them. There is no established rule for determining credit limits, but many retailers try to establish a limit which, when added to the customer's other debts, does not exceed twenty-five percent of his gross income.

Slow payment

No matter how careful a store is in selecting its credit customers, each encounters a number of slow payers. Some people are slow to pay because their financial condition has suddenly changed. Others mismanage their finances, and still others simply refuse to pay. Stores usually try to make arrangements for customers who genuinely want to retain a good credit rating by suggesting ways of liquidating the amounts owed. When customers are totally unable to pay, stores usually write off the account as a bad debt loss. Most stores resort to stringent collection methods for customers who are unwilling to pay. They use collection agencies and lawyers to collect these debts.

To avoid slow payment in general, stores should use a systematic method of collecting amounts owed. First, bills should be sent out promptly. If the customer does not make payment within the time agreed upon, immediate steps should be taken to remind him or her that payment is due. If payment is not received after the second notice, most merchants will follow up by requesting a reason for the lateness. If the customer does not respond after the third notice, the store often resorts to credit collection agencies. In any case, definite time intervals should be established for sending out the various notices, and the length of time between notices should not be great. A basic principle of finance is that as debts become older the likelihood of their collection becomes slimmer.

Summary

Retailers are judged not only on the type and quality of the merchandise they handle but also on the type and quality of their services. Some services are offered without direct charge (attractive displays, adequate parking, and convenient shopping hours), whereas customers may be charged for others (credit, delivery, and installation). Customers often pay for some services they may not use (check cashing, lay away, and baby-sitting). The manager's responsibility is to furnish the services customers expect. Two types of services that may cause permanent customer dissatisfaction, if handled improperly, are customer complaint and adjustment services, and credit services.

Questions and Problems

1. Evaluate this statement: You pay for retail services whether you use them or not.

2. Suggest several methods of making a service pay for itself.

3. To use or to offer credit is un-American. It is symbolic of a decadent society. Do you agree? Why or why not?

4. How would you check the credit worthiness of a retail credit applicant? What would you look for?

5. As a customer, what changes would you like to see made in retail credit procedures? As a retailer, what changes would you like to see made?

Situations and Activities

You are the manager of a self-service liquor store. Your store has 30,000 square feet of selling area. You have been approached by a sales representative who wants you to purchase some uniforms for store personnel. These uniforms are brightly colored and distinctive. You know that at one time most stores required their sales personnel to wear uniforms. Furthermore, you realize that it is sometimes difficult to identify your sales personnel because they wander among customers to help them make selections. You also know that stylish uniforms are being worn by personnel in the airlines, in banks, and in many other industries. Decide whether you should require your personnel to wear uniforms. Take into consideration these factors and any others that might be important to the decision.

You are the manager of a bicycle shop located in a college town. You are considering offering credit to high school and college students to increase sales. Is this a good idea? Would it be a good idea if you were the manager of a clothing store? What types of credit arrangements are possibilities?

A policy used by almost all retailers is "satisfaction guaranteed." How is this term interpreted? Select several different types of retail stores and interview the store managers as to how they implement this policy.

Develop credit policies for a retail store. Do this after you have visited a local credit bureau. Provide explanations for your policies.

Develop a "market basket" of items which might be offered in a full service store and another for a limited service store. Analyze and comment on your findings.

Bibliography

Cole, Robert H. *Consumer and Commercial Credit Management.* Homewood, Ill.: Richard D. Irwin, Inc., 1968.

Customer Services Provided by Department and Speciality Stores. New York: National Retail Merchants Association, 1964.

Halverson, Gerald B. *Can You Afford Delivery Service?* Small Business Administration, Small Marketers Aids, No. 133. Washington, D.C.: U.S. Government Printing Office, 1968.

Judd, Robert C. "The Case for Redefining Services." *Journal of Marketing,* January, 1964, p. 58.

The National Cash Register Company. *Credits and Collections: A Chapter of Better Retailing.* Dayton, Ohio, 1960.

Phelps, Clyde W. *Retail Credit Fundamentals.* 4th ed. International Consumer Credit Association, 1963.

Rathmul, John M. "What is Meant by Services?" *Journal of Marketing.* Vol. 30, October, 1966, pp. 32—36.

Regan, William J. "The Service Revolution." *Journal of Marketing,* Vol. 27, No. 3, July, 1963, pp. 57—58.

Reiff, Wallace W. "Capital Allocation in Credit Decision Making." *Credit and Financial Management,* September, 1967, pp. 20—23.

Welsbans, Merle T. "Using Credit for Profit Making." *Harvard Business Review,* January-February, 1967, pp. 141—156.

seven

THE ENVIRONMENT OF RETAILING: TODAY AND TOMORROW

18

Retailing Under the Law

contents

behavioral objectives

The legal environment touches every aspect of store operations. Laws cover such areas as the regulation of competition, employee relations, sales contracts, customer relations, and products.

Upon completing this chapter, you will be able to do the following:

☐ Explain how antitrust laws affect retailers.

☐ Describe the provisions of the Robinson-Patman Act and explain how they affect retailers.

☐ Describe the provisions of state unfair trade practices acts.

☐ Identify the provisions of the Fair Labor Standards Act.

☐ Describe what retailers should know about a sales contract.

☐ Describe the legal aspects of borrowing and lending of money.

☐ Understand customer liability and product liability, and know how retailers are affected by them.

☐ Summarize the provisions of the Fair Packaging and Labeling Act.

In retailing almost every aspect of day-to-day operations is affected by government regulations. In chapter one we said that the American economic system is characterized by consumer and producer sovereignty—that suppliers of capital and land can use these resources as they wish, that workers can work where they please, and that consumers are free to spend their income where, when, and how they desire. In other words, we said that the economic system of this country is based on a free marketplace and the ownership of private property. And, to a large extent, this is true.

However, in the nineteenth and twentieth centuries Americans found that when there was absolute freedom of action in the marketplace, the economic system failed to function properly. Unrestrained economic activity led to monopolies, which restricted competition and fixed prices. The Constitution gives the federal government power "to regulate interstate commerce . . . among the several states" and "to promote the general welfare"; so the United States government began to regulate the economic system for the protection of consumers. Much of the government's protective regulation was expressed in laws which were designed to encourage and maintain competition and to prevent deceptive, fraudulent, and harmful practices.

Because business activities are governed and restricted by laws, retailers must have some legal knowledge. In this chapter we will try to provide such knowledge by exploring the five areas of retailing most affected by laws: (1) competition, (2) employee relations, (3) sales, purchases, and deliveries, (4) customer relations, and (5) products. We shall also propose guidelines retailers can use to determine whether or not planned activities are legal. Retailers should realize, however, that it is wise to consult an attorney about specific cases.

Competition

By regulating competition, government tries to ensure that no one group gains too much economic power and that consumers have a wide variety of choice. The regulations used by government fall into three categories: (1) antitrust laws, (2) unfair trade practices laws, and (3) price competition laws.

Antitrust laws

In the last half of the nineteenth century firms in industries such as steel, oil, and railroads became so large and economically powerful that they formed combinations and monopolies to reduce competition and otherwise restrain trade.

The Sherman Antitrust Act. The first important legislation designed to combat monopolies was the Sherman Antitrust Act, passed in 1890. Its key provisions are:

Section 1. Every contract, combination, or conspiracy in restraint of trade is illegal.

Section 2. Monopoly and attempts to monopolize are illegal.

Conviction of violation of the Sherman Act is punishable by a fine not exceeding $50,000 and/or by imprisonment not exceeding one year.

Because the provisions of the Sherman Antitrust Act were too vague to be effective, Congress passed the Clayton Act in 1914.

The Clayton Act. The Clayton Act made illegal four types of practices, the effect of which might be to substantially lessen competition or tend to create a monopoly. Its key provisions are found in Sections 2, 3, 7, and 8.

Section 2. It is unlawful to discriminate in price among different purchasers when the effect may be to substantially lessen competition or to tend to create a monopoly. (Section 2 was amended in 1936 by the Robinson-Patman Act.)

Section 3. Tying agreements and exclusive dealings are unlawful when the effect is to substantially reduce competition or to tend to create a monopoly. (In other words, a retailer's supplier who has a product that is in great demand cannot force the retailer to purchase a less desirable product in order to obtain the one in demand if the effect is to lessen competition. Neither can the supplier sell a product on the condition that the retailer not use or not deal in the products of the supplier's competitors.)

Section 7. This section, as amended by the Celler-Kefauver Act in 1950, prohibits the acquisition of the stocks or assets of other corporations (mergers) in any line of commerce in any section of the country if the effect is to substantially reduce competition or to tend to create a monopoly.

Section 8. A person is prohibited from being a member of the board of directors of two or more corporations when the effect would be to substantially lessen competition or to tend to create a monopoly.

The effect of the antitrust laws on retailers. As you can see, the antitrust laws were designed to prevent businesses from engaging in activities that could prove injurious to the public or to their competitors. Furthermore, they protect businesses from the harmful activities of other businesses, suppliers, and manufacturers.

And, retailers do at times run aground of the antitrust laws. In one recent case three major New York specialty stores allegedly conspired to fix prices in women's clothing by using "uniform mark-up lists" from which retail prices were determined. The stores also established clearance dates to reduce the uniform prices and get manufacturers to use the uniform retail prices as "manufacturer's suggested" retail prices. The three stores were fined the maximum $50,000 on no contest pleas. The vice president and merchandise manager of one of the stores was fined $15,000 and sentenced to one day unsupervised probation. Another executive was fined $25,000 for the same charges.

Another recent decision in the area of antitrust involved that of Associated Dry Goods. ADG was ordered to divest Ayr-Way, a division of L. S. Ayres that ADG had purchased.

The FTC felt that the deal eliminated competition between ADG and Ayres in certain parts of the country.

The antitrust laws and associated court rulings have established the following legal guidelines:

1. Retailers cannot put pressure on manufacturers to prevent them from selling products to competitive retailers.
2. Retailers cannot acquire other retail firms if the intent is to substantially lessen competition or to tend to create a monopoly.
3. Retailers cannot conspire to fix the prices of goods they sell. In other words, retailers cannot agree to eliminate price competition among themselves.
4. Retailers cannot undersell other retailers to gain control of a market. This prevents a large chain, for example, from lowering prices to drive smaller competitors in one area out of business while the chain maintains standard prices in other areas.

Another area in which retailers have been accused of being deceptive in their promotion is the misuse of the manufacturer's "cents-off-the-package" deal. The manufacturer sells the product to the retailer at a discount, expecting the discount to be passed on to the customer. The "cents-off" is printed on the product package stating the discount price, for instance, "Price Reflects 25¢ Off the Regular Price." It is suspected tht some retailers do not lower the selling price, keeping the discount for themselves. Therefore, the "cents-off-package" promotion is considered deceptive. The FTC is investigating these practices.

In 1971 the FTC initiated a program for substantiation of advertising claims. An advertiser may be required to submit data to support claims of product safety, performance, quality, or comparative prices. The program is intended to provide information that will allow consumers to make more rational decisions and to discourage advertisers from making unsupported claims.

Also in 1971, the FTC introduced the *corrective advertisement* as a part of a proposed complaint. The corrective advertisement is designed to overcome the effects that misleading advertising may have had on the consumer. If a firm is found to have run deliberately misleading ads, the firm is required to devote a percentage of advertising media budget to running FTC-approved advertisements for a certain period of time. As an example, one retailer was required to run newspaper advertisements with the following statement: "Contrary to my previous ads, neither the Food and Drug Administration nor the Federal Trade Commission nor anyone else has recommended Super B Vitamins. Super B Vitamins are sold on a money-back guarantee, so if you are not fully satisfied return them to me at _____ for a refund."

Unfair trade practices

In 1914 Congress passed, in addition to the Clayton Act, a bill which created the Federal Trade Commission as an independent administrative agency. The Federal Trade Commission, or the FTC, was given jurisdiction over cases arising under Sections 2, 3, 7, and 8 of the Clayton Act. In addition, Section 5, which was passed in 1938 as the Wheeler-Lea Act, and added to the Federal Trade Commission Act, makes "unfair methods of competition in commerce and unfair or deceptive acts or practices in commerce unlawful."

In fulfilling its responsibility to determine what methods, acts, or practices are deceptive or unfair, the FTC has, in recent year, prosecuted many retailers and manufacturers for deceptive advertising. In particular, it has been concerned with deceptive advertising involving food and drugs. Furthermore, retailers have, in increasing numbers, been ordered to cease and desist from technically mispresenting products in advertising and from using list prices to advertise low prices when the advertised merchandise is commonly available at prices below list.

There is pressure on retail stores that advertise specials but don't have sufficient inventory to reasonably cover it. This thin stocking of advertised merchandise falls under generally deceptive practices of the FTC Act. Recently several states have passed bills requiring retailers to give "rain checks" for sold out advertised specials. A "rain check" guarantees the advertised product at the advertised price when the stock is replenished.

The FTC has also attacked problems in areas such as debt collection practices and deceptive packaging, has placed special emphasis on the proper labeling of furs and textiles and has rigorously enforced the Wool Products Labeling Act (1951); the Flammable Fabrics Act (1953); and the Textile Fiber Products Identification Act (1958). The FTC is also responsible for enforcing the price competition laws that are discussed in the next section.

State unfair trade practices laws. Forty-four states have enacted *unfair trade practice laws* more or less like the Federal Trade Commission Act to prevent deceptive and unfair trade practices. The states not having such laws are Alabama, Georgia, Mississippi, Nebraska, Tennessee, and West Virginia. Consumer-complaint clearing houses to facilitate the taking of action under existing laws, and possibly to recommend new legislation have been established in Alabama, Georgia, and Tennessee. The forty-four state laws contain authorization for the enforcement official to conduct investigations and to issue cease-and-desist orders or to obtain court injunctions to halt the use of deceptive or unfair trade practices.

About half of the states also have some form of unfair trade practices act, which is intended to preserve competition by eliminating price-cutting. These acts prohibit middlemen from selling below cost if the effect would be to injure or destroy competition. In most states cost is defined as the actual cost of goods, plus freight, cartage, and a markup to cover the cost of doing business. The specified minimum markup for wholesalers is usually 2 percent and for retailers is usually from 4 to 12 percent. In some states there is no specified minimum markup, and in some the laws apply only to specified products and commodities. Most laws provide exceptions for clearance and closeout sales, sales for business liquidation, and sales of seasonal, damaged, perishable, or deteriorated goods. Regardless of the specific provisions, states have found the laws difficult to enforce.

Price competition laws

Today, the regulation of price competition affects retailers primarily through the Robinson-Patman Act. In the past, retailers also had to be concerned with "fair trade" or *resale price maintenance laws.* As we shall see the "fair trade" laws have been repealed.

The Robinson-Patman Act. In 1936 the Robinson-Patman Act amended Section 2 of the Clayton Act. The amendment ensured equality of treatment to all buyers from a seller when the result of unequal treatment might lead to a lessening of competition or tend to create a monopoly. Passed during the depression, when people considered bigness itself to be harmful, the amendment sought to curb practices of large-scale retailers. Its purpose was to eliminate price discrimination.

The Robinson-Patman Act prohibits price discrimination in interstate commerce among different purchasers of products of like grade and quality when the effect is to lessen or prevent competition or to tend to create a monopoly. In other words, retailers who are competitors are entitled to pay the same price when they buy the same merchandise in the same quantity from the same supplier. The act also contains the following provisions:

1. Price differences are permissible for "differentials which make only due allowance for differences in the cost of manufacture, sale, or delivery resulting from differing methods of quantities in which such commodities are to such purchasers sold or delivered." (Quantity discounts, for example, are permitted if it can be shown that differences in cost are based on different quantities sold. An exception is also made for seasonal obsolescence and physical deterioration.)

2. Price differences are permitted if the intent of the seller is to meet competition in good faith, that is, "to meet an equally low price of a competitor."

3. Buyers are as guilty as sellers if they knowingly induce or receive an unlawful price discrimination.

4. Promotional allowances must be given to all competing buyers on proportionally equal terms. (In other words, a supplier cannot give to only one buyer promotional services, facilities, or payments because this would, in effect, constitute a price reduction.)

5. It is unlawful for a seller to pay, or a buyer to receive, brokerage payments except for services rendered. Retailers cannot receive brokerage fees nor can any company owned or controlled by the retailer.

To insure compliance with the Robinson-Patman Act retailers should observe the following guidelines: (1) make no promises to abide by a vendor's pricing policy; (2) hold no group meetings with other retailers or a vendor at which pricing policies are discussed; (3) have no discussion with the vendor concerning other retailer's resell prices; (4) no participation in vendor or retailer price suggestions or policies.

The death of fair trade. Until 1976, some states had resale price maintenance laws, often called fair trade laws, which permitted retail price fixing. States that had these laws permitted manufacturers to set an exact price at which a retailer must sell the product, or they permitted manufacturers to set the minimum price at which retailers could sell the product.

An agreement between a manufacturer and a retailer to maintain price at or above a minimum level would be a restraint of trade, and would, therefore, be illegal under the Sherman Act. However, in 1937, Section 1 of the Sherman Act was amended by the Miller-Tydings Act which made a price agreement between a manufacturer and a retailer legal if the state had a law that permits it.

The fair trade laws of many states contained a nonsigners provision. If one retailer in a state signed a contract with a manufacturer in which he agreed to sell a particular brand of product at a minimum price, all other retailers that sold the brand in that state were bound to the contract even though they had not signed it.

In 1951 the United States Supreme Court ruled that the nonsigners provision was illegal. In 1952 Congress again amended Section 1 of the Sherman Act. This amendment, called the McGuire-Keogh Fair Trade Enabling Act, made the nonsigners provision legal.

Proponents of fair trade laws believed that such laws are necessary to protect small retailers from chain retailers. In addition, they thought that manufacturers of a product should be able to protect both the reputation of their brand name and their method of distribution by preventing one retailer from using cutthroat competition and loss leaders to discourage other retailers from selling the product. Opponents of fair trade laws argued that they discourage price competition. Consumers who are willing to sacrifice services are not able to obtain a price reduction nor are retailers who deal in large volumes or who have especially efficient operations able to offer reduced prices.

In 1975, Congress agreeing with the opponents of fair trade passed a law effective in 1976 repealing the Miller-Tydings Act and the McGuire-Keogh Fair Trade Enabling Act. A significant aspect of supplier-retailer relationships had come to an end.

Employer—Employee Relations

There are many state, municipal, and federal statutes that affect employee relations. These statutes are usually concerned with job discrimination; labor-management relations; and wages, hours, and working conditions.

Job discrimination

The federal government, most state governments, and many city governments, have passed legislation designed to prevent discrimination in the selection, discharge, promotion, and pay of employees. Discrimination because of race, color, creed, sex, national origin, and, sometimes, age is expressly forbidden. The most well-known of these laws is the Civil Rights Act of 1964, which declared it illegal for an employer

> "to discriminate in matters of compensation against any person otherwise qualified because of race, creed, color, national origin or ancestry."

As a result, equal employment opportunity became a civil right. Following the passage of this federal legislation, states adopted their own versions of the Civil Rights Act and thus created a massive amount of confusing, often contradictory legislation.

Since 1972, all employers, employment agencies, and labor organizations who have 15 or more (previously 25) employees are required to comply.

The Civil Rights Act has required the retailer to become much more responsible in hiring, promoting and firing employees. There are seven areas employers must watch to make sure that they are complying with the intent of the law. These areas are: recruitment sources, application forms, interviewing, testing, hiring, training, and promotion.

In order to comply with the legislation, retailers must be consistent in the application and enforcement of personnel policies and make sure the personnel policies and actions are based upon reasonable and valid points which can be supported in economic terms. Retailers should also be sure to keep records to support policies and reasons for disciplinary actions against personnel. The best policy is to keep up with sensitive areas of discrimination and seek special legal assistance in this area, since it is nearly impossible to keep up on all aspects of the Civil Rights Act.

Labor-management relations

The National Labor Relations Act, or the Wagner Act, of 1935 is applicable to all retail concerns that have a yearly gross volume of business of $500,000 or more. The act contains the following provisions:

1. Employees shall have the right to organize and bargain collectively through representatives of their own choosing, and shall be free from the interference, restraint, or coercion of employers of labor, or their agents, in the designation of such representatives or in self-organization or in other concerted activities for the purpose of collective bargaining or other mutual aid or protection.

2. No employee and no one seeking employment shall be required as a condition of employment to join any company union or to refrain from joining, organizing, or assisting a labor organization of his own choosing . . .

In other words, employers cannot interfere with the efforts of employees to form, join, or assist labor organizations. Neither can they discriminate against employees because of such actions. Furthermore, they must bargain collectively with a duly designated representative of their employees.

Wages and hours

The Fair Labor Standards Act of 1938 deals with minimum wages, equal pay, maximum hours, overtime pay provisions, record keeping and child labor. When the legislation was first enacted, all local retailers were exempt. In 1966, an amendment was added to the act which increased the number of retail establishments under its jurisdiction by reducing the number of exemptions from the legislation and by lowering the necessary sales volume to bring the company under the provisions of this legislation.

Some employees are exempt from minimum wage and overtime provisions. Exemptions include the following:

1. Executive, administrative, and professional employees, and outside salesmen, as defined in regulations of the Secretary of Labor.

2. Employees of retail or service establishments that are primarily engaged in selling automobiles, trucks, or farm implements and employees of any of the following retail or service establishments that make most of their sales within a state:

   a. Hotels, motels, restaurants, motion picture theaters, seasonal amusement and recreational establishments, hospitals and nursing homes, schools for handicapped or gifted children
   b. Establishments that have less than $250,000 in annual sales exclusive of specified taxes
   c. Establishments that have less than $1 million in gross annual sales exclusive of specified taxes or procure less than $250,000 annually in goods for resale that move or have moved across state lines.

3. Employees of retail or service establishments who are employed primarily in connection with particular foods or beverages and employees of particular laundries and drycleaning establishments.

Employees of gasoline service stations and some employees who work for large commissions in retail service establishments are exempt only from the overtime requirements.

Under the FLSA the minimum wage was first established in 1938 at 25¢ per hour, but by 1976, the minimum wage had increased to $2.30. Retailers feel the impact of these increases quite strongly because they hire most new employees into sales clerk positions at whatever the minimum rate is at that time.

The FLSA established a 45 hour work week in the 30's and has now been reduced to a 40 hour week. Employers are required to pay overtime benefits to employees who work over this standard. Today most people take this for granted; however, it was not always a guaranteed right.

The minimum age for most employment was established at 16 years and at 18 years for hazardous occupations. Minors 14 and 15 may be employed outside of school hours in a variety of non-manufacturing and non-mining occupations, but not after 7 p.m. or before 7 a.m.

The equal pay provision requires retailers to pay employees equal wages for doing work of equal skill, effort, and responsibility. Such things as experience, training, education, and ability are acceptable reasons for pay differentials. If an employer is found guilty of not complying with this provision, the employer may be required to repay back wages lost because of the discriminatory pay differences. By the 1970's, the Department of Labor had found 55,000 cases of such non-compliance, and required over 19 million dollars worth of repayments. Nearly all of these payments were to women. Every employer must maintain accurate records of earnings, hours and other data for a period of three years.

Willful violations of the Fair Labor Standards Act can be prosecuted and the violator fined up to $10,000. A second conviction can result in imprisonment.

Workman's compensation and unemployment benefits

Statutes, common law, and case law reflect society's requirement that employers provide safe places for employees to work in and safe equipment for them to use. States have also enacted workman's compensation laws to provide medical expenses for employees who are accidentally injured at work or who suffer from occupational diseases. Compensation laws also make provision for payments to be made to the family of workers who die as a result of their work.

The Social Security Act of 1935 provides a national unemployment insurance plan. Usually an employer of four or more persons is taxed 3.1 percent of the first $3,000 of an employee's wages. The tax is placed in the employer's fund, and former employees, if they qualify, can receive unemployment benefits when they are out of work. To qualify, an employee must usually either be fired or laid off the job. The amounts of the benefits and the length of time they can be drawn vary among states.

Sales, Purchases, and Deliveries

Retailers make hundreds and even thousands of commercial transactions in their dealings with suppliers and manufacturers. Almost every aspect of these transactions takes place in the legal framework provided by the Uniform Commercial Code. This code is now in effect in all states but one, although some sections have been altered by the states to account for local economic and financial conditions.

The Uniform Commercial Code represents an attempt to simplify, clarify, and modernize the laws governing commercial practices and to make them uniform among the states. Because of the code's complexity and the extent of its coverage, a detailed discussion of it is beyond the scope of this text. We have space to discuss only the basic provisions and to summarize the areas covered. Retailers should obtain a copy of the code as enacted in their state.

Provisions of sales contracts

The code restricts "sales" to transactions involving the sale of goods, that is, tangible objects. A sale involves the transferring of the title to goods from a seller to a buyer for a price. Sales contracts include both present sales and contracts to sell goods at a future time. It is the seller's obligation to transfer and deliver and the buyer's obligation to accept and pay for goods according to the terms of the contract. However, if the merchandise or the terms of delivery fail to conform to the contract, the buyer has the right to reject the shipment.

In a sales contract both the buyer and the seller may specify mutually agreeable terms with respect to (1) price, (2) quantity, (3) delivery terms, (4) time for performance, (5) time for payment, (6) buyer inspection, and (7) seller protection. Although a contract should specify all of the terms of an agreement, the code provides rules for interpreting all unspecified terms. For example, the code states that if delivery terms are not specified, the place for delivery is the seller's place of business. Most states require that a contract for sale of personal property of more than $500 be in writing.

Sales contracts involving minors

A contract between a minor (in most states, a person under twenty-one years of age) and a retailer is valid, but minors may, if they desire, disaffirm contracts before they reach the age of twenty-one and for a reasonable time thereafter. Minors need only return the merchandise, if they have it, to void the contract. Minors, however, cannot disaffirm contracts involving necessities such as food, clothing, and shelter.

Advertisements and sales contracts

In general, the courts have ruled that retailer's advertisements are only invitations to customers—that is, that they are not offers of contracts. This means that retailers cannot be held liable if they do not meet the terms in advertisements that contain mistakes in prices or descriptions. It also means that retailers cannot be expected to furnish advertised items if they have run out of stock. Recent FTC actions, however, indicate that retailers may be responsible for having a large enough stock of advertised goods on hand to meet reasonably anticipated demand.

Transfer of title

Contracts sometimes outline the manner in which the title to goods passes from seller to buyer. Because few contracts do this, however, the code defines the rights and duties of the buyer and seller. It is important for retailers to know at what point the title to goods is transferred, because the owner of the goods is responsible for loss or damage before, after, or during transport. There are several shipping terms that are used by retailers to describe transference of title.

The most common shipping term is F.O.B. (free on board). When merchandise is shipped to a retailer F.O.B., the seller pays for freight and other charges until the goods reach the F.O.B. point. At the F.O.B. point, title passes to the retailer. There are two kinds of F.O.B. contracts: shipment contracts and destination contracts. A seller whose place of business is in Denver and who sends a shipment of goods F.O.B., Denver, Colorado, is using a shipment contract. Title to the goods passes to the retailer immediately, and he takes the risk of loss or damage. If loss or damage occurs, the buyer must take action against the carrier, not the seller. An example of a destination contract is F.O.B. Los Angeles, California, if Los Angeles is the place where the buyer is to receive the goods. In this case, the seller is responsible for providing transportation to Los Angeles at his own risk and expense.

Another widely used shipping term is C.I.F. (cost, insurance, and freight). This term indicates that the agreed upon price includes the insurance and freight costs of delivering the merchandise to the shipping point stated after the C.I.F. (for example, C.I.F., Denver). The risk of loss or damage belongs to the retailer after the seller delivers the merchandise to the carrier, sends the bill of lading and the insurance policy to the retailer, and pays the freight. If the merchandise is lost or damaged after the seller fulfills these responsibilities, the retailer must depend on the insurance company for recovery.

Included among shipping terms are "sale with right of return" and "sale on approval." A sale with right of return is completed at the time title passes to the buyer, and the buyer bears the risk of damage or loss even though he or she has the right to return the goods if they are not satisfactory. In a sale on approval a buyer receives goods on approval, title does not pass to the buyer, and the risk of loss is borne by the seller until the sale is consummated.

Customer Relations

The law affects four areas of customer relations: (1) customer injury, (2) customer property, (3) payments by check, and (4) the extension of credit. Another important area of customer relations, shoplifting, has already been discussed in Appendix A.

Customer injury

When retailers open their doors for business and advertise for customers, they invite customers to their stores. To some extent, retailers are responsible for the people thus invited. Although the law does not specifically define the limits of responsibility, in cases based on the common law of torts, of which negligence is a part, there are some guidelines.

Legally, retailers are not responsible for ensuring the safety of customers in their stores, but because customers are invited, retailers must exercise extra care to protect them against injury. When suits have been brought against stores, the courts have usually examined the facts to determine whether reasonable care has been exercised. Decisions in which retailers have been found liable for customer injury have been based on facts that demonstrate a breach of duty to the customer; in other words, the retailer has been negligent by failing to correct situations that could lead to injury. Furthermore, retailers have been found guilty only in situations in which customers have not been guilty of contributory negligence.

Customer property

Often, customers must take off garments to try on clothing. Must the retailer protect the removed garment, and is he or she liable if it is lost? Yes, if customers are being waited on by a clerk. The customer is said to have laid the garments aside at the invitation of the retailer, who is, therefore, liable. If, however, customers wait on themselves without the assistance of store personnel, the retailer is not liable for loss. The courts have held that implied invitation does not apply to personal valuables, such as purses, because customers need not lay aside such valuables to try on garments.

Payments by check

Because the receipt of payments by check can be an especially sensitive area of customer relations, retailers should be aware of their rights and responsibilities in this area. Payments by check are considered to be the same as payments in cash. As in a cash sale, title is transferred when the merchandise is delivered and paid for. Because of this, if merchandise paid for by check is lost or destroyed, even though the bank may not have paid the check, the loss is the customer's.

Checks drawn against inadequate funds are a major concern of retailers. In most states it is at least a misdemeanor for persons to issue a check and receive money or property if they know that they do not have sufficient funds on deposit (that is, if their intent is to defraud). In most states too, retailers can recover merchandise from customers who have paid with a worthless check. It is the responsibility of retailers to deposit checks within a reasonable time after they have been received—usually at least by the day after receipt.

The extension of credit

In the debtor-creditor relationship between customers and retailers, each party has a variety of rights and responsibilities. According to common law, the creditor has the right to be paid and the debtor has a duty to pay. As simple as this may sound, however, these rights and responsibilities are expressed in complex legal language.

Truth-in-lending act. The federal Truth-in-Lending Act of 1969 assists people who purchase on credit or borrow money. The law requires that individuals to whom credit is to be extended be given a disclosure statement. The disclosure statement must inform the borrower of the amount to be financed, the finance charge, the annual percentage rate, the amount of each payment, and the number of payments (see Figure 18.1).

Secured and unsecured transactions. When consumers finance their purchases, they may borrow the money from a bank or obtain financing from the seller. Sometimes financing is given simply on the credit worthiness of the

DISCLOSURE STATEMENT

Loan No._____

The finance charge applies

from_____
        DATE

The First National Bank in Fort Collins

Mason at Oak   Fort Collins, Colorado 80521

Borrowers (Names and Addresses)

(1)_____   (2)_____

_____   _____

_____   _____

STATEMENT OF CHARGES

1. AMOUNT OF LOAN............................. $_____
2. OTHER CHARGES: (ITEMIZED)

_____ _____

_____ _____

_____ _____

3. AMOUNT FINANCED (1 + 2)................... $_____
4. **FINANCE CHARGE** (ITEMIZED)

_____ $_____

_____ _____

_____ _____

Total Finance Charge $_____

5. TOTAL OF PAYMENTS (3 + 4)................... $_____
6. **ANNUAL PERCENTAGE RATE**.................... _____%

Witness:_____

INSURANCE AGREEMENT

Insurance is not required by creditor, and is not provided unless desired by borrower. Insurance may be obtained by borrower through any person of his choice. If borrower desires_____

insurance to be obtained for him by creditor, the cost will be $_____ for the term of the loan.

I desire this insurance.

_____   _____
     DATE   BORROWER'S SIGNATURE

DEFAULT CHARGE: In the event of default on any payment, a charge of twelve percent per annum may be assessed plus ten percent of the amount due for attorney's fees.

SECURITY

A security interest is taken in the following property:

☐ Check here if a separate agreement of even date is executed to secure payment of this note.

I (we) acknowledge receipt of completely filled in executed copies of this disclosure statement and any separate security agreements.

_____   _____
     DATE   BORROWER'S SIGNATURE

N-31

Figure 18.1. The Disclosure Statement insures that the borrower knows what he or she is paying for a loan.

buyer, but in most instances the seller or lender demands that the purchaser's promise to pay be backed with some security. Usually, the retailer asks for a chattel mortgage or a conditional sales contract to retain a security interest in the merchandise being sold and/or in other personal property of the buyer. Under these conditions, the buyer retains possession of the property. Figure 18.2 illustrates a conditional sales contract.

The presence or absence of security is very important. If a debtor fails to pay on an unsecured debt, the creditor can collect the debt only by suing. If a suit occurs and a judgment favorable to the creditor is rendered, the retailer can, by law, resort to some methods of collection. Garnishment of wages and attachment of assets and personal property are two methods used by creditors to collect unpaid debts. These methods are frequently not successful, however, because all states have limitations on garnishment of wages, and some kinds of property are exempt from attachment. All too often, then, judgments are valueless because debtors have few assets that can be reached.

RETAIL INSTALLMENT CONTRACT AND SECURITY AGREEMENT   CONSUMER PAPER

The undersigned Seller hereby sells and the undersigned Buyer hereby purchases the following described goods and services subject to the terms and conditions set forth below and on the reverse side hereof, and Buyer grants to Seller a security interest in said property as security for payment and performance of Buyer's obligations hereunder:

NEW OR USED	MODEL	SERIAL NO.	DESCRIPTION OF GOODS AND SERVICES (IF GOODS, GIVE MAKE OR TRADE NAME)	AMOUNT	
				$	
			TOTAL	$	

BUYER STATES THAT THE ABOVE GOODS AND SERVICES ARE PURCHASED FOR:
☐ PERSONAL, FAMILY OR HOUSEHOLD PURPOSES; ☐ BUSINESS OR COMMERCIAL PURPOSES; ☐ FARM EQUIPMENT.

CREDIT INSURANCE AUTHORIZATION
Dated _____ 19 _____

Buyer understands that Credit Insurance is voluntary and is not required by Seller. Buyer does hereby authorize Seller to arrange for that type of Credit Insurance coverage as indicated.

The cost of credit insurance will be:
Credit Life Insurance only $ _____
Credit Life & Disability $ _____

☐ I want Credit Life Insurance Only
☐ I want Credit Life & Disability
☐ I DO NOT want Credit Insurance

Buyer _____
(PERSON TO BE INSURED)

Buyer acknowledges that he has been advised as to both the cash price and the deferred payment price and realizes the deferred payment price is greater and he has elected to pay the deferred payment price.

In the event of default in the payment of any installment for more than ten days, Buyer agrees to pay a delinquency charge of 5% of such installment with a maximum of $15.00.

Buyer may pay in full at any time before maturity. The Rule of 78's method shall be used to compute the unearned finance charge for refund to Buyer. However, when the earned finance charge is less than the applicable minimum finance charge to which the holder is entitled, the difference is retained and the remainder of the unearned finance charge is refunded to Buyer. The lawful minimum finance charge when the amount financed is $75 or less is $5.00; when more than $75 but less than $500 is $7.50; or $15.00 when the amount financed is $500 or more. If the refund would be less than $1, no refund shall be made.

NOTICE TO THE BUYER: 1. DO NOT SIGN THIS CONTRACT BEFORE YOU READ IT OR IF IT CONTAINS BLANK SPACES. 2. YOU ARE ENTITLED TO AN EXACT COPY OF THE CONTRACT YOU SIGN. 3. UNDER THE LAW YOU HAVE THE RIGHT TO PAY OFF IN ADVANCE THE FULL AMOUNT DUE AND TO OBTAIN A PARTIAL REFUND OF THE FINANCE CHARGE.

BUYER ACKNOWLEDGES THAT THIS CONTRACT WAS COMPLETELY FILLED IN PRIOR TO ITS EXECUTION AND THAT HE RECEIVED A TRUE COPY THEREOF.

(1) CASH PRICE INCLUDING:

$ _____ $ _____ $ _____
DEL. & INSTALLATION   SALES TAX

(2) LESS: TOTAL DOWN PAYMENT .... $ _____

$ _____ $ _____
CASH   +   TRADE-IN

(DESCRIBE TRADE-IN)

(3) UNPAID BALANCE OF CASH PRICE .... $ _____

(4) OTHER CHARGES: _____ $ _____
INSURANCE: _____ Months
If No Premium Charge is Shown Below,
Buyer Has Not Authorized Credit Insurance.

A. CREDIT LIFE $ _____
B. CREDIT DISABILITY $ _____
OFFICIAL FEES .... $ _____

(5) AMOUNT FINANCED .... $ _____

(6) **FINANCE CHARGE** .... $ _____

ANNUAL PERCENTAGE RATE _____ %

(7) TOTAL OF PAYMENTS .... $ _____

(8) DEFERRED PAYMENT PRICE (1 + 4 + 6) .... $ _____

Buyer agrees to pay the "TOTAL OF PAYMENTS" (Item 7 Above) in successive monthly installments on the same day of each month, beginning _____
_____, 19 _____, at the office of Seller or Seller's assignee, as follows: _____ installments of $ _____
and a final installment of $ _____

PROSPECTIVE ASSIGNEE OF THIS CONTRACT IS PACIFIC FINANCE

Dated _____ 19 _____

BUYER _____	SELLER _____
BUYER _____	BY _____ TITLE _____
ADDRESS _____	ADDRESS _____

ORIGINAL

Figure 18.2. Retail Installment Contract and Security Agreement.

If a debtor fails to pay on a secured debt, no suit is required to collect the debt. Creditors may repossess the security and sell it, or they may choose to keep it in full satisfaction of the debt. If they choose to keep it, they must make a proposal to this effect in writing to the debtor. If the debtor objects, the property must be sold. The repossessed property also must be sold if 60 percent of the cash price of merchandise has been paid. After the merchandise has been sold in a reasonable manner, the debtor is entitled to any amount beyond that necessary to fulfill the obligation and reasonable collection costs.

On default, creditors can take possession of collateral if they can do so without "breaching the peace." If the debtor puts up strong resistance to the repossession process, judicial assistance is available.

Products

Retailers must understand the way in which the law affects product warranties, product liability, and packaging and labeling.

Warranties

The Uniform Commercial Code defines retailers' rights and responsibilities with respect to product warranties. It says that in the sale of goods, the warranty is an obligation of the seller with respect to the goods that have been sold. Retailers are responsible for selling merchandise that has a good title, is of proper quality, and is free from defects. With respect to the latter, a warranty covers the present condition of the goods and may cover the performance expected of them.

Implied warranties. Every sale covered by the Uniform Commercial Code carries two implied warranties. Under the warranty of merchantability, goods must be adequate for the ordinary purposes for which they are used. If a retailer knows this purpose and if the buyer is dependent on the retailer's skill and judgment to select goods suitable for that particular use,

an implied warranty of fitness for a particular purpose is created.

Warranty of title is the second implied warranty. In any sale buyers expect retailers to convey a good title to them, and they expect retailers to have the right to sell the goods. In other words, retailers imply that buyers will be able to use the goods free from the claims of any third party. Retailers should realize that a breach of warranty of title provides a basis for a customer to void a sale.

Express warranty. When retailers make statements of fact or promises about a product and buyers might reasonably rely on these facts or promises, an express warranty is created. There is a fine line between statements of facts or promises and mere sales talk about value. Often the distinction is made on the basis of whether or not the statements made during a sale are an expression of opinion or of fact. Courts have recognized the difference between "puffing" and promise. In other words, a statement like "This dress will wear like steel" is "puffing" or sales talk. On the other hand, "this dress will not wear out for two years" is a promise and may create an express warranty.

Product liability

As concern for the safety of consumers grows, an increasing burden is being placed on both manufacturers and retailers. Firms are being forced to find ways of increasing the safety of their products and of giving warnings of dangers involved in using them. Because retailers make implied and, often, express warranties to buyers, buyers are entitled to recover damages for personal injury or property damage that may result from a breach of these warranties. Retailers may be liable for injuries caused by defective products if there has been negligence, misrepresentation, or a breach of warranty.

Negligence. If reasonable care is not exercised in the manufacture and sale of products and the issuance of warning about them, a seller may be liable on the basis of negligence. If an injury is sustained by a customer who uses a product and the court rules that the retailer should have foreseen the possibility of injury, the retailer can be held liable. Even though a defect may have been caused by the manufacturer, both the retailer and the manufacturer may be held responsible.

Misrepresentation. Retailers may publicly misrepresent a product through advertising, selling, or labeling. If so, they are subject to liability for any physical damage sustained by customers who rely on the misrepresentation.

Breach of warranty. In most states suits can be brought on the basis of a breach of implied or expressed warranties. An action based on such a breach does not require proof of negligence on the part of the manufacturer or retailer; it requires only proof that the product was defective and was the proximate cause of injury. It should be pointed out again that statements and promises made in advertising may constitute an express warranty.

Packaging and labeling

Many retailers have products manufactured and/or packaged and labeled to their own specifications. The intent of the Fair Packaging and Labeling Act of 1966 is to regulate interstate and foreign commerce by preventing the use of unfair or deceptive methods of packaging or labeling of particular consumer commodities. This law is based on the premise that "Informed consumers are essential to the fair and efficient functioning of a free market economy. Packages and their labels should enable consumers to obtain accurate information as to the quantity of the contents and should facilitate value comparisons."

The following are the key provisions of the Fair Packaging and Labeling Act:

1. Commodities must be labeled with the identity of the contents and the name and the place of the manufacturer or distributor.

2. The net quantity of the contents must be prominently displayed.
3. If the package is less than four pounds or less than a gallon, the weight must be expressed in both ounces (avoirdupois or fluid) *and* in pounds with any remaining quantity in terms of ounces or decimal fractions of the pound. Liquid measures must be in the largest whole unit with the remainder in fluid ounces or decimal fractions of the quart or pint. Provisions are also made for packages whose contents are specified by length or area and for random weight packages.
4. If the label contains a statement as to the number of servings, it must also state the net weight, measure, or numerical count of each serving.
5. Other statements about quantity should appear on the label if they make qualifications about the contents of the package or if they tend to deceive people about the contents.

These provisions are mandatory. Other provisions state the degree of regulation that should be achieved through administrative discretion:

1. Establish standards for characterization of package sizes (such as "small," "medium," and "large"). These standards do not limit size or content.
2. Regulate the use of printed material on packages that indicates the package is less than other brands or contains more.
3. List the ingredients by their common name and in order of their predominance.
4. Prevent the nonfunctional-slack-fill of packages (other than what is necessary for product protection or caused by automatic packaging).

Summary

This brief overview of the legal environment shows that the actions of the retailer, manufacturer, supplier, and customer are intertwined in a complex maze of law and legal precedent. Retailers must understand what rights they have in pricing merchandise, what provisions they should make for customer relations, what rights and responsibilities they possess when making a sale, and what liabilities they may face in selling products to customers. These are considerations that confront retailers on a day-to-day basis, and retailers must be informed. However, information alone is not sufficient. Retailers should have competent attorneys.

Retailers should also familiarize themselves with areas not covered in this discussion. They must be familiar with local ordinances dealing with certificates of occupancy, fire regulations, zoning, outdoor sign permits, and the like. In addition, federal, state, and local laws regarding trademarks, patents, and copyrights regulate the taking of advantage of an established reputation or deceiving the public.

Questions and Problems

1. What major enforcement problems are associated with price competition laws? With the packaging and labeling law?

2. How do antitrust laws affect retailers?

3. If a customer is injured from a fall on an escalator in a store, what factors would the court consider in determining the store's liability?

4. Evaluate this statement: Most product warranties do not really protect the customer. Obtain copies of the warranties of several products. Are the provisions of the warranty clearly stated?

5. A prominent legislator has proposed that "Packages contain no illustration other than a photograph of container contents." Is this reasonable? Is it in the best interests of the consumer?

Situations and Activities

You are the buyer for private label kitchen appliances for a large chain discount store. Your plans call for purchasing 217,000 electric can openers for the coming year. You believe that several manufacturers will give you a substantial price concession if the order is placed now and if one manufacturer received the entire order. Current economic and market conditions support this belief. However, you are somewhat hesitant to press too hard even though you are in a favorable bargaining position. Why? What legal constraints do you face?

You are the regional manager of five department stores in a major metropolitan area. No store employees have been organized by a union. You are told that the salespeople in one of the stores approached the local manager and requested after-hours use of the community room in the store to hear a presentation by a union organizer. The store manager supposedly "blew his stack" and threatened to fire

immediately anyone that started talking union. What must you do?

Following is a series of buying/selling situations. Describe what provisions (if any) of the Robinson-Patman Act cover the situation. Might these be a violation of the law? If not, why not?

a. A supplier sells the same merchandise to two competing retailers at different prices.

b. A retailer sells identical television sets at a lower price to one consumer than he does to another consumer.

c. A wholesaler and a large chain store buy the same merchandise from the same manufacturer in identical quantities, but the wholesaler is charged a lower price.

d. Retailer 1 purchases 50 swim suits for $1,000 from a manufacturer in April. Retailer 2 buys an identical 50 swim suits from the same manufacturer in September for $400.

e. A supplier sells Retailer 1, 50 cases of canned corn for $200; Retailer 2, 100 cases for $375; Retailer 3, 200 cases for $700; and Retailer 4, 300 cases for $1,300.

f. An independent oil refinery sells oil to two buyers. Buyer 1 is a trucking company that uses the oil in their own trucks. Buyer 2 is a retail service station. The refinery charges the trucker less per quart for the same quantities.

g. Retailer 1 asks a manufacturer to have her own label installed in the manufacturer's line of ladies' dresses. The manufacturer agrees and charges Retailer 1 10% less than Retailer 2, who pays for the dresses with the manufacturer's brand name label.

Select two areas where you believe current laws do not adequately protect the consumer. State the business practice you would like to have corrected; then describe the law you would like to see passed that accomplishes your objective. What problems do you foresee if the law were enacted by your state legislature?

Visit a supermarket, clothing store, and drug store. Carefully note the information contained on labels, packages, information tags, etc. What federal laws require the types of information that you find?

Visit five retailers (of five different types of retail outlets) and ascertain which laws affect them in their day-to-day operations. How are they affected?

Bibliography

Howard, Marshall C. *Legal Aspects of Marketing.* New York: McGraw-Hill, 1964.

Lewis, R. Duffy, and Lewis, J. Norman. *What Every Retailer Should Know About the Law.* New York: Fairchild Publications, 1963.

Myers, Howard A. *Labor Law and Legislation.* Cincinnati: South-Western Publishing, 1968.

U. S. Department of Labor. *Reference Guide to the Fair Labor Standards Act.* Washington, D. C.: U. S. Government Printing Office, 1964.

U. S. Department of Labor. Wage and Hour and Public Contracts Divisions. *Handy Reference Guide to the Fair Labor Standards Act.* WHPC Publication 1122. Washington, D C.: U. S. Government Printing Office, 1964.

U. S. Statutes at Large, Vol. 78, Part l. *Civil Rights Act of 1964, Public Law 88—352.* July 2, 1964.

U. S. Statutes At Large, Vol. 80, Part l. *Fair Packaging and Labeling Act, Public Law 89—755.* November 3, 1966.

Webb, Garn H., and Bianco, Thomas C. *Uniform Commercial Code.* New York: Holt, Rinehart and Winston, 1969.

19

Retailing and Society

contents

behavioral objectives

Retailers should be aware of and concerned about what is happening outside the doors of the store. The external environment of which they are a part plays a significant role in how business will be conducted inside the store. As students of retailing, you should have knowledge of the external influences that affect retailing.

Upon completing this chapter, you will be able to do the following:
☐ Trace the history of business's role in meeting society's needs.
☐ Distinguish among a business ethic, a social ethic, and a business-social ethic.
☐ Explain the difficulties business faces in serving as society's "benevolent overseer."
☐ Describe some social problems and explain how retailing might help alleviate them.

The past three decades have witnessed a period of unprecedented prosperity in the United States. But, in the face of general economic prosperity there have been periods of social unrest. We have seen consumer boycotts, protests, periods of high unemployment, and inflation as symptoms or causes of social pressures.

Retailing cannot help being affected by societal concerns. In many ways, retailing is the first to be attacked (or defended, as the case may be) for causing many of society's ills. Whether the issue involves the problems of the ghetto, consumerism, or ecology, it is retailing with whom people have the most intimate contact, and it is retailing that must often take the brunt of arguments made against business. Unlike manufacturing, which is geographically removed from the consumer, retailing cannot fence out problems. Unlike a bank, it cannot put up guards and grilles to protect its property. If for no other reason than simple self-survival, then, retailing has a great deal at stake in society's welfare.

The Economic Role of Business

The traditional role of business has been an economic one—that of providing goods and services to the ultimate consumer. It was expected to perform this role in a way that made profits for the firm. Only in this way could the business be expected to survive and to continue to provide the goods and services that society wanted.

In performing this task, business relied on its own devices and its own conscience. However, ruthlessness often prevailed and caused some injustices. It was almost acceptable to operate on the basis of *caveat emptor*—"let the buyer beware."

At a time when goods were scarce and the nation needed capital accumulation to further economic growth, such a role may have had its place. Maybe society was forced to take the position that matters of economics were the

problems of business and, as such, should be left entirely in its domain. Maybe society believed that business should have sole responsibility for half of society's needs—the economic half—while government, the church and other social institutions, as instruments of the people, should have responsibility for the other half (see Figure 19.1).

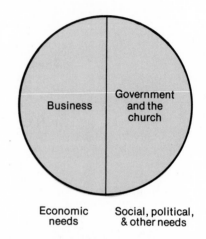

Figure 19.1. Meeting society's needs (the 1800's).

A change in attitudes

Since the early 1900's, society's expectations of business have changed. Ultimately new attitudes were formed. It was no longer sufficient for business simply to provide goods and services; it was expected to do so in an ethical manner. Furthermore, business became responsible for fulfilling social, as well as economic, needs.

Left largely on its own to develop, business promoted some injustices. The injustices created by big business (especially the so-called robber barons, among whom were Hill, Carnegie, Morgan, and Rockefeller) and even in some cases by large retail chain operations became objectionable to society.

At the turn of this century, society began to evaluate business and to take action to ensure that it would act in society's best interests. Specifically, society employed the law to curb bad business practices. In Chapter 18 we discussed some of the laws regulating business practices: the Sherman Act of 1890 and the Clayton Act of 1914, designed to regulate monopolies; the Robinson-Patman Act of 1936, designed to eliminate price discrimination; and the Federal Trade Commission Act of 1914, designed to abolish misrepresentation of goods. Legislation curtailed business's freedom to some degree, and the government assumed an active role in making sure that the economic needs of society were being met (Figure 19.2).

Beginning in the early 1950's, people once again began to object to some business practices. Some people claimed that business was not meeting its *total* obligation to society. Two indictments were associated with this statement. First, business was not performing well enough at those activities it was engaged in. In other words, society was complaining of shoddy merchandise, misleading advertising, the emphasis upon materialistic values, and the general inefficiency and ineffectiveness of business institutions. Second, business felt its responsibility was much more limited in scope than society felt it should be. Society, then, believed that business had a responsibility to help alleviate social ills. Business was given still less freedom in performing its economic role, but it now shared with government some of the responsibility for fulfilling some of society's noneconomic needs (see Figure 19.3).

The Ethics of Business

Although the indictment against business for manufacturing inferior merchandise was not new, the rigor with which it was being leveled was. The second indictment, concerning social responsibility, was foreign to business. Business suddenly had to follow a new moral ethic that was compatible with its new role.

To a large extent, the ethic traditionally held by business was based on survival. The ethic demanded that the businessman give full at-

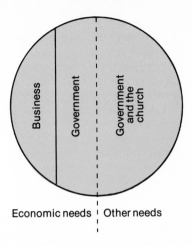

Figure 19.2. Meeting society's needs (the 1900's).

tention to the details of economic life and organization. Virtues such as integrity and honesty were not necessarily demanded of businessmen. In the *business ethic,* the goal of personal gain could tend to overshadow other values.

In a mature society a business ethic tends to be unnecessary and may even be hostile to the total fulfillment of society. An ethic that places importance on the total of society and its survival may be more compatible with society's needs than an ethic based on business's survival. Such a *social ethic* in its extreme interpretation might suggest that business, in addition

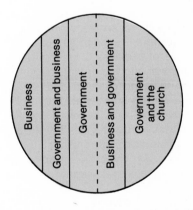

Figure 19.3. Meeting society's needs (the 1950's on).

to its role in meeting the economic needs of society, should play the role of a benevolent overseer in relation to society's other needs. A social ethic implies that business may have an obligation to any or all of the following: the poor, the young, the elderly, minority groups, consumers, the environment, schools, cities, and rural areas.

To place business in the role of benevolent overseer is to make two assumptions. First, it is assumed that business will know precisely what is demanded of it; second, it is assumed that business will have unlimited resources to use in fulfilling societal obligations. The problem with these assumptions, however, is that even if business knew what was demanded of it (and it often doesn't) there are often conflicting demands. In a single decision that management may be responsible for making, it must take into consideration the simultaneous demands of several groups—consumers, workers, stockholders, and so on. When a decision is ultimately made, there may be no "right answer." The business ethic required only that businessmen evaluate the economic gain inherent in a particular situation, but the social ethic requires businessmen to respond to many demands.

To assign to the businessman the role of total provider is both unrealistic and unfair. Business does not have the resources to assume a social godfather role. Such a role assumes that other social institutions such as churches and the government are at least partially unable to provide for society's needs.

On the other hand, to ignore entirely the social role of business is irresponsible. Even from a pragmatic standpoint, business has a stake in initiating changes and working for progress, for this is of benefit both to business and to the total social system. Business could not enjoy the future progress that society might achieve without correspondingly contributing to that progress. Therefore, business must administer its affairs so it acknowledges not only its economic role but also its social role. Of necessity, it must follow both a business and social ethic.

The question that quite naturally arises is: Are a business and a social ethic compatible? The answer to that question is: Yes, if both business and society understand the following:

> For business to best serve society it needs to be aware of its responsibilities and obligations as a business citizen, to respond to new challenges resulting from social upheaval, to work out honest solutions to legitimate problems, and to keep hands firmly on the reins of management so that business can fulfill its primary function as a viable, successful entity within a dynamic, expanding economic system. Business's major contribution to the stability of society is to remain stable and flexible, to provide markets for customers, capacity for producers, jobs for employees, and a fair return for shareholders. Business should do its part in meeting society's needs but business cannot cure social ills by assuming independently the entire burden of social revolution and the faster pace of change that accompanies it.[1]

In a nutshell, the proper role for business is to provide for society's economic well-being and, in addition, be sensitive to all of society's many problems.

Retailing's Involvement with Social Needs

In general, what we have just said about businessmen can be said about retailers, in particular. This is true if for no other reason than that retailing is a subsystem of the total business system, and therefore, that which condemns the total system condemns any part. But maybe what we have said about businessmen and retailers in society is largely irrelevant.

Ten to fifteen years ago, it might have been a new idea for businessmen to be involved in more than the running of their own particular company. But today, and certainly among enlightened businessmen, social morality per-

---

[1]Fernando S. Mostero, "The Insurance Road to Social Responsibility," *Journal of Insurance*, September-October 1971, p. 2.

meates business organizations. It is difficult to conceive how a business could be completely immune to the pressures for social involvement. Therefore, the issue seems to no longer be one of whether business should be socially involved but rather in what way it can make meaningful contributions to society.

Retailers have contributed toward the solutions of social problems in many areas. One of today's greatest unsolved problems is related to the growth of consumerism.

Consumerism

Consumerism is a term encompassing the activities of government, business, independent organizations, and concerned consumers that are designed to protect the rights of consumers.[2] These activities have run the gamut from new consumer protection laws to consumer boycotts. These consumer activities reflect society's rejection of the doctrine of *caveat emptor*—let the buyer beware.

People have become frustrated in their role as consumers because they feel that they have little control over the buying situation. At a time when they possess great consumer sophistication, they often feel abused and even insulted. They are offended, especially when they cannot rely on business to provide needed services for a product, safe products, and truthful information. To them, the free-wheeling nature of the marketplace is a constant source of confusion, irritation, and resentment.[3]

It has been suggested that several factors have enhanced the expression of consumerism. Increased leisure time, income, and education have tended to magnify and intensify the forces of consumerism as the consumer seeks products that fulfill the quest for individuality. Inflation has made it difficult to compare purchases over time. Rising prices lead consumers to expect increased quality that is not there. If unemployment is low and if poorly skilled laborers are employed product quality may decline. Demands for product improvement have led to increased product complexity, which causes increased service difficulties and introduces performance reliability problems.[4]

As technology solved many of the problems of production, and as life styles of consumers changed to meet a society characterized by abundance, business adjusted production to the needs of consumption by turning to a consumer orientation that embodied the idea that the proper way to run a business is to find out the customer's wants and needs, both felt and unfelt, and then to offer a product that fills those needs and wants better than anything else on the market.

There is no question that today business must operate in an aura of consumer consciousness because consumers are exhibiting their intolerance with the system as it now functions. Senator Warren Magnuson outlines three clear and powerful trends. First, mindless product innovation and profitability will no longer satisfy standards of business behavior. Second, business freedom will become increasingly dictated by government controls reflecting emerging concerns over the status of the environment; over consumer rights; even over social values. Third, citizen action through the courts and legislatures by increasingly well-organized and articulate public interest lobbies, and through the politics of confrontation will snowball.[5]

Yet another view of the causes of consumerism has been expressed by the National Goals Research Staff. This organization feels

[2]David A. Aaker and George S. Day, "Introduction: A Guide to Consumerism," in *Consumerism,* David A. Aaker and George S. Day, eds. New York: The Free Press, 1974, p. xvii.

[3]For a vivid account of the abuses that can and do occur in the business system despite the efforts of legislators—and the concern of millions of ethical and responsible businessmen, see Warren G. Magnuson and Jean Carper, *The Dark Side of the Market Place.* Englewood Cliffs, N.J.: Prentice-Hall, 1972.

[4]Richard S. Buskirk and James T. Rothe, "Consumerism—An Interpretation," *Journal of Marketing,* 34, 1970, pp. 61—65.

[5]Warren G. Magnuson, "Consumerism and the Emerging Goals of a New Society," in Ralph M. Gaedeke and Warren W. Etcheson, *Consumerism.* San Francisco: Canfield Press. 1972, p. 6.

that the abundant flow of new consumer goods has been viewed as a clear indication that the economy, with its strong technological base, brings vast direct benefits to the American people. Yet, in the past decade, this virtue has been questioned. Consumerism contends that the rapid introduction of new products produces confusion; that the technical complexity of new products makes it impossible to evaluate their benefits or dangers, and makes them difficult to repair; and that pressure on business firms to introduce new products and services breeds marketing practices of a dubious nature, particularly as promotion has centered on nonprice competition instead of price competition. It can be argued that the consumer just does not have the information with which to make an informed choice.[6]

Basic consumer rights

Society, it seems, is insisting that there must be a consumer bill of rights. The foundation for such a bill of rights was laid when John F. Kennedy, in his first consumer message to Congress in 1962, set forth four basic consumer rights.

1. *The right to safety*—to be protected against the marketing of goods that are hazardous to health or life. The belief in the right to safety has been the basis of many laws that protect the consumer when he cannot be expected to have sufficient knowledge to protect himself. Laws that regulate the quality of the food that we eat, the clothing that we wear, the cosmetics that we buy, all are designed to prevent danger to health and safety and many require clear warnings to be issued if the possibility of danger can occur because of misuse.

2. *The right to be informed*—to be protected against deceitful, fraudulent and misleading information whether in advertising and labeling or other such practices and to be given the facts needed to make an informed choice. This right is fundamental to the economic interests of the consumer. No one questions the fact that the consumer should not be deceived. Not only does the consumer have a right not to be deceived, but he has a right to sufficient information that will allow him to make intelligent purchases.

3. *The right to choose*—to be assured whenever possible of access to a variety of products and services at competitive prices, and, in those industries in which government regulations are substituted for competition, to be assured of satisfactory quality and services at fair prices. Much of the antitrust legislation discussed in the next section has been focused on protecting and encouraging competition. Fundamental to our economic system is the belief that significant numbers of competitors competing in a fair and open market is the critical factor in providing the consumer the right to choose.

4. *The right to be heard*—to be assured that consumer interests will receive full consideration in the formulation of government policies. The Office of Special Assistant to the President for Consumer Affairs is the central focus to insure that consumer interests are given fair consideration in the formulation of government policy and during regulatory proceedings in administrative deliberations.[7]

The preceding discussion, in essence, suggests that the basic consumer civil right is the right to get his money's worth. In theory, a competitive market system and the laws of contracts are designed to ensure that he does.[8]

---

[6]National Goals Research Staff, *"A Report Toward Balanced Growth: Quantity with Quality,"* Gaedeke and Etcheson, pp. 8—15.

[7]"Consumer Advisory Council: First Report," Executive Office of the President, United States Government Printing Office, October 1963.

[8]Philip G. Schrag, "Consumer Rights," in Aaker and Day, pp. 361—371.

Unfortunately, because of faulty quality or scant quantity of merchandise, or because of misleading advertising and high-pressure sales tactics, consumers may still not get their money's worth. Both government and business must continue to express their concern with warranties and guarantees, the handling of consumer complaints, and product performance testing, and must continue to emphasize rectifying fraudulent and deceptive advertising, packaging, pricing and credit practices.

Consumer interests have moved beyond the traditional concerns of fair quality and quantity of the product, including package size, unit pricing, and credit disclosure. Consumers are now also concerned with major social and economic issues such as pollution, welfare systems, health care, poverty, taxes, and the government system. Consumers will soon be involved in all areas of the political, economic, and social spectrums and retailers must learn how to expand their vision.

If retailers make a commitment to excellence where they are best equipped to excel—insisting on products that are fairly priced, that perform as they are supposed to, and meet the claims that are made for them; on warranties that protect the buyer as much as the seller; and on services that truly serve—then they and all business have little to fear. However, if business fails in its responsibilities, legislators will continue to pass laws to establish guidelines for business decisions. In the previous chapter we examined several such laws.

Other social problems

There are other imperfections of concern to our economic system. These concerns primarily involve (1) the lower income consumer, (2) the impersonality of society, and (3) the so-called quality of life.

The low income consumer. The low income consumer has been most vulnerable to shoddy business practices. Because low income consumers are usually poorly educated, less mobile, less value-oriented, and because they do less comparison shopping than the rest of society, they become victims of exploitation in the marketplace. It is these consumers who are most susceptible to exaggerated product claims and high pressure selling techniques.

The impersonality of society. Business has been identified as a symbol of the impersonality of society. When consumers look around them and see with whom they transact business (the corporation) and through what means business is transacted (self-service), they believe business has fostered faceless-to-faceless relationships in society. In addition, they are suspicious of the absence of close relationships, because impersonality can cover deceit.

Quality of life. Quality of life suggests that there be equality, education, and health for all individuals. Some consumer advocates, however, see America as a materialistic society devoid of the spiritual and intellectual values essential to self-fulfillment. They argue that business, more than any other institution, has emphasized consumption and values of happiness and comfort. These emphases are, they believe, materialistic, and they lead to mediocrity. Consumers are concerned that business degrades dignity and personal excellence and, thus, causes or contributes to the lack of dignity and excellence in the public environment. In particular, consumers consider the problems of air, water, and noise pollution as evidence of a deteriorating public environment, resulting in a large measure from the high priority given to material well-being. Consumers seem to be revolting against a "disposable" society.

The retailing response

There are many things that retailers can do to alleviate consumer complaints. In fact, retailers may be in the best position to meet these complaints because they serve as the purchasing agent for the consumer. This gives them a position of power that they can use in behalf of consumers.

Better goods and services. Before retailers attempt to exert power on other businesses to alleviate consumer dissatisfaction, they should first solve their own problems. Consumers have expressed dissatisfaction with retailers primarily for two reasons. First, consumers have been especially irritated with the service (or lack of service) offered by retailers. They complain of ill-informed, indifferent salespeople. They complain of poor postsale services, and they complain of the general lack of attention given to their purchase needs. In many ways, these are the strongest indictments that consumers have against retail operations. When one considers that each of these problems could be easily rectified, the indictments are even more significant. In fact, the indictments may reveal something about the way in which retailers identify with their customers. What may be suggested is that retailing is less than fully customer-oriented.

Second, consumers complain that retailers operate on the premise that they are justified in offering any merchandise as long as it will sell. Consumers argue that retailers are not as concerned with product safety, durability, and warranty as they should be. More than any other institution in the marketplace, retailing has the opportunity to select goods that promote customer welfare. If it did this job well, many consumer criticisms would be eliminated.

Aid in urban affairs. One area in which retailing can play and has to some extent, been playing a significant role is urban affairs. It is in this area that retailing contributes to the solution of problems arising from the social fabric. Retailers have both the personal skill and the commitment required for any meaningful involvement in community activities. The activities that retailers can and do engage in include the following:

1. Assist in training programs for unemployed and minorities
2. Aid in police-community relations
3. Engage in self-policing of sales and credit practices

4. Conduct traffic surveys for better city planning
5. Encourage consumer education and distributive education programs within the community
6. Contribute money for 4-H scholarships, Little League, the city symphony, and so on
7. Work with community leaders and planners before locating a particular store
8. Invest in and improve low income property
9. Encourage entrepreneurship among minority groups
10. Work with city fathers to find ways to alleviate pollution in the community. (Recently many retailers have begun cooperating with cities to implement sign codes as a means of eliminating space pollution.)

It is in these ways, as well as in their concern for the occupational health and safety of their own employees, that retailers can play a role in filling some of society's needs.

Employment opportunities and needs. Because retailers employ such a large segment of the labor force, they have a unique opportunity to make a contribution to society's needs through an improvement in employment opportunities and in helping to make work meaningful. Through enlightened training programs, many retailers have responded to employee needs for greater job variety and increasing of skills which lead to higher wages and greater productivity. With the expansion of numbers and types of stores, the absolute number of job opportunities has also increased significantly.

Where Tomorrow?

As we conclude our look at retailing and society, it is appropriate to pause and speculate about what the future might hold for retailing in the next couple of decades. To note the uncertainty of our speculation the observation of E.

Lawrence Goodman is appropriate.

> If we look back about the same amount of time, it takes us to another significant point in history—the start of the post-war era—when a period of vast economic expansion was beginning.
>
> Yet, what visionary could then have predicted the incredible changes ahead? The increase of education and affluence. Discounting. The deterioration of the central cities, and the problems of the downtown store. Suburbia and shopping centers. Computers. The credit explosion. The national hi-way system. Changes in racial attitudes. Television. The Pill and the new morality.
>
> All that—and more—since the end of World War II. And all profoundly affecting retailing. Certainly the rest of this century will see even greater and faster changes.[9]

The thoughts about the future come from *Grey Matter,* a publication of the Grey Advertising Inc.[10]

Retailers gear to cope with powerful challenges

Every part of retailing, from the smallest shop to the mightiest behemoth, finds itself beset by unprecedented problems. Crosscurrents of change and riptides of recession/inflation are roiling the waters of retailing more dangerously than in years.

How to anticipate change is occupying the attention of the very top echelons of management. Long-range planning is becoming a byword for smaller retailers as well as the giant chains; seat-of-the-pants operations are passé.

Obviously in the brief space of even an expanded issue of *Grey Matter,* we can touch only on what our marketing executives across the U. S. have found most significant in retailing. Why retailing? Because, as we have often

[9]E. Lawrence Goodman, "The Future of Retailing," Paper from the 1973 Region Conventions of the American Association of Advertising Agencies. Eastern Annual Conference. New York, November 14, 1973.

[10]*Grey Matter,* Grey Advertising Inc., Volume 46, No. 6., 1975.

said, "What happens in the world of distribution is of critical concern to everyone in marketing." Here are some key trends.

A New Focus on the Consumer

The retailer is watching the changing consumer more closely than ever. Short-term—here is what he sees:

Retailers face a new, more value-conscious customer. What's more, research shows this is a consumer who—because of high prices, fewer exciting new products—no longer regards shopping as the enjoyable experience it once was.

A further problem surfaces: what the consumer thinks about prices is different from what the retailer knows is true. Housewives believe, for example, that retail food prices (in 1975) are up about 30% over 1974. Actually the increase is only 11% according to a survey by A. C. Nielsen. Unquestionably, retailers need to make more serious and sustained efforts to educate customers about prices.

Other patterns of buying behavior are being affected, too. A study of the American family and money done by Yankelovich, Skelly and White for General Mills indicates that

- 54% spend free time at home instead of going out (which means less eating in restaurants, public entertainment, even shopping opportunities).
- 44% are buying fewer clothing items.
- 38% are spending more time hunting for bargains.
- 34% are repairing things once thrown out.

Long-term, the outlook is for "a more skeptical consumer, more pressed financially, and subjecting buying decisions to different and harder criteria than in the past; changing habitual living patterns to cope with shifting shortages in various areas as well as with the high cost of living; and less thoughtlessly optimistic about the future," as Shirley Wilkens, vice president of The Roper Organization, summarizes its recent findings.

For long range planning, retailers are scrutinizing basic shifts in the demographics, economic status and even psychographic segmentation of the U. S. population.

Class market to become mass

In the past nine years, rising U. S. family earnings have flipped the income distribution pyramid upside down, according to an analysis by Grey subsidiary, Market Horizons. The data: median income for all families in current dollars was up 83% from $6,569 in 1965 to $12,051 in 1974. (Discounting inflation, income in constant dollars rose 28%.) Thus, the proportion of families earning over $10,000 is 61% compared with 23% in 1965—a dramatic turnabout and one that's here to stay.

The Conference Board projects a continued rise in real family income—at the same rate as the past or better. Thus, retailers will face the "class" market increasingly becoming mass. By 1980, some 25 million households should be at or above the $15,000 level (constant dollars)—versus 17 million at last count. This means more disposable income to be tapped at the retail level.

Above-average household incomes more and more result from multiple paychecks. In fact, 68% of homes with earnings of $10,000 minimum had two or more wage earners, affecting retailers' plans for everything from locations near places of employment to store hours. (Some outlets are already clocking two thirds of total sales from 5 to 9 P.M.)

Declining age groups

Despite the current birth dearth (overall projected growth of only 0.8% annually between 1970—90), there's fodder for positive planning by retailers (as well as manufacturers) in terms of opportunities in certain age groups.

The number of newborns to pre-schoolers will continue down till 1980, when the late 50's and early 60's baby crop starts in on parenthood, peaking in 1985. Categories from baby foods and furnishings to tot toys and apparel must fight to grow against population statistics.

In the school agers and early teens groups, there will be growth till after 1985. In fact, the 10—14 group will be down 18%, or 3.6 million kids less from 1975—1985. Tougher sledding for categories from sugared breakfast cereals, school equipment and supplies to bubblegum and teeny-bopper rock.

1975 marks the last growth year for ages 15—19. After 1980, look for sharp declines in teen-oriented products from stereos to skin remedies.

Opportunities Abound

The family formation (20—34) group will expand 21% between 1975 and 1985—twice as fast as the total population. The affluent 30—34 age segment (up 42%) will be the fastest growing. Thus, despite later marriages and smaller families, record levels of new households (many with plural incomes) are going to be formed. Given a healthy economy with unemployment at manageable levels, this is good news for purveyors of home appliances, furnishings and all related household items.

But, meeting needs of this burgeoning market will require a better understanding of their changing lifestyles. More informal living and entertainment patterns, stress on convenience, leisure-orientation, fashion individuality and lack of concern for "lifetime" possessions—all point to reorganizing the way stores select and present their ware. More "instant" furniture and less formal housewares; more "boutiques" within a single store creating total "looks" for different style segments; perhaps an entire department with items from many categories organized around a lifestyle, say "leisure," rather than the more traditional merchandise orientation.

From 1975—1985 the peak income group will grow by 8 million people (23%), making it a major growth segment during the period and an enticing retail prospect.

In the discretionary spenders (50—64), group growth will slow, but they'll still represent nearly 14% of the population at 32 million in 1985. With more discretionary dollars available than ever before in their lives, they'll make a tempting target for travel, leisure, entertainment, retirement homes and furnishings.

The retirement (65 plus) group will be growing by 17% from 1975 to 1985—almost double the population's rate—retired oldsters must spend reduced buying power mainly on essentials. However, the group's size, its growing political power and geriatric needs, such as health care, open up specialized opportunities.

Singles as a special target

Besides the 46.8 million husband-wife units who are prime prospects for retailers, there are 9.3 million households of individual females and 5.7 million households of males living alone or with nonrelatives. Both deserve more attention from marketers. (The average single female spends 50% more on apparel and accessories than her married counterpart.)

Emerging ethnics

Blacks, which now make up 11% of the U. S. and had a growth rate between 1970 and 1974 almost double that of the total population, and the Hispanic segment make increasingly important targets for retailers in many areas. The large-scale exodus of blacks from the rural South mainly to the urban North and West brings rising educational and income levels. While only 24% of black families in the South have incomes over $10,000, approximately 40% of those situated in the Northeast, North Central and Western regions earn that amount and the trend continues. Hispanic families gained 9.7% in median income, to $9,559 last year—versus overall U. S. rise of 6.6% according to recent census figures.

The psychological dimension is vital here. Rising feelings of pride and identity among both blacks and Hispanics are producing more discriminating shoppers, who want recognition for their wants as individuals—in products, in specially oriented ads and displays. As George F. Johnson, president of Johnson Products Co., Inc., the highly successful black toiletries maker, told the Security Analysts: "In many

cases our product development hinges on physiological needs of black consumers. In some, (it) will involve marketing to a style or taste preference."

Alert retailers, particularly those who anticipate changing ethnic mixes in their trading areas, will profit from finding new ways to serve the needs of ethnic customers, from food and fashion to music and cosmetics.

Retailers Think Smaller

The days of explosive, often helter-skelter store building are over. Carefully controlled expansion into smaller population centers and phasing out unprofitable stores and, importantly, remodeling are getting more emphasis.

Mini malls or downtown suburban-style shopping centers are spreading across the land. Improved mass transit, proximity to employment, slowing suburban growth—all point to a boomlet here. According to Thomas M. Macioce, president of Allied Store Corporation, "We may see, within the next decade, many shopping areas located in high density urban areas which will be integrated with other uses, such as offices, hotels and apartments," he predicts.

Specialists in this field are quick to point out that planning of such complexes must be different from suburban center approaches. A must: Better understanding through research, of income, ethnic population, employment and lifestyle patterns in both inner city and environs.

Specialty stores gain

One effect of the profit squeeze will be a return to the oft-neglected principle, inevitably invoked in trying times: "Concentrate on the best and the devil take the rest." Higher turnover on fewer items is the watchword, even if it means phasing out whole divisions.

A heavy gainer is the stocked-in-depth specialty store, concentrating on a single category, i.e., denims, toys, auto supplies or sleepwear. These are sprouting in profusion, especially in malls where supermarkets and general merchandise stores attract one-stop shoppers.

Changing competition

Alert retailers are aware that it's no longer a Macy's versus Gimbels type of slugfest—if it ever was! Department stores feel pressure from specialty stores on one end, discounters on the other. Merchandise lines are being blurred more than ever.

Supermarkets offer a perfect example. They must regard fast food franchisers as a major threat. Insiders predict by 1985 one of every two meals will be eaten out of home versus one of three today.

Manufacturers in the Act

Manufacturers are also getting into the retail act. Texas Instruments, Dallas, opened two outlets for its products; General Telephone & Electronics markets its equipment direct to consumers through "Phone Marts." Home improvement chains by paint marketers Sherwin Williams and Dutch Boy are off and running.

Another form of competition: the burgeoning farmers' market movement. Full-scale versions have sprouted downtown in dozens of cities and dot the suburban landscape from coast to coast. All indications point to continued expansion. Supermarket produce departments need to be alert to the spread of this competition and be able to fight back on price, freshness.

Direct response on the upswing

Buying by mail or phone is on the upswing. Trend is spurred by traffic congestion and parking problems, the surge of women into the labor force, deterioration of sales forces in store, fear of crime and other influences. The credit card explosion has lent major impetus to the purchase of big-ticket items direct. It's attracting the giants; The *New York Times* estimates that at least half of the nation's top 50 corporations now have mail order divisions.

Progressive merchants—unlike those who fear direct marketing's competition—are putting this major sales tool to work. Mail order can gain stores business way beyond their trading areas; even step up store traffic with new customers.

Latest weapon is TV, now becoming a key medium for direct marketers. They spent over $106 million in TV in 1973, up from $20 million in 1969. Eventually we'll see more retailers promote merchandise via direct-response selling on TV and radio.

A new wrinkle: Computer plus tape which can automate telephone selling is being tested in Texas by American Telecom Network Co. It could cut the most of phone solicitation to less than 13¢ a call—under most direct mail.

Automation en route

Automation at the checkout counter is one area being watched by all sectors of marketing. A universal product code has been adopted by 80% of manufacturers. The coded symbol imprinted on packages is read by scanners at computerized cash registers, now in test at dozens of stores. Explosive growth is expected in 1977 and 1978, despite mechanical bugs, threat of legislative restrictions (California passed a one-year law requiring food items be individually price-marked as well as coded) and consumerist opposition. It's a development demanding teamwork between retailers, manufacturers and media. For example, it could be a major weapon against coupon misredemption. Coupons coded to match products and read by scanners could totally eliminate the problem.

Automated checkout can also be used to gauge ad effectiveness in terms of product movement. The Newspaper Advertising Bureau is enlisting manufacturers in a test program with six stores across the country to analyze ad results directly in terms of sales.

Image in Focus

You'll see new emphasis on image projection by stores and chains in every category.

Reasons behind this are many—ranging from the need to project a distinct retail "personality," as opposed to competition, to the necessity for an overall image connoting value, quality, to support expanding private-label activity. Many try for a stronger combination of store promotion, along with specific merchandise sell. Overall strategy and cleaner, easier-to-read look gain favor over cluttered item ads.

Increasingly, the smart retailer is recognizing that he must communicate with consumers through every single one of his contacts with them. Employee attitudes, service policies and store decor are just as vital to the totality of people's perception of a retailer's stance as are the more obvious aspects like merchandise, pricing and advertising.

Changing media mix

Retailers are increasing advertising investments and broadening media mix, with emphasis on TV. A CBS sales division aims at a larger share of retail billings in 1976. Targets include local retailers as well as manufacturer co-op budgets. Radio stations, too, will drive for a larger share of the three billion co-op dollars made available annually to retailers by at least 2,000 companies.

Retailer creative control

Today progressive mass retailers will not accept the proposition of running a newspaper ad prepared by the manufacturer which simply calls for the retailer's logo to be pasted in the space marked 'dealer name.' Instead, retailers rework the ad to reflect the store's image and the manufacturer's product—as it relates to that image. The same must hold true for co-op TV advertising.

A prime requirement of retail advertising is to sell the store along with the product. Retailers who promote their unique images are not me too'ers. They are distinct individuals anxious to preserve their individuality, and make their ads on products into larger store-inspired promotions.

It all adds up to. . .

The retail world is churning. From the boardroom to the selling floor. From the buying function to the store operation. Everyone involved must prepare to face a long-term future of major change.

Summary

Retailers are constantly confronted by a changing environment. However, in recent years, the changes that have occurred have been of such significance that enlightened retailers have had to adjust their operations to meet them. Of particular significance to retailers has been the consumer movement, called consumerism. Consumerism has forced retailers to assume a new responsibility in filling society's needs—a responsibility unheard of in the past. Retailers have had to assume enlarged responsibilities, sometimes along with the government, in eliminating injustices in the marketplace and in achieving a high quality of life for all members of society.

A look at the future of retailing in society shows a picture of challenge with opportunity. The alert retailer will prepare for a long-term future of major change.

Questions and Problems

1. How did riots and civil disorders affect retailing in the urban ghetto?
2. Do the poor pay more? Explain.
3. There is a limit to which a retailer can be socially conscious. Do you agree? Explain.
4. Discuss what might be done to increase customer confidence in retailing.
5. Can retailers truly exercise the function of being buying agents for customers and, therefore, operate in the best interests of consumers? Explain.
6. How will projected changes in retailing affect the stores in your community? Are they making changes which reflect an awareness of social, economic, and demographic changes?

Situations and Activities

You are the assistant manager in a local variety chain store. The company has called a meeting of all store managers and assistants. When you arrive at the meeting, your manager decides that he does not wish to attend; however, it is a required meeting and roll is being taken. He asks you to sign in for him. Will you? Why or why not?

You are the owner-manager of a store located in the downtown area. Your store has been important to the other merchants in the downtown area because of your ability to attract customers from a great distance. Recently, a shopping center has been reported to be coming into town, and you are giving serious consideration to relocating your store in this center. The decision will not be easy to make, because if you leave the downtown area, other stores might follow your lead and leave the remaining merchants in an unfavorable competitive position. In addition, customers who reside near the downtown area will be adversely affected. So, too, will sales people who live near this area. You, however, do not see how you can maintain your present sales volume when the new center comes to town. What will you do?

It is generally held that community and public activities by retailers have added to the prestige and profits of retailers. Select two groups of retailers in your community—those who are active in public affairs and those who are not—and analyze the extent to which retailers should take part in community affairs.

Retailers have a public image to portray. They have a story to tell about their products, financial status, benefits to the community, etc. To what extent are the retailers in your community establishing and carrying out programs to get these messages across? What can and should they do?

You are the owner-manager of a pet shop in a community of 50,000. Recently, a group of interested citizens gathered to develop what they considered to be an appropriate sign code for the city. As a result of their meetings, they have called for legislation that would prohibit the use of any signs not attached to the building and that would limit the size of signs to a size no larger than three feet by five feet. In addition, they are proposing that revolving signs and signs with blinking lights be forbidden. Your store is located in a block with many other retail stores. You have recently paid $3,000 for a new sign, which in your estimation, makes it easier for people to see your store and know what services you offer. What position will you take?

Bibliography

Chamber of Commerce of the United States. *Business and the Consumer: A Program for the Seventies.* Washington, D. C.: Chamber of Commerce, 1970.

Clasen, Earl A. "Marketing Ethics and the Consumer." *Harvard Business Review,* January, 1967, pp. 83—84.

Davis, Keith. "Understanding the Social Responsibility Puzzle." *Business Horizons,* October, 1967, p. 46.

Day, George S. "Consumerism." *Stanford Graduate School of Business Bulletin,* Winter, 1971, p. 12.

Gilbey, J. Gordon. "Your Stake in Urban Affairs." *Stores,* October, 1970, p. 7.

Lagur, William. "Marketing's Changing Social Relationships." *Journal of Marketing,* January, 1969, p. 3.

Mostero, Fernando S. "The Insurance Road to Social Responsibility." *Journal of Insurance,* September-October, 1971, p. 2.

Petrof, John V. "Attitudes of the Urban Poor Toward Their Neighborhood Supermarkets." *Journal of Retailing,* Spring, 1971, pp. 3—17.

Glossary:
How the Retailers Say It*

Accessories women's fashion apparel worn with dresses, coats, suits, sportwear; includes fine and costume jewelry, neckwear, scarfs, handbags, small leather goods, millinery, gloves, hosiery, shoes, handkerchiefs, watches, artificial flowers, ribbons.

Agate Line newspaper advertising unit of measurement: 1 column wide by 1/14 inch deep.

Anticipation paying a bill before it is due, with benefit of extra discount, usually computed at 6% per annum; exception rather than rule.

Assistant Buyer responsible for department's merchandise operation when buyer is in market; filling merchandise requisites for branch stores; analyzing inventory statistics for flagship and each branch store; checking and pricing merchandise in receiving and marketing department; follow-through on advertising details and okaying copy illustrations from merchandise viewpoint.

Association of Buying Offices organization of New York buying office executives to standardize and unify services available to stores; traditionally, manager of NRMA merchandise division is ABO executive secretary.

Automatic Reorder reordering staple merchandise on basis of predetermined minimum quantity; when this minimum is reached, quantity of initial order is again purchased.

Backup Stock additional merchandise available in warehouse or in forward (in-store) stock room; particularly important for runners or best-selling staples.

Balance-and-Mix complete assortment to satisfy wants, needs, pocketbooks of majority of customers; for example, in rugs, includes accent rugs, broadloom rugs, scatter rugs, oriental rugs, remnants.

Balanced Stock and/or **Assortment** makes available what customers want throughout all price zones or price ranges in proportion to that demanded.

Basic Stock items, numbers, or models that must be included in a line or classification; primarily an assortment of bread-and-butter items that enjoy day-to-day customer demand; usually staples, but nonstaple items become basic when, for fashion or fad reasons, they enjoy temporarily increased customer demand; best rule for basic stock is having what customer wants when she wants it.

Beat Last Year's Figures unending battle to sell more every day than was sold on same day a year ago, or at least to meet last year's figures and not fall behind.

Best-Seller, Runner seasonal or year-round item or number in line that sells fast throughout season or year at full markon; merits continuous promotion in displays, advertising, suggestive selling.

Better Business Bureau financed by local media and business interests for purpose of promoting accuracy and honesty in advertising and selling.

---

*A collection of technical words, terms, and titles used in retailing, selected from a larger list published by *Stores,* the NRMA Magazine, September 1969, pp. 49—63. Copyright 1968 by Ralf Shockey & Associates, Inc.

Big Ticket   usually big in physical size and size of price; for example, major appliances, furniture, and other hard goods.

B/L, Bill of Lading   form used by carrier denoting consignor, consignee, number and weight of packages, description, sometimes shipping charges, date, and other information necessary for shipment and receipt of goods into store.

Blanket Order   pre-season order to meet anticipated needs, placed before production has started; buyer orders against blanket order to meet needs as season arrives and progresses.

Bonus, Premium Money, P.M.   additional bonus paid to sales people for selling slow-moving, pre-season, or higher-priced merchandise, or for special promotion; sometimes paid by vendor upon approval by store.

Boutique   small shop, especially one that sells fashionable clothes and accessories for women; recently, department stores have expanded *boutique* to include just about everything from men's wear to home furnishings.

Branch Store   owned and operated by parent or flagship store; generally located in suburban area under name of flagship store.

Brand   word, letter, or group of words or letters composing a name or design or combination of these which identifies the goods as services of one seller and/or distinguishes them from those of competitors; *brand* is a more inclusive, general term than *trademark.*

Brown Goods   radios, televisions, electronics.

Buyer   see **Department Manager.**

Buyer's Market, Soft Market   situation in which manufacturer's inventories are high and demand is low.

Buying Group, Buying Office, Resident Buying Office   organization representing group of noncompeting stores, formed primarily for buying merchandise; may be independent, store-owned, or own the stores. Examples: *Owns stores*—Allied Stores Corp., Associated Dry Goods Corp., Mercantile Stores Co.; *Owned by stores*: Associated Merchandising Corp., Frederick Atkins, Inc.; *Charges stores fee*: Mutual Buying Syndicate, Inc., Felix Lilienthal & Co., Independent Retailers, Inc.

Buying Off the Peg   customers can buy merchandise, particularly ready-to-wear, for immediate "take-with" or for delivery by store; this has not been true in European stores.

Call System   arrangement in some selling departments to give each salesperson, by numerical rotation, equal opportunity to wait on customers; commonly used in men's clothing departments, major appliances, and furniture.

Carry Out, Take-With   merchandise carried from store by customer, expediting delivery and saving delivery expense; particularly significant in branch stores; must be forward stock, immediately available.

C.O.D., Cash on Delivery   transaction whereby customer agrees to pay when goods are delivered.

Cash Register Bank, Fund   monies given to each salesperson for purpose of making change: if prepared at close of business each day by salesperson, it is Single-Bank system; if prepared by cashiers, it is Two-Bank system.

Centralized Buying   all buying done by merchandise staff located in flagship store or buying center, perhaps located in corporate headquarters or warehouse; increasingly influenced by requests, suggestions, opinions of branch store managers and their merchandise staffs.

Cherry Picking   buyer selection of only few numbers from one vendor's line, other numbers from another line, failing to purchase complete line or classification of merchandise from one resource; with rapid development of multi-unit stores, cherry picking from large number of resources becomes economically unsound.

Chopped Ticket   that part of price ticket removed from sold merchandise and forwarded to vendor nightly as step in vendor's computerized stock control for reorders.

Closed-Door Membership Store discount-store operation requiring its customers to qualify as such by type of employment—government employee, public servant, member of union—and by paying initiation fee, annual dues, or both.

Cluster of Stores that which will produce enough sales volume in a geographical area to bear cost of advertising, central warehousing, and distribution and to provide profitable operation.

Column Inch print advertising term: 1 column wide by 1 inch deep.

Comparison Shopper employee in comparison department charged with reporting competitors' activities and merchandise.

Consignment Purchase and Dating purchase wherein title to merchandise does not pass at time of shipment but at expiration of specified period, when buyer is privileged to return to vendor any unsold goods.

Consumerism interest in consumer's welfare; how honestly and well customer is served and informed, how accurate and adequate that information is, how easily it can be understood.

Co-operative Advertising advertising in payment of which manufacturer, importer, or distributor co-operates with retailer.

Co-operative Display Fund definite amount of money provided by vendor, generally matched by store, for development, construction, and installation by store's visual merchandising (display) department to support specific promotion for vendor's products.

Cross-Selling applied to salesperson's selling in more than one department.

Cycle Billing correlation of alphabetical breakdowns to specific days of month to facilitate billing of customer's accounts; each breakdown is a cycle, and billing for cycle occurs on same day each month.

Demonstration Sale presented by vendor's representatives—territorial salesperson, demonstrators, or staff sales trainer—or by member of department's sales personnel to arm departmental staff with facts and selling points and to show better methods of presenting advantages, use, and care of product.

Department Manager, Buyer line management, merchandiser; in one-unit store, has both buying and selling responsibilities; in multi-unit operation, is primarily buyer; analyzes demand; maintains balanced stocks; keeps eye on competition; watches market trends and developments; looks for "hot" new items, manufacturer selling helps, "retail" selling ideas; supervises and deputizes; responsible for profitable operation of department; goes to bat for items, lines, promotions, money to get what is needed.

Departmental Analysis determines (1) whether department is producing its due share of sales volume in that line in store's metromarket, and (2) whether gross margin realized is adequate to cover expenses and contribute to store's profits; when unsatisfactory condition is uncovered, detailed studies aimed at improving performance are made, including resources, markon, cash discount, styling, price lining, customer traffic, selling service, advertising, visual merchandising, departmental layout, workroom expense, customer returns, and adjustments.

Director of Personnel executive responsible for development and activation of store's personnel policies and regulations, in employment, training, and performance reviews.

Discount Merchandising low-margin retailing, generally self-service, selling goods at less than list price.

Distress Merchandise merchandise which, for any reason, must be sold at a sacrifice—at either wholesale or retail level.

Divisional Merchandise Manager executive responsible for merchandising activities of related group of departments; transmits top management policy to line management; supervises department managers (buyers) and managers' assistants; influential decision-making supervisory executive.

Domestics originally applied to yard goods from which sheets, pillow cases, towels, etc., were cut; now broadly encompasses finished products in these classifications.

Double-Truck 2-page advertisement utilizing "gutter" space to make advertisement appear as unit, as opposed to 2 facing pages.

Drop Ship note on order by buyer to ship merchandise directly to specific branch store: "Drop ship to ___ store"; this procedure saves time and expense of vendor's shipping to central warehouse, store's transshipping to designated branch; it also means branch store will not be "out" for a long period; sometimes it is more expensive in terms of freight cost.

End-of-Aisle spaces fronting on main traffic aisles, particularly important location for 4½-second stopper displays to develop impulse sales.

E.O.M., End of Month Terms time allowance for discount reckoned from end of month during which goods were bought, not from date of invoice.

Exclusive Merchandise confined merchandise not available at other stores in that metromarket.

Exurbia areas beyond suburbs but still accessible to major city facilities into which increasing numbers of corporations and their employees' families are moving.

Fact Tag conveys factual information and consumer benefits to sales staff and customers at point of sale; ideally, a self-seller.

Flagging an Account temporarily identifying and suspending an account until brought up to date.

Flash Report total of daily gross sales by departments, prepared at close of each business day.

Floating Display moved from location to location within flagship store or from branch store to branch store.

Floor Limit arbitrary amount established for floor approval of charge purchases without credit authorization when customer presents proper identification.

Flying Squad group of sales people, regular or contingent, with exceptional selling ability and flexibility, who can be added to any regular departmental sales staff when needed; also used in sales-supporting and nonselling areas, such as telmail, complaint departments, during peak load periods.

Forward Stock that stock which is carried in selling department.

Full Line stock of any given classification of goods which includes every variety of style, in every color, in every size, and in every material that customer can reasonably expect to obtain at a given price; consists of four definite categories: (1) staples, (2) style merchandise, (3) novelties, (4) outsizes (for stock that has a size element).

General Merchandise Manager top management; participates in major policymaking; administers policy for entire merchandise division; liaison executive between merchandise division and all other major store divisions; responsible for total store merchandising operation; final work decision-maker.

Glossies prints of merchandise photographs supplied to store's advertising or display department for reproduction.

Graphics illustration, descriptive techniques, including sketches, wash drawings, paintings, water colors, engravings, photographs.

Hard Goods major appliances, including refrigerators, deep freezers, electric and gas ranges, washing machines, dryers, hot-water heaters, air conditioners.

Head of Stock person responsible for arrangement and identification of reserve and forward stocks; generally, someone with promising ability and at junior executive level.

High End most expensive merchandise in classification.

Hot Track Record outstanding promotion or marketing operation exceeding normal performance.

Image, Store Image   reputation of store; feelings of customers toward store.

Impulse Merchandise   articles of merchandise purchased on spur of moment by customer, without predetermined consideration.

Invoice   itemized statement showing merchandise sent to store by supplier.

Items That Pay the Rent   products that sell, and at a profit.

Job Lot   miscellaneous assortment of style, sizes, colors, etc., purchased by store as a "lot" at reduced price.

Kimball Tag   pre-punched tag attached to merchandise and containing size and style information, provided for high-speed processing and counting; used in inventory control reports, recording, and restocking.

Landed Cost   total cost and charges for merchandise on dock after conveyance from foreign port; also total cost to buy and bring to (land in) store.

Lay-Away   method of deferred payment in which merchandise is held by store for customer until completely paid for.

Leased Department   department operated by outside organization, generally on percentage-of-sales basis; lessor must abide by rules, regulations, operations, and objectives of lessee.

Loss Leader   merchandise advertised and sold at, near, or even below cost by store to bring customers into store.

Low End   least expensive merchandise in classification.

Low-Margin Retailing   discount or mass merchandising.

Manifest   shipping form used by carrier for consolidation purposes, listing all pertinent information—consignor, consignee, commodity classification, number and weight of packages, and sometimes cost; used by carrier internally to list contents of particular vehicle, listing same information; also used by stores in transfer operations from central warehouse to branches.

Mannequin   clothes model; styled and three-dimensional representation of human form used in display windows and on ready-to-wear selling floors to display apparel.

Market Penetration   store's share of metromarket in specific department or classification of merchandise; within reason, there is no limit on how deep a penetration successfully operated departments can make.

Market Representative   member of resident-buying-office staff whose major responsibilities are to act as market shopper, analyst, merchandise counsellor to merchandise managers and buyers of office's member stores; also expedites shipment of initial orders and reorders placed by member stores.

Mass Merchandising   self-service store displaying and selling all kinds of merchandise; displays tend to be massive; customers usually push wire carts to collect and carry their own selection of merchandise to cashier checkout counters.

Media Mix   planning use and coordination of advertising and promotional media, such as interior and exterior display, and newspaper, direct mail, radio, television, magazine, transit, and outdoor advertising.

Media Representative   sales and/or service representative from newspapers, radio, television, and direct mail media who services store accounts.

Memorandum and Consignment Selling   vendor agrees to take back goods if not sold in specific period of time; since markdown risk is borne by vendor, buyer's maintenance is equal to his initial markon; under memorandum arrangement, title passes to buyer, ordinarily, when goods are shipped, but vendor assumes contracted obligation of taking back unsold portion of goods at specific time; on consignment purchase, title does not pass to store but instead passes directly from vendor to store's customers—store acts simply as agent for vendor; vendor can control retail price.

Merchandise Mart   building that houses showrooms for manufacturers and importers where, under one roof, store buyers and merchandise managers can inspect lines from resources in minimum time; Merchandise Mart in Chicago is reported to be largest in the world.

Merchandise Specification   buyer sets up or obtains specifications for qualities expressed in necessary technical terms; proper specifications cannot always be determined until needs and expectations of customers have been carefully analyzed and until some experimental work has been done; development of private brands or controlled brands has increased need for rigid specifications prepared for or by store's merchandise divisions.

Metromarket   central city plus suburban areas from which retail store draws major portion of customers.

Model Stock   how much of what to have; stock which has right goods at right time in right quantities at right price; in most classifications, this is three full lines and three price levels which move stock rapidly.

Nailed Down   refers to merchandise advertised at extremely low price which store makes every effort not to sell.

On the Floor   time spent by buyer on selling floor to get "personal touch" with customers, supervise sales personnel, be involved in selling function, devise new floor visual selling ideas; unfortunately, too many buyers are "married to the flagship store," devoting little, if any, time to branch store floor supervision.

On Order   applied to merchandise purchased but not yet received.

One-Stop Shopping   everything customer would need for self, family, home, located under one roof.

Open Order   order placed without price or delivery stipulation; order sent to market representative in resident buying office without specifying vendor.

Open Stock   additional and/or replacement pieces of merchandise (for example, dinnerware) carried in bulk and kept in stock for several years; open stock slows turnover

materially.

Out of Stock   lack of merchandise in store in styles, colors, material content, price lines customers want when they want it.

Peak Season   months or season in which item or line of merchandise is in greatest customer demand, for example, skis during major snow months.

Personal Care Items   merchandise to help improve customer's appearance: hair dryers, electric shavers, saunas, electric hair curlers, hair setters, electric manicure and pedicure sets.

Piece Goods   fabrics for home sewing, including woolens, cottons, synthetics.

P.O.P.   point-of-purchase display and signs.

Pre-Marketing, Pre-Ticketing   marking of merchandise by manufacturer.

Premium Money   see **Bonus.**

Pre-Sold Merchandise   goods for which vendor's national advertising in magazines, newspapers, and via television and radio creates customer acceptance and in-store demand.

Pre-Ticketed   merchandise priced by vendor either on package or on price tickets or tags (often supplied by store to vendor with season letter, price, other necessary information) prior to packing for shipment to store; this saves store time, effort, and money in getting merchandise through receiving and marking room and onto selling floor.

Private Brand   controlled or private-label merchandise developed under store's own brand or developed under resident buying office's label exclusively for member stores.

Profit Squeeze   generally caused by severe competition from other retail stores or by increased wholesale costs, plus selling costs, that cannot be passed on to store's customer.

Publicity Director, Sales Promotion Manager   in large retail store, supervises advertising, display, special activities or events, press and/or public relations managers, and frequently fashion coordinator and comparison shoppers; in medium-size store, managers may report directly to general merchandise manager; in small store, advertising manager may do everything in publicity and promotion.

Pull (verb) refers to advertising, for example, "The ad pulled [produced sales] yesterday," "That type of format doesn't pull."

R.O.G., Receipt of Goods Terms   cash discount terms that begin when merchandise reaches store; designed to benefit retailers far from resource; also permits check of goods prior to due date for discount.

Replenishment Order, Reorder   to fill-in (complete) assortments in specific classification.

Research Director   responsible for all research activities in store operation and customer research; becoming increasingly important function.

Resident Buying Office   see **Buying Group**.

Runner   see **Best Seller**.

Sales Analysis   that part of sales audit which provides totals of sales by sales people, departments, classifications, etc.

Sales Audit   work of checking media from selling floor for purpose of control, reporting, accounting.

Sales Manager   some larger stores are placing responsibility for personal selling efforts, for supervision and on-the-floor training of salespersons, as well as for point-of-purchase signing and demonstrations, with a sales manager; salespeople report to him or his assistants rather than to buyers. See also **Department Manager** and **Section Manager**.

Sales Promotion Manager   see **Publicity Director**.

Sales Slip   slip of paper from roll on cash register showing only dollars-and-cents amount of purchase.

Salon   shop where higher-priced apparel and corresponding accessories are sold.

Seasonal Merchandise   merchandise purchased to meet demands of specific seasons, for example, summer and winter clothing, outdoor furniture.

Section Manager   executive in operating division as management representative with disciplinary and adjustment jurisdiction, budgeting and staffing responsibility within departments under his supervision.

Selling Area   that part of sales floor devoted exclusively to selling; shoe and ready-to-wear stock rooms, fitting rooms, and wrapping stations are considered part of selling area when sales could not be consummated without them.

Share of Market   percent of metromarket sales volume attained by store, department, or classification within department in store.

Short-Hour   employees who work, in both selling and sales-supporting departments, primarily during peak selling hours; many are housewives, students, civil employees, moonlighters.

Showroom   space maintained in various cities by vendors-manufacturers, importers, wholesalers, and distributors where merchandise is displayed for store buyers and merchandise managers to select styles and place orders.

Sleeper   potential "hot item" that, with aggressive promotion, may be developed into a runner.

Soft Goods   ready-to-wear for women, children, men; fashion accessories; piece goods; domestics.

Special Events Director   reports to sales promotion manager, cooperates with advertising and display departments in activating promotions; supervises actual operation of special events.

Special Order   readiness to procure for customer anything not stocked.

Staple Stock   there is always the problem of overlap in defining basic stock versus staple stock; essentially, the difference between basic and staple is assortments versus single items; staple stock is made up of items that are in practically continuous demand; basic stock is an assortment of items that are in current demand; basic stock includes staple stock items.

Stock Book   record of purchases from orders and of sales from stubs of price tickets, usually maintained by buyer.

S.K.U., Stock Keeping Unit represents item of merchandise which is in stock.

Switching Customer when salesperson cannot close a sale, he or she calls buyer or department manager or even another salesperson, who is introduced as a departmental supervisor, to take over the sale; more prevalent in men's clothing, furniture, or major appliance departments.

Take-With see **Carry Out.**

Tickler system in which at specific time a flag or notation indicates that merchandise should be reordered.

Total Look, Total Concept instead of large departments of all kinds of coats, suits, and dresses, development of selling areas—commonly called boutiques—appealing to groups of customers, grouped by age, taste, income; customer no longer has to go all over store to find things "to go with"—she can find everything in one place.

Tracer person in receiving and marking area and traffic department who traces delayed or lost shipments of incoming merchandise; also traces lost deliveries to customers; also the form used in these processes.

Twig small branch store located in community or neighborhood shopping center, generally carrying only women's and children's ready-to-wear and accessories.

Vendor Chargeback when merchandise is returned to vendor, store submits bill to vendor, frequently accompanied by proof of delivery to vendor.

Vignette process of deleting background in photograph used in advertisement.

Visual Merchandising presentation of merchandise to best selling advantage and for maximum traffic exposure, plus projection of customer "ready-to-buy"; not display technique but merchandising strategy.

Walk-Out customer who enters store with acquisitive gleam in eye, walks out dull-eyed and empty-handed; reasons why vary: absence of merchandise information at point-of-sale, lack of informative labeling, items out of stock due to nonexisting basic stock plans, etc.—being fresh out of "serpents in garden," i.e., buying temptations.

Weed-Out eliminating slow-moving items —items for which there is very little customer demand, for example, in ready-to-wear and shoes, eliminating extra-large and extra-small sizes.

White Goods refrigerators, deep freezers, automatic dryers, washing machines, stoves, dish washers; all comparatively big ticket items.

Will Call another name applied to lay-away; also applies to purchases which have been paid for in full but for which customer will return to pick up.

Window Reader sign in display window containing information on fashion or use of merchandise, including department and location of merchandise.

Workroom generally refers to behind-the-scenes room for sales-supporting services, such as alterations and repairs.

Index